CAMBRIDGE ENGLISH PROSE TEXTS

American Colonial Prose

CAMBRIDGE ENGLISH PROSE TEXTS

General editor: GRAHAM STOREY

OTHER BOOKS IN THE SERIES

The Evangelical and Oxford Movements, edited by Elisabeth Jay
Science and Religion in the Nineteenth Century, edited by Tess Cosslett
Burke, Godwin, Paine and the Revolution Controversy, edited by Marilyn Butler
Revolutionary Prose of the English Civil War, edited by Howard Erskine-Hill
and Graham Storey

FORTHCOMING
Romantic Criticial Essays, edited by David Bromwich

American Colonial Prose

John Smith to Thomas Jefferson

Edited by

MARY ANN RADZINOWICZ

The right of the
University of Cambridge
to print and sell
all manner of books
was granted by
Henry VIII in 1534.
The University has printed
and published continuously
since 1584.

CAMBRIDGE UNIVERSITY PRESS

Cambridge

London   New York   New Rochelle

Melbourne   Sydney

Published by the Press Syndicate of the University of Cambridge
The Pitt Building, Trumpington Street, Cambridge CB2 1RP
32 East 57th Street, New York, NY 10022, USA
296 Beaconsfield Parade, Middle Park, Melbourne 3206, Australia

First published 1984

Printed in Great Britain at
the University Press, Cambridge

Library of Congress catalogue card number: 83–20873

British Library cataloguing in publication data

American colonial prose. – Cambridge
English prose texts)
1. American prose literature – Colonial
period, ca. 1600–1775
I. Radzinowicz, Mary Ann
818'.108'08   PS651

ISBN 0 521 24426 9 hard covers
ISBN 0 521 28680 8 paperback

For Ann and William, to acquaint them with
what also is theirs

Contents

Contents

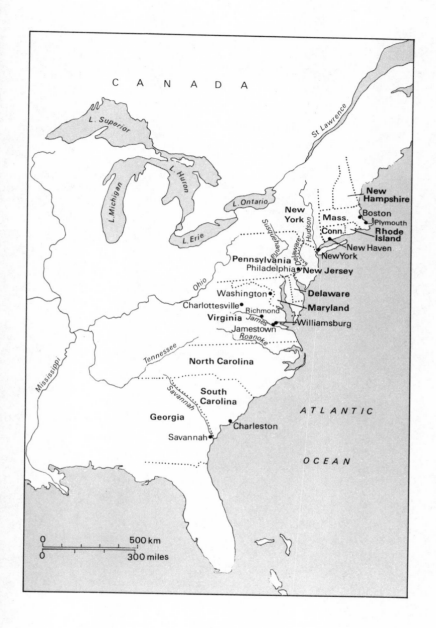

British in Eastern North America 1603–1763 (before Treaty of Paris)

ix

Introduction

When we have said that American colonial prose was written by men who came to and usually remained in an American colony, about American experiences sometimes but not always true or to be found only in the New World, we have said almost all that can be generally affirmed of it. (Even so it was not always written by men: more women in the colonies than in England wrote lasting work.) The interesting Americanness of American colonial prose is not a matter of its stylistic or intellectual or thematic difference from English seventeenth- and eighteenth-century prose, nor a matter of its homogeneity of subject or literary stance, nor a result of any uniform progress towards a recognition in America of a common identity, nor the consequence of a gradually or consistently developing tradition marked by the emergence of individual prose stylists who served as models for subsequent writers. Some of the best of it was not printed in America in the lifetime of the writer; its Americanness was not recognized as such until after the writer's death, and then as much by English as by American readers. American colonial prose is regional in a way English seventeeth- and eighteenth-century prose had long since ceased to be; it registers a halting domestication of a varied land; it bears the marks of where and when in the new continent it was written quite as much as by whom.

In the beginning neither the history nor the literature of a country of immigrants looks like its own, either to the mother country or to the immigrants. To begin with, the continent of North America seemed both to its explorers and their contemporaries at home a vast wilderness dotted with islands of Englishness. If the reality of a culture is established by its dawning consciousness of identity, however, even from the beginning America had a good deal more history than it had literature. The first settlers both in Virginia and Massachusetts landed in British America with a sense that they were making history or fulfilling it, and their first acts included the writing of that history. Historical consciousness is to be found everywhere and literary self-consciousness nowhere in early colonial America; to write of early American literature is to record the activity of the first chroniclers and narrative historians of the new country. Five of the ten writers from whose works I have selected called their writings in some sort 'histories' – John Smith, *Generall Historie of Virginia, New England, and The Summer Isles*; William Bradford, *History of Plimmoth Plantation*; Cotton Mather, *Magnalia Christi Americana*; *or, the Ecclesiastical History of New-England*; William Byrd, *History of the Dividing Line Betwixt Virginia and North Carolina*; and Patrick Tailfer, *A True and Historical Narrative of the Colony of Georgia in America*. Two adapted Tailfer's label 'narrative' to imply descriptive historical interest – Mary Rowlandson, *The Sovereignty and Goodness of God, Together with the Faithfulness of His Promises Displayed; Being a Narrative of the Captivity and Restauration of Mrs. Mary Rowlandson*; Jonathan Edwards, *Personal Narrative*. The remaining three gave, or had given, their books the genre indication 'journal' or 'autobiography' – Sarah Kemble Knight, Benjamin Franklin and Thomas Jefferson – but their works had memorial and chronological ambitions. They were recording, they thought, current history; it is we who see them writing accounts of their achievement of identity.

The 'American' historians came to whatever part of the new continent they found bearing with them the cultural stuff of their English class, religion, region, and generation. What they set down as having happened to them answered to their social, theological, intellectual, and political expectations of what would happen. Predictably, their individual sense of fulfilled prophecy included the common notion of divine guidance. Bradford expected and found God's protection; Mrs Rowlandson, spiritual sustenance in physical trials; Mather, awesome support from his God amidst the backslidings of his people. Their religious expectations were Puritan, but even the Anglicanism dominant in Virginia had a matching prophetic strain represented in George Herbert's lines:

> Religion stands on tiptoe in our land
> Readie to pass to the American strand.
>
> ('The Church Militant', lines 235–6, from *The Temple*)

William Byrd considered 'Tis natural for helpless man to adore his Maker in Some Form or other' and his own form of adoration was to register 'how Fortune delights in bringing great things out of Small'. When, considerably earlier, John Smith wrote in the *True Relation*, his first published work, that 'God (beyond al their expectations) by meanes of the shippes (at which they shot with their Ordinances and Muskets) caused [four hundred Indians] to retire', he but initiated the ascription of divine significance to human events as common in the south as in the north.

Introduction

Had Stuart England been a united and coherent society. American settlers might have exhibited more of a common heritage. We might have been able to say that they transplanted with them a cross-section of the English seventeenth-century mind. We might then have drawn a myth of organic American growth to assert that English consciousness adapted to altered conditions of American life, became gradually less English and more American, and at last by natural evolution smoothly though rebelliously stepped aside from its parentage. That myth is seductively false. Stuart England offered no such homogenous and harmonious 'mind' and the formation of a sense of identity in each colony preceded the emergence of a national or, more properly, federal sense of identity. Each identity was itself the product of an interchange between the widely differing Englishnesses brought to each of the thirteen colonies and the widely differing conditions found in them. The formative years produced characteristics and attitudes which persisted in later generations. Even the persistence of regional traits, however, was uneven; the true myth of American identity must not only recognize the distinctiveness of colonial origins in distinctive strands from inharmonious sources of Stuart Englishness, but allow for the persistent intrusion of cultural pressures from much more homogenous Hanoverian England and elsewhere in Europe. The colonies once planted were permeated by reinfusions from the mother country. The American culture of Jefferson's day would share far more of dominant English enlightenment than the very diverse and scattered writers of the earlier years could share with the unsettled Englishness of Stuart times. The colonies looked to England rather than to each other for intellectual stimulus. The absence of an American public for a good deal of American writing, the effect on much of the prose of its having been addressed either to England or to posterity, is in part the cause of its regionalism. A Virginian would scarcely imagine a Massachusetts audience: no Massachusetts books are to be found, for example, in the largest southern library on record, that belonging to William Byrd and catalogued at Westover in 1777, although it contained a number of English studies of New World history, including John Smith's.

If first there was history and then the literature of history and only subsequently literature itself in America, and if first there were colonial styles and only subsequently a federal style, then in order to have a purchase on the writings which follow we must suggest, however sketchily, the history of the separate settlements of the New World.

I

The North American continent on the eve of its English settlement was a triangular land mass with the widest section located between the twenty-sixth and fifty-fifth parallels. Its eastern seaboard was fringed with bays and inlets and pierced with large rivers – the St Lawrence, Connecticut, Hudson, Delaware, Susquehanna, Potomac – so that landing was easy, a foothold possible, and penetration into the interior more inviting than communication across the capes and peninsulas of the coastline. Behind the coastal plain, thickly forested, was a wild mountain barrier, the Appalachian chain, running virtually the entire length of the English settlement. As the rivers encouraged settlers to travel into the interior, the mountain barrier prompted them to remain in coastal regions and to exploit the environs thoroughly before pushing into the central basin. The very jaggedness of the Atlantic coastline promoted individual colonial identity. Nevertheless the entire continent seemed to lie invitingly open, for all the undeniable evidence that it was already populated. At least fifty million American Indians, and perhaps double that number, inhabited the hemisphere of North, Central and South America, the bulk living in central and southern regions in hundreds of cultural and language groups until Spanish explorers and conquistadores devastated their country and decimated their numbers – by disease as much as by design. The northern half of the western hemisphere and especially the eastern Atlantic seaboard was more thinly settled than the southern, its Indians organized into woodland cultures of hunting, fishing, and gathering tribes who would in turn suffer the same depopulation as the southern half. By the end of the seventeenth century at least ninety per cent of the native population of the eastern seaboard would have been eliminated. Of those woodland tribal groups, Powhatan's Confederacy[1] was especially sophisticated in polity and well-organized in culture. Its civility would not save it.

The confrontation of settlers with the native population would lead very early to the development of sub-genres of colonial history, ranging from military accounts of English and Indian warfare, to missionary diaries, to semi-anthropological surveys of Indian customs, to 'captivity narratives' and the like. By one of the ironies of history, the Indians themselves played a notable role in the conversion of America from a target of exploration to a land for settlement. Raleigh's company in the ill-starred Roanoke expedition (1583), conceived of as an outpost for exploration as much as a plantation, included Sir Thomas Heriot, experimental scientist, who drew up before he returned to England a dictionary of Algonkian Indian words, now lost, which John Smith very probably studied before making his journey to America. Heriot's dictionary accounted for Smith's unexpected proficiency in the language. In 1605 Captain George Waymouth brought five kidnapped Indians from cognate Algonkian tribes to Plymouth, England. The Governor of the Plymouth Forties, Sir Fernando Gorges, retained three and dispatched two to London to the Lord Chief Justice, Sir John Popham. Those Indians strengthened interest in the New World, particularly Virginia. Gorges wrote of them in his *Description of New England* (reprinted in James P. Baxter, *Sir Ferdinando Gorges and His Province of Maine*, 3 vols. Boston, 1890): 'They were all of one nation, but of several parts and several families; this accident must be acknowledged, the means under God of putting on foot, and giving life to all our Plantations.' Probably both Heriot and Smith interviewed the two Algonkians in London; certainly the desire to settle and not simply explore Virginia Britannia was fuelled by the living presence of Indians in England. Smith's subsequent account of his Indian adventures reinforced that desire.

The part of this lightly populated, fertile, temperate continent which in the first hundred years of its settlement would be developed into thirteen colonies was not *terra incognita* in England, when the first small fleet was authorized to set sail, for all that only a century had passed since Colombus had bumped into its southerly fringe by mistake, plunging as he was towards Cathay. In the common English view it was something like the Enchanted Isles. Spanish experience of more southerly America had made it so. By the middle of the sixteenth century, Englishmen interested in America had begun translating Spanish histories and memoirs, including the principal chronicle by Peter Martyr, in the hope of encouraging English efforts to achieve a parallel success. The picture which emerged from such translation and popularization was of an Eden teeming with gentle natives who lived without effort on the earth's natural bounty; if the natives were unfriendly or even cannibalistic, they lacked both gunpowder and ambition, and in all probability would be quickly subdued. That the natives did not at once see the merits of labouring for the new arrivals would present difficulties for which John Hawkins had found a rough solution even before the problem arose in English America: in 1562 he initiated a slave trade between Africa and New Spain[2] which was to continue in English hands with various modifications in the African sources of slaves and the New World location of markets until officially abolished in 1807. But if the Spanish chroniclers emphasized the fertility and commodity of the land, what was conspicuous to Englishmen watching the progress of Spanish conquest was that it would surely contain gold and silver. The Spanish mines of Peru and Mexico were not only objects of envy to the Elizabethans, they were significant goads to emulation. Not all the leading politicians in Elizabeth's court could be persuaded that the New World afforded an opportunity important enough to challenge Spain for; Burleigh, for example, steadily advised the Queen to work out a *modus vivendi* with Spain and concentrate on trade with the continent. But a faction – including such men as Raleigh, Sir Francis Walsingham, Sir Humphrey Gilbert, Sir Francis Drake and his half-brother Sir John Hawkins, and the spokesman–propagandist Richard Hakluyt – was so persuaded. It enjoyed the private support of the Queen; she denied the group only official political endorsement. At first, then, the Englishmen who sailed for the Enchanted Isles or New Eden (as private explorers), were prompted by commerical motives, envy and hatred of Spain, national self-interest and, later, other intermingled acknowledged and unacknowledged motives as different as each man who held them: pious Protestant desires to carry Christianity to the Indians, bourgeois wishes of younger sons to hold land, administrative hopes to relieve the mother country of its dangerous classes of the vagrant, unemployed, and criminal. England had no single embracing policy concerning landholding, land use or taxation, immigration, or regional and local government. The sheer reliance on dissimilar charters and *ad hoc* arrangements would conspire with the geography of North America both to encourage regional diversity and to weaken attachment to England.

Each region spoke for itself during the century and a half between the founding of the colonies and their proclamation of independence. What in the subsequent assertion of an American identity surprises the modern Englishman most is surely the ease with which the Massachusetts settlement retrospectively imposed its version of America upon colonial heterogeneity. Interpreting colonial America from the popular English vantage point has come to mean a deft employment of bifocals – a Puritan halfmoon for short sight, a Yankee lens for long distance. The bent of mind which sees everything south of the Potomac as a cavalier intrusion of little importance should not survive a reading of the following excerpts. The very diversity of English policy towards settlement had much, however, to do with

Introduction

New England's interpretative primacy. New England was more separatist in its inception than Virginia Britannia, and that separatism quickly became identified as the true mark of Americanness. The selections which follow have been chosen to display the birth of American prose – first, as a set of stairs, so to speak, geographically stepping up and down the coastline to produce regional literatures; second, as a series of waves moving down the flow of time from the accession of James I to the Declaration of Independence to produce distinctive preoccupations in each period; third, as an oscillation of continuing influences between the Old and New Worlds to produce a concept of Americanness that took form in England before it achieved substance on the ground of the new continent and was continuously nourished by new arrivals or by the English education of settlers' children; fourth, as a class-structure recapitulating the demography of settlement from landed gentlemen to tradesmen to skilled workers to indentured servants, from learned elders to spiritually excitable youth, from adventurous men to timorous, or adventurous women to nervous; and lastly as a group of genres, commencing with history and current affairs and displaying an increasing self-reflection which did not exclude self-satire.

Self-reflection and self-satire played no part in prompting the first explorers to write of the New World; their motives were promotional and historical, their self-presentation heroic or religious. The contemporary European picture of America deriving from Spain had a strongly southern and optimistic cast; the systematic survey of the North Atlantic coast from the Grand Banks to Florida undertaken by the Portuguese seaman Estevan Gomez in 1524, the failed attempts of De Sota and Coronado to explore the southern interior, the disappointment of Cartier at finding only fool's gold in Canada, the abandonment of the Roanoke Settlement[3] – these and other encounters with reality soon led to sceptical reports of wilderness, warlike Indians, inhospitable climates, and difficult supply routes. North America disappointed the Hispano-Portuguese imperialists; and not only did they say so, they left the northern part of the northern continent strictly alone. North America, it would soon be argued, abandoned by Spain and Portugal, virtually vacant of European foes, geographically accessible to England, potentially profitable to a people by temperament willing to work and not merely plunder, had been, surely, providentially reserved for English possession. The prose of Elizabethan maritime expansion is doubtless a precondition for an American prose but it is not that prose. That prose came into being to display the New World as England's opportunity for settlement. The

7

story properly begins in James I's reign, and with a haphazard royal grant jointly sought by two incompatible groups and given so as to permit each to develop under local circumstances. The two groups consisted on the one hand of a London branch of would-be developers headed by Sir Thomas Smith and augmented by Bristol merchants gathered around Richard Hakluyt, interested in the Chesapeake and North Carolina regions to which Sir Walter Raleigh had gone and whose Roanoke rights they acquired; and on the other hand a West Country group centering on Plymouth headed by Sir Humphrey Gilbert's son, Raleigh Gilbert, and interested in northern New England and the rich fishing areas around Newfoundland. James I granted a royal charter on 10 April 1606 authorizing the London–Bristol group to colonize between the thirty-fourth and forty-first parallels (Cape Fear, North Carolina to New York City) and the Plymouth group to colonize between the thirty-eighth and forty-fifth parallels (the Potomac to Bangor, Maine). Either group was authorized to settle the overlapping area (what was to become Pennsylvania, New Jersey, Delaware and Maryland) so long as they did not encroach within a hundred miles of each other.

The London–Bristol group with southern interests got off the mark first. It dispatched three ships to Virginia, variously estimated to contain 104 to 144 men, of whom 93 can be named. Before they set sail, in accordance with James's *Articles* incorporating the Company, seven councillors were appointed to govern the colony locally, one of whom was Captain John Smith. Upon landing, they built a fort and commemorated their royal benefactor by naming it Jamestown. Despite the granting of a second charter investing control in the 'Treasurer and Company of Adventurers and Planters of the City of London for the first Colony of Viginia' which brought into being a viable joint stock company and enlarged the land grant, and despite the granting of a third charter in 1612 still further enlarging its territory and enriching the stock company with lottery rights, the vicissitudes of that settlement were such that, nearly wiped out on several occasions, the population was only 1,275 person by 1624 – the year of the bankruptcy and dissolution of the Virginia Company, the last year of James I's life, the year at which John Smith concludes his *Generall Historie* and, conveniently, the year of a census.

The Plymouth-based northern group set sail later in 1607, landed 120 men at the Sagadahoc River in Maine and there built a rough village. Those settlers returned to England in disillusionment, half of them in 1608, the other half in 1609. A third, most southerly attempt at settlement was made in 1612 by a subsidiary of the Virginia Company called the Somers Islands or Bermuda Company, reorganized by 1620 into an independent company with perhaps 1,500 people living in Bermuda. Rivalry and factional quarrels between the Virginia and Bermuda adventurers precipitated the investigation by a royal commission which led to the dissolution of the Virginia Company. A fourth attempt brought into being the Newfoundland Company, aiming to establish a permanent base to protect the fisheries of the north. Neither the Bermuda nor Newfoundland company was fertile in developing colonial prose. It was otherwise with the final attempt which led to the colony of Plymouth, Massachusetts in 1620. That attempt resulted from negotiations by representatives of a largish group of English religious dissenters living in Leyden who applied unsuccessfully in 1617 to the Virginia Company for land rights, secured financial backing from the merchant Thomas Watson in 1620 in exchange for an agreement to return all profits to him for the first seven years of their settlement, and with that money behind them set sail in the same year. They embarked with 102 emigrants and just before landing at Plymouth drew up the Mayflower Compact to serve as their instrument of government in place of the formal charter they never received. This group enjoyed a cultural and spiritual homogeneity from the strength of their apocalyptic reading of history; when they got the name 'the Pilgrim Fathers', their grip on the American imagination took its permanent form as the foundation myth of the country's true origin. Although both the Dutch and the French had bases in North America, British America began as three unstable settlements along the James River, at Plymouth, and on Bermuda, the three regions named by Captain John Smith in his *Generall Historie of Virginia, New England and The Summer Isles*, printed in London in 1624. The first extract I have chosen comes from that *Generall Historie* by the eyewitness who sailed with the southern group in 1607; the second, from the *History of Plimmoth Plantation* by an eyewitness who sailed with the pilgrim group on the Mayflower. For his English readers John Smith pictures America as a place of danger, opportunity and exotic strangeness, a ground for heroic conquest and profit; for the elect William Bradford projects America as the locus of the divine testing and perfecting of man.

To complete the staircase of steps up and down the American coast: five further colonies were added to Virginia and Plymouth before the Civil War and Interregnum in England: Massachusetts Bay (1628), Maryland (1634), Connecticut (1635), Rhode Island (1636), and New Haven (1638). Virginia, Plymouth and Massachusetts Bay were each sponsored by English merchants organized into joint stock companies; Connecticut, Rhode Island and New Haven were offshoots of religious impulses from Massachusetts Bay; Maryland, the first colony to be settled by a proprietary grant from Charles I and not by a joint stock company, also had a religious motive, being intended by its founders George and Cecilius Calvert as a refuge for Roman Catholics. Although from 1642 to 1660 emigration from England never ceased – over 75,000 persons landing – no new colonies were founded in that period of English turbulence and the existing colonies were left to their own devices; even Virginia, which had become a royal colony directly under crown control in 1624 after the bankruptcy of the founding stock company, lived largely by itself. The preoccupation of England with its internal troubles resulted in a defensive league of all the New England colonies save Rhode Island in 1643, called the New England Confederation, which lasted until 1684. But the Confederation did not stem, nor seek to stem, the natural development everywhere towards local autonomy, encouraged by England's self-absorption.

With the Restoration came renewed colonial activity. Charles II made a number of proprietary grants on the model of his father's Maryland grant in part to recompense his loyal nobility. Those grants together with the conquest of New Netherlands secured the establishment of Carolina (1664), New York (1664), New Jersey (1665), Pennsylvania (1681), and Delaware (1701). Of the new proprietors only William Penn, the proprietor of Pennsylvania, was driven by religious motives, intending his colony as a refuge for Quakers. But while the King was active in proliferating colonies, his Parliament and Privy Council were equally active in attempts to regulate and organize them. Parliament enacted the Navigation Act of 1660 (a reenactment of Commonwealth navigation acts) to clarify the economic relationship of colonies and England by creating a national monopoly of colonial trade; the Privy Council designated a standing committee, the Lords of Trade, responsible for the administration of all the English colonies. It sat for twenty years during which it vigorously sought to centralize and systematize colonial administration and to convert all colonies into royal colonies. (Upon its recommendation New Hampshire was separated from Massachusetts Bay in 1679 and the charter of Massachusetts forfeited in 1684.) At the accession of James II, the zeal for centralization grew even intenser and the Dominion of New England was created in 1686 to include all the colonies from Maine to Pennsylvania under one government without local representative assemblies. The Glorious Revolution ended not only the rule of James but also the Dominion of New England.

The entire period of the Restoration, then, exhibited a tussle between the centralizing policies of the English government and countervailing forces in each colony. One blinks both at the administrative inventiveness of the central government and its imaginative deficiency in assessing how conditions on the ground might be inimical to stability, the necessary precondition for central government. Among conditions promoting instability, the following now seem the most glaring to modern readers: the concessions of land tenure, religious tolerance and self-government forced upon companies and proprietors in order to recruit and retain settlers, which concessions could not be withdrawn without objection; the discrepancies in social, economic, and political success among the colonies and within each, wildly fluctuating from year to year and leading inevitably to protests; the varying exposures to attacks from Indians, pirate marauders, and foreign powers with a consequent but unsteady determination to find self-reliant means of security; and even the diverse anxieties of founding religious groups against a background of fading purity and zeal, the dilution of doctrine, or the advances of dissent and heresy in their individual colonies. These factors taken together produced volatile and unstable conditions within each colony and in their relations with their neighbours. Such eruptions as King Philip's War,[4] Bacon's Rebellion,[5] Culpeper's Rebellion,[6] Leisler's Rebellion[7] and the Salem Witch Trials can all be traced to one or more of them. Each disturbance occasioned interesting colonial prose comment but one work in particular reflects dramatically the personal insecurity of one woman over a period of three months in 1676 when Indian captors seized her and hurried her westward and northward in 'removes' through the wilderness. Mrs Mary Rowlandson's 'narrative' of 'Captivity and Restauration' reflects the plight of inland settlements in King Philip's War, the tension between frontier and settled communities, the collision between Puritan concepts of fortitude and divine concern on the one hand, and Indian customs or diabolical inspiration on the other. Further, her account introduces another of our governing concerns: the demographic aspect of colonial prose under the influence of class, age, sex, and education.

In disregard of local conditions, the Duke of York pitted himself against regionalism when, on the death of his brother Charles II, he became James II. His remote experiences as proprietor of New York from 1664 undoubtedly shaped his centralizing policy: not for nothing was he known as the king 'who never learned anything and never forgot anything'. When the Anglo-Dutch war loomed closer in Europe in 1664, English warships had seized New York and the

Hudson River and the Duke of York had been given title to the wide domain between the Connecticut and Delaware Rivers; upon his accession he drove into brief being the Dominion of New England meant to unite New York, New Jersey, Connecticut, Rhode Island, Massachusetts, New Hampshire, and the territory of Maine under the direct rule of an appointed governor general. Just as arbitrarily and personally as James's English subjects were to be ruled according to his concept of kingship, so were his colonial subjects to be ruled. When his subjects at home drove James from the throne and invited his daughter Mary and her husband William of Orange to take his place, the impact of that Glorious Revolution upon the new colonies was enormous. It constitutes but one of the strong reinfusions of English thought which shaped America and its literature. The next three writers I have included – Cotton Mather, Sarah Kemble, and William Byrd – not only reflect geographical and demographic influences on American prose, they may also serve to indicate the permeability of the colonies to successive tides of English pre-occupations.

By the end of the Glorious Revolution, all of the thirteen colonies were in position save Georgia (1732), although Carolina was not formally divided into two until 1729 and not until 1728 was North Carolina's border clearly marked off from Virginia by a joint commission of Virginians and Carolinians including William Byrd II. Maine was still only a northern province of Massachusetts Bay in 1688 and would remain so until 1820. Delaware and New Jersey were likewise provinces of, respectively, Pennsylvania and New York. Plymouth would be absorbed into Massachusetts in 1691 just as New Haven had been absorbed into Connecticut in 1662. The five decades between the Virginia settlement and the Restoration were decades of plantation and population growth (by 1660 probably 200,000 Englishmen were resident in America); the next five decades between 1660 and 1710 were years of enlargement during which the colonies notably differentiated themselves from each other but even more notably commenced to distinguish themselves from the mother country. By 1710 a sufficient number of people in the colonies had begun to speak of themselves as 'Americans' for the usage to be common. England the while sought to gather the colonies into something like an empire. The Glorious Revolution was pivotal in both processes and can with hindsight be seen to have supplied the model of the American Revolution when it came. The remaining five or so decades are represented below by Edwards, Franklin, Tailfer, and Jefferson to indicate why and how it came. If the result was the birth of a nation, it was neither a stylistic nor a thematic *e pluribus unum*.

Time and place, then, govern the tone, materials, dominant themes and self-presentation of the first American writers who were at the outset English writers of American 'history'. That those Anglo-American writers did not come to seem to produce a second-class sub-set of English seventeenth-century prose – or, as Matthew Arnold thought, a provincial Macedonian school within a Greek literature – is partly owing to the contrast between what that history was meant to discover (seen by English eyes) and what it actually discovered (its American scenes). We have looked briefly at the colonial foundation. A look at the mythology of colonial foundation, or if one prefers, the historiography, will reveal the five theses this collection exemplifies: regionalism, periodicity, successive cultural replantation, demographic inscription, and genre transformation.

II

The two first-generation writers, Smith of Virginia and Bradford of Plymouth, were eyewitnesses of great prominence in their respective settlements, though Smith perhaps overstated and Bradford under-stated that prominence. John Smith's *Generall Historie* has primacy of time: as early as 1621 he planned its compilation from materials he had himself already written and from the accounts of fellow explorers and administrators; it was printed in London in 1624. Book One traces the history of British North America from the first English landing in 1170 by Madoc, Prince of Wales, down to 1605, Smith's materials being drawn from Hakluyt and other sources to describe the scene before he himself took the stage as principal actor. Book Two Smith 'writ with his own hand'; it is a revised and expanded version of his *A Map of Virginia* (1612). Book Three reprinted part two of the *Map of Virginia* augmented with material of his own and others' devising, including *The Proceedings of the English Colonie in Virginia* (1612). Book Four he put together from miscellaneous sources, some of his own writing. Book Five he took wholesale from a manuscript written by a Bermuda administrator. Book Six he wrote from his own *Description of New England* (1616) and *New England Trials* (1620, 1622). The whole compilation was intended to be a veracious success story of the conquest of the wilderness delivered in 'the stile of a Souldier' but punctuated and elevated by verse interjections and flights of rhetoric.

Books Two and Three intensified the saga-like suspense entailed in repeated efforts to bring the land under control by dramatizing the romantic human interest tale of Pocahontas. That she made more and longer appearances in the *Generall Historie* than in its sources has sometimes been taken to reduce its historical value, revision towards wonder being equated with mendacity. Smith's conception of reality was persistently at odds with what he found, however, and no phrase occurs with more regularity in the book than 'beyond all their expectations'. The interweaving of anticipated truths (an Indian princess) with unexpected abnormal experiences (the cannibalism, for example, of starving English settlers) is precisely what makes Smith's history so interesting. He could not avoid anticipating an Indian monarchic though savage court; neither, however, could he avoid noticing the craven incompetence of his civilized company. The ever higher value he gave the Pocahontas story in each telling does not – as Henry Adams, for example, severely thought – prove him a poor historian; it reveals an imaginative and shaping preconception allowed to assert itself in a retrospective reconsideration of his adventures. Furthermore if the text to which he everywhere addressed himself was the perfect viability of Virginia Britannia, his subtext was 'how it came to passe there was no better speed and successe in those proceedings' (p. 42). His apology in general terms relied on the Elizabethan commonplaces of the fall of man and the wheel of fortune. More specifically, against the commodity of the land Smith variously balanced the inadequacies, sloth, and mutinies of the settlers. His annalistic account is of a place where everything encourages prosperity save a people too frightened, too conventional, too incompetent, too ill-chosen for their task to capitalize on what God and nature so abundantly offered. If his sense of self is theatrical, he was not only the playwright but a principal actor, and his readers come to share his irritation that so few participated in his sense of occasion. When the place fell short of their anticipations, most wished to leave; Smith portrayed it as not only answering his expectations but exceeding his dreams. To English readers his extemporized version of a dependent yeoman kingdom naturally became a model for future colonies.

Without exaggeration or simplification, Bradford's *History of Plimmoth Plantation* represents in every respect the opposite. Smith's impetus to settle America can be read from *A Description of New England* printed in London in 1616: heroic fame was his spur, fame bought by success and paid for in good economic coin, fame open to any man of great heart and small means:

Introduction

Who can desire more content, that hath small meanes; or but only his merit to advance his fortune, then to tread, and plant that ground hee hath purchased by the hazard of his life? If he have but the taste of virtue, and magnanimitie, what to such a minde can bee more pleasant, then planting and building a foundation for his Posteritie, gotte from the rude earth, by Gods blessing and his own industrie, without prejudice to any? If hee have any graine of faith or zeale in Religion, what can hee doe lesse hurtfull to any; or more agreeable to God, then to seeke to convert those poore Salvages to know Christ, and humanitie, whose labors with descretion will triple requite thy charge and paines? What so truely sutes with honour and honestie, as the discovering things unknowne? erecting Townes, peopling Countries, informing the ignorant, reforming things unjust, teaching virtue; and gaine to our Native mother-countrie a kingdom to attend her; finde imployment for those that are idle, because they know not what to doe: so farre from wronging any, as to cause Posteritie to remember thee; and remembring thee, ever honour that remembrance with praise?

(Travels and works of Captain John Smith, vol. 2)

(Just as converting Indians to Christianity is seen first as holy work but quickly as the means of establishing peonage, the shift of pronoun from 'hee' to 'they' prepares for the maze of sliding pronouns by which all are exhorted to heroism for '*our* Native mother-countrie'.) But though he addressed himself to propaganda for New England as roundly as for Virginia, Smith saw the geographical differences between them. In New England he found 'high craggy clifty Rocks and stony Iles', 'a Country rather to affright than delight one'. 'How to describe a more plaine spectacle of desolation, or more barren, I know not', he wrote, 'yet are those rocky Iles furnished with good Woods, Springs, Fruits, Fish and Fowles, and the Sea the strangest Fish-pond I ever saw.' He emphasizes the abundance by describing as the 'strangest Fish-pond' what Bradford saw as 'a maine barr and goulfe to separate us from all the civill parts of the World', a 'vast and furious ocean'.

Bradford has another motive, another dream of commonwealth, another sense of the new land and another pattern of historiography to present in his annals. Smith's tacit assumption is the identity of classical epic and contemporary plantation, of Roman and English imperial success; Bradford's is the parallel between the Hebrew chosen people and the Plymouth settlers. Smith's theme assumes the continuous Englishness of Virginia in slow growth, the restocking of its population, the supply of its people until self-sufficient, the management of its polity all to come from England. Virginia Britannia by his reading is the classical and perfect model of New World colonialism. When he falls into a Biblical idiom, his is a modest, unapocalyptic, worldly parodic Hebraism as in The First Book, *The Generall Historie*: 'My purpose is not to perswade children from their parents; men from their wives; nor servants from

their masters: but only such as with free consent may be spared.'
Bradford was the official spokesman for the Pilgrim settlers to whom
he gave their name and for whom he reflected their own sense of
momentous and providential importance. For thirty-three years the
governor, he wrote as a permanent resident of a place intended for the
divine testing and perfection of man, not a mini-kingdom chartered
to return a profit to England but a colony of God's making, responsible to the King of kings for spiritual obedience.

Always a settler and never an entrepreneur, Bradford addressed
himself to the task of recording, not for publication to an English
audience, but for the memorial use of future generations, an exact
account of a climactic moment in Satan's eternal war as he writes in
Plimmoth Plantation, chapter 1, 'to ruinate and destroy the kingdom
of Christ'. His text is not man's success in taming the natural
abundance of the land, it is the strict covenant of God Almighty with
his Puritan saints to protect them in the harshest of places and bring
them first into local purity of worship and conduct them at length into
life eternal. The very resistance of America to settlement authentic-
ated its parallel with the testing of Israel in the old dispensation.
Bradford's more difficult circumstances proved his greater spiritual
advantages: the pilgrims could not

as it were, goe up to the tope of Pisgah, to vew from this willdernes a more goodly
cuntrie to feed their hopes; for which way soever they turned their eyes (save upward to
the heavens) they could have little solace or content in respecte of any outward objects.
For summer being done, all things stand upon them with a wetherbeaten face; and the
whole countrie, full of woods and thickets, represented a wild and savage heiw. (p. 64)

Bradford wrote to record the building of New Jerusalem in a
difficult land, conceiving of the pilgrims as sowers of an imminent
perfect reformation. Listing the motives for their removal to New
England, he cited 'great hopes ... for the propagating, and
advancing the gospell of the Kingdom of Christ in the remote parts of
the world; yea, though they should be but even as stepping-stones,
unto others of the performing of so great a work' (*Plimmoth Plantation*, chapter 4). The arrival of more Leyden settlers in 1629 signified
'the beginning of a larger harvest unto the Lord in the increase of his
churches and people in these parts, to the ... almost wonder of the
world that of so small beginnings so great things should insue'
(chapter 20). Bradford concluded his record in 1646 when episco-
pacy was abolished in England. On the back of a page in his first
chapter he then wrote:

Full litle did I thinke, that the downfall of the Bishops ... had been so neare, when I first
begane these scribled writings (which was aboute the year 1630, and so peeced up at

times of leasure afterward) or that I should have lived to have seene, or heard of the same; but it is the lords doing and ought to be marvelous in our eyes!....

Doe you not now see the fruits of your labours, O all yee servants of the lord? that have suffered for his truth, and have been faithfull witneses of the same, and yee litle handfull amongst the rest, the least amongest the thousands of Israel? You have not only had a seed time, but many of you have seene the joyfull Harvest.

Bradford wrote of a spiritual success story which he expected from the moment he landed. But the unity of text implied by his apocalyptic historiography, together with the veracity and simplicity enjoined on him by his message – 'That which I shall endevore to menefest in a plaine stile; with singuler regard unto the simple trueth in all things, at least as near as my slender Judgemente can attaine the same' – cannot conceal a subtext of disappointment, perhaps best revealed in another overleaf comment on his text:

I have been happy, in my first time, to see, and with much comforte to injoye, the blessed fruits of this sweete communion, but it is now a parte of my miserie in old age, to find and feele the decay and wante therof (in a great measure), and with greefe and sorrow of hart to lamente and bewaile the same.

That subtext recounts a story of gradual decline in spirituality amongst the pilgrims. Bradford's audience then becomes not posterity but the new generation, to be recalled to better ways. It is as though embarking on *Paradise Regained*, Bradford could not prevent his work's registering *Paradise Lost*.

Smith's history cobbled together other men's accounts in hasty expediency; Bradford frequently inserts letters and documents but he chooses brevity or amplification with the implied audience of the next generation in mind. He explains, for example, that he has

bene the larger in these things, and so shall crave leave in some like passages following, (thoug in other things I shal labour to be more contracte) that their children may see with what difficulties their fathers wrastled in going throug these things in their first beginnings, and how God brought them along notwithstanding all their weaknesses and infirmities. As also that some use may be made of herof in after times by others in shuch like waightie imployments.

(*Plimmoth Plantation*, chapter 6)

Of course full documentation adds veracity and interest, as Bradford knows – when he writes in chapter 14 '(desiring rather to manefest things in their words and apprehensions, then in my owne, as much as may, without tediousness)' – but the principal value Bradford sees in excerpting from current accounts is the value of conveying the past into the present stream of time so as to evoke the past for emulation. His rather different portrait drawing in the two biographies of Robinson and Brewster[8] illustrates not only the two stages of his hopes but also his governing didacticism, his aim to place ideal heroes before the younger generation. Robinson from the purer past is represented as an exemplary ancestor, 'in every way ... a commone father'; Brewster dying in a more dangerous present is described throughout in cautionary tones –

> none did more offend and displease him than shuch as would hautily and proudly carry and lift up themselves, being risen from nothing, and haveing litle els in them to comend them but a few fine cloaths, or a litle riches more then others... He had a singuler good gift in prayer, both publick and private, in ripping up the hart and conscience before God, in the humble confession of sinne...For the governmente of the church ... he was carfull to supress any errour or contention that might begine to rise up amongst them; and accordingly God gave good success to his indeavors herein all his days, and he saw the fruite of his labours in that behalfe.
>
> (*Plimmoth Plantation*, chapter 33)

In brief, the greater the distance between Bradford's expectations and his experience, his apocalyptic certainty and his daily life, the deeper grew his sense of moral danger. His account stretches between the poles of belief and horror, from 'the first breaking out of the light of the gospell in our Honourable Nation of England' to Plymouth church in 1644 seen as 'an anciente mother, growne olde, and forsaken of her children ... like a widow left only to trust in God'.

Even in smaller respects the contrast between Smith and Bradford seems perfect. The Pocahontas story in Smith, a kind of Dido episode in his epic, is balanced by the Squanto story in Bradford, a parable of a pagan, saved by providentially saving others. Virginia Indians stand religion on its head: 'There is', Smith writes, 'yet in Virginia no place discovered to bee so Savage in which the Savages have not a religion... But their chiefe God they worship is the Divell.' Their propensity for worship gives hope for conversion but meanwhile 'in lamentable ignorance doe these poore soules sacrifice themselves to the Divell, not knowing their Creator'. On the other hand, Indian government, although savage, is monarchic, stable, and orderly: 'Although the countrie people be very barbarous; yet have they amongst them such government, as that their Magistrates for good commanding, and their people for due subjection and obeying, excell many places that would be considered very civill.' Bradford's Squanto (guide, interpreter and teacher, the instrument by which a binding peace treaty was concluded with Massasoit, lasting thirty odd years) however, does come to know God. His brotherhood and helpfulness display God's providence just as Pocahontas's beauty and princely compassion authenticate Smith's chivalric heroism. In *Plimmoth Plantation*, chapter 13 Squanto dies, 'desiring the Governor to pray for him, that he might goe to the Englishmens God in heaven and bequeathed sundrie of his things to sundry of his English freinds, as remembrances of his love; of whom they had great loss'. As the Pocahontas story brightens in Smith's eyes with each telling, so the Bradfordian sense of cyclical lapse gradually infects his account of the Indians too: base settlers teach them wampumpeag coinage, sell them firearms, prompt their contempt; their tribal conflicts and commercial dealings with the Dutch and French contaminate the accord with the English; and gradually the language in which Bradford describes them darkens.

Bradford presents the gradual deterioration in Indian–English relations as a parallel to the morally dangerous increased prosperity of the settlement. At first Plymouth, organized in common landholding, mimed its religious separatism in its political isolation. It throve in spiritual opportunities but not in agricultural productivity. In chapter 14 when the Governor (Bradford never refers to himself by name or in the first person) yielded to pressure and allotted annual small-holdings to be farmed by family groups, it 'made all hands very industrious ... and gave farr better content'. Platonic communism being ruled out by the corrupt desire for property, 'God in his wisdome saw another course fiter for them.' Annual land allocation was succeeded by seven-year allotments given 'as nere the towne as might be ... that they might be kept close together, both for more saftie and defence, and the better improvement of the generall imployments'. Within twelve years prosperity led to wider dispersal of the population, 'For now as their stocks increased and the increse vendible, ther was no longer any holding them togeather, but now they must of necessitie goe to their great lots; they could not other wise keep their katle.' Bradford fought dispersal by giving 'some good farms to spetiall persons, that would promise to live at Plimoth, and lickly to be helpfull to the church or comonewealth'. But 'within a few years those that had thus gott footing ther rente them selves away'. Such prosperity and dispersal Bradford fears 'will be the ruine of New England ... and will provock the Lords displeasure against them'. His modern reader cannot but notice, however, that in Plymouth ownership of land always passed from Indian into English hands and never vice versa; dispersal inevitably created frontiers of collision with other colonies, other tribes and other kinds of settlement; private landholding, unlike trade in furs and fish which made for a common source of income, led to competitive individualism. These changes and those darkly viewed by Bradford resulted inevitably in the situation delineated in Mary Rowlandson's narrative.

Mary Rowlandson's narrative covers twelve weeks in 1675 and shows the regional distinction of Massachusetts from Plymouth, the

Introduction

concerns of a new period, and the emergence of the American woman writer. She was the daughter of Salem settlers who moved on to Lancaster when it was incorporated in 1653, where she married the Reverend Joseph Rowlandson, its first ordained minister. Salem had been planted in 1626 on poor land lacking a harbour. When in 1630 John Winthrop and 400 others arrived in four ships representing the Massachusetts Bay Company, they quickly saw the inconvenience and preferred to settle around Boston, whose virtually ice-free port guaranteed the prosperity from seaborne trade that Bradford feared from agriculture. Winthrop stands in the same relationship to Massachusetts as Bradford does to Plymouth. His journal, begun at Southampton when the expedition was about to set sail, was kept intermittently until his death in 1649.

Winthrop recorded his shipboard sermon to his fellow passengers as they sailed towards Massachusetts: 'wee shall be as a City upon a Hill. The eies of all people are uppon us' (*A Model of Christian Charity*, printed by Massachusetts Historical Society, 1838). He spoke to rural and urban middle-class families not so much escaping Laudian persecution[9] and separating themselves from the Church of England (although Winthrop acknowledged that persecution, poor economic conditions caused by land enclosure, depression in the textile industry and inflation were God's means of weaning them from their native land) as intending to display to the whole world the congruity between commonwealth in polity, and congregationalism in religion, God's plan for mankind. Their journey was to be an example to those in England. Typically they were nuclear family units, two parents, a few children, a servant; the cost of migration discouraged the young, the unmarried, the unskilled. And when Massachusetts Bay was settled in 1630, Plymouth became provincial at a stroke. It held out as an independent colony only until 1691, when – together with the twenty-one towns it had spawned – it was absorbed into Massachusetts.

Women were vital to the early success of the Massachusetts experiment; in the renewed wave of migration after the Restoration, they never constituted less than one-quarter of the emigrants. They walk through pages of Winthrop's journal, not always favourably noticed, but noticed. Women settlers were largely literate; they were regularly called 'yoke-fellows', as was Mary Rowlandson, in a locution implying some sexual equality reinforced by the ascription to them in memorial sermons of a number of asexual virtues – prayerfulness, industry, charity, modesty, serious reading, and godly writing. It is not clear that Bradford shared the Massachusetts sense of the value of women. They first appear in his text as seasick on the way to Holland, detained by Hull authorities 'for no other cause ... but that they must goe with their husbands', then released because 'all were wearied and tired with them'. When removal to America is proposed, Bradford lists amongst the objections made that 'the length of the voiage was shuch, as the weake bodys of women ... could never be able to endure'; he confutes most of the objections but not that one. The landing at Cape Cod notably omits any separate mention of them:

> Being thus arived in a good harbor and brought safe to land, they fell upon their knees and blessed the God of heaven, who had brought them over the vast and furious ocean, and delivered them from all the periles and miseries therof, againe to set their feete on the firme and stable earth, their proper elemente. (p. 64)

Winthrop's matter-of-fact arrival ten years later (recorded in his journal, *The Winthrop Papers*, ed. A. Forbes, 5 vols., Boston, 1929–45) is sociably aware of the ladies:

> We that were of the assistants, and some other gentlemen, and some of the women, and our captain, returned with [the welcoming Salem citizens] to Nahumkeck, where we supped with a good venison pasty and good beer, and at night we returned to our own ship, but some of the women stayed behind. In the mean time most of our people went on shore upon the land of Cape Ann, which lay near us, and gathered store of fine strawberries.

Women make such exceedingly rare appearances in Bradford that you can count them on one hand: some decline 'to doe servise for other men [than their husbands], as dresing their meate, washing their cloaths, etc.'; Mrs Oldham's purity is contrasted to her husband's duplicity; Mr Lyford debauches a chaste maid who repents heartily; Morton and his Merrymount men amongst other wickednesses take Indian consorts; Gardiner keeps a concubine disguised as a cousin; Arthur Peach gets a servant girl with child; some women are shaken up during an earthquake. Winthrop, not always gallant, does not fail to remark the presence of women or rely on their useful gifts; unlike Bradford who uses the feminine third person singular almost exclusively for marine vessels, Winthrop naturally extends it to women as man's weaker vessel but essential helpmeet and even earthly joy.

Mary Rowlandson accepts the well-defined diminished sense of personal value but displays the valour implied in Winthrop's understanding of women, shown in his remarking in his journal of the nervous breakdown of the wife of Governor Hopkins of Connecticut,

> if she had attended her household affairs, and such things as belong to women, and not gone out of her way and calling to meddle in such things as are proper for men, whose minds are stronger etc., she had kept her wits, and might have improved them usefully and honorably in the place God had set her.

Mary Rowlandson was taken captive for ransom, used as a servant and carried into Vermont towards Canada in a withdrawal through twenty 'removes' in the wilderness. Her narrative presents her captivity as a recollected account chronologically ordered in twenty thousand words, shaped by frequent scriptural references from which she draws typological significance for herself and the puritan community. The account contains layers of signification, of which the ground is a direct and vigorous episodic relation of day-to-day experience. Upon that captivity narrative is raised a form of spiritual autobiography, evidencing God's providence in testing her own place among the elect. Further imposed upon the spiritual autobiography is the typical pattern of the Puritan experience in New England and upon that, the religious emblem of the soul attacked by Satan.

On the level of sheer event, Mary Rowlandson, writing frankly and pithily, shows herself quick-tongued, resourceful, and healthily self-centered. Maternal only to her own children, she extends no pity to sick papooses but grieves at her son's boil; she not only eats her own bit of horsefoot quickly, she then dispatches that of an English child: 'the Child could not bite it, it was so tough and sinewy, but lay sucking, gnawing, chewing and slabbering of it in the mouth and hand, then I took it of the Child, and eat it my self, and savoury it was to my taste' (p. 90). Her hopes and fears veer reasonably from high to low; she recounts naturally and succinctly her persistent search for food, her attachment to two or three friendly Indians, her satisfaction in having shaken her nicotine addiction and the like. She is calm about her normal human weakness:

I had often before this said, that if the Indians should come, I should chuse rather to be killed by them then taken alive but when it came to the tryal my mind changed; their glittering weapons so daunted my spirit, that I chose rather to go along with those (as I may say) ravenous Beasts, then that moment to end my dayes. (p. 82)

She is not heroic in her own eyes but a woman among others, dragged from her home and meaning to do what she can to survive.

On the level of spiritual autobiography, however, Mary Rowlandson's commonsensical self-identification as womanish but tough collapses at the third remove, when given a Bible on the Sabbath, she hits upon a Deuteronomy passage, 'and when I had read it, my dark heart wrought on this manner, That there was no mercy for me, that the blessings were gone, and the curses come in their room, and that I had lost my opportunity' (p. 87). Instantly her natural sense of self as victim undergoes the common transfer amongst women to a sense of herself as villain, captivity representing God's condemnation of her spiritual complacency and frivolity. Fortunately for her nervous health, the Puritan culture that prompted her feminine sense of complicity in her suffering offered the alternative concept of God's merciful chastisement. When that thought of chastisement not condemnation crosses her mind, the narrative discovers its spiritual purpose: the presentation of the Lord's dealing with one of the elect in a conversion experience, and by extension with his whole puritan community, and by further extension against Satan in the world. (She commences in the singular 'no mercy for me' but concludes in the significant plural: 'mercy promised if we would return to him by repentence'. She sees enemy Indians as 'hell-hounds', their singing and dancing 'hellish', their celebrations 'lively resemblances of hell'; they lie like the 'Father of Lies' and like the devil-as-lion, they roar and seek to devour the settlers.) In the end of her account Mary Rowlandson is restored to her husband much improved by her Pilgrim's Progress: 'And I hope I can say in some measure, As David did, *It is good for me that I have been afflicted*' (p. 101). By her conversion she can now liken herself to the man David 'in some measure' whereas formerly she feared her lightness; her address to her theme bears the marks of her region, time, and sex; the theme, the marks of her confrontation with the reality of her Indian captors interpreted as God's opportunity and the devil's intervention.

Another visit to Massachusetts two decades later allows us to add to the themes of regionalism, periodicity, and demographic inscription, the themes of genre transformation and re-Englishing. (Cotton Mather used Bradford's manuscript in his own history.) Mather's *Magnalia Christi Americana: or, the Ecclesiastical History of New England* was written between 1693 and 1697, and published in London in 1702. In seven books it outlines New England history from the Plymouth settlement to its own day, briefly memorializes officials and lengthily depicts 'Famous Divines', recites the history of 'Harvard-Colledge' and the lives of its clerical graduates, registers the 'Acts and Monuments' of the Puritan churches, gives the 'Faithful Record' of 'many Illustrious, Wonderful Providences' of God to the elect, and concludes with 'The Wars of the Lord' against Antinomians,[10] Quakers, Indians, false clergymen and the like. The order of the work is topical and then chronological, the structure separating into books and short essays some of the materials Bradford took up in his annalistic plan. The style claims to be 'simple, submiss, humble' (p. 113), 'without figure of rhetorick', and Mather commends the 'very plain, studiously avoiding obscure and foreign terms, and unnecessary citations of Latin sentences' in others; but it is in fact profuse, allusive, contrived, and ornate. Mather's overt theme is heroic – 'I write the WONDERS of the CHRISTIAN RELIGION, flying from the depravations of Europe to the American Strand' (p. 104); his latent theme is elegiac lament – *De tristibus* may be a proper title for the book I am now writing.' His professed model is 'incomparable Plutarch'; his actual model, Jeremiah and the gloomier prophets. Elsewhere in *Magnatia* by showing the 'Declension' of the present generation from the virtues of its fathers, he seeks to preach reform:

I saw a fearful *degeneracy* creeping, I cannot say, but rushing in upon those churches; I saw to multiply continually our dangers, of our losing no small points in our *first faith*, as well as our *first love*, and of our giving up the *essentials* of that church order, which was the very end of these colonies; I saw a visible *shrink* in all orders of men from among us, from that *greatness*, and that *goodness*, which was in the *first grain* that our God brought from *three sifted kingdoms*, into this land, when it was a *land not sown*.

That the old days and ways were best was his message for America; to it he joined for England the message that New England gave the world 'great examples of the methods and measures wherein an Evangelical Reformation is to be prosecuted' (p. 107). Although New England remained the 'city in the wilderness' on which all eyes, including God's, were fixed, its mission in the world given by Christ so that 'He might there, *to* them first, and then *by* them, give a *specimen* of many good things, which He would have His Churches elsewhere aspire and arise unto' (p. 108), Mather did not speak of it as a type for the New Jerusalem or regard it as a blueprint for England.

His *Magnalia* is more than a typical jeremiad, however, as the enormous self-consciousness of the Introduction conveys. Although doubtful and perplexed the text clearly belongs to the era that followed the Glorious Revolution. Addressing both an English and an American audience, Mather gives an account not only of God's intentions but of American achievements in civility and polity. His egregious self-display shows off Harvard learning to England as much as his own learning to his own people. Describing the first settlement he emphasizes that 'PERSECUTION' sent the Puritans to the Bay colony: 'It was indeed a *Banishment*, rather than a Removal, which was undergone by the glorious Generation.' The purest part of the church was thereby exiled: like Winthrop and the non-separating congregationalists of Massachusetts, he considers the New England churches a part of the Church of England. If the church continued to please God, the nation would be blessed; when it did not, God would remove his blessing. The church would forever survive, the nation might 'soon after this, *Come to Nothing*'. However, contemplating New England's purposes, Mather is neither reactionary bigot nor conservative doom-watcher and can conceive of the need for positive change; he knows that the altered political circumstances of the Glorious Revolution enjoin a new religious toleration, unlike the separating intolerance he described and endorsed in the earlier days. His own ecumenicalism is prepared to accommodate a good deal, if not amongst Anglicans, 'those IDUMAEANS, whose Religion is all Ceremony' or elsewhere 'Children of Unperswadeableness'. He decries 'an unhappy Narrowness of Soul'; unfortunately he could not always avoid it himself.

Mather made full use of Bradford's manuscript in his first book; he coloured his style, however, by quite other principles. In comparison with contemporary English style, his is remarkably old-fashioned. John Oldmixon in *The British Empire in America* (1708) for example, aspiring to ease and correctness, scorned Mather's 'Punns, Anagrams, Acrosticks, Miracles and Prodigies' and justly thought his book like one of those 'School Boy Exercises [of] Forty Years Ago'. Mather decorated his work with alliterative repetition, echoes of sound, violent capitalizations and italics, and puns on the names of his subjects – Urian Oakes's name leads to a digression on oak trees and Harvard, 'a rendezvous of Happy Druids'. Those reflect his boyhood training by Ezekiel Cheever, himself partly trained at Cambridge in Milton's day, as well as his study at Harvard, also patterned on Cambridge. His style owes nothing to the example of Bradford and much to a re-Englishing already half a century behind his own historical moment. He was a learned man, writing hastily, engaged in a heroic but also cautionary task, driving himself out of a persistent fear of 'idleness, of which there never came any goodness! idleness which is "the reproach of any people"'. There is no doubt that he considered himself a modernist, defending the 'reasonableness' of Christianity, interesting himself in the new science, commending a purified change. If his style looks backward, some things in his book look forward; the shifts from current annalistic history to essayistic topical history and from typology[11] to biography are both significant of things to come.

William Byrd of Virginia stands in contrast to Cotton Mather much as Smith did earlier to Bradford. Doubtless their sheer psychological and temperamental incompatibility accounts for a good deal of the difference, as a glance at Mather's diary (or 'Revised Memorials' as he called the records meant to be read by his survivors for their improvement) in contrast to Byrd's, written in shorthand cypher and detailing experiences Pepys would not find foreign, reveals. Byrd records as a typical day:

I arose at 5 o'clock and read two chapters in Hebrew and some Greek in Anacreon. I said my prayers and ate milk and strawberries. . . . I read some Italian in the evening and took a walk about the plantation, I scolded at G-r-l for telling a lie. I said my prayers and had good health, good thoughts and good humor, thanks be to God Almighty.

An equally typical Mather entry runs:

Being prostrate, in the Dust on my Study-floor, after many Fears of a sad, woful Heart, that the Holy Spirit of the Lord Jesus Christ, grieved by my Miscarriages, would forsake mee utterly, that Spirit of the Lord made an inexpressible Descent upon mee. A Stream of Tears gushed out of my Eyes, upon my Floor, while I had my Soul inexpressibly irradiated with Assurances.

Byrd's casual irreverence about how the colonies came to be settled – 'As it happen'd some Ages before to be the fashion to Santer to the Holy Land, and go upon other Quixot Adventures, so it was now grown the Humour to take a Trip to America' (p. 144) – would have horrified Mather. The only common intellectual ground between the two I have observed is their bibliophilia (Mather's library contained over 3,000 books, Byrd's over 3,500), their contempt for sloth, and their strong consciousness of oligarchic descent. Nevertheless the salient differences continue to witness to the regionalism, the changing period concerns, the marks of social class, the gradual genre changes and the re-Englishing so important in the American tradition.

Like Smith's a hundred years earlier, Byrd's text is nature's abundance; given the changed circumstances of his period, his sub-text is not so much man's ineptitude as the progressive possibilities of improvement. His father, who developed a large frontier estate on the James river where he grew tobacco and traded in slaves, sugar, molasses, and rum, sent him to be educated in England first at Felsted and then after a Grand Tour (with a longish sojourn in Holland to learn good business methods) at the Middle Temple. Byrd several times returned to England but from 1704 his residence was Westover, where he increased the family estate from 26,000 to 180,000 acres and lived like a New World princeling, his cavalier tastes improved by his Enlightenment interests. In 1737 he laid out a town on the Byrd property at the James Falls and named it Richmond, the very name expressive of his way of thinking. Like Mather he became a member of the Royal Society, his pamphlet on the plague (almost the only prose work he published in his lifetime) perhaps analogous to Mather's promotion of smallpox vaccination. And if the taint of witchcraft somewhat undeservedly hangs over Mather, who was in fact more moderate than most, so the taint of slavery undeservedly hangs over Byrd, for he would have run the estate with white indentured servants if he could have got and kept them, augmented by the children of intermarriage with Indians if he could have brought that about. He considered that slavery confirmed the pride and sloth of white people, their resulting poverty making criminals of them, and that the increasing number of blacks forced a severity on the whites repugnant to a good-natured man. He believed too that the whites' rejection of intermarriage alienated the Indians, made them fierce, and weakened the colonial stock.

Byrd's most important works are the three groups of travel journals in the Westover manuscripts, *History of the Dividing Line . . . Run in the Year of our Lord 1728*, *A Progress to the Mines* (1732) and *A Journey to the Land of Eden, A.D. 1733*, a satire on his Carolina neighbours of 'Lubberland' in the ironic manner of his acquaintance Swift though far less biting. The first (from which I extract) is a journal Byrd kept in the woods when he was one of the Virginia commissioners appointed to settle the boundary dispute between Virginia and North Carolina. He intended to write it up more formally as a history of how the commissioners executed their task. That overt theme cloaks his true southern theme: a fecund land absurdly mismanaged by, among others, 'Riprobates of good Familys', the leaders 'always engaged in Factions and Quarrels, while the rest detested Work more than Famine' (p. 145), but ready to be improved when men used their energies to drain swamps, cut canals, plant orchards, grow flax, and see to the local administration of justice. Byrd's sheer stylistic competence ought to have secured for the opening pages of the *History of the Dividing Line*, an account of the generation of all the original colonies from the one Virginia, the authority of foundation myth, 'shewing how the other British Colonies on the Main have, one after the other, been carved out of Virginia' (p. 143). Byrd's style is quick, witty, informal, and conversational. Droll understatement – 'and so Private Interest got the better of Public Spirit; and I wish that were the only Place in the World where such politicks are fashionable' (p. 153) – is varied with shrewdly mocked deflation – 'Not only the Gun-Powder-Treason, but every other Plot, both pretended and real, that has been trump't up in England ever Since, has helpt to People his Lordship's Propriety' (p. 150). Having outlined the foundations of Virginia and North Carolina and coming to the surveying of the border, Byrd records whatever catches his alert eye. He indulges his taste for natural history – 'A vertuoso might divert himself here very well, in picking up Shells of various Hue and Figure, and amongst the rest, that Species of Conque Shell which the Indian Peak [wampum in Massachusetts] is made of' (p. 158); gossip – 'not far from the Inlet, dwelt a Marooner, that Modestly call'd himself a Hermit, tho' he forfeited that Name by Suffering a wanton Female to cohabit with

Him... Thus did these Wretches live in a dirty State of Nature, and were mere Adamites, Innocence only excepted' (pp. 158–9); descriptive social anthropology – 'Thus, considering the foul and pernicious effects [yaws], of Eating Swine's Flesh in a hot Country, it was wisely forbidden and made an Abomination to the Jews, who liv'd much in the same Latitude with Carolina' (p. 162); comparative history, likening Carolina's shelter of fugitive slaves, debtors, and criminals 'to increase their People' to Rome's 'which was made a City of Refuge for all Debtors and Fugitives, and from that wretched Beginning grew up in time to be Mistress of a great Part of the World' (p. 163). In such locutions as 'a vertuoso' and 'a dirty State of Nature' as in his fastidious tolerance and scepticism, Byrd displays the verbal and intellectual currency of an English gentleman. Everywhere he notes condescendingly the intolerable laziness and disorderly freedom of the Carolinian in contrast to the Virginian. Perhaps nothing makes clearer the bent of his mind than his sardonic description of the slovenliness and backwardness of the Lubberlanders:

One thing maybe said for the Inhabitants of that province, that they are not troubled with any Religious Fumes, and have the least Superstition of any People living. They do not know Sunday from any other day, any more than Robinson Crusoe did, which would give them a great Advantage were they given to be industrious. But they keep so many Sabbaths every week, that their disregard of the Seventh Day has no manner of cruelty in it, either to Servants or Cattle. (p. 168)

Byrd's prose strives so successfully for ease and correctness that it might have served for a model to his fellow Virginians. But it remained a private gentlemanly exercise unpublished in his own day, and inaugurated no native tradition. A reader of Burnett, Eachard, Addison, Hobbes, Boyle, Cowley, Bentley, Etherege, Halifax, Locke, Otway, Dryden, Sprat, Gay, Defoe, Congreve, Vanbrugh, Pope, Newton, Fielding, Swift, and Prior; of the *Spectator*, the *Philosophical Transactions of the Royal Society*, *The Monthly Mercury*, and *The Gentleman's Magazine*, Byrd set himself a daily pattern of methodical study, never intermitting to read Hebrew and Greek, interspersed with Latin, Italian, and French. He occasionally translated and drafted essays for his own amusement. Yet one cannot doubt that had he remained in England, little more than feuilletons suitable for the journals he read would have been produced. Not only his eye but what it looked upon makes up his value.

The unpublished journal of Sarah Kemble Knight, recounting a horseback business trip (to help settle a niece's estate) from Boston to New York and home again in the year 1704, may be compared both to Mary Rowlandson's unwilling travels and Byrd's surveying journey. Madam Knight was a business woman, recorder of public documents and teacher; the unverified tradition that Benjamin Franklin attended her school may suggest the middle-class shrewd Yankee in her self-projection. Her travelogue, written up from a daily diary, shows the intent to publish in such name-dropping locutions as: 'I stayed a day here longer than I intended by the Commands of the Honerable Governor Winthrop to stay and take a supper with him whose wonderful civility I may not omitt'. It was designed as a humorous guidebook of recreational utility, neither like Rowlandson to quicken the religious nor like Byrd to inform the literate. Hence Madam Knight projects herself variously as a 'fearful female travailler', a literary flourisher of lyrical *aperçus*, a competent, hardheaded business woman, and an ironic social commentator. Each of her postures is self-consciously unstable. As a 'fearful female travailler' she uses ironically the religious paralleling so significant to Mary Rowlandson:

The Canoo was very small and shallow, so that when we were in she seem'd redy to take in water, which greatly terrified mee, and caused me to be very circumspect, sitting with my hands fast on each side . . . not daring so much as to lodg my tongue a hair's breadth more on the side of my mouth than tother, nor so much as think on Lott's wife. (p. 126)

As prose poet she is also role-subversive like a demi-Fielding: 'Now was the Glorious Luminary, wth his swift Coursers arrived at his Stage, leaving poor me wth the rest of this part of the lower world in darkness' (p. 127). These two humorous poses rotate around the shrewdest, that of the factual recorder of useful commercial information: '[New Yorkers] are not strict in keeping the Sabbath as in Boston. . . But seem to deal with great exactness as farr as I see or Deall with' (p. 138), and on the return journey that voice asserts its dominance. But her most interesting voice is that of social commentator and here she most invites comparison with Byrd. She registers her sense of regional superiority to Connecticut folk, for example, like Byrd observing his Lubbers (or for that matter like Mrs Trollope on the *Domestic Manners of the Americans* more than a century later):

Being at a merchants house, in comes a tall country fellow, wth his alfogeos^a full of Tobacco; for they seldom Loose their Cudd, but keep Chewing and Spitting as long as they'r eyes are open. . .At last, like the creature Balaam Rode on, he opened his mouth and said: have You any Ribinen for Hatbands to sell I pray? (pp. 135–6)

When it was first published, her journal was taken for fiction and indeed Madam Knight shows the novelist's power to render dialogue in dialect; she names characters satirically, sets them in typical motion and puts them to speech. 'Jone Tawdry' 'curtsees' fifty times, and then

^a Saddlebags, and so by extension, cheeks.

says, 'Law you ... its right Gent, do You, take, tis dreadful pretty.'
Her sense of the comical is both folk and snobbish, producing such
anecdotes as that of the two rural justices sitting on a bench of
pumpkins to adjudicate a theft by a slave and the receiving of the
stolen goods by an Indian, in which the justices are a very Dogberry
and Verges. From her alternations of vernacular Yankeeism and
various literary workings-up emerges a picture of a country already
advanced in secularization and social stratification. Such dangers she
does not perceive. Her land is neither wilderness nor Eden, her future
neither apocalypse nor millennium. Her Boston is far from a Holy
City but neither is it *primum inter pares*;[b] it is incomparable. She scoffs
at Quakers and foreigners, at bumpkins, Indians, and blacks. She is
not an intellectual and owes little to literary values from a mother
country across the Atlantic. But neither has she begun to mythologize
a federal nation. Regionalism is too strong an element in her make-up
even for her instinctive hypothesis of economic progress to suggest to
her a future homogenous and prosperous America. What she has
done, however, is to put on record under all the posed self-
deprecations of gender the social ease of womanly competence in her
times. That Mather's picture of the church triumphant though the
nation die was published in the very year she made her journey must
suggest a redirection of colonial interests towards the secular, the
exploitative, and the independent, which would leave the Mather
position high and dry. But the year before that journey, Jonathan
Edwards was born; the national possibilities in the conjunction of
Edwards and Franklin are next to be explored.

There is nothing in common between the all too easy consciences of
William Byrd's 'good health, good thoughts, and good humor,
thanks be to God Almighty' or Madam Knight's 'I Blest myself that I
was not one of this miserable crew' and Jonathan Edwards's 'I have
been before God; and have given myself, and all that I am and have to
God, so that I am not in any respect my own: I can challenge no right
in myself.... I have given myself clear away, and have not retained any
thing as my own.' The interesting question is, of course, what signs of
accommodation between the Great Awakening and a transplanted
Enlightenment can be found in him. And the answer to this question
is found in the different concerns which distinguish Edwards from the
earlier Mather and can perhaps even be detected in some lessening in
the regionalism which characterizes the earlier period. Edwards
addressed himself to problems specific to his own eighteenth century
from a position richly indebted to his New England forefathers. His

b The first among equals.

eulogy of his uncle, Colonel John Stoddard, as a 'strong rod of the community' because he was 'thoroughly established in those religious principles and doctrines of the first fathers of New England' is easily transferable to him. Honouring those principles, Edwards like Mather agreed that his generation's commitment to Puritanism had diminished into a lukewarm formalism in religious practice, a moralization of faith, and an optimistic rationalism in religion, all of them changes which he subsumed under the conventionally available term Arminianism. [12] The work of his life was to counter that diminution, recall his generation to a revived Calvinism, assail Arminian doctrines, and by both moving and teaching his readers redirect them into effectual piety. Just as precocious and dedicated a young person as Mather, he used his considerable intellectual and personal powers – deep if not broad, strong if not varied – to stir America to a Great Awakening. In treatises on Original Sin, Freedom of the Will, and the Religious Affections, he opposed Arminian positions and addressed the general problems of the nature and destiny of man. His *Personal Narrative* was intended to play a didactic part in this life work.

Edwards's fundamental intellectual conviction involved an act categorically separating the human and the divine, nature and the supernatural, to assert the sovereignty of God and the incapacity of man to achieve true religion by any power of his own, save the reception of God's grace. His *Personal Narrative*, a retrospective account of his own conversion experiences, intended to be exemplary and informative, is a consistent reworking from his own diary of his personal efforts to conceptualize emotions felt twenty years earlier as a young man at Yale College. The recasting creates a unified text with an overriding theme; the narrative is not intended to develop the day-to-day religious experiences of the author as they occurred in the past, but rather to recreate a mature assessment of those experiences in form and language influenced by later readings, by conversations with awakened sinners in his subsequent Northampton parish, and by the intellectual preoccupations of the time of composition. Consulting his diary, Edwards is careful to distinguish the 'I' of the present narrative from the younger 'I' of the diary. He lets the reader watch him in retrospection: 'My support was in contemplations on the heavenly state; as I find in my Diary of May 1, 1723' (p. 184). The mature 'I' discovers in the immature diarist an unreliable but ardent subject of God's activity; the boyish 'I' tends dangerously towards spiritual self-reliance, takes 'self-righteous' pleasure in performing religious duties, seeks salvation as the 'main Business' of his life oblivious to the self-preoccupation in his calculated religion. Yet the younger man's energetic seeking cannot be utterly dismissed for it leads to a positive change in his behaviour: 'I was brought wholly to break off all former wicked ways, and all ways of known outward sin' (p. 179). Nonetheless the older man perceives even that change as lacking salvatory grace: 'But yet, it seems to me, I sought after a miserable manner; which has made me sometimes since to question, whether ever it issued in that which was saving; being ready to doubt, whether such miserable seeking ever succeeded' (p. 179). Contrariwise, the mature 'I' discovers in recollection positive signs of grace in experiences overlooked by the immature 'I': 'But it never came into my thought, that there was any thing spiritual, or of a saving nature in this' (p. 180). To secure the unity of the work, Edwards opens with a summary sentence predicting the outcome of the narrative: 'I had a variety of concerns and exercises about my soul from my childhood; but had two more remarkable seasons of awakening, before I met with that change by which I was brought to those new dispositions, and that new sense of things, that I have since had' (p. 178). His theme is the necessity to distinguish genuinely saving, religious affections from unsaving, apparently religious affections, and to conceptualize the true affections into a knowing faith. His technical device is to dramatize the new vision through the differences between the 'old' and 'new' man under the appearance of the 'young' and 'mature' writer, without obliterating signs of the new man in the young man, since his implied audience is composed of those at diverse stages in their own spiritual development.

Edwards has to record that in the beginning he resisted the Calvinist doctrine of God's sovereignty, God choosing to save some and leave the rest to be 'everlastingly tormented in Hell'; when the resistance vanished, and the doctrine seemed 'exceedingly pleasant, bright, and sweet', then Edwards strove to express his 'inward, sweet delight in God and divine things' (p. 180). In psalm-influenced parallelism and repetition, he then struggles to 'sing, or chaunt forth my meditations; or, to speak my thoughts in soliloquies with a singing Voice', showing how 'God's excellency, his wisdom, his purity, and love, seemed to appear in every thing; in the sun, moon and stars; in the clouds, and blue sky; in the grass, flowers, trees; in the water, and all nature; which used greatly to fix my mind' (p. 181). The affective content is not meant to obliterate the conceptual but to derive from and intensify it. Nor, of course, could Edwards's 'new sense' provide only ecstasy: when turned upon his own depravity, it aroused passionate nausea. Both positive and negative rhapsody in Edwards is an expressive experiment in the creation of affective symbolism.

The significance of Edwards's self-offering in the *Personal narrative*, its fusion of conception and emotion, is greater even than the presentation of the core of his religious philosophy applied to his own experience. I have been arguing the diversity (especially regional) in early American colonial prose. It might be thought that something like a single dominant line should soon emerge, or a voice fuller than local voices representing an emergent American identity. Were that so, Edwards would surely be consigned to the losing side, his stance giving ground to a triumphant secularism, expansionism, exploitativeness, and optimism. Edwards's conviction of sin, however, and his cultivated self-excoriation is not only heart-honest; it is also common to a dark line of American writing that re-surfaces in Melville and Hawthorne. Furthermore, to see religious awakening as God's outpouring of grace in America is to tap a radical millenarian politics only apparently at odds with Edwards's conservative theology. In undertaking his heroic task of awakening mankind to God's irresistible sovereignty, Edwards played a role in democratizing religion, broadening its social basis to incorporate any person, however rare, in whom conversion occurred, and extending its hegemony to Americans in many other colonies. (After all, the least interesting aspect of regionalism is its complacency, whether Madam Knight's or William Byrd's, though the palm for complacency must surely go to New England.) Awakenings in Pennsylvania, Virginia, the Carolinas, and elsewhere followed punctually on his and drew upon the same affective rhetoric. If the Great Awakening in the end lost Edwards's analytic drive and slid into a persistent American backwoods evangelism, its bequest was at the least a corporate experience.

If Edwards can be seen as an introspective counter-current to eighteenth-century enlightenment who nonetheless honoured enlightenment with its most searching personal examination, Benjamin Franklin can be read as his natural antithesis − a relaxed embracer of enlightenment concepts of scepticism, rationalism, liberalism, and utilitarianism, who because he could never take seriously either predestination or the uselessness of good works made only a jesting critic of awakenings. Virtually all of our general theses are of interest in his case. Period interests emerge in the plot line of his *Autobiography*: the making of a self-made man. A new version of regionalism can be seen emerging there: loyalty not to the polis of one's birth (for he left Boston cheerfully enough) but the polis of one's choice (for he tirelessly worked to make Philadelphia a centre of literate civility). Re-Englishing is conveyed in Franklin's description of learning to write by imitating first Defoe, then Addison, then Shaftesbury, Pope, and Roscommon. Class marks emerge in an embourgeoisement of style, where the marks of class are marks of changing one's class, 'Having emerg'd from the Poverty and Obscurity in which I was born and bred, to a State of Affluence and some Degree of Reputation in the World' (p. 192). But the most interesting is the genre transformation of autobiography at Franklin's hands, since it subsumes the others.

Whatever Franklin overtly says of his motives for writing autobiography – and he opens with his motives, giving them fairly and fully as the pleasure in anecdotes proposed to his family, as the utitlity of example for the same implied audience, as the pleasure to himself in reliving a felicitous life, as the self-indulgence in self-display should a larger audience choose to read him, and finally as the gratification of vanity – autobiography as Franklin conceives of it is the celebration of the successful achievement of self-hood. An optimistic saga describes a hero at the centre of an environment which presents such obstacles and problems as do not suppress the protagonist but arouse his inner resources so that he more and more dominates that environment and forces from it public recognition. In Franklin's version of autobiography the outside world watches the single actor, is hostile, scoffs, becomes interested and finally pays homage; the protagonist feels his own reality and individualism in a self-recollection tinged with tolerant self-judgment: 'this I therefore reckon one of the first Errata of my life' (pp. 204–5); he also can easily put his self-awareness to one side for objective on-looking: 'I who stood by and heard all, saw immediately' (p. 209). The story of self-fulfilment contains little emotional introspection but a good deal of novelistic self-observation. Both the design and style converge in a self-presentation not unlike that of Defoe's Moll Flanders or Robinson Crusoe, Fielding's Tom Jones or Joseph Andrews, though perfectly unlike that of Richardson's Pamela, for all that the Franklin 1744 reprint of her story was the first novel to be published in America. Franklin wrote Part One in a fortnight in England visiting his friend Jonathan Shipley, Bishop of St Asaph. The tradition that what he wrote during the day he read aloud to amuse the family each evening speaks to the unified presentation of comic epic imitating his boyhood and early career in America, the consistency of the writing persona who observes the boy and young man he has been, not so as to conceal what he became or his judgment of what he once was but not at all to allow that theme to muffle the principal source of interest: a highly individual, totally external twenty-five year course of events in a new country. The successful adult shows himself helping first his profession, then his city, and finally his nation become itself. There is no inconsistency and little irony in the double perspective of youth and maturity; in the autobiography as Franklin produces it in Part One (Part Two exhibits his moral earnestness) converge the novel of the achievement of individuality and the Plutarchian life of anecdote marshalled under a developmental scheme. It is neither exemplary typology, nor conversion story, nor mock confession, nor serious confession. Humour is incidental to it, though its theme is festive and celebratory; the recollecting persona does not enter covet and melancholy judgment upon the younger subject, nor does Franklin work from a more documentary source than memory – as does Edwards. Unlike his putative schoolmistress Madam Knight he seeks no effects from literary parody and gains none from conflicting personae. Unlike Byrd, he includes himself amongst bumpkins at the outset but does not expect to remain in their company. Although he shares Jefferson's interest in self and national improvement and although the thrust for independence is clearer in his work than anything we have read thus far, Franklin's autobiography is chiefly interesting for its acute pragmatic intelligence in describing and recreating social change so as to promote it. For Franklin simply assumed that the free and fulfilled self was the nucleus of a free and fulfilled society; he called his times 'The Age of Experiment' and thought self-fulfilment man's chief experimental interest, naturally furthering the concomitant American experiment to perpetuate a free society.

Georgia was an experiment in founding a wholly benevolent society. In the voice of the three pamphleteers who produced *A True and Historical Narrative of the Colony of Georgia* a new libertarian pragmatism pits itself satirically against the benevolent enlightened imperial orthodoxy of the mother country. In 1732 England had a good many reasons for founding Georgia, the last colony before the American Revolution. In international terms, the colony, founded in a region previously claimed and occupied by Spain, made an imperial statement of expansionist intentions to be heard by Spain to the south and France to the west. In American colonial terms, the colony, founded on land once ceded to but not settled by Carolina, protected the frontiers of that useful proprietorship. But in national English terms, the colony was meant to serve as a haven for debtors to the relief of English prisons, and as a model community to bear witness to enlightened English benevolence. It was the only colony run by a charitable Board of Trustees without hope of financial return, the only colony to ban slavery, the only colony to prohibit hard liquor. Its first charter proclaimed its military and philanthropic purposes, restricted land-holding to not more than 500 acres in order to create a society of smallfarmers, and granted liberty of conscience to all save Roman Catholics. James Oglethorpe, well known in England as a penal reformer, sailed as one of the trustees on the ship *Anne* with 100 emigrants in 1732 and made the first settlement at Savannah, purchasing a tract of land from the Creek Indians for that purpose. To create a social utopia might not have been incompatible with building a military outpost, but the colonists from the outset were dissatisfied with the economic and social arrangements made for them, and their dissatisfaction centered on land tenure, slave labour, and rum. (Just to the north in South Carolina they could see a prosperous economy based on large plantations worked by slaves which invited emulation and made competition difficult; trade in lumber with the West Indies was inviting but required the exchange in rum, a commodity the colony could neither drink nor re-export.) For Patrick Tailfer and his fellow Scottish collaborators David Douglas and Hugh Anderson, the crux of the problem with Georgia was that they could have no hand themselves in making their own economic and social arrangements, but the thrust of their pamphlet was against land, slave, and rum provisions. To secure 'reform' – for so they styled their ambitions – the group built into the overt satirical strategy of *A True and Historical Narrative* the conflict between anticipation and actuality which coloured the histories of Smith and Bradford. Writing with Franklin's sceptical pragmatism, they altered the genre 'regional history' to target holy men as the obstacle to real progress. If Savannah is their 'city on a hill', God-fearing men are not their friends.

   A True and Historical Narrative opens with a mock dedication to the founder of the colony, extolling in egregious mock flattery Oglethorpe's peculiar brand of philanthropy, who to preserve his colony from the dangers of riches, the anxieties of ambition and the perplexities of law and to secure for it the advantages of humility and sobriety planted a genteel, paternalistic, charity-driven colonial dictatorship. Between the dedication and the text, a preface prints excerpts first from a promotional pamphlet printed in England in 1733 entitled *A New and Accurate Account of the Provinces of South Carolina and Georgia*, and then from Samuel Wesley's eulogistic poems on the colony. Against that carefully adjusted perspective, the 'true . . . narative' then compares point by point what was declared to have been accomplished and what the authors say was actually accomplished. A strategy of complete truth telling allows the satirists to promote their alternative economic and social plans for Georgia under the guise of stripping away pretence. Their argument in favour of colonial rights against incompetent external folly produces a mordant, and partisan document. The self-consciousness of the strategy is almost entire: the writers know the degree of exaggeration on either side of their analysis. Nevertheless they write not so much re-Englishing an American style in imitation of, say, Swift's Drapier's letters as unselfconsciously fuelling their irritation from the energy of the region from which they come. All are 'North Britons', all have enjoyed the condescension of the English to Scotland, all know that Scots were brought to Georgia because Scots make good fighters and philanthropy needs stiffening from a sector seen in England as raw, energetic, and bellicose. The full history of Scotland's anti-English contribution to American independence is still to be written; when it is, Tailfer, Douglas, and Anderson should be recorded therein. Certainly the Anglo-Irish peer, the Earl of Egmont, writing a contemporary hostile critique of the pamphlet, was clear that a major component in their mutinous pride was their Scottish origin; he called them a 'Scotch Club', 'Grumbletonians', 'a company of proud, idle and turbulent spirited Scotch' and he charged them with 'on all occasions [showing] an Inveteracy to this present Government, finding fault with all the measures that have been taken since the [Glorious] Revolution, excepting during the few years of Lord Bolingbroke's Ministry'. Their satirical drive for independence is a far cry from Thomas Jefferson's declaration of it, save perhaps in one respect; like Jefferson, the pamphleteers understand the value of consolidating all their indictable offences in the person of a single foe, a fictionalized Him – for the pamphleteers James Oglethorpe, for Jefferson George III.

The Declaration of Independence was like the 'true narrative' intended to be a committee production. On 7 June 1776 Richard Henry Lee, Virginia's senior delegate to the Continental Congress meeting in Philadelphia, introduced for their consideration a series of three resolutions, the first of which proclaimed that 'these United Colonies are, and of right ought to be, free and independent States'. A few days later a committee composed of Thomas Jefferson, John Adams, Benjamin Franklin, Roger Sherman and Robert R. Livingston was appointed to 'prepare a declaration to the effect of the first resolution'. Jefferson wrote a first draft, into which Franklin and Adams introduced a few changes; it was reported to Congress on 28 June; Lee's resolution was adopted on 2 July; Jefferson's declaration, on 4 July 1776. It was printed as a broadsheet on the following day.

Introduction

The theme, structure, plot, and rhetoric were Jefferson's. He had prepared himself for the task by composing two years earlier the pamphlet *A Summary View of the Rights of British America*, containing as its theme the position: 'Single acts of tyranny may be ascribed to the accidental opinion of the day; but a series of oppressions, begun at a distinguished period, and pursued unalterably through every change of ministers, too plainly prove a deliberate, systematic plan of reducing us to slavery.' Jefferson's premises there – the proper limits of sovereignty have been exceeded, over a number of years England has taken unlawful actions against her colonies, the King has become a tyrant, natural rights have been disregarded, an innocent people has been oppressed, a conspiratorial plan has been followed, a hostile strategy has been evolved, its object is the enslavement of free men, to resist enslavement is a moral obligation – inform the tripartite, balanced oration he took but a fortnight to draft. Although the genre – political oration or public soliloquy – is not one we have met before, in fact Jefferson is writing history or inventing history in his declaration.

The Declaration opens and closes symmetrically so as to focus upon its central historical revision. The opening two paragraph preamble and political credo is set forth in 350 words; the central indictment presenting a list of twenty-seven historic grievances runs to a little over 600 words; the concluding proposition and pledges are covered in 327 words. The first paragraph contains a single sentence the tone and syntax of which dramatize the rational control of justified moral passion, the control of a whole American republic facing the arbitrary passions of an egotistical monarch. Jefferson opens in a recognizable universe of enlightenment theory, like Franklin's universe. He writes,

> When in the course of human events, it becomes necessary for one people to dissolve the political bands which have connected them with another, and to assume among the powers of the earth the separate and equal station to which the laws of nature and of nature's God entitle them, a decent respect to the opinions of mankind requires that they should declare the causes which impel them to the Separation. (p. 270)

That announces to 'mankind' the purpose with which Jefferson concludes the introduction: 'To prove this, let Facts be submitted to a candid World.' His 'one people' are not the wilful subjects of the sentence; they are constrained by 'causes' requiring them 'to dissolve political bands' and 'to assume' new responsibilities; they live in a systematic enclosed and reasonable universe containing 'the course of human events' and have lived quietly there in the past though an accumulated identifiable set of pressures at a given moment or a 'When' now exacts of them a responsive double deed, 'to dissolve ...

38

and to assume'. That 'people', however, are controlledly cognizant of decency and respectfulness; their constraint does not relieve them of the need to display 'decent respect to the opinions of mankind', the 'candid world'. Hence they are obliged by a third necessity, their restrained civility, to 'declare the causes which impel them to the Separation'. Those causes exist in relation to a universe of meaning; to declare them, Jefferson next shifts from the impersonal 'one people' to the personal 'We' to set forth his sense of what the 'laws of nature and of nature's God' imply. He draws out the implications in a communal recitation of a political faith. The newly constituted 'We' hold a set of 'truths to be self-evident' not for 'one people' alone but for 'all men'; all know the conditions of human creation and their self-determined share in absolute human rights. Apart from equality, the rights to 'life, liberty and the pursuit of happiness' authorize them to institute, alter or abolish governments brought into being by them to secure their 'safety and happiness'. Nor are they lacking in 'Prudence . . . and experience' enough not to understand the value of a reasonable conservatism in preserving political continuity; '*But* when a long train of abuses and usurpations, pursuing invariably the same object, evinces a design to reduce them under absolute despotism', then 'it is their right, it is their duty to throw off such government' (p. 270). The greater warmth of 'throw off' in comparison with the earlier 'to dissolve' is justified by the 'patient sufferance of these colonies', the fearful conspiracy to establish 'an absolute tyranny' which they face, and especially their constitution into a 'We', a personal heroic *res publica*.

The middle section of the Declaration does not so much summon up 'facts to be submitted to a candid world' as it creates those facts. George III wears a face in the text so very like the face of Charles I in Milton's *Tenure of Kings and Magistrates* that no English reader can fail to notice the rhetoric of revolution common to Jefferson and Milton. George is variously shown as arbitrary, erratic, anarchic, warlike, acquisitive, piratical, provocative, crafty, and brutal; his crimes include conspiracy, harassment, obstruction of justice, theft, arson, kidnapping, murder, and treason; his victims are law-abiding, just, peaceful, high-principled, patient, brotherly, patriotic, decent, humane and long-suffering, Every conceivable complaint of the innocent is laid at the door of the 'present King of Great Britain', never named but always recorded as 'He' in a litany of mounting horrors. Increasing seriousness is augmented by increasing horror until the list concludes by his turning loose mercenaries, fomenting fratricide ('He has constrained our fellow citizens taken captive on the high seas, to bear arms against their country, to become the executioners of their friends and brethren, or to fall themselves by their hands'), and stirring up 'the merciless Indian savages' against 'all ages, sexes and conditions' (p. 272).

Jefferson's draft recorded in his *Autobriography* added to George's crimes the ultimate crime against human nature itself – the endorsing of slavery and the suppressing of American attempts to abolish it: '*And that this assemblage of horrors might want no fact of distinguished die, he is now exciting those very people to rise in arms among us, and to purchase that liberty of which he has deprived them, by murdering the people on whom he also obtruded them: thus paying off former crimes committed against the* LIBERTIES *of one people, with crimes which he urges them to commit against the* LIVES *of another*' (p. 272). The Continental Congress deleted Jefferson's crowning indictment in deference to the objections of slave owners and slave traders. (For himself Jefferson was elsewhere to write on that issue, 'Indeed I tremble for my country when I reflect that God is just; that his justice cannot sleep forever. . . The Almighty has no attribute which can take sides with us in such a contest.') Upon the created basis of such a heinous catalogue Jefferson then builds the conclusion: a solemn declaration, 'appealing to the supreme judge of the world for the rectitude of our intentions' and mutual 'pledge to each other [of] our lives, our fortunes, and our sacred honor'.

To 'a candid world' whatever prose in the New World would be written beyond this moment would assume a rather different character from the prose we have examined. It would continue to resonate with the tones of regionalism, the themes of its current moments, the class and gender marks of those who wrote it, re-Englishments not stopping short of the peculiar influence of writers who returned to England to live, and 'anxious' transformations of genre. Nevertheless it would not be American *colonial* prose, for an acknowledged political confederation would colour its reading and call it simply *American*. Jefferson's encompassing 'We' has superseded the previous founders, heroes, victims, prophets. His sense of destiny in a 'separate but equal Station' has superseded the previous destinies. If the colonies at his moment of writing are still only individual states, in less than ten years the various anxieties of one state about another would assist in the writing of a constitution compelling them towards the union Jefferson only posits. And then would ensue all those efforts of native and foreign literary historians to define an 'Americanness' which in the early years can only be acknowledged as heterogeneous and time-shifting.

Captain John Smith, 'The Generall Historie of Virginia, New England and The Summer Isles'

John Smith (?1579–1631) was born in Lincolnshire, hankered after the sea like many born to the land, and sought a seafarer's career by soldiering on the continent where he first became the subject of his own heroic invention, fighting as he put it 'beyond all men's expectations'. In Turkey in an action piously coloured by religious motives, he killed three Turks in single combat, was captured and sold into slavery, beat out his owner's brains to escape and fled towards England in a long detour by way of Russia. In Turkish Transylvania he suffered from his persistent irresistability to women when he attracted the pasha's wife; in Russia, he tells us, the same problem arose with the czarina. Once back in England Smith sought other worlds to conquer and settled upon Virginia. An original member of the Virginia Company of London, Smith sailed late in 1606 for the new colony in a company containing other adventurers and fortune-seekers. His own gifts of command and the natural divisions among ambitious men led him to be suspected of mutiny; he was in and out of favour but seized sufficient control to handle the exploration and trade which gave the colonists their fragile toehold. In 1608 he was made president of the council that governed the colony. He saw his gifts as nearer those of Achilles than Ulysses, however, although he sent back by the vessel that brought him when it was plying home a second time the business-like *True Relation*, printed at once and the source text for his own later *Generall Historie*. Hence he continued exploring rather than presiding and the dissension mounted.

In 1609, Smith returned to England and in 1610 he again wrote of Virginia to defend himself from his critics. Self-defence, of course, stimulated further recollections of his own heroic dash. In 1614 he was given charge of an expedition to explore New England, publishing an account of that coastal endeavour in 1616 in *A Description of New England*. He wished a further voyage but was thwarted by French pirates. In 1624 he published *The Generall Historie*, presenting himself in its dedication as the hero as much as the author; his story

ought to have been clad in better robes than my rude military hand can cut out in paper ornaments. But because, of the most things therein, I am no compiler by hearsay, but have been a real actor, I take myself to have a property in them; and therefore have been bold to challenge them to come under the reach of my own rough pen.

An even more picaresque account of his life from his point of view came out in an autobiography published in 1631, the year of his death.

Smith's eagerness not only to do justice to himself but to the new country, and to open to all courageous men the possibility of fame and fortune fuelled a prose not itself a model for subsequent American writing which, put to the service of a 'matter of America', did influence American writing. The persistence of the Indian maiden in American poetry as well as in American prose bears witness to Smith's success in myth-making.

My text reprints the Edward Arber edition, Glasgow, James MacLehose and Sons, 1907. It is taken from The Third Booke and covers events of 1607, the first year of the Virginia settlement.

The Third Booke

The Proceedings
And Accidents of The English Colony in Virginia, Extracted from the Authors following, by William Simons, Doctour of Divinitie

Chapter I

It might well be thought, a Countrie so faire (as Virginia is) and a people so tractable, would long ere this have beene quietly possessed, to the satisfaction of the adventurers, & the eternizing of the memory of those that effected it. But because all the world doe see a defailement; this following Treatise shall give satisfaction to all indifferent Readers, how the businesse hath bin carried: where no doubt they will easily understand and answer to their question, how it came to passe there was no better speed and successe in those proceedings.

Captaine Bartholomew Gosnoll, one of the first movers of this plantation, having many yeares solicited many of his friends, but found small assistants; at last prevailed with some Gentlemen, as Captaine John Smith, Mr. Edward-maria Wingfield, Mr. Robert Hunt, and divers others, who depended a yeare upon his projects, but nothing could be effected, till by their great charge and industrie, it came to be apprehended by certaine of the Nobilitie, Gentry, and Marchants, so that his Majestie by his letters patents, gave commission for establishing Councels, to direct here; and to governe, and to execute there. To effect this, was spent another yeare, and by that, three ships were provided, one of 100 Tuns, another of 40. and a Pinnace of 20. The transportation of the company was committed to Captaine Christopher Newport, a Marriner well practised for the Westerne parts of America. But their orders for government were put in a box, not to be opened, nor the governours knowne untill they arrived in Virginia.

On the 19 of December, 1606. we set sayle from Blackwall, but by unprosperous winds, were kept six weekes in the sight of England; all which time, Mr. Hunt our Preacher, was so weake and sicke, that few expected his recovery. Yet although he were but twentie myles from his habitation (the time we were in the Downes) and notwithstanding the stormy weather, nor the scandalous imputations (of some few, little better then Atheists, of the greatest ranke amongst us) suggested against him, all this could never force from him so much as a seeming desire to leave the busines, but preferred the service of God, in so good a voyage, before any affection to contest with his godlesse foes, whose disasterous designes (could they have prevailed) had even then overthrowne the businesse, so many discontents did then arise, had he not with the water of patience, and his godly exhortations (but chiefly by his true devoted examples) quenched those flames of envie, and dissention.[1]

We watered at the Canaries, we traded with the Salvages at Dominica; three weekes we spent in refreshing our selves amongst these west-India Isles; in Gwardalupa we found a bath so hot, as in it we boyled Porck as well as over the fire. And at a little Isle called Monica, we tooke from the bushes with our hands, neare two hogsheads full of Birds in three or foure houres. In Mevis, Mona, and the Virgin Isles, we spent some time, where with a lothsome beast like a Crocodil, called a Gwayn, Tortoises, Pellicans, Parrots, and fishes, we daily feasted. Gone from thence in search of Virginia, the company was not a little discomforted, seeing the Marriners had 3 dayes passed their reckoning and found no land, so that Captaine Ratliffe (Captaine of the Pinnace) rather desired to beare up the helme to returne for England, then make further search. But God the guider of all good actions, forcing them by an extreame storme to hull all night, did drive them by his providence to their desired Port, beyond all their expectations, for never any of them had seene that coast.[2] The first land they made they called Cape Henry; where thirtie of them recreating themselves on shore, were assaulted by five Salvages, who hurt two of the English very dangerously. That night was the box opened, and the orders read, in which Bartholomew Gosnoll, John Smith, Edward Wingfield, Christopher Newport, John Ratliffe, John Martin, and George Kendall, were named to be the Councell, and to choose a President amongst them for a yeare, who with the Councell should governe... Untill the 13 of May they sought a place to plant in, then the Councell was sworne, Mr. Wingfield was chosen President, and an Oration made, why Captaine Smith was not admitted of the Councell as the rest.

Now falleth every man to worke, the Councell contrive the Fort, the rest cut downe trees to make place to pitch their Tents; some provide clapbord to relade the ships, some make gardens, some nets, &c. The Salvages often visited us kindly. The Presidents overweening jealousie would admit no exercise at armes, or fortification, but the boughs of trees cast together in the forme of a halfe moone by the extraordinary paines and diligence of Captaine Kendall, Newport, Smith, and twentie others, were sent to discover the head of the river:

by divers small habitations they passed, in six dayes they arrived at a Towne called Powhatan, consisting of some twelve houses, pleasantly seated on a hill; before it three fertile Isles, about it many of their cornefields, the place is very pleasant, and strong by nature, of this place the Prince is called Powhatan, and his people Powhatans, to this place the river is navigable: but higher within a myle, by reason of the Rockes and Isles, there is not passage for a small Boat, this they call the Falles, the people in all parts kindly intreated them, till being returned within twentie myles of James towne, they gave just cause of jealousie, but had God not blessed the discoverers otherwise then those at the Fort, there had then beene an end of that plantation; for at the Fort, where they arrived the next day, they found 17 men hurt, and a boy slaine by the Salvages, and had it not chanced a crosse barre shot from the Ships strooke down a bough from a tree amongst them, that caused them to retire, our men had all beene slaine, being securely all at worke, and their armes in dry fats.

Hereupon the President was contented the Fort should be pallisadoed, the Ordnance mounted, his men armed and exercised, for many were the assaults, and ambuscadoes of the Salvages, & our men by their disorderly stragling were often hurt, when the Salvages by the nimblenesse of their heeles well escaped. What toyle we had, with so small a power to guard our workemen adayes, watch all night, resist our enemies, and effect our businesse, to relade the ships, cut downe trees, and prepare the ground to plant our Corne, &c, I referre to the Readers consideration. Six weekes being spent in this manner, Captaine Newport (who was hired onely for our transportation) was to returne with the ships. Now Captaine Smith, who all this time from their departure from the Canaries was restrained as a prisoner upon the scandalous suggestions of some of the chiefe (envying his repute) who fained he intended to usurpe the government, murther the Councell, and make himselfe King, that his confederats were dispersed in all the three ships, and that divers of his confederats that revealed it, would affirme it, for this he was committed as a prisoner: thirteene weekes he remained thus suspected, and by that time the ships should returne they pretended out of their commisserations, to referre him to the Councell in England to receive a check, rather then by particulating his designes make him so odious to the world, as to touch his life, or utterly overthrow his reputation. But he so much scorned their charitie, and publikely defied the uttermost of their crueltie, he wisely prevented their policies, though he could not suppresse their envies, yet so well he demeaned himselfe in this businesse, as all the company did see his innocency, and his adversaries malice, and those suborned to accuse him, accused his accusers of subornation; many untruthes were alledged against him; but being so apparently disproved, begat a generall hatred in the hearts of the company against such unjust Commanders, that the President was adjudged to give him 200l. so that all he had was seized upon, in part of satisfaction, which Smith presently returned to the Store for the generall use of the Colony. Many were the mischiefes that daily sprung from their ignorant (yet ambitious) spirits; but the good Doctrine and exhortation of our Preacher Mr. Hunt reconciled them, and caused Captaine Smith to be admitted of the Councell; the next day all received the Communion, the day following the Salvages voluntarily desired peace, and Captaine Newport returned for England with newes; leaving in Virginia 100. the 15 of June 1607.

. . .

Chap. II
What happened till the first supply

Being thus left to our fortunes, it fortuned that within ten dayes scarce ten amongst us could either goe, or well stand, such extreame weaknes and sicknes oppressed us. And thereat none need marvaile, if they consider the cause and reason, which was this; whilest the ships stayed, our allowance was somewhat bettered, by a daily proportion of Bisket, which the sailers would pilfer to sell, give, or exchange with us, for money, Saxefras,[a] furres, or love. But when they departed, there remained neither taverne, beere house, nor place of reliefe, but the common Kettell. Had we beene as free from all sinnes as gluttony, and drunkennesse, we might have beene canonized for Saints; But our President would never have beene admitted, for ingrossing to his private, Oatmeale, Sacke, Oyle, Aquavitæ, Beefe, Egges, or what not, but the Kettell; that indeed he allowed equally to be distributed, and that was halfe a pint of wheat, and as much barely boyled with water for a man a day, and this having fryed some 26. weekes in the ships hold, contained as many wormes as graines; so that we might truely call it rather so much bran then corne, our drinke was water, our lodgings Castles in the ayre: with this lodging and dyet, our extreame toile in bearing and planting Pallisadoes, so strained and bruised us, and our continuall labour in the extremitie of the heat had so weakned us, as were cause sufficient to have made us as miserable in our native Countrey, or any other place in the world. From May, to September, those that escaped, lived upon Sturgeon, and Sea-crabs, fiftie in this

---

[a] Saxefras: sassefras, the dried bark of a North American tree used as a spice.

time we buried ... But now was all our provision spent, the Sturgeon gone, all helps abandoned, each houre expecting the fury of the Salvages; when God the patron of all good indevours, in that desperate extremitie so changed the hearts of the Salvages, that they brought such plenty of their fruits, and provision, as no man wanted.

And now where some affirmed it was ill done of the Councell to send forth men so badly provided, this incontradictable reason will shew them plainely they are too ill advised to nourish such ill conceits; first, the fault of our going was our owne, what could be thought fitting or necessary we had, but what we should find, or want, or where we should be, we were all ignorant, and supposing to make our passage in two monethes, with victuall to live, and the advantage of the spring to worke; we were at Sea five monethes, where we both spent our victuall and lost the opportunitie of the time, and season to plant, by the unskilfull presumption of our ignorant transporters, that understood not at all, what they undertooke.

Such actions have ever since the worlds beginning beene subject to such accidents, and every thing of worth is found full of difficulties, but nothing so difficult as to establish a Common wealth so farre remote from men and meanes, and where mens mindes are so untoward as neither doe well themselves, nor suffer others.[3] But to proceed.

The new president and Martin, being little beloved, of weake judgement in dangers, and lesse industrie in peace, committed the managing of all things abroad to Captaine Smith: who by his owne example, good words, and faire promises, set some to mow, others to binde thatch, some to build houses, others to thatch them, himselfe alwayes bearing the greatest taske for his owne share, so that in short time, he provided most of them lodgings, neglecting any for himselfe. This done, seeing the Salvages superfluitie beginne to decrease (with some of his workemen) shipped himselfe in the Shallop to search the Country for trade. The want of the language, knowledge to mannage his boat without sailes, the want of a sufficient power, (knowing the multitude of the Salvages) apparell for his men, and other necessaries, were infinite impediments, yet no discouragement. Being but six or seaven in company he went downe the river to Kecoughtan, where at first they scorned him, as a famished man, and would in derision offer him a handfull of Corne, a peece of bread, for their swords and muskets, and such like proportions also for their apparell. But seeing by trade and courtesie there was nothing to be had, he made bold to try such conclusions as necessitie inforced, though contrary to his Commission: Let fly his muskets, ran his boat on shore, whereat they all fled into the woods. So marching towards their houses, they might see great heapes of corne: much adoe he had to restraine his hungry souldiers from present taking of it, expecting as it hapned that the Salvages would assault them, as not long after they did with a most hydeous noyse. Sixtie or seaventie of them, some blacke, some red, some white, some party-coloured, came in a square order, singing and dauncing out of the woods, with their Okee[b] (which was an Idoll made of skinnes, stuffed with mosse, all painted and hung with chaines and copper) borne before them: and in this manner being well armed, with Clubs, Targets, Bowes and Arrowes, they charged the English, that so kindly received them with their muskets loaden with Pistoll shot, that downe fell their God, and divers lay sprauling on the ground; the rest fled againe to the woods, and ere long sent one of their Quiyoughkasoucks to offer peace, and redeeme their Okee. Smith told them, if onely six of them would come unarmed and loade his boat, he would not only be their friend, but restore them their Okee, and give them Beads, Copper, and Hatchets besides: which on both sides was to their contents performed: and then they brought him Venison, Turkies, wild foule, bread, and what they had, singing and dauncing in signe of friendship till they departed.[4] In his returne he discovered the Towne and Country of Warraskoyack.

> Thus God unboundlesse by his power,
> Made them thus kind, would us devour.

Smith perceiving (notwithstanding their late miserie) not any regarded but from hand to mouth (the company being well recovered) caused the Pinnace to be provided with things fitting to get provision for the yeare following; but in the interim he made 3. or 4. journies and discovered the people of Chickahamania: yet what he carefully provided the rest carelessly spent. Wingfield and Kendall living in disgrace, seeing all things at randome in the absence of Smith, the companies dislike of their presidents weaknes, and their small love to Martins never mending sicknes, strengthened themselves with the sailers, and other confederates to regaine their former credit and authority, or at least such meanes abord the Pinnace, (being fitted to saile as Smith had appointed for trade) to alter her course and to goe for England. Smith unexpectedly returning had the plot discovered to him, much trouble he had to prevent it, till with store of sakre and musket shot he forced them stay or sinke in the river, which action cost the life of captaine Kendall. These brawles are so disgustfull, as some will say they were better forgotten, yet all men of good judgement will conclude, it were better their basenes should be

---

[b] Okee: Indian sacred icon. Smith's own gloss is adequate.

manifest to the world, then the busines beare the scorne and shame of their excused disorders. The President and captaine Archer not long after intended also to have abandoned the country, which project also was curbed, and suppressed by Smith. The Spaniard never more greedily desired gold then he victuall, nor his souldiers more to abandon the Country, then he to keepe it. But finding plentie of Corne in the river of Chickahamania where hundreds of Salvages in divers places stood with baskets expecting his comming. And now the winter approaching, the rivers became so covered with swans, geese, duckes, and cranes, that we daily feasted with good bread, Virginia pease, pumpions, and putchamins, fish, fowle, and diverse sorts of wild beasts as far as we could eate them: so that none of our Tuftaffaty humorists desired to goe for England. But our Comædies never endured long without a Tragedie; some idle exceptions being muttered against Captaine Smith, for not discovering the head of Chickahamania river, and taxed by the Councell, to be too slow in so worthy an attempt. The next voyage hee proceeded so farre that with much labour by cutting of trees in sunder he made his passage, but when his Barge could passe no farther, he left her in a broad bay out of danger of shot, commanding none should goe a shore till his returne: himselfe with two English and two Salvages went up higher in a Canowe, but hee was not long absent, but his men went a shore, whose want of government, gave both occasion and opportunity to the Salvages to surprise one George Cassen, whom they slew, and much failed not to have cut of the boat and all the rest. Smith little dreaming of that accident, being got to the marshes at the rivers head, twentie myles in the desert, had his two men slaine (as is supposed) sleeping by the Canowe, whilst himselfe by fowling sought them victuall, who finding he was beset with 200. Salvages, two of them hee slew, still defending himselfe with the ayd of a Salvage his guid, whom he bound to his arme with his garters, and used him as a buckler, yet he was shot in his thigh a little, and had many arrowes that stucke in his cloathes but no great hurt, till at last they tooke him prisoner. When this newes came to James towne, much was their sorrow for his losse, fewe expecting what ensued. Sixe or seven weekes those Barbarians kept him prisoner, many strange triumphes and conjurations they made of him, yet hee so demeaned himselfe amongst them, as he not onely diverted them from surprising the Fort, but procured his owne libertie, and got himselfe and his company such estimation amongst them, that those Salvages admired him more then their owne Quiyouckosucks. The manner how they used and delivered him, is as followeth.

The Salvages having drawne from George Cassen whether Captaine Smith was gone, prosecuting that opportunity they followed him with 300. bowmen, conducted by the King of Pamaunkee, who in divisions searching the turnings of the river, found Robinson and Emry by the fire side, those they shot full of arrowes and slew. Then finding the Captaine, as is said, that used the Salvage that was his guide as his shield (three of them being slaine and divers other so gauld) all the rest would not come neere him. Thinking thus to have returned to his boat, regarding them, as he marched, more then his way, slipped up to the middle in an oasie creeke & his Salvage with him, yet durst they not come to him till being neere dead with cold, he threw away his armes. Then according to their composition they drew him forth and led him to the fire, where his men were slaine. Diligently they chafed his benummed limbs. He demanding for their Captaine; they shewed him Opechankanough, King of Pamaunkee, to whom he gave a round Ivory double compass Dyall. Much they marvailed at the playing of the Fly and Needle, which they could see so plainely, and yet not touch it, because of the glasse that covered them. But when he demonstrated by that Globe-like Jewell, the roundnesse of the earth, and skies, the spheare of the Sunne, Moone, and Starres, and how the Sunne did chase the night round about the world continually; the greatnesse of the Land and Sea, the diversitie of Nations, varietie of complexions, and how we were to them Antipodes, and many other such like matters, they all stood as amazed with admiration. Notwithstanding, within an houre after they tyed him to a tree, and as many as could stand about him prepared to shoot him, but the King holding up the Compass in his hand, they all laid downe their Bowes and Arrowes, and in a triumphant manner led him to Orapaks, where he was after their manner kindly feasted, and well used.

Their order in conducting him was thus; Drawing themselves all in fyle, the King in the middest had all their Peeces and Swords borne before him. Captaine Smith was led after him by three great Salvages, holding him fast by each arme: and on each side six went in fyle with their Arrowes nocked. But arriving at the Towne (which was but onely thirtie or fortie hunting houses made of mats, which they remove as they please, as we our tents) all the women and children staring to behold him, the souldiers first all in fyle performed the forme of a Bissom[c] so well as could be, and on each flanke, officers as Serjeants to see them keepe their orders. A good time they continued this exercise, and then cast themselves in a ring, dauncing in such

[c] Bissom: besom, here a broom-shaped file of men in a fanned out procession.

severall Postures, and singing and yelling out such hellish notes and screeches; being strangely painted, every one his quiver of Arrowes, and at his backe a club; on his arme a Fox or an Otters skinne, or some such matter for his vambrace; their heads and shoulders painted red, with Oyle and Pocones mingled together, which Scarlet-like colour made an exceeding handsome shew; his Bow in his hand, and the skinne of a Bird with her wings abroad dryed, tyed on his head, a peece of copper, a white shell, a long feather, with a small rattle growing at the tayles of their snaks tyed to it, or some such like toy. All this while Smith and the King stood in the middest guarded, as before is said, and after three dances they all departed. Smith they conducted to a long house, where thirtie or fortie tall fellowes did guard him, and ere long more bread and venison was brought him then would have served twentie men, I thinke his stomacke at that time was not very good; what he left they put in baskets and tyed over his head. About midnight they set the meate againe before him, all this time not one of them would eate a bit with him, till the next morning they brought him as much more, and then did they eate all the old, & reserved the new as they had done the other, which made him thinke they would fat him to eat him. Yet in this desperate estate to defend him from the cold, one Maocassater brought him his gowne, in requitall of some beads and toyes Smith had given him at his first arrivall in Virginia.

Two dayes after a man would have slaine him (but that the guard prevented it) for the death of his sonne, to whom they conducted him to recover the poore man then breathing his last. Smith told them that at James towne he had a water would doe it, if they would let him fetch it, but they would not permit that; but made all the preparations they could to assault James towne, craving his advice, and for recompence he should have life, libertie, land, and women. In part of a Table booke he writ his minde to them at the Fort, what was intended, how they should follow that direction to affright the messengers, and without fayle send him such things as he writ for. And an Inventory with them. The difficultie and danger, he told the Salvages, of the Mines, great-gunnes, and other Engins exceedingly affrighted them, yet according to his request they went to James towne, in as bitter weather as could be of frost and snow, and within three dayes returned with an answer.

But when they came to James towne, seeing men sally out as he had told them they would, they fled; yet in the night they came againe to the same place where he had told them they should receive an answer, and such things as he had promised them, which they found accordingly, and with which they returned with no small expedition, to the wonder of them all that heard it, that he could either divine, or the paper could speake: then they led him to the Youthtanunds, the Mattapanients, the Payankatanks, the Nantaughtacunds, and Onaw-manients upon the rivers of Raphanock, and Patawomek, over all those rivers, and backe againe by divers other severall Nations, to the Kings habitation at Pamaunkee...

Not long after, early in a morning a great fire was made in a long house, and a mat spread on the one side, as on the other; on the one they caused him to sit, and all the guard went out of the house, and presently came skipping in a great grim fellow, all painted over with coale, mingled with oyle; and many Snakes and Wesels skins stuffed with mosse, and all their tayles tyed together, so as they met on the crowne of his head in a tassell; and round about the tassell was as a Coronet of feathers, the skins hanging round about his head, backe, and shoulders, and in a manner covered his face; with a hellish voyce and a rattle in his hand. With most strange gestures and passions he began his invocation, and environed the fire with a circle of meale; which done, three more such like devils came rushing in with the like antique tricks, painted halfe blacke, halfe red: but all their eyes were painted white, and some red stroakes like Mutchato's, along their cheekes: roundabout him those fiends daunced a pretty while, and then came in three more as ugly as the rest; with red eyes, and white stroakes over their blacke faces, at last they all sat downe right against him; three of them on the one hand of the chiefe priest, and three on the other. Then all with their rattles began a song, which ended, the chiefe Priest layd downe five wheat cornes: then strayning his armes and hands with such violence that he sweat, and his veynes swelled, he began a short Oration: at the conclusion they all gave a short groane; and then layd down three graines more. After that, began their song againe, and then another Oration, ever laying downe so many cornes as before, till they had twice incirculed the fire; that done, they tooke a bunch of little stickes prepared for that purpose, continuing still their devotion, and at the end of every song and Oration, they layd downe a sticke betwixt the divisions of Corne. Till night, neither he nor they did either eate or drinke, and then they feasted merrily, with the best provisions they could make. Three dayes they used this Ceremony; the meaning whereof they told him, was to know if he intended them well or no. The circle of meale signified their Country, the circles of corne the bounds of the sea, and the stickes his Country. They imagined the world to be flat and round, like a trencher, and they in the middest. After this they brought him a bagge of gunpowder, which they carefully preserved till the next spring, to plant as they did their corne; because they would be acquainted with the nature of that seede...

At last they brought him to Meronocomo, where was Powhatan their Emperor. Here more then two hundrd of those grim Courtiers stood wondering at him, as he had beene a monster; till Powhatan and his trayne had put themselves in their greatest braveries. Before a fire upon a seat like a bedsted, he sat covered with a great robe, made of Rarowcun skinnes, and all the tayles hanging by. On either hand did sit a young wench of 16 or 18 yeares, and along on each side the house, two rowes of men, and behind them as many women, with all their heads and shoulders painted red; many of their heads bedecked with the white downe of Birds; but every one with something: and a great chayne of white beads about their necks. At his entrance before the King, all the people gave a great shout. The Queene of Appamatuck was appointed to bring him water to wash his hands, and another brought him a bunch of feathers, in stead of a Towell to dry them: having feasted him after their best barbarous manner they could, a long consultation was held, but the conclusion was, two great stones were brought before Powhatan: then as many as could layd hands on him, dragged him to them, and thereon laid his head, and being ready with their clubs, to beate out his braines, Pocahontas the Kings dearest daughter, when no intreaty could prevaile, got his head in her armes, and laid her owne upon his to save him from death: whereat the Emperour was contented he should live to make him hatchets, and her bells, beads, and copper; for they thought him aswell of all occupations as themselves.[5] For the King himselfe will make his owne robes, shooes, bowes, arrowes, pots; plant, hunt, or doe any thing so well as the rest.

> They say he bore a pleasant shew,
> But sure his heart was sad.
> For who can pleasant be, and rest,
> That lives in feare and dread:
> And having life suspected, doth
> It still suspected lead.

Two dayes after, Powhatan having disguised himselfe in the most fearefull manner he could, caused Capt. Smith to be brought forth to a great house in the woods, and there upon a mat by the fire to be left alone. Not long after from behinde a mat that divided the house, was made the most dolefullest noyse he ever heard; then Powhatan more like a devill then a man with some two hundred more as blacke as himselfe, came unto him and told him now they were friends, and presently he should goe to James towne, to send him two great gunnes, and a gryndstone, for which he would give him the Country of Capahowosick, and forever esteeme him as his sonne Nantaquoud. So to James towne with 12 guides Powhatan sent him. That night they quarterd in the woods, he still expecting (as he had done all this long time of his imprisonment) every houre to be put to one death or other: for all their feasting. But almightie God (by his divine providence) had mollified the hearts of those sterne Barbarians with compassion. The next morning betimes they came to the Fort, where Smith having used the Salvages with what kindnesse he could, he shewed Rawhunt, Powhatans trusty servant two demi-Culverings & a millstone to carry Powhatan: they found them somewhat too heavie; but when they did see him discharge them, being loaded with stones, among the boughs of a great tree loaded with Isickles, the yce and branches came so tumbling downe, that the poore Salvages ran away halfe dead with feare. But at last we regained some conference with them, and gave them such toyes; and sent to Powhatan, his women, and children such presents, as gave them in generall full content. Now in James Towne they were all in combustion, the strongest preparing once more to run away with the Pinnace; which with the hazzard of his life, with Sakre falcon[d] and musket shot, Smith forced now the third time to stay or sinke. Some no better then they should be, had plotted with the president, the next day to have put him to death by the Leviticall law, for the lives of Robinson and Emry, pretending the fault was his that had led them to their ends: but he quickly tooke such order with such Lawyers, that he layd them by the heeles till he sent some of them prisoners for England. Now ever once in foure or five dayes, Pocahontas with her attendants, brought him so much provision, that saved many of their lives, that els for all this had starved with hunger.

> Thus from numbe death our good God sent reliefe,
> The sweete asswager of all other griefe.

His relation of the plenty he had seene, especially at Werawocomoco, and of the state and bountie of Powhatan, (which till that time was unknowne) so revived their dead spirits (especially the love of Pocahontas) as all mens feare was abandoned. Thus you may see what difficulties still crossed any good indevour: and the good successe of the businesse being thus oft brought to the very period of destruction; yet you see by what strange means God hath still delivered it. As for the insufficiency of them admitted in Commission, that error could not be prevented by the electors; there being no

---

[d] Sakre falcon: a light ship's cannon.

other choise, and all strangers to each others education, qualities, or disposition. And if any deeme it a shame to our Nation to have any mention made of those inormities, let them peruse the Histories of the Spanyards Discoveries and Plantations, where they may see how many mutinies, disorders, and dissentions have accompanied them, and crossed their attempts: which being knowne to be particular mens offences; doth take away the generall scorne and contempt, which malice, presumption, covetousnesse, or ignorance might produce; to the scandall and reproach of those, whose actions and valiant resolutions deserve a more worthy respect.

. . .

Chap. III
The Arrivall of the first supply, with their
Proceedings, and the Ships returne

All this time our care was not so much to abandon the Countrey; but the Treasurer and Councell in England, were as diligent & carefull to supply us. Two good ships they sent us, with neare a hundred men, well furnished with all things could be imagined necessary, both for them and us; The one commanded by Captaine Newport: the other by Captaine Francis Nelson, an honest man, and an expert Marriner. But such was the lewardnesse of his Ship (that though he was within the sight of Cape Henry) by stormy contrary winds was he forced so farre to Sea, that the West Indies was the next land, for the repaire of his Masts, and reliefe of wood and water. But Newport got in and arrived at James Towne, not long after the redemption of Captaine Smith. To whom the Salvages, as is sayd, every other day repaired, with such provisions that sufficiently did serve them from hand to mouth: part alwayes they brought him as Presents from their Kings, or Pocahontas; the rest he as their Market Clarke set the price himselfe, how they should sell: so he had inchanted these poore soules being their prisoner; and now Newport, whom he called his Father arriving, neare as directly as he foretold, they esteemed him as an Oracle, and had them at that submission he might command them what he listed. That God that created all things they knew he adored for his God: they would also in their discourses tearme the God of Captaine Smith.

Thus the Almightie was the bringer on,
The guide, path, terme, all which was God alone.

But the President and Councell so much envied his estimation among the Salvages, (though we all in generall equally participated with him of the good thereof,) that they wrought it into the Salvages understandings (by their great bounty in giving foure times more for their commodities then Smith appointed) that their greatnesse and authoritie as much exceeded his, as their bountie and liberalitie. Now the arrivall of this first supply so overjoyed us, that wee could not devise too much to please the Marriners. We gave them libertie to trucke or trade at their pleasures. But in a short time it followed, that could not be had for a pound of Copper, which before was sould us for an ounce: thus ambition and sufferance cut the throat of our trade, but confirmed their opinion of the greatnesse of Capt. Newport, (wherewith Smith had possessed Powhatan) especially by the great presents Newport often sent him, before he could prepare the Pinnace to goe and visit him: so that this great Savage desired also to see him. A great coyle there was to set him forward. When he went he was accompanied with Captaine Smith, & Mr. Scrivener... with thirtie or fortie chosen men for their guard...

These ... comming a-shore, landed amongst a many of creekes, over which they were to passe such poore bridges, onely made of a few cratches, thrust in the ose, and three or foure poles laid on them, and at the end of them the like, tyed together onely with barkes of trees, that it made them much suspect those bridges were but traps. Which caused Smith to make diverse Salvages goe over first, keeping some of the chiefe as hostage till halfe his men were passed, to make a guard for himselfe and the rest. But finding all things well, by two or three hundred Salvages they were kindly conducted to their towne. Where Powhatan strained himselfe to the utmost of his greatnesse to entertaine them, with great shouts of joy, Orations of protestations; and with the most plenty of victualls he could provide to feast them. Sitting upon his bed of mats, his pillow of leather imbrodered (after their rude manner with pearle and white Beads) his attyre a faire robe of skinnes as large as an Irish mantell: at his head and feete a handsome young woman: on each side his house sat twentie of his Concubines, their heads and shoulders painted red, with a great chaine of white beads about each of their neckes. Before those sat his chiefest men in like order in his arbour-like house, and more then fortie platters of fine bread stood as a guard in two fyles on each side the doore. Foure or five hundred people made a guard behinde them for our passage; and Proclamation was made, none upon paine of death to presume to doe us any wrong or discourtesie. With many pretty Discourses to renew their old acquaintance, this great King and our Captaine spent the time till the ebbe left our Barge aground. Then renewing their feasts with feates, dauncing and singing, and such like mirth, we quartered that night with Powhatan. The next day Newport came a shore and received as much content as those people could give him: a boy named Thomas Salvage was then given unto Powhatan, whom Newport called his sonne; for whom Powhatan gave him Namontack his trustie servant, and one of a shrewd, subtill capacitie. Three or foure dayes more we spent in feasting, dauncing, and trading, wherein Powhatan carried himselfe so proudly, yet discreetly (in his salvage manner) as made us all admire his naturall gifts, considering his education. As scorning to trade as his subjects did; he bespake Newport in this manner.[6]

Captaine Newport it is not agreeable to my greatnesse, in this pedling manner to trade for trifles; and I esteeme you also a great Werowance. Therefore lay me downe all your commodities together; what I like I will take, and in recompence give you what I thinke fitting their value. Captaine Smith being our interpreter, regarding Newport as his father, knowing best the disposition of Powhatan, tould us his intent was but onely to cheate us; yet Captaine Newport thinking to out brave this Salvage in ostentation of greatnesse, and so to bewitch him with his bountie, as to have what he listed, it so hapned, that Powhatan having his desire, valued his corne at such a rate, that I thinke it better cheape in Spaine: for we had not foure bushells for that we expected to have twentie hogsheads. This bred some unkindnesse betweene our two Captaines; Newport seeking to please the unsatiable desire of the Salvage, Smith to cause the Salvage to please him; but smothering his distast to avoyd the Salvages suspition, glanced in the eyes of Powhatan many trifles, who fixed his humor upon a few blew beades. A long time he importunately desired them, but Smith seemed so much the more to affect them, as being composed of a most rare substance of the coulour of the skyes, and not to be worne but by the greatest kings in the world. This made him halfe madde to be the owner of such strange Jewells: so that ere we departed, for a pound or two of blew beades, he brought over my king for 2. or 300. Bushells of corne; yet parted good friends. The like entertainment we found of Opechankanough king of Pamaunkee, whom also he in like manner fitted (at the like rates) with blew beads, which grew by this meanes, of that estimation, that none durst weare any of them but their great kings, their wives and children. And so we returned all well to James towne, where this new supply being lodged with the rest, accidentally fired their quarters and so the towne, which being but thatched with reeds, the fire was so fierce as it burnt their Pallisado's, (though eight or ten yards distant) with their Armes, bedding, apparell, and much private provision. Good Master Hunt our Preacher lost all his Library and all he had but the cloathes on his backe: yet none never heard him repine at his losse. This happned in the winter in that extreame frost, 1607. Now though we had victuall sufficient I meane onely of Oatmeale, meale and corne, yet the Ship staying 14. weekes when shee might as wel have beene gone in 14. dayes, spent a great part of that, and neare all the rest that was sent to be landed. When they departed what there discretion could spare us, to make a little poore meale or two, we called feastes, to relish our mouthes: of each somwhat they left us, yet I must confesse, those that had either money, spare clothes credit to give billes of paiment, gold rings, furrs, or any such commodities, were ever welcome to this removing taverne, such was our patience to obay such vile Commanders, and buy our owne provisions at 15 times the value, suffering them feast (we bearing the charge) yet must not repine, but fast, least we should incure the censure of factious and seditious persons: and then leakage, shiprats, and other casuallties occasioned them losse, but the vessels and remnants (for totals) we were glad to receave with all our hearts to make up the account, highly commending their providence for preserving that, least they should discourage any more to come to us. Now for all this plenty our ordynary was but meale and water, so that this great charge little releeved our wants, whereby with the extremitie of the bitter cold frost and those defects, more then halfe of us dyed; I cannot deny but both Smith and Skrivener did their best to amend what was amisse, but with the President went the major part, that there hornes were to short. But the worst was our guilded refiners with their golden promises made all men their slaves in hope of recompences; there was no talke, no hope, no worke, but dig gold, wash gold, refine gold, loade gold, such a bruit of gold, that one mad fellow desired to be buried in the sands least they should by there art make gold of his bones: little neede there was and lesse reason, the ship should stay, there wages run on, our victualls consume 14. weekes, that the Mariners might say, they did helpe to build such a golden Church that we can say the raine washed neere to nothing in 14. dayes. Were it that captaine Smith would not applaude all those golden inventions, because they admitted him not to the sight of their trialls nor golden consultations, I know not; but I have heard him oft question with Captaine Martin & tell him, except he could shew him a more substantiall triall, he was not inamoured with their durty skill, breathing out these and many other passions, never any thing did more torment him, then to see all necessary busines neglected, to fraught such a drunken ship with so much guilded durt...

> Oh cursed gold those, hunger-starved movers,
> To what misfortunes lead'st thou all those lovers!
> For all the China wealth, nor Indies can
> Suffice the minde of an av'ritious man.

Chap. IIII
The Arrivall of the Phœnix; her returne; and other Accidents

The authoritie now consisting in Captaine Martin, and the still sickly President, the sale of the Stores commodities maintained his estate, as an inheritable revenew. The spring approaching, and the Ship departing, Mr. Scrivener and Captaine Smith devided betwixt them the rebuilding James towne; the repairing our Pallizadoes; the cutting downe trees; preparing our fields; planting our corne, and to rebuild our Church, and recover our Store house. All men thus busie at their severall labours, Master Nelson arrived with his lost Phœnix; lost (I say) for that we all deemed him lost. Landing safely all his men, (so well he had mannaged his ill hap,) causing the Indian Isles to feede his company, that his victuall to that we had gotten, as is said before, was neare after our allowance sufficient for halfe a yeare. He had not any thing but he freely imparted it, which honest dealing (being a Marriner) caused us admire him: we would not have wished more then he did for us. Now to relade this ship with some good tydings, the President (not holding it stood with the dignitie of his place to leave the Fort) gave order to Captaine Smith to discover and search the commodities of the Monacans Countrey beyond the Falls. Sixtie able men was allotted them, the which within six dayes, Smith had so well trained to their armes and orders, that they little feared with whom they should incounter: yet so unseasonable was the time, and so opposit was Captaine Martin to any thing, but onely to fraught this ship also with his phantasticall gold, as Captaine Smith rather desired to relade her with Cedar, (which was a present dispatch) then either with durt, or the hopes and reports of an uncertaine discovery, which he would performe when they had lesse charge and more leisure.

> But, The God of Heav'n, He eas'ly can
> Immortalize a mortall man,
> With glory and with fame.
> The same God, ev'n as eas'ly may
> Afflict a mortall man, I say,
> With sorrow and with shame.

Whilst the conclusion was a resolving, this hapned.

Powhatan (to express his love to Newport) when he departed,

presented him with twentie Turkies, conditionally to returne him twentie swords, which immediately was sent him; now after his departure he presented Captaine Smith with the like luggage, but not finding his humor obeyed in not sending such weapons as he desired, he caused his people with twentie devices to obtaine them. At last by ambuscadoes at our very Ports they would take them perforce, surprise us at worke, or any way; which was so long permitted, they became so insolent there was no rule; the command from England was so strait not to offend them, as our authoritie-bearers (keeping their houses) would rather be any thing then peace-breakers. This charitable humor prevailed, till well it chanced they medled with Captaine Smith, who without farther deliberation gave them such an incounter, as some he so hunted up and downe the Isle, some he so terrified with whipping, beating, and imprisonment, as for revenge they surprised two of our forraging disorderly souldiers, and having assembled their forces, boldly threatned at our Ports to force Smith to redeliver seven Salvages, which for their villanies he detained prisoners, or we were all but dead men. But to try their furies he sallied out amongst them, and in lesse then an houre, he so hampred their insolencies, they brought them his two men, desiring peace without any further composition for their prisoners. Those he examined, and caused them all beleeve, by severall vollies of shot one of their companions was shot to death, because they would not confesse their intents and plotters of those villanies. And thus they all agreed in one point, they were directed onely by Powhatan to obtaine him our weapons, to cut our owne throats, with the manner where, how, and when, which we plainly found most true and apparant: yet he sent his messengers, and his dearest daughter Pocahontas with presents to excuse him of the injuries done by some rash untoward Captaines his subjects, desiring their liberties for this time, with the assurance of his love for ever. After Smith had given the prisoners what correction he thought fit, used them well a day or two after, & then delivered them Pocahontas, for whose sake onely he fayned to have saved their lives, and gave them libertie. The patient Councell that nothing would move to warre with the Salvages, would gladly have wrangled with Captaine Smith for his crueltie, yet none was slaine to any mans knowledge, but it brought them in such feare and obedience, as his very name would sufficiently affright them; where before, wee had sometime peace and warre twice in a day, and very seldome a weeke, but we had some trecherous villany or other.

The fraught of this Ship being concluded to be Cedar, by the diligence of the Master, and Captaine Smith, she was quickly reladed:

Master Scrivener was neither idle nor slow to follow all things at the Fort; the Ship being ready to set sayle, Captaine Martin being alwayes very sickly, and unserviceable, and desirous to injoy the credit of his supposed Art of finding the golden Mine, was most willingly admitted to returne for England.

Governor William Bradford, 'The History of Plimmoth Plantation'

William Bradford (1590–1657) was born in Yorkshire, the son of a well-to-do farmer who died when he was a baby. At twelve years old to the sorrow of his well-placed yeoman family, he joined a prayer group or separatist congregation at Scrooby that met at William Brewster's house. By 1606 the group had left the Church of England. Local persecution and their own zeal led the congregation to migrate to Holland with the Reverend John Robinson, a Cambridge graduate who renounced his holy orders in order to minister to them. There they lived briefly at Amsterdam and then for ten years at Leyden, eventually in comfortable circumstances. The zeal which brought them to Leyden propelled them from it and Bradford was involved in the protracted negotiations which culminated in the voyage to Plymouth, Massachusetts in 1620. *Plimmoth Plantation*, which Bradford wrote in two principal bursts of composition commencing in 1630 and bringing the narrative down to 1646, describes the Scrooby group's affairs from their earliest persecutions in England, through their exile, their journey, their landing and their successful settlement until protected by the larger and even more successful Massachusetts Bay Colony to the north.

Bradford's history is silent about Bradford's life, however. Among the details it neglects to record are that his first wife was drowned within sight of land while he was exploring the waters around Cape Cod choosing a place to settle. She either slipped or cast herself from the deck. (Bradford remarried in 1623 in a ceremony which Massasoit and a good number of warriors attended.) A few months after their arrival, the first governor, John Carver, died and Bradford was elected to succeed him in the post he filled for thirty of the years between 1622 and 1656. As one of the principal actors, Bradford ascribes the difficult but successful foundation to the hand of God and not to his undeniable vigour and courage. His reticence in giving primacy to his Maker extends to his never using his name personally in the text or mentioning his wives and children. Unlike Smith who announces a plain style but elevates it rhetorically and falls into verse to clinch an episode, Bradford holds to a severe and chastened style. He intended no immediate publication but sought to make a written record to contain the chronicle of his people's godly exodus for the use of further generations and a prophetic warning to them of the need for constant fidelity and vigilance. Although unpublished, his book was made available to other colonial historians and thus its literary strategies became disseminated. No direct influence need be argued, however, for the readers of this chronicle were themselves imbued with the common strength of the Puritan tradition.

Briefly, Bradford's prose aims at strict and austere truth and lucidity unadorned by trope or scheme. He left a manuscript book of poems of equal plainness and three 'Dialogues' between young men born at Plymouth and 'sundry ancient men' of the original group as well. The place of figurative language is filled in his prose by Biblical allusion. Puritan typology permits Bradford to chart the symbolic significance of the incidents and actions he records and to present them as 'special providences' of God. Although his certainty that literal facts communicate spiritual realities leads to interpretations unlike the interpretations of later American transcendentalists, his persistent and allusive double vision is not unlike that of Emerson or Emily Dickinson in promoting a significant symbolic style. Furthermore, that Nathaniel Morton para-phrased the most moving and eloquent sections of Book One in *New England's Memoriall* (Cambridge, 1669) and that Increase and Cotton Mather, William Hubbard, Thomas Prince and Thomas Hutchinson drew on it variously in their own histories led to the pervasiveness of his version of the 'matter of America'. His account is of the inspired acts of men who 'knew they were pilgrims'; it was for Cotton Mather, who wrote the only biography of Bradford we had until 1955, to remind us that he was a man 'of more than ordinary piety, wisdom and courage'.

My text reprints the edition made for the Massachusetts Historical Society and published by Houghton Mifflin in 1912.

The 9 Chap[ter]

Of their vioage, and how they passed the sea, and of their safe arrivall at Cape Codd

SEPT^R: 6.[a] These troubles being blowne over, and now all being compacte togeather in one shipe, they put to sea againe with a prosperus winde, which continued diverce days togeather, which was some incouragmente unto them; yet according to the usuall maner many were afflicted with sea-sicknes. And I may not omite hear a spetiall worke of Gods providence. Ther was a proud and very profane yonge man, one of the sea-men, of a lustie, able body, which made him the more hauty; he would allway be contemning the poore people in their sicknes, and cursing them dayly with gree[v]ous execrations, and did not let to tell them, that he hoped to help to cast halfe of them over board before they came to their jurneys end, and to make mery with what they had; and if he were by any gently reproved, he would curse and swear most bitterly. But it pl[e]ased God before they came halfe seas over, to smite this yong man with a greeveous disease, of which he dyed in a desperate maner, and so was him selfe the first that was throwne overbord. Thus his curses light on his owne head; and it was an astonishmente to all his fellow, for they noted it to be the just hand of God upon him[1]

After they had injoyed faire winds and weather for a season, they were incountred many times with crosse winds, and mette with many feirce stormes, with which the shipe was shroudly shaken, and her upper works made very leakie; and one of the maine beames in the midd ships was bowed and craked, which put them in some fear that the shipe could not be able to performe the vioage. So some of the cheefe of the company, perceiveing the mariners to feare the suffisien-

---

[a] The date is 1620. Chapter Nine is the last chapter of Book One of the history.

cie of the shipe, as appeared by their mutterings, they entred into serious consulltation with the m[aste]r and other officers of the ship, to consider in time of the danger; and rather to returne then to cast them selves into a desperate and inevitable perill. And truly ther was great distraction and differance of oppinion amongst the mariners them selves; faine would they doe what could be done for their wages sake, (being now halfe the seas over,) and on the other hand they were loath to hazard their lives too desperatly. But in examening of all oppinions, the m[aste]r and others affirmed they knew the ship to be stronge and firme underwater; and for the buckling of the maine beame, ther was a great iron scrue the passengers brought out of Holland, which would raise the beame into his place; the which being done, the carpenter and m[aste]r affirmed that with a post put under it, set firme in the lower deck, and otherways bounde, he would make it sufficiente. And as for the decks and uper workes they would calke them as well as they could, and though with the workeing of the ship they would not longe keepe stanch, yet ther would otherwise be no great danger, if they did not overpress her with sails. So they commited them selves to the will of God, and resolved to proseede. In sundrie of these stormes the winds were so feirce, and the seas so high, as they could not beare a knote of saile, but were forced to hull, for diverce days togither. And in one of them, as they thus lay at hull, in a mighty storme, a lustie yonge man (called John Howland) coming upon some occasion above the grattings, was, with a seele[b] of the shipe throwne into [the] sea; but it pleased God that he caught hould of the top-saile halliards, which hunge over board, and rane out at length; yet he held his hould (though he was sundrie fadomes under water) till he was hald up by the same rope to the brime of the water, and then with a boathooke and other means got into the shipe againe, and his life saved; and though he was something ill with it, yet he lived many years after, and became a profitable member both in church and commone wealthe.[2] In all this viage ther died but one of the passengers ... But to omite other things, (that I may be breefe,) after longe beating at sea they fell with that land which is called Cape Cod: the which being made and certainly knowne to be it, they were not a litle joyfull. After some deliberation had amongst them selves and with the m[aste]r of the ship, they tacked aboute and resolved to stande for the southward (the wind and weather being faire) to finde some place aboute Hudsons river for their habitation. But after they had sailed that course aboute halfe the day, they fell amongst deangerous shoulds and roring breakers, and they were so farr intangled ther with

b Seele: pitch or roll.

as they conceived them selves in great danger; and the wind shrinking upon them withall, they resolved to bear up againe for the Cape, and thought them selves hapy to gett out of those dangers before night overtooke them, as by Gods good providence they did. And the next day they gott into the Cape-harbor wher they ridd in saftie. . .ᶜ

Being thus arived in a good harbor and brought safe to land, they fell upon their knees and blessed the God of heaven, who had brought them over the vast and furious ocean, and delivered them from all the periles and miseries therof, againe to set their feete on the firme and stable earth, their proper elemente. And no marvell if they were thus joyefull, seeing wise Seneca was so affected with sailing a few miles on the coast of his owne Italy; as he affirmed, that he had rather remaine twentie years on his way by land, then pass by sea to any place in a short time; so tedious and dreadfull was the same unto him.

But hear I cannot but stay and make a pause, and stand half amazed at this poore peoples presente condition; and so I thinke will the reader too, when he well considers the same. Being thus passed the vast ocean, and a sea of troubles before in their preparation (as may be remembred by that which wente before), they had now no freinds to wellcome them, nor inns to entertaine or refresh their weatherbeaten bodys, no houses or much less townes to repaire too, to seeke for succoure. It is recorded in scripture as a mercie to the apostle and his shipwraked company, that the barbarians shewed them no smale kindnes in refreshing them, but these savage barbarians, when they mette with them (as after will appeare) were readier to fill their sides full of arrows then other wise. And for the season it was winter, and they that know the winters of that cuntrie know them to be sharp and violent, and subjecte to cruell and feirce stormes, deangerous to travill to known places, much more to serch an unknown coast. Besides, what could they see but a hidious and desolate wildernes, full of wild beasts and willd men? and what multitudes ther might be of them they knew not. Nether could they, as it were, goe up to the tope of Pisgah, to vew from this willdernes a more goodly cuntrie to feed their hopes; for which way soever they turnd their eyes (save upward to the heavens) they could have litle solace or content in respecte of any outward objects. For summer being done, all things stand upon them with a wetherbeaten face; and the whole countrie, full of woods and thickets, represented a wild and savage heiw. If they looked behind them, ther was the mighty ocean which they had passed, and was now as a maine barr and goulfe to seperate them from all the civill parts of the world. If it be said they had a ship to sucour them, it is trew; but

ᶜ The arrival was on 11 November 1620, the journey of the Mayflower having lasted sixty-five days.

what heard they daly from the m[aste]r and company? but that with
speede they should looke out a place with their shallop, wher they
would be at somenear distance; for the season was shuch as he would
not stirr from thence till a safe harbor was discovered by them wher
they would be, and he might goe without danger; and that victells
consumed apace, but he must and would keepe sufficient for them
selves and their returne. Yea, it was muttered by some, that if they gott
not a place in time, they would turne them and their goods a shore and
leave them. Let it also be considered what weake hopes of supply and
succoure they left behinde them, that might bear up their minds in
this sade condition and trialls they were under; and they could not but
be very smale. It is true, indeed, the affections and love of their
brethren at Leyden was cordiall and entire towards them, but they
had litle power to help them, or them selves; and how the case stoode
betweene them and the marchants at their coming away, hath allready
been declared. What could now sustaine them but the spirite of God
and his grace? May not and ought not the children of these fathers
rightly say: *Our faithers were English men which came over this great
ocean, and were ready to perish in this willdernes,*[d] *but they cried unto the
Lord, and he heard their voyce, and looked on their adversitie, etc. Let them
therfore praise the Lord, because he is good, and his mercies endure forever.
Yea, let them which have been redeemed of the Lord, shew how he hath
delivered them from the hand of the oppressour. When they wandered in the
deserte [and] willdernes out of the way, and found no citie to dwell in, both
hungrie, and thirstie, their sowle was overwhelmed in them. Let them
confess before the Lord his loving kindnes, and his wonderfull works before
the sons of men.*[3]

The 10 Chap[ter]

Showing how they sought out a place of habitation, and what befell them theraboute

Being thus arrived at Cap-Cod the 11 of November, and necessitie
calling them to looke out a place for habitation, (as well as the maisters
and mariners importunitie,) they having brought a large shalop with
them out of England, stowed in quarters in the ship, they now gott
her out and sett their carpenters to worke to trime her up; but being
much brused and shatered in the shipe with foule weather, they saw

[d] Deu. 26: 5, 7.

she would be longe in mending. Wherupon a few of them tendered them selves to goe by land and discovere those nearest places, whilst the shallop was in mending; and the rather because as they wente into that harbor ther seemed to be an opening some 2 or 3 leagues of, which the maister judged to be a river. It was conceived ther might be some danger in the attempte, yet seeing them resolute, they were permited to goe, being 16 of them well armed, under the conduct of Captein Standish, having shuch instructions given them as was thought meete.[4] They sett forth the 15 of Nove[m]b[e]r: and when they had marched aboute the space of a mile by the sea side, they espied 5 or 6 persons with a dogg coming towards them, who were salvages; but they fled from them, and ranne up into the woods, and the English followed them, partly to see if they could speake with them, and partly to discover if ther might not be more of them lying in ambush. But the Indeans seeing them selves thus followed, they againe forsooke the woods, and rane away on the sands as hard as they could, so as they could not come near them, but followed them by the tracte of their feet sundrie miles, and saw that they had come the same way. So, night coming on, they made their randevous and set out their sentinels, and rested in quiete *that night*, and the next morning followed their tracte till they had headed a great creeke, and so left the sands, and turned an other way into the woods. But they still followed them by geuss, hopeing to find their dwellings; but they soone lost both them and them selves, falling into shuch thickets as were ready to tear their cloaths and armore in peeces, but were most distressed for wante of drinke. But at length they found water and refreshed them selves, being the first New-England water they drunke of, and was now in thir great thirste as pleasante unto them as wine or bear had been in for-times. Afterwards they directed their course to come to the other shore, for they knew it was a necke of land they were to crosse over, and so at length gott to the sea-side, and marched to this supposed river, and by the way found a pond of clear fresh water, and shortly after a good quantitie of clear ground wher the Indeans had formerly set corne, and some of their graves. And proceeding furder they saw new-stuble wher corne had been set the same year, also they found wher latly a house had been, wher some planks and a great ketle was remaining, and heaps of sand newly padled with their hands, which they, digging up, found in them diverce faire Indean baskets filled with corne, and some in eares, faire and good, of diverce collours, which seemed to them a very goodly sight, (haveing never seen any shuch before). This was near the place of that supposed river they came to seeck; unto which they wente and found it to open it selfe into 2 armes with a high cliffe of sand in the enterance, but more like to be crikes of salte water then any fresh, for ought they saw; and that ther was good harborige for their shalope; leaving it further to be discovered by their shalop when she was ready. So their time limeted them being expired, they returned to the ship, least they should be in fear of their saftie; and tooke with them parte of the corne, and buried up the rest, and so like the men from Eshcoll carried with them of the fruits of the land, and showed their breethren; of which, and their returne, they are marvelusly glad, and their harts incouraged.

After this, the shalop being got ready, they set out againe for the better discovery of this place, and the m[aste]r of the ship desired to goe him selfe, so ther went some 30 men, but found it to be no harbor for ships but only for boats; ther was allso found 2 of their houses covered with matts, and sundrie of their implements in them, but the people were rune away and could not be seen; also ther was found more of their corne, and of their beans of various collours. The corne and beans they brought away, purposing to give them full satisfaction when they should meete with any of them (as about some 6 months afterward they did, to their good contente).[5] And here is to be noted a spetiall providence of God, and a great mercie to this poore people, that hear they gott seed to plant them corne the next yeare, or els they might have starved, for they had none, nor any liklyhood to get any till the season had beene past (as the sequell did manyfest). Neither is it lickly they had had this, if the first viage had not been made, for the ground was now all covered with snow, and hard frosen. But the Lord is never wanting unto his in their greatest needs; let his holy name have all the praise.

The month of November being spente in these affairs, and much foule weather falling in, the 6 of *Desem[be]r* they sente out their shallop againe with 10 of their principall men, and some sea men, upon further discovery, intending to circulate that deepe bay of Cap-Codd. The weather was very could, and it frose so hard as the sprea of the sea lighting on their coats, they were as if they had been glased; yet *that night* betimes they gott downe into the botome of the bay, and as they drue nere the shore they saw some 10 or 12 Indeans very busie aboute some thing. They landed aboute a league or 2 from them, and had much a doe to put a shore any wher, it lay so full of flats. Being landed, it grew late, and they made them selves a barricado with loggs and bowes as well as they could in the time, and set out their sentenill and betooke them to rest, and saw the smoake of the fire the savages made that night. When *morning* was come they devided their company, some to coast along the shore in the boate, and the rest

67

marched throw the woods to see the land, if any fit place might be for their dwelling. They came allso to the place wher they saw the Ind[i]ans the night before, and found they had been cuting up a great fish like a grampus, being some 2 inches thike of fate like a hogg, some peeces wher of they had left by the way; and the shallop found 2 more of these fishes dead on the sands, a thing usuall after storms in that place, by reason of the great flats of sand that lye of. So they ranged up and doune all that day, but found no people, nor any place they liked. When the sune grue low, they hasted out of the woods to meete with their shallop, to whom they made signes to come to them into a *creeke* hardby, the which they did at highwater; of which they were very glad, for they had not seen each other all that day, since the morning. So they made them a barricado (as usually they did every night) with loggs, stakes, and thike pine bowes, the height of a man, leaving it open to leeward, partly to shelter them from the could and wind (making their fire in the midle, and lying round aboute it), and partly to defend them from any sudden assaults of the savages, if they should surround them. So being very weary, they betooke them to rest. But aboute *midnight* they heard a hideous and great crie, and their senti-nell caled, Arme, arme; so they bestired them and stood to their armes, and shote of a cupple of moskets, and then the noys seased. They concluded it was a companie of wolves, or such like willd beasts; for one of the sea men tould them he had often heard shuch a noyse in New-found land. So they rested till about 5 of the clock in the *morning*; for the tide, and ther purpos to goe from thence, made them be stiring betimes. So after praier they prepared for breakfast, and it being day dawning, it was thought best to be carring things downe to the boate. But some said it was not best to carrie the armes downe, others said they would be the readier, or they had laped them up in their coats from the dew. But some 3 or 4 would not cary theirs till they wente them selves, yet as it fell out, the water being not high enough, they layed them downe on the banke side, and came up to breakfast. But presently, all on the sudain, they heard a great and strange crie, which they knew to be the same voyces they heard in the night, though they varied their notes, and one of their company being abroad came runing in, and cried, Men, Indeans, Indeans; and withall, their arowes came flying amongst them. Their men rane with all speed to recover their armes, as by the good providence of God they did. In the mean time, of those that were ther ready, tow muskets were discharged at them, and 2 more stood ready in the enterance of ther randevoue, but were comanded not to shoote till they could take full aime at them; and the other 2 charged againe with all speed, for ther were only 4 had armes ther, and defended the baricado which was first assalted. The crie of the Indeans was dreadfull, espetially when they saw ther men rune out of the randevoue towourds the shallop, to recover ther armes the Indeans wheeling aboute upon them. But some running out with coats of malle on, and cutlashess in their hands, they soone got their armes, and let flye amongs them, and quickly stopped their violence. Yet ther was a lustie man, and no less valiante, stood behind a tree within halfe a musket shot, and let his arrows flie at them. He was seen shoot 3 arrowes, which were all avoyded. He stood 3 shot of musket, till one taking full aime at him, and made the barke or splinters of the tree fly about his ears, after which he gave an extraordinary shrike, and away they wente all of them. They left some to keep the shalop, and followed them aboute a quarter of a mille, and shouted once or twise, and shot of 2 or 3 peces, and so returned. This they did, that they might conceive that they were not affrade of them or any way discouraged. Thus it pleased God to vanquish their enimies, and give them deliverance: and by his spetial providence so to dispose that not any one of them were either hurte, or hitt, though their arrows came close by them, and on every side [of] them, and sundry of their coats, which hunge up in the barricado, were shot throw and throw. Aterwards they gave God sollemne thanks and praise for their deliverance, and gathered up a bundle of their arrows, and sente them into England afterward by the m[aste]r of the ship, and called that place the first encounter. From hence they departed. and costed all along, but discerned no place likly for harbor . . . After some houres sailing, it begane to snow and raine, and about the midle of the afternoone, the wind increased, and the sea became very rough, and they broake their rudder, and it was as much as 2 men could doe to steere her with a cupple of oares. But their pillott bad them be of good cheere, for he saw the harbor; but the storme increasing, and night drawing on, they bore what saile they could to gett in, while they could see. But herwith they broake their mast in 3 peeces, and their saill fell over bord, in a very grown sea, so as they had like to have been cast away; yet by Gods mercie they recovered them selves, and having the floud with them, struck into the harbore. But when it came too, the pillott was deceived in the place, and said, the Lord be mercifull unto them, for his eyes never saw that place before; and he and the m[aste]r mate would have rune her a shore, in a cove full of breakers, before the winde. But a lusty seaman which steered, bad those which rowed, if they were men, about with

69

her, or ells they were all cast away; the which they did with speed. So
he bid them be of good cheere and row lustly, for ther was a faire
sound before them, and he doubted not but they should find one
place or other wher they might ride in saftie. And though it was *very
darke*, and rained sore, yet in the end they gott under the lee of a smalle
iland, and remained ther all *that night* in saftie. But they knew not this
to be an iland till morning, but were divided in their minds; some
would keepe the boate for fear they might be amongst the Indians;
others were so weake and could, they could not endure, but got a
shore, and with much adoe got fire, (all things being so wett,) and the
rest were glad to come to them; for after midnight the wind shifted to
the north-west, and it frose hard. But though this had been a day
and night of much trouble and danger unto them, yet God gave them
a *morning* of comforte and refreshing (as usually he doth to his
children), for the next day was a faire sunshininge day, and they found
them sellves to be on an iland secure from the Indeans, wher they
might drie their stufe, fixe their peeces, and rest them selves, and gave
God thanks for his mercies, in their manifould deliverances. And this
being the *last day of the weeke*, they prepared ther to keepe the *Sabath*.
On *Munday* they sounded the harbor, and founde it fitt for shipping;
and marched into the land, and found diverse cornfeilds, and litle
runing brooks, a place (as they supposed) fitt for situation; at least it
was the best they could find, and the season, and their presente
necessitie, made them glad to accepte of it. So they returned to their
shipp againe with this news to the rest of their people, which did
much comforte their harts.[6]

On the *15 of Desem[be]r:* they wayed anchor to goe to the place they
had discovered, and came within 2 leagues of it, but were faine to bear
up againe; but the *16 day* the winde came faire, and they arrived safe in
this harbor. And after wards tooke better view ofthe place, and
resolved wher to pitch their dwelling; and the *25 day* begane to erecte
the first house for commone use to receive them and their goods.

The 2 Booke

The rest of this history (if God give me life, and opportunitie) I
shall, for brevitis sake, handle by way of annalls, noteing only
the heads of principall things, and passages as they fell in order
of time, and may seeme to be profitable to know, or to make use
of. And this may be as the 2 Booke

The remainder of Anno 1620

I shall a litle returne backe and begine with a combination made by them before they came a shore, being the first foundation of their govermente in this place; occasioned partly by the discontented and mutinous speeches that some of the strangers amongst them had let fall from them in the ship;[e] That when they came a shore they would use their owne libertie; for none had power to command them, the patente they had being for Virginia, and not for New england, which belonged to an other Goverment, with which the Virginia Company had nothing to doe. And partly that shuch an acte by them done (this their condition considered) might be as firme as any patent, and in some respects more sure.

The forme was as followeth

In the name of God, Amen. We whose names are underwriten, the loyall subjects of our dread soveraigne Lord, King James, by the grace of God, of Great Britaine, Franc, and Ireland king, defender of the faith, etc.

Haveing undertaken, for the glorie of God, and advancemente of the Christian faith, and honour of our king and countrie, a voyage to plant the first colonie in the Northerne parts of Virginia, doe by these presents solemnly and mutualy in the presence of God, and one of another, covenant and combine our selves togeather into a civill body politick, for our better ordering and preservation and furtherance of the ends aforesaid; and by vertue hearof to enacte, constitute, and frame shuch just and equall lawes, ordinances, acts, constitutions, and offices, from time to time, as shall be thought most meete and convenient for the generall good of the Colonie, unto which we promise all due submission and obedience. In witnes wherof we have hereunder subscribed our names at Cap-Codd the 11 of November, in the year of the raigne of our soveraigne lord, King James, of England, France, and Ireland, the eighteenth, and of Scotland the fiftie fourth. Anno Dom. 1620.

After this they chose, or rather confirmed, Mr. John Carver (a man godly and well approved amongst them) their Governour for that year. And after they had provided a place for their goods, or comone store, (which were long in unlading for want of boats, foulnes of the winter weather, and sicknes of diverce,) and begune some small cottages for their habitation, as time would admitte, they mette and consulted of lawes and orders, both for their civill and military Govermente, as the necessitie of their condition did require, still adding therunto as urgent occasion in severall times, and as cases did require.

In these hard and difficulte beginings they found some discontents and murmurings arise amongst some, and mutinous speeches and carriages in other; but they were soone quelled and overcome by the

---

[e] The 'strangers' were recruits for the journey taken on in England, not part of the Leyden group.

wisdome, patience, and just and equall carrage of things by the Gov[erno]r and better part, which clave faithfully togeather in the maine. But that which was most sadd and lamentable was, that in 2 or 3 moneths time halfe of their company dyed, espetialy in Jan: and February, being the depth of winter, and wanting houses and other comforts;[7] being infected with the scurvie and other diseases, which this long voiage and their inacomodate condition had brought upon them; so as ther dyed some times 2 or 3 of a day, in the aforesaid time; that of 100 and odd persons, scarce 50 remained. And of these in the time of most distres, ther was but 6 or 7 sound persons, who, to their great comendations be it spoken, spared no pains, night nor day, but with abundance of toyle and hazard of their owne health, fetched them woode, made them fires, drest them meat, made their beads, washed their lothsome cloaths, cloathed and uncloathed them; in a word, did all the homly and necessarie offices for them which dainty and quesie stomacks cannot endure to hear named; and all this willingly and cherfully, without any grudging in the least, shewing herein their true love unto their freinds and bretheren. A rare example and worthy to be remembred. Tow of these 7 were Mr. William Brewster, ther reverend Elder, and Myles Standish, ther Captein and military comander, unto whom my selfe, and many others, were much beholden in our low and sicke condition. And yet the Lord so upheld these persons, as in this generall calamity they were not at all infected either with sicknes, or lamnes. And what I have said of these, I may say of many others who dyed in this generall vissitation, and others yet living, that whilst they had health, yea, or any strength continuing, they were not wanting to any that had need of them. And I doute not but their recompence is with the Lord.

But I may not hear pass by an other remarkable passage not to be forgotten. As this calamitie fell among the passengers that were to be left here to plant, and were hasted a shore and made to drinke water, that the sea-men might have the more bear, and one in his sicknes desiring but a small cann of beere[f] it was answered, that if he were their owne father he should have none; the disease begane to fall amongst them also, so as allmost halfe of their company dyed before they went away, and many of their officers and lustyest men, as the boatson, gunner, 3 quarter-maisters, the cooke, and others. At which the m[aste]r was something strucken and sent to the sick a shore and tould the Gov[erno]r he should send for beer for them that had need of it, though he drunke water homward bound. But now amongst his company ther was farr another kind of carriage in this miserie then

---

[f] Bradford himself.

amongst the passengers; for they that before had been boone companions in drinking and joyllity in the time of their health and
wellfare, begane now to deserte one another in this calamitie saing,
they would not hasard ther lives for them, they should be infected by
coming to help them in their cabins, and so, after they came to lye by
it, would doe litle or nothing for them, but if they dyed let them dye.
But shuch of the passengers as were yet abord shewed them what
mercy they could, which made some of their harts relente, as the
boatson (and some others), who was a prowd yonge man, and would
often curse and scofe at the passengers; but when he grew weak, they
had compasion on him, and helped him; then he confessed he did not
deserve it at their hands, he had abused them in word and deed. O!
saith he, you, I now see, shew your love like Christians indeed one to
another, but we let one another lye and dye like doggs. Another lay
cursing his wife, saing if it had not ben for her he had never come this
unlucky viage, and anone cursing his felows, saing he had done this
and that, for some of them, he had spente so much, and so much,
amongst them, and they were now weary of him, and did not help
him, having need. Another gave his companion all he had, if he died,
to help him in his weaknes; he went and got a litle spise and made him
a mess of meat once or twise, and because he dyed not so soone as he
expected, he went amongst his fellows, and swore the rogue would
cousen him, he would see him chooked before he made him any more
meate; and yet the pore fellow dyed before morning.

All this while the Indians came skulking about them, and would
sometimes show them selves aloofe of, but when any aproached near
them, they would rune away. And once they stoale away their tools
wher they had been at worke, and were gone to diner. But about the
16 of March a certaine Indian came bouldly amongst them, and spoke
to them in broken English, which they could well understand, but
marvelled at it. At length they understood by discourse with him, that
he was not of these parts, but belonged to the eastrene parts, wher
some English-ships came to fhish, with whom he was aquainted, and
could name sundrie of them by their names, amongst whom he had
gott his language.[8] He became prof[i]table to them in aquainting
them with many things concerning the state of the cuntry in the
east-parts wher he lived, which was afterwards profitable unto them;
as also of the people hear, of their names, number, and strength; of
their situation and distance from this place, and who was cheefe
amongst them. His name was *Samasett;* he tould them also of another
Indian whose name was *Squanto*, a native of this place, who had been
in England and could speake better English then him selfe. Being,

after some time of entertainmente and gifts, dismist, a while after he came againe, and 5 more with him, and they brought againe all the tooles that were stolen away before, and made way for the coming of their great Sachem, called *Massasoyt;* who, about 4 or 5 *days after*, came with the cheefe of his freinds and other attendance, with the aforesaid *Squanto.* With whom, after frendly entertainment, and some gifts given him, they made a peace with him (which hath now continued this 24 years) in these terms.

    1. That neither he nor any of his, should injurie or doe hurte to any of their people[e].

    2. That if any of his did any hurte to any of theirs, he should send the offender, that they might punish him.

    3. That if any thing were taken away from any of theirs, he should cause it to be restored; and they should doe the like to his.

    4. If any did unjustly warr against him, they would aide him; if any did warr against them, he should aide them.

    5. He should send to his neighbours confederates, to certifie them of this, that they might not wrong them, but might be likewise comprised in the conditions of peace.

    6. That when ther men came to them, they should leave their bows and arrows behind them.[9]

After these things he returned to his place caled *Sowams,* some 40 *mile* from this place, but *Squanto* continued with them, and was their interpreter, and was a spetiall instrument sent of God for their good beyond their expectation. He directed them how to set their corne, wher to take fish, and to procure other comodities, and was also their pilott to bring them to unknowne places for their profitt, and never left them till he dyed. He was a *native of this place,* and scarce any left alive besides him selfe. He was caried away with diverce others by one *Hunt,*[10] a m[aster] of a ship, who thought to sell them for slaves in Spaine; but he got away for England, and was entertained by a marchante in London and imployed to New-found-land and other parts, and lastly brought hither into these parts by one Mr. *Dermer,* a gentle-man imployed by Sir Ferdinando Gorges and others, for discovery, and other designes in these parts. Of whom I shall say some thing, because it is mentioned in a booke set forth Anno: 1622. by the Presidente and Counsell for New-England, that he made the peace betweene the salvages of these parts and the English: of which this plantation, as it is intimated, had the benefite.

. . .

But to returne. The spring now approaching, it pleased God the mortalitie begane to cease amongst them, and the sick and lame recovered apace, which put as [it] were new life into them; though they had borne their sadd affliction with much patience and contentednes, as I thinke any people could doe. But it was the Lord which upheld them, and had beforehand prepared them; many having long borne the yoake, yea from their youth. Many other smaler maters I omite, sundrie of them having been allready published in a Jurnall made by one of the company; and some other passages of jurneys and relations allredy published, to which I referr those that are willing to know them more perticulerly. And being now come to the 25 of March I shall begine the year 1621.

Anno 1621

They now begane to dispatch the ship away which brought them over, which lay tille aboute this time, or the begining of Aprill. The reason on their parts why she stayed so long, was the necessitie and danger that lay upon them, for it was well towards the ende of Desember before she could land any thing hear, or they able to receive any thing a shore. Afterwards, the 14 of Jan[uary] the house which they had made for a generall randevoze by casu[a]lty fell afire, and some were faine to retire abord for shilter. Then the sicknes begane to fall sore amongst them, and the weather so bad so they could not make much sooner any dispatch. Againe, the Gov[ernor] and cheefe of them, seeing so many dye, and fall downe sick dayly, thought it no wisdom to send away the ship, their condition considered, and the danger they stood in from the Indeans, till they could procure some shelter; and therfore thought it better to draw some more charge upon them selves and freinds, then hazard all. The m[aste]r and seamen likewise, though before they hasted the passengers a shore to be goone, now many of their men being dead, and of the ablest of them, (as is before noted,) and of the rest many lay sick and weake, the m[aste]r durst not put to sea, till he saw his men begine to recover, and the hart of winter over.

Afterwards they (as many as were able) began to plant ther corne, in which servise Squanto stood them in great stead, showing them both the maner how to set it, and after how to dress and tend it. Also he tould them excepte they gott fish and set with it (in these old grounds) it would come to nothing, and he showed them that in the midle of Aprill they should have store enough come up the brooke, by which they begane to build, and taught them how to take it, and wher to get other provisions necessary for them; all which they found true by triall and experience. Some English seed they sew, as wheat and pease, but it came not to good, eather by the badnes of the seed, or latenes of the season, or both, or some other defecte. In this month of *Aprill* whilst they were bussie about their seed, their Gov[ernor] (Mr. John Carver) came out of the feild very sick, it being a hott day; he complained greatly of his head, and lay downe, and within a few howers his sences failed, so as he never spake more till he dyed, which was within a few days after. Whoss death was much lamented, and caused great heavines amongst them, as ther was cause. He was buried in the best maner they could, with some vollies of shott by all that bore armes; and his wife, being a weak woman, dyed within 5 or 6 weeks after him.

Shortly after William Bradford was chosen Gov[rno]r in his stead, and being not yet recoverd of his ilnes, in which he had been near the point of death, Isaack Allerton was chosen to be an Asistante unto him, who, by renewed election every year, continued sundry years togeather, which I hear note once for all.

May 12 was the first mariage in this place, which, according to the laudable custome of the Low-cuntries, in which they had lived, was thought most requisite to be performed by the magistrate, as being a civill thing, upon which many questions aboute inheritances doe depende, with other things most proper to their cognizans, and most consonante to the scriptures, Ruth 4 and no wher found in the gospell to be layed on the ministers as a part of their office...[11]

Haveing in some sorte ordered their bussines at home, it was thought meete to send some abroad to see their new freind Massasoyet, and to bestow upon him some gratuitie to bind him the faster unto them; as also that hearby they might veiw the countrie, and see in what maner he lived, what strength he had aboute him, and how the ways were to his place, if at any time they should have occasion. So the 2 *of July* they sente Mr. Edward Winslow and Mr. Hopkins, with the fore said Squanto for ther guid, who gave him a suite of cloaths, and a horse-mans coate, with some other small things, which were kindly accepted; but they found but short commons, and came both weary and hungrie home. For the Indeans used then to have nothing so much corne as they have since the English have stored them with their hows, and seene their industrie in breaking up new-grounds therwith. *They found his place to be 40 myles from hence,* the soyle good, and the people not many, being dead and abundantly wasted in the late great mortalitie which fell in all these parts aboute *three years* before the coming of the English, wherin thousands of them dyed; they not being able to burie one another, ther sculs and bones were found in many places lying still above ground, where their houses and dwellings had been; a very sad spectackle to behould. But they brought word that the Narighansets lived but on the other side of that great bay, and were a strong people, and many in number, living compacte togeather, and had not been at all touched with this wasting plague.

About the *later end of this month*, one John Billington lost him selfe in the woods, and wandered up and downe some 5 days, living on beries and what he could find. At length he light on an Indean plantation, 20 miles south of this place, called *Manamet*. They conveid him furder of, to *Nawssett*, among those peopl[e] that had before set upon the English when they were costing, whilest the ship lay at the Cape, as is before noted. But the Gove[rno]r caused him to be enquired for among the Indeans, and at length Massassoyt sent word wher he was, and the Gov[rno]r sent a shalop for him, and had him delivered. Those people also came and made their peace; and they gave full satisfaction to those whose corne they had found and taken when they were at Cap-Codd.

Thus ther peace and aquaintance was prety well establisht with the natives aboute them; and ther was an other Indean called *Hobamack* come to live amongst them, a proper lustie man, and a man of accounte for his vallour and parts amongst the Indeans, and continued very faithfull and constant to the English till he dyed. He and Squanto being gone upon bussines amonge the Indeans, at their returne (whether it was out of envie to them or malice to the English) ther was a Sachem called Corbitant, alyed to Massassoyte, but never any good freind to the English to this day, mett with them at an Indean towne caled Namassakett 14 miles to the west of this place, and begane to quarell with them, and offered to stabe Hobamack; but being a lusty man, he cleared him selfe of him, and came running away all sweating and tould the Gov[erno]r what had befalne him, and he feared they had killed Squanto, for they threatened them both, and for no other cause but because they were freinds to the English, and servisable unto them. Upon this the Gove[rno]r taking counsell, it was conceivd not fitt to be borne; for if they should suffer their freinds and messengers thus to be wronged, they should have none would cleave to them, or give them any inteligence, or doe them serviss afterwards; but nexte they would fall upon them selves. Where upon it was resolved to send the Captaine and 14 men well armed, and to goe and fall upon them in the night; and if they found that Squanto was kild, to cut of Corbitants head, but not to hurt any but those that had a hand in it. Hobamack was asked if he would goe and be their guid, and bring them ther before day. He said he would, and bring them to the house wher the man lay, and show them which was he.

So they set forth the 14 *of August*, and beset the house round; the Captin giving charg to let none pass out, entred the house to search for him. But he was goone away that day, so they mist him; but understood that Squanto was alive, and that he had only threatened to kill him, and made an offer to stabe him but did not. So they withheld and did no more hurte, and the people came trembling, and brought them the best provissions they had, after they were aquainted by Hobamack what was only intended. Ther was 3 sore wounded which broak out of the house, and asaid to pass through the garde. These they brought home with them, and they had their wounds drest and cured, and sente home. After this they had many gratulations from diverce sachims, and much firmer peace; yea, those of the Iles of Capawack sent to make frendship; and this Corbitant him selfe used the mediation of Massassoyte to make his peace, but was shie to come neare them a longe while after.

After this, the 18 of Sep[t]ember they sente out ther shalop to the Massachusets, with 10 men, and Squanto for their guid and inter-preter, to discover and view that bay, and trade with the natives; the which they performed, and found kind entertainement. The people were much affraid of the Tarentins, a people to the eastward which used to come in harvest time and take away their corne, and many times kill their persons. They returned in saftie, and brought home a good quan[ti]ty of beaver, and made reporte of the place, wishing they had been ther seated; (but it seems the Lord, who assignes to all men the bounds of their habitations, had apoynted it for an other use). And thus they found the Lord to be with them in all their ways, and to blesse their outgoings and incommings, for which let his holy name have the praise forever, to all posteritie.

They begane now to gather in the small harvest they had, and to fitte up their houses and dwellings against winter, being all well recovered in health and strength, and had all things in good plenty; for as some were thus imployed in affairs abroad, others were excersised in fishing, aboute codd, and bass, and other fish, of which they tooke good store, of which every family had their portion. All the sommer ther was no wante. And now begane to come in store of foule, as winter aproached, of which this place did abound when they came first (but afterward decreased by degrees). And besides water foule, ther was great store of wild Turkies, of which they tooke many, besides venison, etc. Besides they had aboute a peck a meale a weeke to a person, or now since harvest, Indean corne to that proportion. Which made many afterwards write so largely of their plenty hear to their freinds in England, which were not fained, but true reports.

Mary Rowlandson, 'The Sovereignity and Goodness of God, Together with the Faithfulness of His Promises Displayed; Being a Narrative of the Captivity and Restauration of Mrs. Mary Rowlandson'

It is not clear whether Mary White Rowlandson (c. 1635–78) was born in England before her parents sailed to America or in Massachusetts once they arrived. Her parents first settled near Salem and then pushed on to Lancaster, Massachusetts where they held a good amount of land. Lancaster was a frontier village of about fifty families, exposed to Indian attacks during the years of King Philip's War (see Introduction, note 4). In 1656, she married the local Congregational minister, Joseph Rowlandson. Virtually all that we know of her for certain – that she was the mother of three children, for example – comes from her own *Narrative*, the account of her three months of captivity by the Narragansett Indians during the late winter and spring of 1675. It was printed six years after the event, presumably after her death. If she died, as is thought, in 1678, she survived her experience for only two years during which she and her husband transferred to Wethersfield, Connecticut. The book was her only known attempt at writing, but it represents a very common genre, of which for its vividness and firmness it is the best representative. It was enormously popular, running to three editions in the year of its first appearance and more than thirty since.

Like Bradford, Mrs Rowlandson allegorizes her experience by way of the Puritan typology, a rationalizing mythology underpinned by God's having covenanted with his elect to so shape their lives that all their experiences would be meaningful and explicable. That mythology supplied her with the pattern by which she gives shape and large meaning to her ordeal; she herself lends it drama and effect. From the typology is derived her sense of participating in the prophesied Christian struggle of good and evil, God and Satan, the church and the excluded. She herself unselfconsciously but not inartistically places within that pattern – nonetheless piercingly real to her for all its ghostly biblicism – the realistic details of the sudden attack at dawn; the shooting, scalping and mutilation; the sounds and sights of destruction, first visible by the light of the fired houses; the capture itself; the abrupt removals, herself wounded and carrying her six-year-old dying child; the subsequent terrors and intermittent rough mercies; her ransomed release, the drunken celebration of the Indians, and her final return to what was left of her family. Those realistic details account for the long popularity of her narrative and indeed for the persistence of the genre, a genre able to offer something far more sensational than yet another allegorical confirmation of God's unwithdrawing hand. It says much for her skill that all that is necessary in the way of antecedent action is conveyed in the narrative itself. Towards the end of January a friendly Indian warned the town of an attack planned within three weeks; Mrs

Rowlandson was left unprotected when her husband departed with some others to bring help; the attack came before their return. Her sense of the meaning of her experience is adequately conveyed in the first part of her comprehensive title, *The Sovereignty and Goodness of God, Together with the Faithfulness of His Promise Displayed...* No irony should be read into such pious observations as those summarizing her experience at the end, for example: 'I can but admire to see the wonderfull providence of God in preserving the heathen for farther affliction to our poor Countrey.' What her title does not predict is the spirit of the woman who confessed 'Before I knew what affliction meant, I was ready sometimes to wish for it.' That spirit includes savagery in her presentation of the Indians as diabolical savages.

My text is taken from *Narratives of the Indian Wars, 1675–1699*, edited by Charles H. Lincoln, New York, Charles Scribner's Sons, 1913. (Volume entitled: *Original Narratives of Early American History*.)

A Narrative of the Captivity and Restauration of Mrs Mary Rowlandson

On the tenth of February 1675 Came the Indians with great numbers upon Lancaster: Their first coming was about Sun-rising; hearing the noise of some Guns, we looked out; several Houses were burning, and the Smoke ascending to Heaven. There were five person taken in one house, the Father, and the Mother and a sucking Child, they knockt on the head; the other two they took and carried away alive. Their were two others, who being out of their Garison upon some occasion were set upon; one was knockt on the head, the other escaped: Another their was who running along was shot and wounded, and fell down; he begged of them his life, promising them Money (as they told me) but they would not hearken to him but knockt him in head, and stript him naked, and split open his Bowels. Another seeing many of the Indians about his Barn, ventured and went out, but was quickly shot down. There were three others belonging to the same Garison who were killed; the Indians getting up upon the roof of the Barn, had advantage to shoot down upon them over their Fortification. Thus these murtherous wretches went on, burning, and destroying before them.

At length they came and beset our own house, and quickly it was the dolefullest day that ever mine eyes saw. The House stood upon the edg of a hill; some of the Indians got behind the hill, others into the Barn, and others behind any thing that could shelter them; from all which places they shot against the House, so that the Bullets seemed to fly like hail; and quickly they wounded one man among us, then another, and then a third, About two hours (according to my observation, in that amazing time) they had been about the house before they prevailed to fire it (which they did with Flax and Hemp, which they brought out of the Barn, and there being no defence about the House, only two Flankers[a] at two opposite corners and one of them not finished) they fired it once and one ventured out and quenched it, but they quickly fired it again, and that took. Now is the dreadfull hour come, that I have often heard of (in time of War, as it was the case of others) but now mine eyes see it. Some in our house were fighting for their lives, others wallowing in their blood, the House on fire over our heads, and the bloody Heathen ready to knock us on the head, if we stirred out. Now might we hear Mothers and Children crying out for themselves, and one another, Lord, What shall we do? Then I took my Children (and one of my sisters, hers) to go forth and leave the house: but as soon as we came to the dore and appeared, the Indians shot so thick that the bulletts rattled against the House, as if one had taken an handfull of stones and threw them, so that we were fain to give back. We had six stout Dogs belonging to our Garrison, but none of them would stir, though another time, if any Indian had come to the door, they were ready to fly upon him and tear him down. The Lord hereby would make us the more to acknowledge his hand, and to see that our help is always in him. But out we must go, the fire increasing, and coming along behind us, roaring, and the Indians gaping before us with their Guns, Spears and Hatchets to devour us. No sooner were we out of the House, but my Brother in Law (being before wounded, in defending the house, in or near the throat) fell down dead, wherat the Indians scornfully shouted, and hallowed, and were presently upon him, stripping off his cloaths, the bulletts flying thick, one went through my side, and the same (as would seem) through the bowels and hand of my dear Child in my arms. One of my elder Sisters Children, named William, had then his Leg broken, which the Indians perceiving, they knockt him on head. Thus were we butchered by those merciless Heathen, standing amazed, with the blood running down to our heels. My eldest Sister being yet in the House, and seeing those wofull sights, the Infidels haling Mothers one way, and Children another, and some wallowing in their blood: and her elder Son telling her that her Son William was dead, and my self was wounded, she said, And, Lord, let me dy with them; which was no sooner said, but she was struck with a Bullet, and fell down dead over the threshold. I hope she is reaping the fruit of her good labours, being faithfull to the service of God in her place. In her younger years she lay under much trouble upon spiritual accounts, till it pleased God to make that precious Scripture

[a] Flankers were wooden projections from which blank walls or curtains could be hung.

take hold of her heart, 2 Cor. 12.9. *And he said unto me, my Grace is sufficient for thee.* More then twenty years after I have heard her tell how sweet and comfortable that place was to her. But to return: The Indians laid hold of us, pulling me one way, and the Children another, and said, Come go along with us; I told them they would kill me: they answered, If I were willing to go along with them, they would not hurt me.

Oh the dolefull sight that now was to behold at this House! *Come, behold the works of the Lord, what dissolations he has made in the Earth.* Of thirty seven persons who were in this one House, none escaped either present death, or a bitter captivity, save only one, who might say as he, Job 1. 15, *And I only am escaped alone to tell the News.* There were twelve killed, some shot, some stab'd with their Spears, some knock'd down with their Hatchets. When we are in prosperity, Oh the little that we think of such dreadfull sights, and to see our dear Friends, and Relations ly bleeding out their heart-blood upon the ground. There was one who was chopt into the head with a Hatchet, and stript naked, and yet was crawling up and down. It is a solemn sight to see so many Christians lying in their blood, some here, and some there, like a company of Sheep torn by Wolves, All of them stript naked by a company of hell-hounds, roaring, singing, ranting and insulting, as if they would have torn our very hearts out; yet the Lord by his Almighty power preserved a number of us from death, for there were twenty-four of us taken alive and carried Captive.

I had often before this said, that if the Indians should come, I should chuse rather to be killed by them then taken alive but when it came to the tryal my mind changed; their glittering weapons so daunted my spirit, that I chose rather to go along with those (as I may say) ravenous Beasts, then that moment to end my dayes; and that I may the better declare what happened to me during that grievous Captivity, I shall particularly speak of the severall Removes we had up and down the Wilderness.

The first Remove

Now away we must go with those Barbarous Creatures, with our bodies wounded and bleeding, and our hearts no less than our bodies. About a mile we went that night, up upon a hill within sight of the Town, where they intended to lodge. There was hard by a vacant house (deserted by the English before, for fear of the Indians). I asked them whither I might not lodge in the house that night to which they answered, what will you love English men still? this was the dole-fullest night that ever my eyes saw. Oh the roaring, and singing and danceing, and yelling of those black creatures in the night, which made the place a lively resemblance of hell. And as miserable was the wast that was there made, of Horses, Cattle, Sheep, Swine, Calves, Lambs, Roasting Pigs, and Fowl (which they had plundered in the Town) some roasting, some lying and burning, and some boyling to feed our merciless Enemies; who were joyful enough though we were disconsolate. To add to the dolefulness of the former day, and the dismalness of the present night: my thoughts ran upon my losses and sad bereaved condition. All was gone, my Husband gone (at least separated from me, he being in the Bay,[b] and to add to my grief, the Indians told me they would kill him as he came homeward) my Children gone, my Relations and Friends gone, our House and home and all our comforts within door, and without, all was gone, (except my life) and I knew not but the next moment that might go too. There remained nothing to me but one poor wounded Babe, and it seemed at present worse than death that it was in such a pitiful condition, bespeaking Compassion, and I had no refreshing for it, nor suitable things to revive it. Little do many think what is the savageness and bruitishness of this barbarous Enemy, I even those that seem to profess more than others among them, when the English have fallen into their hands.

Those seven that were killed at Lancaster the summer before upon a Sabbath day, and the one that was afterward killed upon a week day, were slain and mangled in a barbarous manner by one-ey'd John, and Marlborough's Praying Indians,[c] which Capt. Mosely brought to Boston, as the Indians told me.

The second Remove[1]

But now, the next morning, I must turn my back upon the Town. and travel with them into the vast and desolate Wilderness, I knew not whither. It is not my tongue, or pen can express the sorrows of my heart, and bitterness of my spirit, that I had at this departure: but God was with me, in a wonderfull manner, carrying me along, and bearing up my spirit, that it did not quite fail. One of the Indians carried my

---

[b] Massachusetts Bay. The Reverend Joseph Rowlandson had gone to seek protection for the settlement. An appeal was made to Captain Wadsworth at Marlborough, the nearest garrison, but help arrived too late.

[c] Marlborough's Praying Indians – the settlement of Christian converts at Marlborough. Mrs Rowlandson's hostility to Indians particularly includes the 'praying Indians'. Attempts to convict or exonerate them of guilt in this kidnapping raid have not been decisive.

poor wounded Babe upon a horse, it went moaning all along, I shall dy, I shall dy. I went on foot after it, with sorrow that cannot be exprest. At length I took it off the horse, and carried it in my armes till my strength failed, and I fell down with it: Then they set me upon a horse with my wounded Child in my lap, and there being no furniture upon the horse back, as we were going down a steep hill, we both fell over the horses head, at which they like inhumane creatures laught, and rejoyced to see it, though I thought we should there have ended our dayes, as overcome with so many difficulties. But the Lord renewed my strength still, and carried me along, that I might see more of his Power; yea, so much that I could never have thought of, had I not experienced it.

After this it quickly began to snow, and when night came on, they stopt: and now down I must sit in the snow, by a little fire, and a few boughs behind me, with my sick Child in my lap; and calling much for water, being now (through the wound) fallen into a violent Fever. My own wound also growing so stiff, that I could scarce sit down or rise up; yet so it must be, that I must sit all this cold winter night upon the cold snowy ground, with my sick Child in my armes, looking that every hour would be the last of its life; and having no Christian friend near me, either to comfort or help me. Oh, I may see the wonderful power of God, that my Spirit did not utterly sink under my affliction: still the Lord upheld me with his gracious and mercifull Spirit, and we were both alive to see the light of the next morning.

The third remove.

The morning being come, they prepared to go on their way. One of the Indians got up upon a horse, and they set me up behind him, with my poor sick Babe in my lap. A very wearisome and tedious day I had of it; what with my own wound, and my Childs being so exceeding sick, and in a lamentable condition with her wound. It may be easily judged what a poor feeble condition we were in, there being not the least crumb of refreshing that came within either of our mouths, from Wednesday night to Saturday night, except only a little cold water. This day in the afternoon, about an hour by Sun, we came to the place where they intended, *viz.* an Indian Town, called Wenimesset, Norward of Quabaug. When we were come, Oh the number of Pagans (now merciless enemies) that there came about me, that I may say as David, Psal. 27. 13, *I had fainted, unless I had believed*, etc. The next day was the Sabbath: I then remembered how careless I had been of Gods holy time, how many Sabbaths I had lost and mispent, and how evily I had walked in Gods sight; which lay so close unto my spirit, that it was easie for me to see how righteous it was with God to cut off the thread of my life, and cast me out of his presence for ever. Yet the Lord still shewed mercy to me, and upheld me; and as he wounded me with one hand, so he healed me with the other. This day there came to me one Robbert Pepper (a man belonging to Roxbury) who was taken in Captain Beers his Fight, and had been now a considerable time with the Indians; and up with them almost as far as Albany, to see king Philip, as he told me, and was now very lately come into these parts. Hearing, I say, that I was in this Indian Town, he obtained leave to come and see me. He told me, he himself was wounded in the leg at Captain Beers his Fight; and was not able some time to go, but as they carried him, and as he took Oaken leaves and laid to his wound, and through the blessing of God he was able to travel again. Then I took Oaken leaves and laid to my side, and with the blessing of God it cured me also; yet before the cure was wrought, I may say, as it is in Psal. 38. 5, 6. *My wounds stink and are corrupt, I am troubled, I am bowed down greatly, I go mourning all the day long.* I sat much alone with a poor wounded Child in my lap, which moaned night and day, having nothing to revive the body, or cheer the spirits of her, but in stead of that, sometimes one Indian would come and tell me one hour, that your Master will knock your Child in the head, and then a second, and then a third, your Master will quickly knock your Child in the head.

This was the comfort I had from them, miserable comforters are ye all, as he said. Thus nine dayes I sat upon my knees, with my Babe in my lap, till my flesh was raw again; my Child being even ready to depart this sorrowfull world, they bade me carry it out to another Wigwam (I suppose because they would not be troubled with such spectacles) Whither I went with a very heavy heart, and down I sat with the picture of death in my lap. About two houres in the night my sweet Babe like a Lambe departed this life, on Feb. 18, 1675. It being about six yeares, and five months old. It was nine dayes from the first wounding, in this miserable condition, without any refreshing of one nature or other, except a little cold water. I cannot, but take notice, how at another time I could not bear to be in the room where any dead person was, but now the case is changed; I must and could ly down by my dead Babe, side by side all the night after. I have thought since of the wonderfull goodness of God to me, in preserving me in the use of my reason and senses, in that distressed time, that I did not use wicked and violent means to end my own miserable life. In the morning, when they understood that my child was dead they sent for me home to my Masters Wigwam:[2] (by my Master in this writing, must be understood Quanopin, who was a Saggamore, and married King Phillips wives Sister; not that he first took me, but I was sold to him by another Narrhaganset Indian, who took me when first I came out of the Garison). I went to take up my dead child in my arms to carry it with me, but they bid me let it alone: there was no resisting, but goe I must and leave it. When I had been at my masters wigwam, I took the first opportunity I could get, to go look after my dead child: when I came I askt them what they had done with it? then they told me it was upon the hill: then they went and shewed me where it was, where I saw the ground was newly digged, and there they told me they had buried it: there I left that Child in the Wilderness, and must commit it, and my self also in this Wilderness-condition, to him who is above all. God having taken away this dear Child, I went to see my daughter Mary, who was at this same Indian Town, at a Wigwam not very far off, though we had little liberty or opportunity to see one another. She was about ten years old, and taken from the door at first by a praying Ind and afterward sold for a gun. When I came in sight, she would fall a weeping; at which they were provoked, and would not let me come near her, but bade me be gone; which was a heart-cutting word to me. I had one Child dead, another in the Wilderness, I knew not where, the third they would not let me come near to: *Me* (as he said) *have ye bereaved of my Children, Joseph is not, and Simeon is not, and ye will take Benjamin also, all these things are against me.* I could not sit still in this condition, but kept walking from one place to another. And as I was going along, my heart was even overwhelm'd with the thoughts of my condition, and that I should have Children, and a Nation which I knew not ruled over them. Whereupon I earnestly entreated the Lord, that he would consider my low estate, and shew me a token for good, and if it were his blessed will, some sign and hope of some relief. And indeed quickly the Lord answered, in some measure, my poor prayers: for as I was going up and down mourning and lamenting my condition, my Son came to me, and asked me how I did; I had not seen him before, since the destruction of the Town, and I knew not where he was, till I was informed by himself, that he was amongst a smaller percel of Indians, whose place was about six miles off; with tears in his eyes, he asked me whether his Sister Sarah was dead; and told me he had seen his Sister Mary; and prayed me, that I would not be troubled in reference to himself. The occasion of his coming to see me at this time, was this: There was, as I said, about six miles from us, a smal Plantation of Indians, where it seems he had been during his Captivity: and at this time, there were some Forces of the Ind. gathered out of our company, and some also from them (among whom was my Sons master) to go to assault and burn Medfield: In this time of the absence of his master, his dame brought him to see me. I took this to be some gracious answer to my earnest and unfeigned desire. The next day, *viz.* to this, the Indians returned from Medfield, all the company, for those that belonged to the other smal company, came thorough the Town that now we were at. But before they came to us, Oh! the ourtragious roaring and hooping that there was: They began their din about a mile before they came to us. By their noise and hooping they signified how many they had destroyed (which was at that time twenty three.) Those that were with us at home, were gathered together as soon as they heard the hooping, and every time that the other went over their number, these at home gave a shout, that the very Earth rung again: and thus they continued till those that had been upon the expedition were come up to the Sagamores Wigwam; and then, Oh, the hideous insulting and triumphing that there was over some Englishmens scalps that they had taken (as their manner is) and brought with them. I cannot but take notice of the wonderfull mercy of God to me in those afflictions, in sending me a Bible. One of the Indians that came from Medfield fight, had brought some plunder, came to me, and asked me, if I would have a Bible, he had got one in his Basket. I was glad of it, and asked him, whether he thought the Indians would let me read? he answered, yes: So I took the Bible, and in that melancholy time, it came into my mind to read first the 28. Chap. of Deut.,[d] which I did, and when I had read it, my dark heart wrought on this manner, That there was no mercy for me, that the blessings were gone, and the curses come in their room, and that I had lost my opportunity. But the Lord helped me still to go on reading till I came to Chap. 30 the seven first verses, where I found, There was mercy promised again, if we would return to him by repentance; and though we were scatered from one end of the Earth to the other, yet the Lord would gather us together, and turn all those curses upon our Enemies. I do not desire to live to forget this Scripture, and what comfort it was to me.

. . .

The fourth Remove.

And now I must part with that little Company I had. Here I parted from my Daughter Mary, (whom I never saw again till I saw her in Dorchester, returned from Captivity), and from four little Cousins

---

[d] Deuteronomy 28 recites blessings for obedience to God and curses for disobedience.

and Neighbours, some of which I never saw afterward: the Lord only knows the end of them... But to return to my own Journey; we travelled about half a day or little more, and came to a desolate place in the Wilderness, where there were no Wigwams or Inhabitants before; we came about the middle of the afternoon to this place, cold and wet, and snowy, and hungry, and weary, and no refreshing, for man, but the cold ground to sit on, and our poor Indian cheer.

Heart-aking thoughts here I had about my poor Children, who were scattered up and down among the wild beasts of the forrest: My head was light and dissey (either through hunger or hard lodging, or trouble or altogether) my knees feeble, my body raw by sitting double night and day, that I cannot express to man the affliction that lay upon my Spirit, but the Lord helped me at that time to express it to himself. I opened my Bible to read, and the Lord brought that precious Scripture to me, Jer. 31. 16. *Thus saith the Lord, refrain thy voice from weeping, and thine eyes from tears, for thy work shall be rewarded, and they shall come again from the land of the Enemy.* This was a sweet Cordial to me, when I was ready to faint, many and many a time have I sat down, and weept sweetly over this Scripture. At this place we continued about four dayes.

The fifth Remove.

The occasion (as I thought) of their moving at this time, was, the English Army, it being near and following them: For they went, as if they had gone for their lives, for some considerable way, and then they made a stop, and chose some of their stoutest men, and sent them back to hold the English Army in play whilst the rest escaped: And then, like Jehu, they marched on furiously, with their old, and with their young: some carried their old decrepit mothers, some carried one, and some another. Four of them carried a great Indian upon a Bier; but going through a thick Wood with thim, they were hindered, and could make no hast; whereupon they took him upon their backs, and carried him, one at a time, till they came to Bacquaug River. Upon a Friday, a little after noon we came to this River. When all the company was come up, and were gathered together, I thought to count the number of them, but they were so many, and being somewhat in motion, it was beyond my skil. In this travel, because of my wound, I was somewhat favoured in my load; I carried only my knitting work and two quarts of parched meal: Being very faint I asked my mistriss to give me one spoonfull of the meal, but she would not give me a taste. They quickly fell to cutting dry trees, to make Rafts to carry them over the river: and soon my turn came to go over: By the advantage of some brush which they had laid upon the Raft to sit upon, I did not wet my foot (which many of themselves at the other end were mid-leg deep) which cannot but be acknowledged as a favour of God to my weakned body, it being a very cold time. I was not before acquainted with such kind of doings or dangers. *When thou passeth through the waters I will be with thee, and through the Rivers they shall not overflow thee*, Isai. 43. 2. A certain number of us got over the River that night, but it was the night after the Sabbath before all the company was got over. On the Saturday they boyled an old Horses leg which they had got, and so we drank of the broth, as soon as they thought it was ready, and when it was almost all gone, they filled it up again.

The first week of my being among them, I hardly ate any thing; the second week, I found my stomach grow very faint for want of something; and yet it was very hard to get down their filthy trash: but the third week, though I could think how formerly my stomach would turn against this or that, and I could starve and dy before I could eat such things, yet they were sweet and savoury to my taste. I was at this time knitting a pair of white cotton stockins for my mistriss; and had not yet wrought upon a Sabbath day; when the Sabbath came they bade me go to work; I told them it was the Sabbath-day, and desired them to let me rest, and told them I would do as much more to morrow; to which they answered me, they would break my face. And here I cannot but take notice of the strange providence of God in preserving the heathen: They were many hundreds, old and young, some sick, and some lame, many had Papooses at their backs, the greatest number at this time with us, were Squaws, and they travelled with all they had, bag and baggage, and yet they got over this River aforesaid; and on Munday they set their Wigwams on fire, and away they went: On that very day came the English Army after them to this River, and saw the smoak of their Wigwams, and yet this River put a stop to them. God did not give them courage or activity to go over after us; we were not ready for so great a mercy as victory and deliverance; if we had been, God would have found out a way for the English to have passed this River, as well as for the Indians with their Squaws and Children, and all their Luggage. *Oh that my People had hearkened to me, and Israel had walked in my ways, I should have subdued their Enemies, and turned my hand against their Adversaries*, Psal. 81: 13, 14. . .[3]

The eighteenth Remove.

We took up our packs and along we went, but a wearisome day I had of it. As we went along I saw an English-man stript naked, and lying dead upon the ground, but knew not who it was. Then we came to another Indian Town, where we stayed all night. In this Town there were four English Children, Captives; and one of them my own Sisters. I went to see how she did, and she was well, considering her Captive-condition. I would have tarried that night with her, but they that owned her would not suffer it. Then I went into another Wigwam, where they were boyling Corn and Beans, which was a lovely sight to see, but I could not get a taste thereof. Then I went to another Wigwam, where there were two of the English Children; the Squaw was boyling Horses feet, then she cut me off a little piece, and gave one of the English Children a piece also. Being very hungry I had quickly eat up mine, but the Child could not bite it, it was so tough and sinewy, but lay sucking, gnawing, chewing and slabbering of it in the mouth and hand, then I took it of the Child, and eat it my self, and savoury it was to my taste. Then I may say as Job, Chap. 6. 7. *The things that my soul refused to touch, are as my sorrowfull meat*. Thus the Lord made that pleasant refreshing, which another time would have been an abomination. Then I went home to my mistresses Wigwam; and they told me I disgraced my master with begging, and if I did so any more, they would knock me in head: I told them, they had as good knock me in head as starve me to death.

The nineteenth Remove

They said, when we went out, that we must travel to Wachuset this day. But a bitter weary day I had of it, travelling now three dayes together, without resting any day between. At last, after many weary steps, I saw Wachuset hills, but many miles off. Then we came to a great Swamp, through which we travelled, up to the knees in mud and water, which was heavy going to one tyred before. Being almost spent, I thought I should have sunk down at last, and never gat out; but I may say, as in Psal. 94. 18, *When my foot slipped, thy mercy, O Lord, held me up*. Going along, having indeed my life, but little spirit, Philip, who was in the Company, came up and took me by the hand, and said, Two weeks more and you shal be Mistress again. I asked him, if he spake true? he answered, Yes, and quickly you shal come to your master again; who had been gone from us three weeks. After many weary steps we came to Wachuset, where he was: and glad I was to see him. He asked me, When I washt me? I told him not this month, then he fetcht me some water himself, and bid me wash, and gave me the Glass to see how I lookt; and bid his Squaw give me something to eat: so she gave me a mess of Beans and meat, and a little Ground-nut Cake. I was wonderfully revived with this favour shewed me, Psal. 106. 46, *He made them also to be pittied, of all those that carried them Captives.*

My master had three Squaws, living sometimes with one, and sometimes with another one, this old Squaw, at whose Wigwam I was, and with whom my Master had been those three weeks. Another was Wattimore, with whom I had lived and served all this while: A severe and proud Dame she was, bestowing every day in dressing her self neat as much time as any of the Gentry of the land: powdering her hair, and painting her face, going with Neck-laces, with Jewels in her ears, and Bracelets upon her hands: When she had dressed her self, her work was to make Girdles of Wampom and Beads. The third Squaw was a younger one, by whom he had two Papooses. By that time I was refresht by the old Squaw, with whom my master was, Wettimores Maid came to call me home, at which I fell a weeping. Then the old Squaw told me, to encourage me, that if I wanted victuals, I should come to her, and that I should ly there in her Wigwam. Then I went with the maid, and quickly came again and lodged there. The Squaw laid a Mat under me, and a good Rugg over me; the first time I had any such kindness shewed me. I understood that Wettimore thought, that if she should let me go and serve with the old Squaw, she would be in danger to loose, not only my service, but the redemption-pay also. And I was not a little glad to hear this; being by it raised in my hopes, that in Gods due time there would be an end of this sorrowfull hour. Then came an Indian, and asked me to knit him three pair of Stockins, for which I had a Hat, and a silk Handkerchief. Then another asked me to make her a shift, for which she gave me an Apron.

Then came Tom and Peter,^e with the second Letter from the Council, about the Captives. Though they were Indians, I gat them by the hand, and burst out into tears; my heart was so full that I could not speak to them; but recovering my self, I asked them how my husband did, and all my friends and acquaintance? they said, They are all very well but melancholy. They brought me two Biskets, and a pound of Tobacco. The Tobacco I quickly gave away; when it was all gone, one asked me to give him a pipe of Tobacco, I told him it was all gone; then began he to rant and threaten. I told him when my Husband came I would give him some: Hang him Rogue (sayes he) I will knock out his brains, if he comes here. And then again, in the same breath they would say, That if there should come an hundred without Guns, they would do them no hurt. So unstable and like mad men they were. So that fearing the worst, I durst not send to my

e Tom Dublet (Nepanet) and Peter Conway (Tatatiquinea), Christian Indians who conducted the negotiations for ransom.

Husband, though there were some thoughts of his coming to
Redeem and fetch me, not knowing what might follow. For there was
little more trust to them then to the master they served. When the
Letter was come, the Saggamores met to consult about the Captives,
and called me to them to enquire how much my husband would give
to redeem me, when I came I sate down among them, as I was wont to
do, as their manner is: Then they bade me stand up, and said, they
were the General Court. They bid me speak what I thought he would
give. Now knowing that all we had was destroyed by the Indians, I
was in a great strait: I thought if I should speak of but a little, it would
be slighted, and hinder the matter: if of a great sum. I knew not where
it would be procured: yet at a venture, I said Twenty pounds, yet
desired them to take less; but they would not hear of that, but sent
that message to Boston, that for Twenty pounds I should be
redeemed.   . . .

The twentieth Remove[4]

It was their usual manner to remove, when they had done any
mischief, lest they shoud be found out: and so they did at this time.
We went about three or four miles, and there they built a great
Wigwam, big enough to hold an hundred Indians, which they did in
preparation to a great day of Dancing. They would say now amongst
themselves, that the Governour would be so angry for his loss at
Sudbury, that he would send no more about the captives, which made
me grieve and tremble. My Sister being not far from the place where
we now were, and hearing that I was here, desired her master to let her
come and see me, and he was willing to it, and would go with her: but
she being ready before him, told him she would go before, and was
come within a Mile or two of the place; Then he overtook her, and
began to rant as if he had been mad; and made her go back again in the
Rain; so that I never saw her till I saw her in Charlestown. But the
Lord requited many of their ill doings, for this Indian her Master, was
hanged afterward at Boston. The Indians now began to come from all
quarters, against their merry dancing day. Among some of them came
one Goodwife Kettle: I told her my heart was so heavy that it was
ready to break: so is mine too said she, but yet said, I hope we shall
hear some good news shortly. I could hear how earnestly my Sister
desired to see me, and I as earnestly desired to see her: and yet neither
of us could get an opportunity. My Daughter was also now about a
mile off, and I had not seen her in nine or ten weeks, as I had not seen
my Sister since our first taking. I earnestly desired them to let me go
and see them: yea, I intreated, begged, and perswaded them, but to let

me see my Daughter; and yet so hard hearted were they, that they would not suffer it. They made use of their tyrannical power whilst they had it: but through the Lords wonderfull mercy, their time was now but short.

On a Sabbath day, the Sun being about an hour high in the afternoon, came Mr. John Hoar (the Council permitting him, and his own foreward spirit inclining him) together with the two fore-mentioned Indians, Tom and Peter, with their third Letter from the Council. When they came near, I was abroad: though I saw them not, they presently called me in, and bade me sit down and not stir. Then they catched up their Guns, and away they ran, as if an Enemy had been at hand; and the Guns went off apace. I manifested some great trouble, and they asked me what was the matter? I told them, I thought they had killed the English-man (for they had in the mean time informed me that an English-man was come) they said, No; They shot over his Horse and under, and before his Horse; and they pusht him this way and that way, at their pleasure: shewing what they could do: Then they let them come to their Wigwams. I begged of them to let me see the English-man, but they would not. But there was I fain to sit their pleasure. When they had talked their fill with him, they suffered me to go to him. We asked each other of our welfare, and how my Husband did, and all my Friends? He told me they were all well, and would be glad to see me. Amongst other things which my Husband sent me, there came a pound of Tobacco: which I sold for nine shillings in Money: for many of the the Indians for want of Tobacco, smoaked Hemlock, and Ground-Ivy. It was a great mistake in any, who thought I sent for Tobacco: for through the favour of God, that desire was overcome. I now asked them, whether I should go home with Mr. Hoar? They answered No, one and another of them: and it being night, we lay down with that answer; in the morning, Mr Hoar invited the Saggamores to Dinner; but when we went to get it ready, we found that they had stollen the greatest part of the Provision Mr. Hoar had brought, out of his Bags, in the night. And we may see the wonderfull power of God, in that one passage, in that when there was such a great number of the Indians together, and so greedy of a little good food; and no English there, but Mr. Hoar and my self: that there they did not knock us in the head, and take what we had: there being not only some Provision, but also Trading-cloth, a part of the twenty pounds agreed upon: But instead of doing us any mischief, they seemed to be ashamed of the fact, and said, it were some Matchit Indian[f] that did it. Oh, that we could believe that there is no thing too hard for God! God shewed his

---

[f] Bad Indian.

Power over the Heathen in this, as he did over the hungry Lyons when Daniel was cast into the Den. Mr. Hoar called them betime to Dinner, but they ate very little, they being so busie in dressing themselves, and getting ready for their Dance: which was carried on by eight of them, four Men and four Squaws: My master and mistress being two. He was dressed in his Holland shirt, with great Laces sewed at the tail of it, he had his silver Buttons, his white Stockins, his Garters were hung round with Shillings, and he had Girdles of Wampom upon his head and shoulders. She had a Kersey Coat, and covered with Girdles of Wampom from the Loins upward: her armes from her elbows to her hands were covered with Bracelets; there were handfulls of Necklaces about her neck, and severall sorts of Jewels in her ears. She had fine red Stokins, and white Shoos, her hair pow- dered and face painted Red, that was alwayes before Black. And all the Dancers were after the same manner. There were two other singing and knocking on a Kettle for their musick. They keept hopping up and down one after another, with a Kettle of water in the midst, standing warm upon some Embers, to drink of when they were dry. They held on till it was almost night, throwing out Wampom to the standers by. At night I asked them again, if I should go home? They all as one said No, except my Husband would come for me. When we were lain down, my Master went out of the Wigwam, and by and by sent in an Indian called James the Printer,g who told Mr. Hoar, that my Master would let me go home to morrow, if he would let him have one pint of Liquors. Then Mr. Hoar called his own Indians, Tom and Peter, and bid them go and see whither he would promise it before them three: and if he would, he should have it; which he did, and he had it. Then Philip smeling the business cal'd me to him, and asked me what I would give him, to tell me some good news, and speak a good word for me. I told him, I could not tell what to give him, I would any thing I had, and asked him what he would have? He said, two Coats and twenty shillings in Mony, and half a bushel of seed Corn, and some Tobacco. I thanked him for his love: but I knew the good news as well as the crafty Fox. My Master after he had had his drink, quickly came ranting into the Wigwam again, and called for Mr. Hoar, drinking to him, and saying, He was a good man: and then again he would say, Hang him Rogue: Being almost drunk, he would drink to him, and yet presently say he should be hanged. Then he called for me. I trembled to hear him, yet I was fain to go to him, and he drank to me, shewing no incivility. He was the first Indian I saw drunk all the

---

g A Praying Indian who assisted in the printing of Eliot's Indian Bible at Cambridge, Massa- chusetts.

while that I was amongst them. At last his Squaw ran out, and he after her, round the Wigwam, with his mony jingling at his knees: But she escaped him; But having an old Squaw he ran to her: and so through the Lords mercy, we were no more troubled that night. Yet I had not a comfortable nights rest: for I think I can say, I did not sleep for three nights together. The night before the Letter came from the Council, I could not rest, I was so full of feares and troubles, God many times leaving us most in the dark, when deliverance is nearest: yea, at this time I could not rest night nor day. The next night I was overjoyed, Mr. Hoar being come, and that with such good tidings. The third night I was even swallowed up with the thoughts of things, *viz.* that ever I should go home again; and that I must go, leaving my Children behind me in the Wilderness; so that sleep was now almost departed from mine eyes.

On Tuesday morning they called their General Court (as they call it) to consult and determine, whether I should go home or no: And they all as one man did seemingly consent to it, that I should go home; except Philip, who would not come among them.

But before I go any further, I would take leave to mention a few remarkable passages of providence, which I took special notice of in my afflicted time.

1. Of the fair opportunity lost in the long March, a little after the Fort-fight, when our English Army was so numerous, and in pursuit of the Enemy, and so near as to take several and destroy them: and the Enemy in such distress for food, that our men might track them by their rooting in the earth for Ground-nuts, whilest they were flying for their lives. I say, that then our Army should want Provision, and be forced to leave their pursuit and return homeward: and the very next week the Enemy came upon our Town, like Bears bereft of their whelps, or so many ravenous Wolves, rending us and our Lambs to death. But what shall I say? God seemed to leave his People to themselves, and order all things for his own holy ends. *Shal there be evil in the City and the Lord hath not done it? They are not grieved for the affliction of Joseph, therefore shal they go Captive, with the first that go Captive.* It is the Lords doing, and it should be marvelous in our eyes.

2. I cannot but remember how the Indians derided the slowness, and dulness of the English Army, in its setting out. For after the desolations at Lancaster and Medfield, as I went along with them, they asked me when I thought the English Army would come after them? I told them I could not tell: It may be they will come in May, said they. Thus did they scoffe at us, as if the English would be a quarter of a year getting ready.

3. Which also I have hinted before, when the English Army with new supplies were sent forth to pursue after the enemy, and they understanding it, fled before them till they came to Baquaug River, where they forthwith went over safely: that that River should be impassable to the English. I can but admire to see the wonderfull providence of God in preserving the heathen for farther affliction to our poor Countrey. They could go in great numbers over, but the English must stop: God had an over-ruling hand in all those things.

4. It was thought, if their Corn were cut down, they would starve and dy with hunger: and all their Corn that could be found, was destroyed, and they driven from that little they had in store, into the Woods in the midst of Winter; and yet how to admiration did the Lord preserve them for his holy ends, and the destruction of many still amongst the English! strangely did the Lord provide for them; that I did not see (all the time I was among them) one Man, Woman, or Child, die with hunger.

Though many times they would eat that, that a Hog or a Dog would hardly touch; yet by that God strengthned them to be a scourge to his People.

The chief and commonest food was Ground-nuts: They eat also Nuts and Acorns, Harty-choaks, Lilly roots, Ground-beans, and several other weeds and roots, that I know not.

They would pick up old bones, and cut them to pieces at the joynts, and if they were full of wormes and magots, they would scald them over the fire to make the vermine come out, and then boile them, and drink up the Liquor, and then beat the great ends of them in a Morter, and so eat them. They would eat Horses guts, and ears, and all sorts of wild Birds which they could catch: also Bear, Vennison, Beaver, Tortois, Frogs, Squirrels, Dogs, Skunks, Rattle-snakes; yea, the very Bark of Trees; besides all sorts of creatures, and provision which they plundered from the English. I can but stand in admiration to see the wonderful power of God, in providing for such a vast number of our Enemies in the Wilderness, where there was nothing to be seen, but from hand to mouth. Many times in a morning, the generality of them would eat up all they had, and yet have some further supply against they wanted. It is said, Psal. 81. 13, 14. *Oh, that my People had hearkned to me, and Israel had walked in my wayes, I should soon have subdued their Enemies, and turned my hand against their Adversaries.* But now our perverse and evil carriages in the sight of the Lord, have so offended him, that instead of turning his hand against them, the Lord feeds and nourishes them up to be a scourge to the whole Land.

5. Another thing that I would observe is, the strange providence of

God, in turning things about when the Indians was at the highest, and the English at the lowest. I was with the Enemy eleven weeks and five dayes, and not one Week passed without the fury of the Enemy, and some desolation by fire and sword upon one place or other. They mourned (with their black faces) for their own lossess, yet triumphed and rejoyced in their inhumane, and many times devilish cruelty to the English. They would boast much of their Victories; saying, that in two hours time they had destroyed such a Captain, and his Company at such a place; and such a Captain and his Company in such a place; and such a Captain and his Company in such a place: and boast how many Towns they had destroyed, and then scoffe, and say, They had done them a good turn, to send them to Heaven so soon. Again, they would say, This Summer that they would knock all the Rogues in the head, or drive them into the Sea, or make them flie the Countrey: thinking surely, Agag-like, *The bitterness of Death is past.* Now the Heathen begins to think all is their own, and the poor Christians hopes to fail (as to man) and now their eyes are more to God, and their hearts sigh heaven-ward: and to say in good earnest, *Help Lord, or we perish:* When the Lord had brought his people to this, that they saw no help in any thing but himself: then he takes the quarrel into his own hand: and though they had made a pit, in their own imaginations, as deep as hell for the Christians that Summer, yet the Lord hurll'd them selves into it. And the Lord had not so many wayes before to preserve them, but now he hath as many to destroy them.

But to return again to my going home, where we may see a remarkable change of Providence: At first they were all against it, except my Husband would come for me; but afterwards they assented to it, and seemed much to rejoyce in it; some askt me to send them some Bread, others some Tobacco, others shaking me by the hand, offering me a Hood and Scarfe to ride in; not one moving hand or tongue against it. Thus hath the Lord answered my poor desire, and the many earnest requests of others put up unto God for me. In my travels an Indian came to me, and told me, if I were willing, he and his Squaw would run away, and go home along with me: I told him No: I was not willing to run away, but desired to wait Gods time, that I might go home quietly, and without fear. And now God hath granted me my desire. O the wonderfull power of God that I have seen, and the experience that I have had: I have been in the midst of those roaring Lyons, and Salvage Bears, that feared neither God, nor Man, nor the Devil, by night and day, alone and in company: sleeping all sorts together, and yet not one of them ever offered me the least abuse of unchastity to me, in word or action. Though some are ready to say,

I speak it for my own credit; But I speak it in the presence of God, and to his Glory. Gods Power is as great now, and as sufficient to save, as when he preserved Daniel in the Lions Den; or the three Children in the fiery Furnace. I may well say as his Psal. 107. 12, *Oh give thanks unto the Lord for he is good, for his mercy endureth for ever.* Let the Redeemed of the Lord say so, whom he hath redeemed for the hand of the Enemy, especially that I should come away in the midst of so many hundreds of Enemies quietly and peacably, and not a Dog moving his tongue. So I took my leave of them, and in coming along my heart melted into tears, more then all the while I was with them, and I was almost swallowed up with the thoughts that ever I should go home again. About the Sun going down, Mr. Hoar, and my self, and the two Indians came to Lancaster, and a solemn sight it was to me. There had I lived many comfortable years amongst my Relations and Neighbours, and now not one Christian to be seen, nor one house left standing. We went on to a Farm house that was yet standing, where we lay all night: and a comfortable lodging we had, though nothing but straw to ly on. The Lord preserved us in safety that night, and raised us up again in the morning, and carried us along, that before noon, we came to Concord. Now was I full of joy, and yet not without sorrow: joy to see such a lovely sight, so many Christians together, and some of them my Neighbours: There I met with my Brother, and my Brother in Law, who asked me, if I knew where his Wife was? Poor heart! he had helped to bury her, and knew it not; she being shot down by the house was partly burnt: so that those who were at Boston at the desolation of the Town, and came back afterward, and buried the dead, did not know her. Yet I was not without sorrow, to think how many were looking and longing, and my own Children amongst the rest, to enjoy that deliverance that I had now received, and I did not know whither ever I should see them again. Being recruited with food and raiment we went to Boston that day, where I met with my dear Husband, but the thoughts of our dear Children, one being dead, and the other we could not tell where, abated our comfort each to other. I was not before so much hem'd in with the merciless and cruel Heathen, but now as much with pittiful, tender-hearted and compassionate Christians. In that poor, and destressed, and beggerly condition I was received in, I was kindly entertained in severall Houses: so much love I received from several (some of whom I knew, and others I knew not) that I am not capable to declare it. But the Lord knows them all by name: The Lord reward them seven fold into their bosoms of his spirituals, for their temporals. The twenty pounds the price of my redemption was raised by some Boston Gentlemen, and Mrs. Usher, whose bounty and religious charity, I would not forget to make mention of. Then Mr. Thomas Shepard of Charlstown received us into his House, where we continued eleven weeks; and a Father and Mother they were to us. And many more tender-hearted Friends we met with in that place. We were now in the midst of love, yet not without much and frequent heaviness of heart for our poor Children, and other Relations, who were still in affliction. The week following, after my coming in, the Governour and Council sent forth to the Indians again; and that not without success; for they brought in my Sister, and Good-wife Kettle: Their not knowing where our Children were, was a sore tryal to us still, and yet we were not without secret hopes that we should see them again. That which was dead lay heavier upon my spirit, than those which were alive and amongst the Heathen; thinking how it suffered with its wounds, and I was no way able to relieve it; and how it was buried by the Heathen in the Wilderness from among all Christians. We were hurried up and down in our thoughts, sometime we should hear a report that they were gone this way, and sometimes that; and that they were come in, in this place or that: We kept enquiring and listning to hear concerning them, but no certain news as yet. About this time the Council had ordered a day of publick Thanks-giving though I thought I had still cause of mourning, and being unsettled in our minds, we thought we would ride toward the Eastward, to see if we could hear any thing concerning our Children. And as we were riding along (God is the wise disposer of all things) between Ipswich and Rowly we met with Mr. William Hubbard who told us that our Son Joseph was come in to Major Waldrens, and another with him, which was my Sisters Son. I asked him how he knew it? He said, the Major himself told him so. So along we went till we came to Newbury; and their Minister being absent, they desired my Husband to Preach the Thanks giving for them; but he was not willing to stay there that night, but would go over to Salisbury, to hear further, and come again in the morning; which he did, and Preached there that day. At night, when he had done, one came and told him that his Daughter was come in at Providence: Here was mercy on both hands: Now hath God fulfiled that precious Scripture which was such a comfort to me in my distressed condition. When my heart was ready to sink into the Earth (my Children being gone I could not tell whither) and my knees trembled under me, And I was walking through the valley of the shadow of Death: Then the Lord brought, and now has fulfilled that reviving word unto me: *Thus saith the Lord, Refrain thy voice from weeping, and thine eyes from tears, for thy*

Work shall be rewarded, saith the Lord, and they shall come again from the Land of the Enemy. Now we were between them, the one on the East, and the other on the West: Our Son being nearest, we went to him first, to Portsmouth, where we met with him, and with the Major also: who told us he had done what he could, but could not redeem him under seven pounds; which the good People thereabouts were pleased to pay. The Lord reward the Major, and all the rest, though unknown to me, for their labour of Love. My Sisters Son was redeemed for four pounds, which the Council gave order for the payment of. Having now received one of our Children, we hastened toward the other; going back through Newbury, my Husband preached there on the Sabbath-day: for which they rewarded him many fold.

On Munday we came to Charlstown, where we heard that the Governour of Road-Island had sent over for our Daughter, to take care of her, being now within his Jurisdiction: which should not pass without our acknowledgments. But she being nearer Rehoboth than Road-Island, Mr. Newman went over, and took care of her, and brought her to his own House. And the goodness of God was admirable to us in our low estate, in that he raised up passionate Friends on every side to us, when we had nothing to recompance any for their love. The Indians were now gone that way, that it was apprehended dangerous to go to her: But the Carts which carried Provision to the English Army, being guarded, brought her with them to Dorchester, where we received her safe: blessed be the Lord for it, For great is his Power, and he can do whatsoever seemeth him good. Her coming in was after this manner: She was travelling one day with the Indians, with her basket at her back; the company of Indians were got before her, and gone out of sight, all except one Squaw; she followed the Squaw till night, and then both of them lay down, having nothing over them but the heavens, and under them but the earth. Thus she travelled three dayes together, not knowing whither she was going: having nothing to eat or drink but water, and green Hirtle-berries. At last they came into Providence, where she was kindly entertained by several of that Town. The Indians often said, that I should never have her under twenty pounds: But now the Lord hath brought her in upon free-cost, and given her to me the second time. The Lord make us a blessing indeed, each to others. Now have I seen that Scripture also fulfilled, Deut. 30:4, 7. *If any of thine be driven out to the outmost parts of heaven, from thence will the Lord thy God gather thee, and from thence will he fetch thee. And the Lord thy God will put all these curses upon thine enemies, and on them which hate thee, which persecuted thee.* Thus hath the Lord brought me and mine out of that horrible pit, and hath set us in the midst of tender-hearted and compassionate Christians. It is the desire of my soul, that we may walk worthy of the mercies received, and which we are receiving.

Our Family being now gathered together (those of us that were living) the South Church in Boston hired an House for us: Then we removed from Mr. Shepards, those cordial Friends, and went to Boston, where we continued about three quarters of a year: Still the Lord went along with us, and provided graciously for us. I thought it somewhat strange to set up House-keeping with bare walls; but as Solomon sayes, *Mony answers all things,* and that we had through the benevolence of Christian-friends, some in this Town, and some in that, and others: And some from England, that in a little time we might look, and see the House furnished with love. The Lord hath been exceeding good to us in our low estate, in that when we had neither house nor home, nor other necessaries; the Lord so moved the hearts of these and those towards us, that we wanted neither food, nor raiment for our selves or ours, Prov. 18. 24. *There is a Friend which sticketh closer than a Brother.* And how many such Friends have we found, and now living amongst? And truly such a Friend have we found him to be unto us, in whose house we lived, *viz.* Mr. James Whitcomb, a Friend unto us near hand, and afar off.

I can remember the time, when I used to sleep quietly without workings in my thoughts, whole nights together, but now it is other wayes with me. When all are fast about me, and no eye open, but his who ever waketh, my thoughts are upon things past, upon the awfull dispensation of the Lord towards us; upon his wonderfull power and might, in carrying of us through so many difficulties, in returning us in safety, and suffering none to hurt us. I remember in the night season, how the other day I was in the midst of thousands of enemies, and nothing but death before me: It is then hard work to perswade my self, that ever I should be satisfied with bread again. But now we are fed with the finest of the Wheat, and, as I may say, With honey out of the rock: In stead of the Husk, we have the fatted Calf: The thoughts of these things in the particulars of them, and of the love and goodness of God towards us, make it true of me, what David said of himself, Psal. 6. 5. *I watered my Couch with my tears.* Oh! the wonderfull power of God that mine eyes have seen, affording matter enough for my thoughts to run in, that when others are sleeping mine eyes are weeping.

I have seen the extrem vanity of this World: One hour I have been in health, and wealth, wanting nothing: But the next hour in sickness and wounds, and death, having nothing but sorrow and affliction.

Before I knew what affliction meant, I was ready sometimes to wish for it. When I lived in prosperity, having the comforts of the World about me, my relations by me, my Heart chearfull, and taking little care for any thing; and yet seeing many, whom I preferred before my self, under many tryals and afflictions, in sickness, weakness, poverty, losses, crosses, and cares of the World, I should be sometimes jealous least I should have my portion in this life, and that Scripture would come to my mind, Heb. 12. 6. *For whom the Lord loveth he chasteneth, and scourgeth every Son whom he receiveth.* But now I see the Lord had his time to scourge and chasten me. The portion of some is to have their afflictions by drops, now one drop and then another; but the dregs of the Cup, the Wine of astonishment, like a sweeping rain that leaveth no food, did the Lord prepare to be my portion. Affliction I wanted, and affliction I had, full measure (I thought) pressed down and running over; yet I see, when God calls a Person to any thing, and through never so many difficulties, yet he is fully able to carry them through and make them see, and say they have been gainers thereby. And I hope I can say in some measure, As David did, *It is good for me that I have been afflicted.* The Lord hath shewed me the vanity of these outward things. That they are the Vanity of vanities, and vexation of spirit; that they are but a shadow, a blast, a bubble, and things of no continuance. That we must rely on God himself, and our whole dependance must be upon him. If trouble from smaller matters begin to arise in me, I have something at hand to check my self with, and say, why am I troubled? It was but the other day that if I had had the world, I would have given it for my freedom, or to have been a Servant to a Christian. I have learned to look beyond present and smaller troubles, and to be quieted under them, as Moses said, Exod. 14. 13. *Stand still and see the salvation of the Lord.*

Finis.

Cotton Mather, 'Magnalia Christi Americana: or, the Ecclesiastical History of New-England; from its first planting, in the year 1620, unto the year of our Lord 1698'

Cotton Mather (1663–1728) was born in Boston, Massachusetts, on 12 March 1663, the first of our American prose writers certainly born in America and one who never left his own country for so much as a visit to England. He was the son of Increase Mather and the grandson of John Cotton and Richard Mather, all three remarkable, admired and vigorous New England ministers. His distinguished lineage placed upon him a double burden: to achieve equal distinction and to preserve the power of his family. His own gifts of intellect and energy might have ensured both had he been born in his grandfathers' period when Massachusetts Bay was more nearly a Holy Commonwealth living by 'the New England way' worked out, prominently among others, by Richard Mather. As it was the times were changing both politically and spiritually – in his view the latter clearly for the worst – and despite all the promise of his youth, exactitude of his training and energy of his dedication, he made little difference in the direction of change, swimming valiantly, it seemed, against the current. His personal gifts were promising. He entered Harvard at twelve, already noted for his command of Latin, Greek, and Hebrew. Against his inclination he at first studied medicine, considering his stammer a bar to the church; when he overcame the stammer, he thought God removed it to reserve him for holy orders and changed to divinity. He graduated in 1678, the youngest man to have taken a degree, and spent the next four years as assistant preacher in his father's church, the Second Church of Boston. He was ordained and made co-minister in 1685 and he married his first wife in 1686. She bore him nine children, of whom four survived infancy, before her death in 1702. He married again in 1703 and his second wife bore him six children, of whom two survived infancy, before her death in 1713. He married again in 1715, but his third wife almost at once became insane. His last thirteen years of life were dark and difficult. His father died in 1723. His son Increase ('Cresy') 'went to the dogs', disgraced the family and was lost at sea in 1724. That year marked also the death of another child so that of his fifteen only two in the end survived him. He was harassed by financial difficulties, compounded by the burden of three widowed sisters. But through those dark years, Mather lived as he had always lived, writing, preaching, fasting, and steadily accumulating a store of good deeds. At his death he had written about five hundred books. In one year, he was not only an active pastor while writing fourteen publications, he also kept twenty vigils and sixty fasts. At his death he knew the principal ancient and modern languages, including two Indian dialects, had kept 450 fasts, had never wavered in his religious faith and had accumulated the largest private New England library.

Mather's personality is as difficult to grasp as his entire *œuvre* would be to read, but his obsessive horror of sin, his violent asceticism, his compulsive production of books and deeds of virtue, his amativeness and love of children, his quarrelsomeness and haughtiness (which prompted him to confess, 'Proud thoughts fly blow my best performances.') went hand in hand with a genuinely curious and thoughtful cast of mind. He may have been careful to square his affections with his theology, writing 'I do not apprehand, that Heaven requires me utterlie to lay aside my fondness for my lovelie Consort', but clearly they ran strong. His consuming interest in history, especially history as biography, in tracing God's management of his universe, was allied to an interest in describing and experimenting on nature. Nor was he an impractical visionary – Franklin commended his pragmatic system for the daily production of benevolent acts set forth in *Bonifacius* (or *Essays to Do Good*, 1710) – or an unchanging conservative, although he adjusted his changes in position throughout his life always towards the centre, until at the end a sort of mystical enthusiasm began to emerge in his thinking and to cloud his certainty that all God's ways in the world are accessible to human reason. He has not always been able to attract and hold modern readers, despite his undoubted centrality; but in *Grandfather's Chair*, Hawthorne responds to him in a sympathetic and respectful manner that is still worth consulting for its balance.

I have described Mather's style as old-fashioned, ornate and incapable of reaching the plainness he commended. Both in *Magnalia* and in his handbook for pastors, *Manuductio ad Ministerium* a much later work, Mather lets us see that his style is as it is by conscious choice. In the latter work, he wrote:

> There will always be those who will think that the real excellency of a book will never lie in saying of little; that the less one has for his money in a book, 'tis really the more valuable for it. . .And if a more massy way of writing be never so much disgusted at this day, a better gust will come on.

But the 'better gust' that might relish Mather's 'more massy way of writing' has not yet 'come on' in his own country.

My text reprints the second edition of the *Magnalia* Hartford, Connecticut, Silas Andrus and Son, 1855. The first edition appeared in London in 1702 in a folio volume of 788 pages.

A General Introduction[1]

'Ἐρῶ δὲ τοῦτο, τῆς τῶν ἐντευξομένων ὠφελείας ἕνεκα
Dicam hoc propter utilitatem eorum qui Lecturi sunt hoc opus,
– Theodorit[a]

1. I write the Wonders of the Christian Religion, flying from the depravations of Europe, to the American Strand; and, assisted by the Holy Author of that Religion, I do with all conscience of Truth, required therein by Him, who is the Truth itself, report the wonderful displays of His infinite Power, Wisdom, Goodness, and Faithfulness, wherewith His Divine Providence hath irradiated an Indian Wilderness.

I relate the Considerable Matters, that produced and attended the First Settlement of Colonies, which have been renowned for the

---

[a] 'I say this for the benefit of those who will read this book.' Mather subjoins a Latin translation to the Greek original.

degree of REFORMATION, professed and attained by Evangelical Churches, erected in those *ends of the earth;* and a *Field* being thus prepared, I proceed unto a relation of the *Considerable Matters* which have been acted thereupon.

I first introduce the *Actors,* that have in a more exemplary manner served those Colonies; and give Remarkable Occurrences, in the exemplary LIVES of many Magistrates, and of more Ministers, who so lived as to leave unto Posterity *examples* worthy of everlasting remembrance.

I add hereunto, the Notables of the only Protestant University that ever *shone* in that hemisphere of the New World; with particular instances of Criolians, in our Biography, provoking the whole world with vertuous objects of emulation.

I introduce then, the *Actions* of a more eminent importance, that have signalized those Colonies: whether the Establishments, directed by their Synods; with a rich variety of Synodical and Ecclesiastical Determinations; or, the Disturbances, with which they have been from all sorts of temptations and enemies tempestuated; and the Methods by which they have still weathered out each horrible tempest.

And into the midst of these Actions, I interpose an entire Book, wherein there is, with all possible veracity, a Collection made of Memorable Occurrences, and amazing Judgments and Mercies befalling many particular persons among the people of New-England.

Let my readers expect all that I have promised them, in this *Bill of Fare;* and it may be they will find themselves entertained with yet many other passages, above and beyond their expectation, deserving likewise a room in History: in all which, there will be nothing but the Author's too mean way of preparing so great entertainments, to reproach the Invitation.

2. The reader will doubtless desire to know, what it was that

> ———tot Volvere casus
> Insignes Pietate Viros, tot adire Labores,
> Impulerit.[b]

And our History shall, on many fit occasions which will be therein offered, endeavour, with all historical fidelity and simplicity, and with as little offence as may be, to satisfy him. The sum of the matter is, that from the very beginning of the REFORMATION in the English Nation, there hath always been a generation of Godly Men, desirous to pursue the Reformation of Religion, according to the Word of God, and the

[b] Drove forth those pious heroes to withstand
The seas's rough rage and rougher toil on land. Virgil

Example of the best Reformed Churches; and answering the character of Good Men, given by Josephus, in his Paraphrase on the words of Samuel to Saul, μηδὲν ἀλλ' πζάχθῆσεσθαι καλῶς ὑφ' ἑαυτῶν νομιζοντες, ἢ ὅ τι ἄν ποιήσωσι τοῦ Θεοῦ κεκελεύκοτος. (They think they do nothing right in the service of God, but what they do according to the command of God.) And there hath been another generation of men, who have still employed the *power* which they have generally still had in their hands, not only to stop the progress of the desired Reformation, but also, with innumerable vexations, to persecute those that most heartily wished well unto it. There were many of the Reformers, who joyned with the Reverend JOHN FOX, in the *complaints* which he then entred in his Martyrology, about the 'baits of Popery' yet left in the Church; and in his wishes, 'God take them away, or ease us from them, for God knows they be the cause of much blindness and strife amongst men!' They zealously decreed the *policy* of complying always with the ignorance and vanity of the *People;* and cried out earnestly for purer Administrations in the house of God, and more *conformity* to the *Law of Christ* and *primitive Christianity:* while others would not hear of going any further than the first Essay of Reformation. 'Tis very certain, that the first Reformers never intended that what they did should be the absolute boundary of Reformation, so that it should be a sin to proceed any further; as, by their own going beyond Wicklift, and changing and growing in their own Models also, and the confessions of Cranmer, with the *Scripta Anglicana* of Bucer, and a thousand other things, was abundantly demonstrated. But after a fruitless expectation, wherein the truest friends of the Reformation long waited for to have that which Heylin himself owns to have been the design of the first Reformers, followed as it should have been, a party very unjustly arrogating to themselves the venerable name of *The Church of England*, by numberless oppressions, grievously smote those their Fellow-Servants. Then 'twas that, as our great OWEN hath expressed it, 'Multitudes of pious, peaceable Protestants, were driven, by their severities, to leave their native country, and seek a refuge for their lives and liberties, with freedom for the worship of God, in a wilderness, in the ends of the earth.'

3. It is the History of these PROTESTANTS that is here attempted: PROTESTANTS that highly honoured and affected the Church of ENGLAND, and humbly petition to be a *part* of it: but by the mistake of a few powerful brethren, driven to seek a place for the exercise of the Protestant Religion, according to the light of their consciences, in the desarts of America. And in this attempt I have proposed, not only

to preserve and secure the interest of Religion in the Churches of that little country NEW-ENGLAND, so far as the Lord Jesus Christ may please to bless it for that end, but also to offer unto the Churches of the Reformation, abroad in the world, some small Memorials, that may be serviceable unto the designs of Reformation, whereto, I believe, they are quickly to be awakened. I am far from any such boast, concerning these Churches, *that they have need of nothing;* I wish their works were more *perfect before God.* Indeed, that which Austin called 'the perfection of Christians', is like to be, until the term for the anti-christian apostasie be expired, 'the perfection of Churches' too; *ut agnoscant se nunquam esse perfecta.*[c] Nevertheless, I perswade myself, that *so far as they have attained,* they have given great examples of the methods and measures wherein an Evangelical Reformation is to be prosecuted, and of the qualifications requisite in the instruments that are to prosecute it, and of the difficulties which may be most likely to obstruct it, and the most likely Directions and Remedies for those obstructions. It may be, 'tis not possible for me to do a greater service unto the Churches on the *best Island* of the universe, than to give a distinct relation of those great examples which have been occurring among Churches of *exiles,* that were driven out of that Island, into an horrible wilderness, meerly for their being well-willers unto the Reformation. When that blessed Martyr Constantine was carried, with other Martyrs, in a *dung-cart,* unto the place of execution, he pleasantly said, 'Well, yet we are a precious odour to God in Christ'. Though, the Reformed Churches in the American Regions have, by very injurious representations of their brethren, (all which they desire to forget and forgive!) been many times thrown into a *dung-cart;* yet, as they have been a 'precious odour to God in Christ', so, I hope, they will be a precious odour unto His people; and not only *precious,* but *useful* also, when the History of them shall come to be considered. A Reformation of the Church is seeming on, and I cannot but thereupon say, with the dying Cyrus to his children in *Xenophon,* Ἐκ τῶν προγεγεννημένων μανδάνετε, αὐτὴ γὰρ ἀρίστη διδασκαλία. (Learn from the things that have been done already, for this is the best way of learning.) The reader hath here an account of the 'things that have been done already'. Bernard, upon that clause in the Canticles, ['O thou fairest among women!'] has this ingenious gloss: *Pulchram, non omnimode quidem, sed pulchram inter mulieres eam docet; videlicet cum distinctime, quatenus ex hoc amplius reprimatur, et sciat quid*

---

[c] To acknowledge their imperfections.

desit sibi.[d] Thus, I do not say, that the Churches of New-England are the most *regular* that can be; yet I do say, and am sure, that they are very like unto those that were in the first ages of Christianity. And if I assert that, in the Reformation of the Church, the state of it in those first Ages is to be not a little considered, the great Peter Ramus, among others, has emboldened me. For when the Cardinal of Lorrain, the *Mæcenas* of that great man, was offended at him, for turning Protestant, he replied: *Inter Opes illas, quibus me ditâsti, has etiam in æternum recordabor, quod Beneficio Poessiacæ Responsionis tuæ didici, de quindecim a Christo sæculis, primum vere esse aureum; Reliqua, quo longius abscederent, esse nequiora, atque deteriora: tum igitur cum fieret optio, Aureum sæculum delegi.*[e] In short, the *first* Age was the *golden* Age: to return unto *that*, will make a man a Protestant, and I may add, a Puritan. 'Tis possible that our Lord Jesus Christ carried some thousands of Reformers into the retirements of an American desart, on purpose that, with an opportunity granted unto many of his faithful servants, to enjoy the precious *liberty* of their Ministry, though in the midst of many temptations all their days, He might there, *to* them first, and then *by* them, give a *specimen* of many good things, which He would have His Churches elsewhere aspire and arise unto; and *this* being done, he knows not whether there be not *all done*, that New-England was planted for; and whether the Plantation may not, soon after this, *come to nothing*. Upon that expression in the sacred Scripture, 'Cast the unprofitable servant into outer darkness', it hath been imagined by some, that the *Regiones exteræ,*[f] of America, are the *Tenebræ exteriores,*[g] which the unprofitable are there condemned unto. No doubt, the authors of these Ecclesiastical impositions and severities, which drove the English Christians into the dark regions of America, esteemed those Christians to be a very unprofitable sort of creatures. But behold, ye European Churches, there are golden Candlesticks [more than twice seven times seven!] in the midst of this 'outer darkness': unto the upright children of Abraham, here hath arisen *light in darkness*. And, let us humbly speak it, it shall be profitable for you to consider the *light* which, from the midst of this 'outer darkness', is now to be darted over unto the other side of the

[margin note, handwritten] New World, or, End of World destroyed

---

[d] The sacred writer calls her fair, not in an absolute sense, but fair among women; implying a distinction, in order that his praise may have due qualification, and that she may apprehend her deficiencies.

[e] Among the many favours with which your bounty has enriched me, I shall keep one in everlasting remembrance – I mean the lesson I have learned through your reply to the Poissy Conference, that of the fifteen centuries since Christ, the first was truly the golden age of the Church, and that the rest have been successive periods of degeneracy; when therefore I had the power of choosing between them, I preferred the golden age.

[f] Remote regions.   [g] Outer darkness.

Atlantick Ocean. But we must therewithal ask your Prayers, that these 'golden Candlesticks' may not quickly be 'removed out of their place!'[2]

4. But whether New-England may *live* any where else or no, it must *live* in our History! HISTORY, in general, hath had so many and mighty commendations from the pens of those numberless authors, who, from Herodotus to Howel, have been the professed writers of it, that a tenth part of them transcribed, would be a furniture for a *Polyanthea in folio*.[h] We, that have neither liberty, nor occasion, to quote these commendations of History, will content ourselves with the opinion of one who was not much of a professed historian, expressed in that passage, whereto all mankind subscribe, *Histoira est Testis temporum, Nuntia vetustatis, Lux veritatis, vita memoriæ, magistra vitæ*.[i] But of all History it must be confessed, that the palm is to be given unto Church History; wherein the dignity, the suavity, and the utility of the subject is transcendent. I observe, that for the description of the whole world in the Book of Genesis, that first-born of all historians, the great Moses, implies but one or two chapters, whereas he implies, it may be seven times as many chapters, in describing that one little Pavilion, the Tabernacle. And when I am thinking what may be the reason of this difference, methinks it intimates unto us, that the Church wherein the service of God is performed, is much more precious than the world, which was indeed created for the sake and use of the Church. 'Tis very certain, that the greatest entertainments must needs occur in the History of the people whom the Son of God hath redeemed and purified unto himself, as a peculiar people, and whom the Spirit of God, by supernatural operations upon their minds, does cause to live like strangers in this world, conforming themselves unto the Truths and Rules of his Holy Word, in expectation of a Kingdom, whereto they shall be in another and a better World advanced. Such a people our Lord Jesus Christ hath procured and preserved in all ages visible; and the dispensations of his wondrous Providence towards this People, (for, 'O Lord, thou dost lift them up and cast them down!') their calamities, their deliverances, the dispositions which they have still discovered, and the considerable *persons* and *actions* found among them, cannot but afford matters of *admiration* and *admonition*, above what any other story can pretend unto: 'tis nothing but Atheism in the hearts of men, that can perswade them otherwise...But for the manner of my treating this *matter*, I must now give some account.[3]

---

[h] Anthology.

[i] 'History is Time's witness, the messenger of antiquity, the lamp of truth, the embodied soul of memory, the guide of human life.' Like some other tags quoted from memory, Mather slightly transposes Cicero's word order.

5. *Reader!* I have done the part of an impartial historian, albeit not without all occasion perhaps, for the rule which a worthy writer, in his *Historica*, gives to every reader, *Historici legantur cum moderatione et venia, et cogitetur fieri non posse ut in omnibus circumstantiis sint lyncei.*[j] Polybius complains of those historians, who always made either the Carthagenians brave, or the Romans base, or *e contra*, in all their actions, as their affection for their own party led them. I have endeavoured, with all good conscience, to decline this writing meerly for a party, or doing like the dealer in History, whom Lucian derides, for always calling the captain of his own party an Achilles, but of the adverse party a Thersites: nor have I added unto the just provocations for the complaint made by the Baron Maurier, that the greatest *part* of Histories are but so many panegyricks composed by interested hands, which elevate iniquity to the heavens, like Paterculus, and like Machiavel, who propose Tiberius Cesar, and Cesar Borgia, as examples fit for imitation, whereas true History would have exhibited them as horrid monsters – as very devils. 'Tis true, I am not of the opinion that one cannot merit the name of an impartial historian, except he write bare *matters of fact* without all *reflection;* for I can tell where to find this given as the definition of History, *Historia est rerum gestarum, cum laude aut vituperatione, narratio;*[k] and if I am not altogether a Tacitus, when *vertues* or *vices* occur to be matters of reflection, as well as of relation, I will, for my vindication, appeal to Tacitus himself, whom Lipsius calls one of the prudentest (though Tertullian, long before, counts him one of the *lyingest*) of them who have enriched the world with History: he says, *Precipuum munus Annalium reor, ne virtutes sileantur, utque pravis Dictis, Factisque ex posteritate et Infamia metus sit.*[l] I have not commended any person, but when I have really judged, not only that he *deserved* it, but also that it would be a benefit unto posterity to know wherein he deserved it: and my judgment of desert, hath not been biassed by persons being of my own particular judgment, in matters of disputation, among the Churches of God. I have been as willing to wear the name of *Simplicius Verinus*, throughout my whole undertaking, as he that, before me, hath assumed it: nor am I like Pope Zachary, impatient so much as to hear of any Antipodes. That spirit of a Schlusselbergius, who falls foul with fury and reproach on all who differ from him; the spirit of an Heylin, who seems to count no obloquy too hard for a reformer; and the spirit of

---

[j] Historians should be read with moderation and indulgence, and one must keep in mind that they cannot in all circumstances be as keen-sighted as Lynceus.

[k] History is the account of great events, with praise or blame.

[l] I regard it the primary function of history to record virtues, and to hold up before depravity, whether of word or deed, the fear of obloquy.

those (folio-writers there are, some of them, in the English nation!) whom a noble Historian stigmatizes, as, 'Those hot-headed, passionate bigots, from whom, 'tis enough, if you be of a religion contrary unto theirs, to be defamed, condemned and pursued with a thousand calumnies.' I thank Heaven I hate it with all my heart. But how can the *lives* of the commendable be written without commending them of, is that law of History, given in one of the eminentest pieces of antiquity we now have in our hands, wholly antiquated, *Maxime proprium est Historiæ, Laudem rerum egregie gestarum persequi*[m] nor have I, on the other side, forbore to mention many *censurable* things, even in the best of my friends, when the things, in my opinion, were not good; or so bore away for Placentia, in the course of our story, as to pass by Verona; but been mindful of the direction which Polybius gives to the historian: 'It becomes him that writes an History, sometimes to extol enemies in his praises, when their praise worthy actions bespeak it, and at the same time to reprove the best friends, when their deeds appear worthy of a reproof; in-as-much as History is good for nothing, if truth (which is the very eye of the animal) be not in it.' Indeed, I have thought it my duty upon all accounts, (and if it have proceeded unto the degree of a fault, there is, it may be, something in my temper and nature that has betrayed me therein,) to be more sparing and easie, in thus mentioning of censurable things, than in my other liberty: a writer of Church-History should, I know, be like the builder of the temple, one of the tribe of Naphthali; and for this I will also plead my Polybius in my excuse: 'It is not the work of an historian, to commemorate the vices and villainies of men, so much as their just, their fair, their honest actions; and the readers of History get more good by the objects of their emulation, than of their indignation.' Nor do I deny that, though I cannot approve the conduct of Josephus; (whom Jerom not unjustly nor inaptly calls 'the Greek Livy',) when he left out of his Antiquities, the story of the *golden Calf*, and I don't wonder to find Chamier, and Rivet, and others, taxing him for his partiality towards his country-men; yet I have left unmentioned some censurable occurrences in the story of our Colonies, as things no less unuseful than improper to be raised out of the grave, wherein Oblivion hath now buried them; lest I should have incurred the *pasquil* bestowed upon Pope Urban, who, employing a committee to rip up the old errors of his predecessors, one clapped a pair of spurs upon the heels of the statue of St. Peter; and a label from the statue of St. Paul opposite thereunto, upon the bridge, asked him, 'Whither he was bound?' St. Peter answered, 'I

[m] It is the chief property of history to praise exceptionally noble deeds.

apprehend some danger in staying here; I fear they'll call me in question for denying my Master.' And St. Paul replied, 'Nay, then I had best be gone too, for they'll question me also for persecuting the Christians before my conversion.' Briefly, my pen shall reproach none that can give a good word unto any good man that is not of their own faction, and shall fall out with none but those that can agree with no body else, except those of their own schism. If I draw any sort of men with charcoal, it shall be because I remember a notable passage of the best Queen that ever was in the world, our late Queen Mary. Monsieur Juvien, that he might justifie the Reformation in Scotland, made a very black representation of their old Queen Mary; for which, a certain sycophant would have incensed our Queen Mary against that Reverend person, saying, 'Is it not a shame that this man, without any consideration for your royal person, should dare to throw such infamous calumnies upon a Queen, from whom your Royal Highness is descended?' But that excellent Princess replied, 'No, not at all; is it not enough that, by fulsome praises, great persons be lulled asleep all their lives; but must flattery accompany them to their very graves? How should they fear the judgment of posterity, if historians be not allowed to speak the truth after their death?' But whether I do myself commend, or whether I give my reader an opportunity to censure, I am careful above all things to do it with truth; and as I have considered the words of Plato, *Deum indigne et graviter ferre, cum quis ei similem, hoc est, virtute præstantem, vituperet, aut laudet contrarium,*[n] so I have had the Ninth Commandment of a greater law-giver than Plato, to preserve my care of Truth from first to last. If any mistake have been any where committed, it will be found meerly *circumstantial*, and wholly *involuntary;* and let it remembered, that though no historian ever merited better than the incomparable Thuanus, yet learned men have said of *his* work, what they never shall truly say of *ours*, that it contains *multa falsissima et indigna.*[o] I find Erasmus himself mistaking *one* man for *two*, when writing of the ancients. And even our own English writers too are often mistaken, and in matters of a very late importance, as Baker, and Heylin, and Fuller, (professed historians) tell us that Richard Sutton, a single man, founded the Charter-House; whereas his name was Thomas, and he was a married man. I think I can recite such mistakes, it may be *sans* number occurring in the most credible writers; yet I hope I shall *commit* none such. But although I thus challenge, as my due, the character of an

---

[n] It is offensive to God when dishonour is cast on such as resemble him in loftiness of virtue, or when praise is given to the opposite.
[o] Much that is very false and unworthy.

impartial, I doubt I may not challenge that of an *elegant* historian. I cannot say whether the style wherein this Church-History is written, will please the modern criticks: but if I seem to have used ἁπλαστᾳη συνταξει γραφης,[p] a simple, submiss, humble style, 'tis the same that Eusebius affirms to have been used by Hegesippus, who, as far as we understand, was the first author (after Luke) that ever composed an entire body of Ecclesiastical History, which he divided into five books, and entituled, ὑπομνηματα των ἐκκλησιαστικῶν πραξ-εων.[q] Whereas others, it may be, will reckon the *style* embellished with too much of *ornament*, by the multiplied references to other and former concerns, closely couched, for the observation of the attentive, in almost every paragraph; but I must confess, that I am of his mind who said, *Sicuti sal modice cibis aspersus Condit, et gratiam saporis addit, ita si paulum antiquitatis admiscueris, Oratio fit venustior*[r] And I have seldom seen that way of writing faulted, but by those who, for a certain odd reason, sometimes find fault that 'the grapes are not ripe'. These embellishments (of which yet I only — *Veniam pro laude peto*[s]) are not the puerile spoils of Polyanthea's; but I should have asserted them to be as choice *flowers* as most that occur in ancient or modern writings, almost unavoidably putting themselves into the author's hand, while about his work, if those words of Ambrose had not a little frighted me, as well as they did Baronius, *Unumquemque Fallunt sua scripta.*[t] I observe that learned men have been so terrified by the reproaches of pedantry, which little smatterers at reading and learning have, by their quoting humours, brought upon themselves, that, for to avoid all approaches towards that which those feeble creatures have gone to imitate, the best way of writing has been most injuriously deserted. But what shall we say? The best way of writing under heaven shall be the worst, when Erasmus, his monosyllable tyrant, will have it so! and if I should have resigned my self wholly to the judgment of *others,* what way of writing to have taken, the story of the two statues made by Policletus tells me what may have been the issue: he contrived one of them according to the rules that best pleased himself, and the other according to the fancy of every one that looked upon his work: the former was afterwards applauded by all, and the latter derided by those very persons who had given their directions for it. As for such unaccuracies as the critical may discover, *Opere in longo.*[u] I

---

[p] The simplest style of writing.
[q] Memorials of ecclesiastical transactions.
[r] As a little salt seasons food and improves its flavour, so a seasoning of antiquity heightens style.
[s] Ask pardon for this self-praise.
[t] Every writer forms mistaken judgments of his own works.
[u] In a long work.

appeal to the courteous for a favourable construction of them; and certainly they will be favourably judged of, when there is considered the variety of my other imployments; which have kept me in continual hurries, I had almost said like those of the ninth sphere, for the few months in which this Work has been digesting. It was a thing well thought, by the wise designers of Chelsea-Colledge, wherein able historians were one sort of persons to be maintained; that the Romanists do in one point condemn the Protestants; for among the Romanists, they don't burden their Professor with any *Parochial incumbrances;* but among the Protestants, the very same individual man must preach, catechize, administer the Sacraments, visit the afflicted, and manage all the parts of Church-discipline; and if any books for the service of Religion be written, persons thus extreamly incumberd must be the writers. Now, of all the Churches under heaven, there are none that expects so much *variety* of service from their Pastors as those of New-England; and of all the Churches in New-England, there are none that require more than those in Boston, the metropolis of the English America; whereof *one* is, by the Lord Jesus Christ, committed unto the care of the unworthy hand by which this History is compiled. Reader, give me leave humbly to mention, with him in Tully, *Antequam de re, Pauca de me.*[v] Constant sermons, usually more than once, and perhaps three or four times in a week, and all the other duties of a pastoral watchfulness, a very large flock has all this while demanded of me; wherein, if I had been furnished with as many heads as a Typheus, as many eyes as an Argos, and as many hands as a Briareus, I might have had work enough to have employed them all; nor hath my station left me free from obligations to spend very much time in the Evangelical service of *others* also. It would have been a great *sin* in me to have *omitted*, or *abated*, my just cares, to *fulfil my Ministry in these things*, and in a manner *give my self wholly to them*. All the time I have had for my Church-History, hath been perhaps only, or chiefly, that which I might have taken else for less profitable recreations; and it hath all been done by *snatches*. My reader will not find me the person intended in his Littany, when he says, *Libera me ab homine unius negotii*,[w] nor have I spent thirty years in shaping this my History, as Diodorus Siculus did for his, [and yet both Bodinus and Sigonius complain of the σφαλματα],[x] attending it. But I wish I could have enjoyed, entirely for this work, one quarter of the little more than two years which have rolled away since I began it; whereas I have

---

[v] Before I talk of my subject, I must say a few things of myself.
[w] Deliver me from a man of one idea.
[x] Mistakes.

been forced sometimes wholly to throw by the work whole months together, and then resume it, but by a stolen hour or two in the day, not without some hazard of incurring the *title* which Coryat put upon his History of his Travels, '*Crudities hastily gobbled up in five months.*' Protogenes being seven years in drawing a picture, Apelles, upon the sight of it, said, 'The grace of the work was much allayed by the length of the time.' Whatever else there may have been to take off the 'grace of the work' now in the reader's hands, (whereof the *pictures* of great and good men make a considerable part,) I am sure there hath not been the 'length of the time' to do it. Our English Martyrologer counted it a sufficient *apology* for what meanness might be found in the first edition of his 'acts and monuments', that it was 'hastily rashed up in about fourteen months', and I may apologize for this collection of our 'acts and monuments', that I should have been glad, in the little more than two years which have ran out since I entred upon it, if I could have had one half of 'about fourteen months' to have entirely devoted thereunto. But besides the *time*, which the daily services of my own first, and then many other Churches, have necessarily called for, I have lost abundance of precious time through the feeble and broken state of my health, which hath unfitted me for hard study; I can do nothing to purpose at lucubrations. And yet, in this time also of the two or three years last past, I have not been excused from the further diversion of publishing (though not so many as they say Mercurius Trismegistus did, yet) more than a score of other *books*, upon a copious variety of other subjects, besides the composing of several more, that are not yet published.[4]

...

Unto thee, therefore, O thou Son of God, and King of Heaven, and Lord of all things, whom all the glorious Angels of Light unspeakably love to glorifie; I humbly offer up a poor History of Churches, which own thee alone for their Head, and Prince, and Law-Giver; Churches which thou has purchased with thy own blood, and with wonderful dispensations of thy Providence hitherto protected and preserved; and of a people which thou didst form for thy self, to shew forth thy praises. I bless thy great Name, for thy inclining of me to, and carrying of me through, the work of this History: I pray thee to sprinkle the book of this History with thy blood, and make it acceptable and profitable unto thy Churches, and serve thy Truths and Ways among thy people, by that which thou hast here prepared; for 'tis THOU *that hast prepared it for them.* AMEN.

> *Quid sum? Nil. – Quis sum? Nullus – Sed gratia* CHRISTI,
> *Quod sum, quod vivo, quodque laboro, facit.*[y]

y What am I? Nothing. The grace of Christ alone
   Lives in my life, and does what I have done.

Galeacius Secundus.[z5]

The Life of William Bradford, Esq, Governour of Plymouth Colony.

Omnium Somnos illius vigilantia defendit; omnium otium, illius Labor; omnium Delitias, illius Industria; omnium vacationem, illius occupatio.[a]

1. It has been a matter of some observation, that although Yorkshire be one of the largest shires in England; yet, for all the *fires* of martyrdom which were kindled in the days of Queen Mary, it afforded no more *fuel* than one poor *Leaf;* namely, John Leaf, an apprentice, who suffered for the doctrine of the Reformation at the same time and stake with the famous John Bradford. But when the reign of Queen Elizabeth would not admit the Reformation of worship to proceed unto those degrees, which were proposed and pursued by no small number of the faithful in those days, Yorkshire was not the least of the shires in England that afforded suffering *witnesses* thereunto. The Churches there gathered were quickly molested with such a raging persecution, that if the spirit of separation in them did carry them unto a further *extream* than it should have done, one blameable cause thereof will be found in the *extremity* of that persecution. Their troubles made that *cold* country too *hot* for them, so that they were under a necessity to *seek* a retreat in the Low Countries; and yet the watchful malice and fury of their adversaries rendred it almost impossible for them to *find* what they sought. For them to leave their native soil, their lands and their friends, and go into a strange place, where they must hear foreign language, and live meanly and hardly, and in other imployments than that of husbandry, wherein they had been educated, *these* must needs have been such discouragements as could have been conquered by none, save those who 'sought first the kingdom of God, and the righteousness thereof.' But that which would have made these discouragements the more unconquerable unto an ordinary faith, was the terrible zeal of their enemies to guard all ports, and search all ships, that none of them should be carried off. I will not relate the sad things of this kind then *seen* and *felt* by this people of God; but only exemplifie those trials with one short story. Divers of this people having hired a Dutchman,

---

z The second shield-bearer.

a His vigilance secures others' slumbers; his toil, others' rest; his industry, others' pleasures; his diligence, others' leisures.

then lying at Hull, to carry them over to Holland, he promised faithfully to take them in between Grimsly and Hull; but they coming to the place a day or two too soon, the appearance of such a multitude alarmed the officers of the town adjoining, who came with a great body of soldiers to seize upon them. Now it happened that one boat full of men had been carried aboard, while the women were yet in a bark that lay aground in a creek at low water. The Dutchman perceiving the storm that was thus beginning ashore, swore by the sacrament that he would stay no longer for any of them; and so taking the advantage of a fair wind then blowing, he put out to sea for Zealand. The women thus left near Grimsly-common, bereaved of their husbands, who had been hurried from them, and forsaken of their neighbours, of whom none durst in this fright stay with them, were a very rueful spectacle; some crying for *fear*, some shaking for *cold*, all dragged by troops of armed and angry men from one Justice to another, till not knowing what to do with them, they even dismissed them to shift as well as they could for themselves. But by their singular *afflictions*, and by their Christian *behaviours*, the *cause* for which they exposed themselves did gain considerably. In the mean time, the men at sea found reason to be glad that their families were not with them, for they were surprized with an horrible tempest, which held them for fourteen days together, in seven whereof they saw not sun, moon or star, but were driven upon the coast of Norway. The mariners often despaired of life, and once with doleful shrieks gave over all, as thinking the vessel was foundred; but the vessel rose again, and when the mariners with sunk hearts often cried out, 'We sink! we sink!' the passengers, without such distraction of mind, even while the water was running into their mouths and ears, would chearfully shout, 'Yet, Lord, thou canst save! Yet, Lord, thou canst save!' And the Lord accordingly brought them at last safe unto their desired haven: and not long after helped their distressed relations thither after them, where indeed they found upon almost all accounts *a new world*, but a world in which they found that they must live like strangers and pilgrims.[6]

2. Among those devout people was our William Bradford, who was born *Anno* 1588, in an obscure village called Ansterfield, where the people were as unacquainted with the Bible, as the Jews do seem to have been with *part* of it in the days of Josiah; a most ignorant and licentious *people*, and *like unto their priest*. Here, and in some other places, he had a comfortable inheritance left him of his honest parents, who died while he was yet a child, and cast him on the education, first of his grand parents, and then of his uncles, who devoted him, like his

ancestors, unto the affairs of husbandry. Soon a long sickness kept him, as he would afterwards thankfully say, from the *vanities of youth*, and made him the fitter for what he was afterwards to undergo. When he was about a dozen years old, the reading of the Scriptures began to cause great impressions upon him; and those impressions were much assisted and improved, when he came to enjoy Mr. Richard Clifton's illuminating ministry, not far from his abode; he was then also further befriended, by being brought into the company and fellowship of such as were then called professors; though the young man that brought him into it did after become a prophane and wicked *apostate*. Nor could the wrath of his uncles, nor the scoff of his neighbours, now turned upon him, as one of the *Puritans*, divert him from his pious inclinations.

3. At last, beholding how fearfully the evangelical and apostolical *church-form*, whereinto the churches of the primitive times were cast by the good spirit of God, had been *deformed* by the apostacy of the succeeding times; and what little progress the Reformation had yet made in many parts of Christendom towards its recovery, he set himself by reading, by discourse, by prayer, to learn whether it was not his duty to withdraw from the communion of the parish-assemblies, and engage with some society of the faithful, that should keep close unto the *written word* of God, as the *rule* of their worship. And after many distresses of mind concerning it, he took up a very deliberate and understanding resolution, of doing so; which resolution he chearfully prosecuted, although the provoked rage of his friends tried all the ways imaginable to reclaim him from it, unto all whom his answer was:

Were I like to endanger my life, or consume my estate by any ungodly courses, your counsels to me were very seasonable; but you know that I have been diligent and provident in my calling, and not only desirous to augment what I have, but also to enjoy it in your company; to part from which will be as great a cross as can befal me. Nevertheless, to keep a good conscience, and walk in such a way as God has prescribed in his Word, is a thing which I must prefer before you all, and above life it self. Wherefore, since 'tis for a good cause that I am like to suffer the disasters which you lay before me, you have no cause to be either angry with me, or sorry for me; yea, I am not only willing to part with every thing that is dear to me in this world for this cause, but I am also thankful that God has given me an heart to do, and will accept me so to suffer for him.[7]

Some lamented him, some derided him, *all* disswaded him: nevertheless, the more they did it, the more fixed he was in his purpose to seek the ordinances of the gospel, where they should be dispensed with most of the *commanded purity;* and the sudden deaths of the chief relations which thus lay at him, quickly after convinced him what a folly it had been to have quitted his profession, in expectation of any satisfaction from them. So to Holland he attempted a removal.

4. Having with a great company of Christians hired a ship to transport them for Holland, the master perfidiously betrayed them into the hands of those persecutors, who rifled and ransacked their goods, and clapped their persons into prison at Boston, where they lay for a month together. But Mr. Bradford being a young man of about eighteen, was dismissed sooner than the rest, so that within a while he had opportunity with some others to get over to Zealand, through *perils*, both by *land* and *sea* not inconsiderable; where he was not long ashore ere a viper seized on his hand – that is, an officer – who carried him unto the magistrates, unto whom an envious passenger had accused him as having *fled* out of England. When the magistrates understood the true cause of his coming thither, they were well satisfied with him; and so he repaired joyfully unto his brethren at Amsterdam, where the difficulties to which he afterwards stooped in learning and serving of a Frenchman at the working of silks, were abundantly compensated by the delight where-with he sat under the shadow of our Lord, in his purely dispensed ordinances. At the end of two years, he did, being of age to do it, convert his estate in England into money; but setting up for himself, he found some of his designs by the *providence* of God frowned upon, which he judged a *correction* bestowed by God upon him for certain decays of *internal piety*, whereinto he had fallen; the consumption of his *estate* he thought came to prevent a consumption in his *virtue*. But after he had resided in Holland about half a score years, he was one of those who bore a part in that hazardous and generous enterprise of removing into New-England, with part of the English church at Leyden, where, at their first landing, his dearest consort accidentally falling over-board, was drowned in the harbour; and the rest of his days were spent in the services, and the temptations, of that American wilderness.[8]

5. Here was Mr. Bradford, in the year 1621, unanimously chosen the governour of the plantation: the difficulties whereof were such, that if he had not been a person of more than ordinary piety, wisdom and courage, he must have sunk under them. He had, with a laudable industry, been laying up a treasure of experiences, and he had now occasion to use it: indeed, nothing but an *experienced* man could have been suitable to the necessities of the people. The potent nations of the Indians, into whose country they were come, would have cut them off, if the blessing of God upon *his* conduct had not quelled them; and if his prudence, justice and moderation had not over-ruled

them, they had been ruined by their own distempers. One specimen of his demeanour is to this day particularly spoken of. A company of young fellows that were newly arrived, were very unwilling to comply with the governour's order for working abroad on the publick account; and therefore on Christmas-day, when he had called upon them, they excused themselves, with a pretence that it was against their conscience to *work* such a day. The governour gave them no answer, only that he would spare them till they were better informed; but by and by he found them all at *play* in the street, sporting themselves with various diversions; whereupon commanding the instruments of their games to be taken from them, he effectually gave them to understand, '*That it was against his conscience that they should play whilst others were at work:* and that if they had any devotion to the day, they should show it at home in the exercises of religion, and not in the streets with pastime and frolicks'; and this gentle reproof put a final stop to all such disorders for the future.

6. For two years together after the beginning of the colony, whereof he was now governour, the poor people had a great experiment of 'man's not living by bread alone'; for when they were left all together without one morsel of bread for many months one after another, still the good providence of God relieved them, and supplied them, and this for the most part out of the *sea*. In this low condition of affairs, there was no little exercise for the prudence and patience of the governour, who chearfully bore his part in all: and, that industry might not flag, he quickly set himself to settle *propriety* among the new-planters; foreseeing that while the whole country laboured upon a common stock, the husbandry and business of the plantation could not flourish, as Plato and others long since dreamed that it would, if a *community* were established. Certainly, if the spirit which dwelt in the old puritans, had not inspired these new-planters, they had sunk under the burden of these difficulties; but our Bradford had a double portion of that spirit.

7. The plantation was quickly thrown into a storm that almost overwhelmed it, by the unhappy actions of a minister sent over from England by the adventurers concerned for the plantation; but by the blessing of Heaven on the conduct of the governour, they weathered out that storm. Only the adventurers hereupon breaking to pieces, threw up all their concernments with the infant-colony; whereof they gave this as one reason, 'That the planters dissembled with his Majesty and their friends in their petition, wherein they declared for a church-discipline, agreeing with the French and others of the reforming churches in Europe.' Whereas 'twas now urged, that they had admitted into their communion a person who at his admission utterly

renounced the Churches of England, (which person, by the way, was *that* very man who had made the complaints against them,) and therefore, though they denied the *name* of Brownists, yet they were the thing. In answer hereunto, the very words written by the governour were these:

Whereas you tax us with dissembling about the *French discipline*, you do us wrong, for we both hold and practice the *discipline* of the French and other Reformed Churches (as they have published the same in the *Harmony of Confessions*) according to our means, is effect and substance. But whereas you would tie us up to the *French discipline* in every circumstance, you derogate from the *liberty* we have in Christ Jesus. The Apostle Paul would have none to *follow him* in any thing, but wherein he *follows* Christ; much less ought any Christian or church in the world to do it. The French may err, we may err, and other churches may err, and doubtless do in many *circumstances*. That honour therefore belongs only to the *infallible Word of God*, and *pure Testament of Christ*, to be propounded and followed as the only rule and pattern for direction herein to all churches and Christians. And it is too great arrogancy for any man or church to think that he or they have so sounded the Word of God unto the bottom, as precisely to set down the church's discipline without error in substance or circumstance, that no other without blame may digress or differ in any thing from the same. And it is not difficult to shew that the Reformed Churches differ in many *circumstances* among themselves.

By which words it appears how far he was free from that rigid spirit of separation, which broke to pieces the Separatists themselves in the Low Countries, unto the great scandal of the reforming churches. He was indeed a person of a well-tempered spirit, or else it had been scarce possible for him to have kept the affairs of Plymouth in so good a temper for thirty-seven years together; in every one of which he was chosen their governour, except the three years wherein Mr. Winslow, and the two years wherein Mr. Prince, at the choice of the people, took a turn with him.

8. The leader of a people in a wilderness had need be a Moses; and if a Moses had not led the people of Plymouth Colony, when this worthy person was their governour, the people had never with so much unanimity and importunity still called him to lead them. Among many instances thereof, let this one piece of self-denial be told for a memorial of him, wheresoever this History shall be considered: The Patent of the Colony was taken in his name, running in these terms: 'To William Bradford, his heirs, associates, and assigns'. But when the number of the freemen was much increased, and many new townships erected, the General Court there desired of Mr. Bradford, that he would make a surrender of the same into their hands, which he willingly and presently assented unto, and confirmed it according to their desire by his hand and seal, reserving no more for himself than was his proportion, with others, by agreement. But as he found the providence of Heaven many ways recompensing his many acts of self-denial, so he gave this testimony to the faithfulness of the divine

promises: 'That he had forsaken friends, houses and lands for the sake of the gospel, and the Lord gave them him again'. Here he prospered in his estate; and besides a worthy son which he had by a former wife, he had also two sons and a daughter by another, whom he married in this land.

9. He was a person for study as well as action; and hence, notwithstanding the difficulties through which he passed in his youth, he attained unto a notable skill in languages: the Dutch tongue was become almost as vernacular to him as the English; the French tongue he could also manage; the Latin and the Greek he had mastered; but the Hebrew he most of all studied, 'Because', he said, 'he would see with his own eyes the ancient oracles of God in their native beauty.' He was also well skilled in History, in Antiquity, and in Philosophy; and for Theology he became so versed in it, that he was an irrefragable disputant against the *errors*, especially those of Anabaptism, which with trouble he saw rising in his colony; wherefore he wrote some significant things for the confutation of those errors. But the *crown* of all was his holy, prayerful, watchful, and fruitful walk with God, wherein he was very exemplary.

10. At length he fell into an indisposition of body, which rendred him unhealthy for a whole winter; and as the spring advanced, his health yet more declined; yet he felt himself not what he counted sick, till one day; in the night after which, the God of heaven so filled his mind with ineffable consolations, that he seemed little short of Paul, rapt up unto the unutterable entertainments of Paradise. The next morning he told his friends, 'That the good Spirit of God had given him a pledge of his happiness in another world, and the first-fruits of his eternal glory'; and on the day following he died, May 9, 1657, in the 69th year of his age – lamented by all the colonies of New-England, as a common blessing and father to them all.

O mihi si Similis Contingat Clausula Vitæ!^b

Plato's brief description of a governour, is all that I will now leave as his character, in an

EPITAPH

Νομευς Τροφος ἀγελης ἀνθρωπινης.^c

MEN are but flocks: BRADFORD beheld their need,
And long did them at once both rule and feed.

---

^b O that life's end may be as sweet to me.
^c Shepherd and feeder of the human flock. The life has clearly been patterened in the conversion and vocation stages both Bradford and Mather expected for the elect.

Sarah Kemble Knight, 'The Private Journal of a Journey from Boston to New York, in the Year 1704'

Madam Knight (1666–1727) was born, as was Cotton Mather, in Boston and only three years later than he; her world was the world looking forward, however, just as resolutely as his the world looking backward. She was the daugher of Thomas Kemble, a successful Boston merchant, reportedly an agent of Cromwell in selling prisoners of war. When she recorded the journal of her trip to New York and back, she was the widow of a shipmaster Richard Knight, whom she married when he was already considerably her senior. They had one child, a daughter Elizabeth, who in turn inherited from her mother a goodish estate. On her husband's death, Madam Knight became a court scrivener and from learning something of the law thereby seems to have been employed in settling estates and other semi-legal matters. Thereafter she kept a school in Boston which by tradition both Benjamin Franklin and Samuel Mather attended. She also managed a shop and a boarding house in the city. When the death of a relative left her with an estate to settle, she set off on 2 October 1704 to ride on horseback from Boston to New York, returning to Boston five months later on 3 March 1705. The way she managed her travels through backwoods' frontier New England and acquitted herself in prosperous New York bears witness to the strength of character and enterprise of an unusual woman of thirty-eight. Her society put few impediments in the way of such a woman. Her journey may also therefore suggest the new forms of economic exploitation and secular sophistication swiftly altering the quality of New England life. Her personal attitude towards social change is utterly unlike Cotton Mather's but rather like William Byrd's: the improvement of large areas of ignorance, backwardness, and inefficiency strikes her as altogether possible and desirable. Although she gives herself airs on account of her Bostonianism, she notices well enough what can be made of Connecticut. We are not surprised to learn, then, that she moved to Connecticut in 1712 for reasons of good husbandry. She quickly acquired property in both Norwich and New London, engaged in Indian trading and farming, kept a shop and an inn and at her death in 1727 left an estate of about £1,800 (including two slaves), then a considerable sum.

At the outset of her journal Madam Knight does not reveal a very complex or interesting mind – she is too snobbish, flippant, self-assured and brightly gay to interest us much in her psyche. What gives to her opening pages a decisive interest is not the mental world of the writer; that she virtually discards as a subject while assuming a series of contrasting, unstable roles. Although her courageous and practical address to existence is valuable and makes all else possible, she initially offers little more than a swiftly humorous unrolling of New England frontier life. With introspection absent from the account, interest resides in her amusing presentation of the emergence of another America, living side by side with Mather's and replacing it step by step. Fifty miles outside Boston, she feels herself among aliens and sets about recording their oddities as if she were a British traveller in foreign parts, now and then nearly lecturing her readers on subjects about what ought to be done to bring this or that place up to scratch. Her ability to play diverse roles in her own journal – frail woman, mock lyricist, comic novelist, and commercial traveller – is reflected in equally vigorous role-playing on the journey: now the governor's guest, now the slightly cross and censorious schoolmistress on the outside laughing on the inside at her effect on barmaid and guide, now the head of her family meeting New York entrepreneurs on their own ground, now the brisk cataloguer of distinctions in dress, accent, architecture.

As the journal continues, however, and the controlling personality beneath her roles is strengthened and comes to dominate the account, the reader's respect for Madam Knight and his way of reading both change. It is not simply that she stands up so well to mid-winter danger and discomfort on the road, it is the amount of social and cultural territory she manages so swiftly and pragmatically to cover which leads to deepening interest. Her initial attitude towards prose style and self-presentation – an attitude of artful concealment and contrivance – yields to a noncommital assurance that the things to be experienced in her world are essentially interesting and that she is as valuable a reporter as anyone on the scene.

My text is a reprint of the first edition (New York, 1825) printed in Albany by Frank H. Little in 1865.

The Journal of Madam Knight

Monday, Octb'r. ye second, 1704. – About three o'clock afternoon, I begun my Journey from Boston to New Haven; being about two Hundred Mile. My Kinsman, Capt. Robert Luist, waited on me as farr as Dedham, where I was to meet ye Western post.

I vissitted the Reverd. Mr. Belcher, ye Minister of ye town, and tarried there till evening, in hopes ye post would come along. But he not coming, I resolved to go to Billingses where he used to lodg, being 12 miles further. But being ignorant of the way, Mad^m Billings, seing no persuasions of her good spouses or hers could prevail with me to Lodg there that night, Very kindly went wyth me to ye Tavern, where I hoped to get my guide, And desired the Hostess to inquire of her guests whether any of them would go with mee. But they being tyed by the Lipps to a pewter engine,[a] scarcely allowed themselves time to say what clownish...

[*Here half a page of the MS. is gone.*]

...Peices of eight, I told her no, I would not be accessary to such extortion.

Then John shan't go, sais shee. No, indeed, shan't hee; And held forth at that rate a long time, that I began to fear I was got among the Quaking tribe, beleeving not a Limbertong'd sister among them could outdo Madm. Hostes.

Upon this, to my no small surprise, son John arrose, and gravely demanded what I would give him to go with me? Give you, sais I, are you John? Yes, says he, for want of a Better, And behold! this John look't as old as my Host, and perhaps had bin a man in the last

---

[a] Drinking from pewter mugs. Madam Knight is fastidiously facetious.

Century. Well, Mr. John, sais I, make your demands. Why, half a pss. of eight and a dram, sais John. I agreed, and gave him a Dram (now) in hand to bind the bargain.

My hostess catechis'd John for going so cheep, saying his poor wife would break her heart...

[*Here another half page of the MS. is gone.*]

His shade on his Hors resembled a Globe on a Gate post. His habitt, Hors and furniture, its looks and goings Incomparably answered the rest.

Thus Jogging on with an easy pace, my Guide telling mee it was dangero's to Ride hard in the Night, (wh^{ch} his horse had the sence to avoid,) Hee entertained me with the Adventurs he had passed by late Rideing, and eminent Dangers he had escaped, so that, Remembring the Hero's in Parismus and the Knight of the Oracle, I didn't know but I had mett wth a Prince disguis'd.[1]

When we had Ridd about an how'r, wee come into a thick swamp, wch. by Reason of a great fogg, very much startled mee, it being now very Dark. But nothing dismay'd John: Hee had encountered a thousand and a thousand such Swamps, having a Universall Knowledge in the woods; and readily Answered all my inquiries wch. were not a few.

In about an how'r, or something more, after we left the Swamp, we come to Billinges, where I was to Lodg. My Guide dismounted and very Complasantly help't me down and shewd the door, signing to me wth his hand to Go in; wch I Gladly did – But had not gone many steps into the Room, ere I was Interogated by a young Lady I understood afterwards was the Eldest daughter of the family, with these, or words to this purpose, (viz.) Law for mee – what in the world brings You here at this time a night? – I never see a woman on the Rode so Dreadfull late, in all the days of my versall life. Who are You? Where are You going? I'me scar'd out of my witts – with much now of the same Kind. I stood aghast, Prepareing to reply, when in comes my Guide – to him Madam turn'd, Roreing out: Lawfull heart, John, is it You? – how de do! Where in the world are you going with this woman? Who is she? John made no Ansr. but sat down in the corner, fumbled out his black Junk, and saluted that instead of Debb; she then turned agen to mee and fell anew into her silly questions, without asking me to sitt down.

I told her she treated me very Rudely, and I did not think it my duty to answer her unmannerly Questions. But to get ridd of them, I told her I come there to have the post's company with me to-morrow on my Journey, &c. Miss star'd awhile, drew a chair, bid me sitt, And then run up stairs and putts on two or three Rings, (or else I had not seen them before,) and returning, sett herself just before me, showing the way to Reding.[b] that I might see her Ornaments, perhaps to gain the more respect. But her Granam's new Rung sow, had it appeared, would affected me as much. I paid honest John wth money and dram according to contract, and Dismist him, and pray'd Miss to shew me where I must Lodg. Shee conducted me to a parlour in a little back Lento,[c] wch was almost filled wth the bedsted, wch was so high I was forced to climb on a chair to gitt up to ye wretched bed that lay on it; on wch having Stretcht my tired Limbs, and lay'd my head on a Sad-colour'd pillow, I began to think on the transactions of ye past day.

Tuesday, October ye third, about 8 in the morning, I with the Post proceeded forward without observing any thing remarkable; And about two, afternoon, Arrived at the Post's second stage, where the western Post mett him and exchanged Letters. Here, having called for something to eat, ye woman bro't in a Twisted thing like a cable, but something whiter; and laying it on the bord, tugg'd for life to bring it into a capacity to spread; wch having wth great pains accomplished, shee serv'd in a dish of Pork and Cabage, I suppose the remains of Dinner. The sause was of deep Purple, wch I tho't was boil'd in her dye Kettle; the bread was Indian, and every thing on the Table service Agreeable to these. I, being hungry, gott a little down; but my stomach was soon cloy'd, and what cabbage I swallowed serv'd me for a Cudd the whole day after.

Having here discharged the Ordnary for self and Guide, (as I understood was the custom,) About Three afternoon went on with my Third Guide, who Rode very hard: and having crossed Providence Ferry, we come to a River wch they Generally Ride thro'. But I dare not venture; so the Post got a Ladd and Cannoo to carry me to tother side, and hee rid thro' and Led my hors. The Cannoo was very small and shallow, so that when we were in she seem'd redy to take in water, which greatly terrified mee, and caused me to be very circumspect, sitting with my hands fast on each side, my eyes stedy, not daring so much as to lodg my tongue a hair's breadth more on one side of my mouth then tother, nor so much as think on Lott's wife, for a wry thought woud have oversett our wherry; But was soon put out of this pain, by feeling the Cannoo on shore, wch I as soon almost saluted with my feet; and Rewarding my sculler, again

---

b Waving her hand around.
c Lean-to or attached single-storey building.

mounted and made the best of our way forwards. The Rode here was very even and ye day pleasant, it being now near Sunsett.

. . .

Now was the Glorious Luminary, wth his swift Courses arrived at his Stage, leaving poor me wth the rest of this part of the lower world in darkness, with which *wee* were soon Surrounded. The only Glimering we now had was from the spangled Skies, Whose Imperfect Reflections rendered every Object formidable. Each lifeless Trunk. with its shatter'd Limbs, appear'd an Armed Enymie; and every little stump like a Ravenous devourer. Nor could I so much as discern my Guide, when at any distance, which added to the terror.

Thus, absolutely lost in Thought, and dying with the very thoughts of drowning, I come up wth the post, who I did not see till even with his Hors: he told mee he stopt for mee; and wee Rode on Very deliberatly a few paces, when we entred a Thickett of Trees and Shrubbs, and I perceived by the Hors's going we were on the descent of a Hill, w^{ch}, as wee come neerer the bottom, twas totaly dark wth the Trees that surrounded it. But I knew by the Going of the hors wee had entred the water, wch my Guide told mee was the hazzardos River he had told me off; and hee, Riding up close to my Side, Bid me not fear – we should be over Imediatly. I now ralyed all the Courage I was mistriss of, Knowing that I must either Venture my fate of drowning, or be left like ye Children in the wood. So, as the Post bid me, I gave Reins to my Nagg; and sitting as Stedy as Just before in the Cannoo, in a few minutes got safe to the other side, which hee told mee was the Narragansett country.

Here We found great difficulty in Travailing, the way being very narrow, and on each side the Trees and bushes gave us very unpleasent welcome wth their Branches and bow's, wch wee could not avoid, it being so exceeding dark. My Guide, as before so now, putt on harder than I, wth my weary bones, could follow; so left mee and the way beehind him. Now Returned my distressed aprehensions of the place where I was: the dolesome woods, my Company next to none. Going I knew not whither, and encompased wth Terrifying darkness; The least of which was enough to startle a more Masculine courage. Added to which the Reflections, as in the afternoon of ye day that my Call was very Questionable, wch till then I had not so Prudently as I ought considered. Now, coming to ye foot of a hill, I found great difficulty in ascending; But being got to the Top, was there amply recompenced with the friendly Appearance of the Kind Conductress of the night, Just then Advancing above the Horisontall Line. The Raptures wch the Sight of that fair Planett produced in mee, caus'd mee, for the Moment, to forgett my present wearyness and past toils; and Inspir'd me for most of the remaining way with very divirting thot's, some of which, with the other Occurances of the day, I reserved to note down when I should come to my Stage. My tho'ts on the sight of the moon were to this purpose:

> Fair Cynthia, all the Homage that I may
> Unto a Creature, unto thee I pay;
> In Lonesome woods to meet so kind a guide,
> To Mee's more worth than all the world beside.
> Some Joy I felt just now, when safe got or'e
> Yon Surly River to this Rugged shore,
> Deeming Rough welcomes from these clownish Trees,
> Better than Lodgings wch Nereidees.
> Yet swelling fears surprise; all dark appears –
> Nothing but Light can disipate those fears.
> My fainting vitals can't lend strength to say,
> But softly whisper, O I wish 'twere day.
> The murmer hardly warm'd the Ambient air,
> E're thy Bright Aspect rescues from dispair:
> Makes the old Hagg her sable mantle loose,
> And a Bright Joy do's through my Soul diffuse.
> The Boistero's Trees now Lend a Passage Free,
> And pleasent prospects thou giv'st light to see.

From hence wee kept on, with more ease y^n before: the way being smooth and even, the night warm and serene, and the Tall and thick Trees at a distance, especially w^n the moon glar'd light through the branches, fill'd my Imagination wth the pleasent delusion of a Sumpteous citty, fill'd wth famous Buildings and churches, wth their spiring steeples, Balconies, Galleries and I know not what.

. . .

Being come to mr. Havens', I was very civilly Received, and courteously entertained, in a clean comfortable House; and the Good woman was very active in helping off my Riding cloths, and then ask't what I would eat. I told her I had some Chocolett if shee would prepare it; which with the help of some Milk, and a little clean brass Kettle, she soon effected to my satisfaction. I then betook me to my Apartment, wch was a little Room parted from the Kitchen by a single bord partition; where, after I had noted the Occurrances of the past day, I went to bed, which, tho' pretty hard, Yet neet and handsome. But I could get no sleep, because of the Clamor of some of the Town tope-ers in next Room, Who were entred into a strong debate concerning ye Signifycation of the name of their Country, (viz.) *Narraganset*. One said it was named so by ye Indians, because there grew a Brier there, of a prodigious Highth and bigness, the like hardly ever known, called by the Indians Narragansett; And quotes an

Indian of so Barberous a name for his Author, that I could not write it. His Antagonist Replyed no – It was from a Spring it had its name, wch hee well knew where it was, which was extreem cold in summer, and as Hott as could be imagined in the winter, which was much resorted too by the natives, and by them called Narragansett, (Hott and Cold,) and that was the originall of their places name – with a thousand Impertinances not worth notice, wch He utter'd with such a Roreing voice and Thundering blows with the fist of wickedness on the Table, that it peirced my very head. I heartily fretted, and wish't 'um tongue tyed; but wth as little succes as a freind of mine once, who was (as shee said) kept a whole night awake, on a Jorny, by a country Left,^d and a Sergent, Insigne and a Deacon, contriving how to bring a triangle into a Square. They kept calling for tother Gill wch while they were swallowing, was some Intermission; But presently, like Oyle to fire, encreased the flame. I set my Candle on a Chest by the bed side, and setting up, fell to my old way of composing my Resentments, in the following manner:

> I ask thy Aid, O Potent Rum!
> To Charm these wrangling Topers Dum.
> Thou hast their Giddy Brains possest –
> The man confounded wth the Beast –
> And I, poor I, can get no rest.
> Intoxicate them with thy fumes:
> O still their Tongues till morning comes.

And I know not but my wishes took effect; for the dispute soon ended wth 'tother Dram; and so Good night!

Wednesday, Octob^r 4th. About four in the morning, we set off for Kingston (for so was the Town called) with a french Docter in our company. Hee and ye Post put on very furiously, so that I could not keep up with them, only as now and then they'd stop till they see mee. This Rode was poorly furnished wth accommodations for Travellers, so that we were forced to ride 22 miles by the post's account, but neerer thirty by mine, before wee could bait so much as our Horses, wch I exceedingly complained of. But the post encourag'd mee, by saying wee should be well accommodated anon at mr. Devills, a few miles further. But I questioned whether we ought to go to the Devil to be helpt out of affliction. However, like the rest of Deluded souls that post to ye Infernal denn, Wee made all possible speed to this Devil's Habitation; where alliting, in full assurance of good accommodation, wee were going in. But meeting his two daughters, as I suposed twins, they so neerly resembled each other, both in features

---

^d Lieutenant.

and habit. and look't as old as the Divel himselfe, and quite as Ugly, We desired entertainm't, but could hardly get a word out of 'um, till with our Importunity, telling them our necesity, &c. they call'd the old Sophister, who was as sparing of his words as his daughters had bin, and no, or none, was the reply's hee made us to our demands. Hee differed only in this from the old fellow in to'ther Country: hee let us depart. However, I thought it proper to warn poor Travailers to endeavour to Avoid falling into circumstances like ours, wch at our next Stage I sat down and did as followeth:

> May all that dread the cruel feind of night
> Keep on, and not at this curs't Mansion light.
> 'Tis Hell; 'tis Hell! and Devills here do dwell:
> Here dwells the Devil – surely this's Hell.
> Nothing but Wants: a drop to cool yo'r Tongue
> Cant be procur'd these cruel Feinds among.
> Plenty of horrid Grins and looks sevear.
> Hunger and thirst, But pitty's bannish'd here –
> The Right hand keep, if Hell on Earth you fear!

. . .

From hence we proceeded (about ten forenoon) through the Naragansett country, pretty Leisurely; and about one afternoon come to Paukataug River, wch was about two hundred paces over, and now very high, and no way over to to'ther side but this. I darid not venture to Ride thro, my courage at best in such cases but small, And now at the Lowest Ebb, by reason of my weary, very weary, hungry and uneasy Circumstances. So takeing leave of my company, tho' wth no little Reluctance, that I could not proceed wth them on my Jorny, Stop at a little cottage Just by the River, to wait the Waters falling, wch the old man that lived there said would be in a little time, and he would conduct me safe over. This little Hutt was one of the wretchedest I ever saw a habitation for human creatures. It was suported with shores enclosed with Clapbords, laid on Lengthways, and so much asunder, that the Light come throu' every where; the doore tyed on wth a cord in ye place of hinges; The floor the bear earth; no windows but such as the thin covering afforded, nor any furniture but a Bedd wth a glass Bottle hanging at ye head on't; an earthan cupp, a small pewter Bason, A Bord wth sticks to stand on, instead of a table, and a block or two in ye corner instead of chairs. The family were the old man, his wife and two Children; all and every part being the picture of poverty. Notwithstanding both the Hutt and its Inhabitance were very clean and tydee: to the crossing the Old Proverb, that bare walls make giddy hows-wifes.

I Blest myselfe that I was not one of this misserable crew; and the

Impressions their wretchedness formed in me caused mee on ye very
Spott to say:

> Tho' Ill at ease. A stranger and alone.
> All my fatigu's shall not extort a grone.
> These Indigents have hunger with their ease;
> Their best is wors behalfe than my disease.
> Their Misirable hutt wch Heat and Cold
> Alternately without Repulse do hold;
> Their Lodgings thyn and hard, their Indian fare,
> Their mean Apparel which the wretches wear,
> And their ten thousand ills wch can't be told,
> Makes nature er'e 'tis midle age'd look old.
> When I reflect, my late fatigues do seem
> Only a notion or forgotten Dreem.

I had scarce done thinking, when an Indian-like Animal come to the
door, on a creature very much like himselfe, in mien and feature, as
well as Ragged cloathing; and having 'litt, makes an Awkerd Scratch
wth his Indian shoo, and a Nodd, sitts on ye block, fumbles out his
black Junk, dipps it in ye Ashes, and presents it piping hott to his
muscheeto's, and fell to sucking like a calf, without speaking, for near
a quarter of an hower. At length the old man said how do's Sarah do?
who I understood was the wretches wife and Daughter to ye old man:
he Replyed – as well as can be expected, &c. So I remembred the old
say, and suposed I knew Sarah's case. Butt hee being, as I understood,
going over the River, as ugly as hee was, I was glad to ask him to show
me ye way to Saxtons, at Stoningtown; wch he promising, I ventur'd
over wth the old man's assistance; who having rewarded to content,
with my Tattertailed guide, I Ridd on very slowly thro' Stoningtown,
where the Rode was very Stony and uneven. I asked the fellow, as we
went, divers questions of the place and way. &c. I being arrived at my
country Saxtons, at Stonington, was very well accommodated both as
to victuals and Lodging, the only Good of both I had found since my
setting out. Here I heard there was an old man and his Daughter to
come that way, bound to N. London; and being now destitute of a
Guide, gladly waited for them, being in so good a harbour, and
accordingly, Thirsday, Octob^r ye 5th, about 3 in the afternoon, I sat
forward with neighbour Polly and Jemima, a Girl about 18 years old,
who hee said he had been to fetch out of the Narragausetts, and said
they had Rode thirty miles that day, on a sory lean jade, wth only a
Bagg under her for a pillion, which the poor Girl often complain'd
was very uneasy.

Wee made Good speed along wch made poor Jemima make many a
sow'r face, the mare being a very hard trotter; and after many a hearty

and bitter Oh, she at length Low'd out: Lawful Heart father! this bare mare hurts mee Dingeely, I'me direfull sore I vow; with many words to that purpose: – poor Child sais Gaffer – she us't to serve your mother so. I don't care how mother us't to do, quoth Jemima, in a passionate tone, at which the old man Laught, and kik't his Jade o' the side, which made her Jolt ten times harder.

About seven that Evening, we come to New London Ferry: here, by reason of a very high wind, we mett with great difficulty in getting over – the Boat tos't exceedingly, and our Horses capper'd at a very surprizing Rate, and sett us all in a fright: especially poor Jemima, who desired her father to say so jack to the Jade, to make her stand. But the careless parent, taking no notice of her repeated desires, She Rored out in a Passionate manner: Pray suth father, Are you deaf? Say so Jack to the Jade, I tell you. The Dutiful Parent obey's; saying so Jack, so Jack, as gravely as if hee'd bin to saying Catechise after Young Miss, who with her fright look't of all coullers in ye Rain Bow.

Being safely arrived at the house of Mrs. Prentices in N. London, I treated neighbour Polly and daughter for their divirting company, and bid them farewell; and between nine and ten at night waited on the Rev^d Mr. Gurdon Saltonstall, minister of the town, who kindly Invited me to Stay that night at his house, where I was very handsomely and plentifully treated and Lodg'd; and made good the Great Character I had before heard concerning him: viz. that he was the most affable, courteous Genero's and best of men.

Friday, Octo^r 6th. I got up very early, in Order to hire somebody to go with mee to New Haven, being in great parplexity at the thoughts of proceeding alone; which my most hospitable entertainer observing, himself went, and soon return'd wth a young Gentleman of the town, who he could confide in to Go with mee; and about eight this morning, wth Mr. Joshua Wheeler my new Guide, takeing leave of this worthy Gentleman, Wee advanced on toward Seabrook. The Rodes all along this way are very bad, Incumbred wth Rocks and mountainos passages, wch were very disagreeable to my tired carcass; but we went on with a moderate pace wch made ye Journey more pleasent.

. . .

From hence wee went pretty briskly forward, and arriv'd at Saybrook ferry about two of the Clock afternoon; and crossing it, wee call'd at an Inn to Bait, (foreseeing we should not have such another Opportunity till we come to Killingsworth.) Landlady come in, with her hair about her ears, and hands at full pay scratching. Shee told us shee had some mutton wch shee would broil, wch I was glad to hear; But I suppose forgot to wash her scratchers; in a little time shee brot it in; but it being pickled, and my Guide said it smelt strong of head sause, we left it, and p^d sixpence a piece for our Dinners, wch was only smell.

So wee putt forward with all speed, and about seven at night come to Killingsworth, and were tollerably well with Travillers fare, and Lodgd there that night.

Saturday, Oct. 7th, we sett out early in the Morning, and being something unaquainted wth the way, having ask't it of some wee mett . . . and we soon after came into the Rhode, and keeping still on, without any thing further Remarkabell, about two a clock afternoon we arrived at New Haven, where I was received with all Posible Respects and civility. Here I discharged Mr. Wheeler with a reward to his satisfaction, and took some time to rest after so long and toilsome a Journey; And Inform'd myselfe of the manners and customs of the place, and at the same time employed myselfe in the afair I went there upon.

They are Govern'd by the same Laws as wee in Boston, (or little differing,) thr'out this whole Colony of Connecticot, And much the same way of Church Government, and many of them good, Sociable people, and I hope Religious too; but a little too much Independant in their principalls,^{e} and, as I have been told, were formerly in their Zeal very Riggid in their Administrations towards such as their Lawes made Offenders, even to a harmless Kiss or Innocent merriment among Young people.[2] Whipping being a frequent and counted an easy Punishment, about wch as other Crimes, the Judges were absolute in their Sentances. They told mee a pleasant story about a pair of Justices in those parts, wch I may not omit the relation of.

A negro Slave belonging to a man in ye Town, stole a hogs head from his master, and gave or sold it to an Indian, native of the place. The Indian sold it in the neighbourhood, and so the theft was found out. Thereupon the Heathen was Seized, and carried to the Justices House to be Examined. But his worship (it seems) was gone into the feild, with a Brother in office, to gather in his Pompions.^{f} Whither the malefactor is hurried, And Complaint made, and satisfaction in the name of Justice demanded. Their Worships cann't proceed in form without a Bench: whereupon they Order one to be Imediately erected, which, for want of fitter materials, they made with pompions – which being finished, down setts their Worships, and the Malefactor call'd, and by the Senior Justice Interrogated after the following manner. You Indian why did You steal from this man? You sho'dn't

---

^{e} That is, of a separatist congregational organization.
^{f} Pumpkins.

do so – it's a Grandy wicked thing to steal. Hol't Hol't cryes Justice Jun[r] Brother, You speak negro to him. I'le ask him. You sirrah, why did You steal this man's Hoggshead? Hoggshead, (replys the Indian.) me no stomany.[g] No? says his Worship; and pulling off his hatt, Patted his own head with his hand, sais, Tatapa[h] – You, Tatapa – you; all one this. Hoggshead all one this. Hah! says Netop,[i] now me stomany that. Whereupon the Company fell into a great fitt of Laughter, even to Roreing. Silence is comanded, but to no effect: for they continued perfectly Shouting. Nay, sais his worship, in an angry tone, if it be so, *take me off the Bench*.

Their Diversions in this part of the Country are on Lecture days and Training days mostly: on the former there is Riding from town to town.

And on training dayes The Youth divert themselves by Shooting at the Target, as they call it. (but it very much resembles a pillory,) where hee that hitts neerest the white has some yards of Red Ribbin presented him, w[ch] being tied to his hattband, the two ends streeming down his back, he is Led away in Triumph, wth great applause, as the winners of the Olympiack Games. They generally marry very young: the males oftener as I am told under twentie than above; they generally make public wedings, and have a way something singular (as they say) in some of them. viz. Just before Joyning hands the Bridegroom quitts the place, who is soon followed by the Bridesmen, and as it were, dragg'd back to duty – being the reverse to y[e] former practice among us, to steal m[e] Pride.

There are great plenty of Oysters all along by the sea side, as farr as I Rode in the Collony, and those very good. And they Generally lived very well and comfortably in their famelies. But too Indulgent (especially y[e] farmers) to their slaves: suffering too great familiarity from them, permitting y[m] to sit at table and eat with them, (as they say to save time,) and into the dish goes the black hoof as freely as the white hand. They told me that there was a farmer lived nere the Town where I lodgd who had some difference wth his slave, concerning something the master had promised him and did not punctualy perform; w[ch] caused some hard words between them: But at length they put the matter to Arbitration and Bound themselves to stand to the award of such as they named – w[ch] done, the Arbitrators Having heard the Allegations of both parties. Order the master to pay 40[s] to black face, and acknowledge his fault. And so

---

[g] A corruption of understand.
[h] I cannot tell.
[i] Friend.

the matter ended: the poor master very honestly standing to the award.[3]

There are every where in the Towns as I passed, a Number of Indians the Natives of the Country, and are the most salvage of all the salvages of that kind that I had ever Seen[4] little or no care taken (as I heard upon enquiry) to make them otherwise. They have in some places Landes of theire owne, and Govern'd by Law's of their own making; – they marry many wives and at pleasure put them away, and on the ye least dislike or fickle humor, on either side, saying *stand away* to one another is a sufficient Divorce. And indeed those uncomely *Stand aways* are too much in Vougue among the English in this (Indulgent Colony) as their Records plentifully prove, and that on very trivial matters, of which some have been told me, but are not proper to be Related by a Female pen, tho some of that foolish sex have had too large a share in the story.

If the natives committ any crime on their own precints among themselves, ye English takes no Cognezens of. But if on the English ground, they are punishable by our Laws. They mourn for their Dead by blacking their faces, and cutting their hair, after an Awkerd and frightfull manner; But can't bear You should mention the names of their dead Relations to them: they trade most for Rum, for wch they^d hazzard their very lives; and the English fit them Generally as well, by seasoning it plentifully with water.

They give the title of merchant to every trader; who Rate their Goods according to the time and spetia they pay in: viz. Pay, mony, Pay as mony, and trusting. *Pay* is Grain, Pork, Beef, &c. at the prices sett by the General Court that Year; *mony* is pieces of Eight, Ryalls, or Boston or Bay shillings (as they call them,) or Good hard money. as sometimes silver coin is termed by them: also Wampom. viz Indian beads wch serves for change. *Pay as mony* is provisions, as afores^d one Third cheaper then as the assembly or Gene^l Court setts it; and *Trust* as they and the merch^t agree for time.

Now, when the buyer comes to ask for a comodity, sometimes before the merchant answers that he has it, he sais, *is Your pay redy?* Perhaps the Chap Reply's Yes: what do You pay in? say's the merchant. The buyer having answered, then the price is set; as suppose he wants a sixpenny knife, in pay it is 12d – in pay as money eight pence, and hard money its own price, viz. 6d. It seems a very Intricate way of trade and what Lex Mercatoria had not thought of.

Being at a merchants house, in comes a tall country fellow wth his alfogeos^j full of Tobacco; for they seldom Loose their Cudd, but keep

---

^j A corruption of the Spanish *alforja*, saddlebag, or the Portuguese *alforges* (pl.), wallets.

Chewing and Spitting as long as they'r eyes are open – he advanc't to the midle of the Room, makes an Awkward Nodd, and spitting a Large deal of Aromatick Tincture, he gave a scrape with his shovel like shoo, leaving a small shovel full of dirt on the floor, made a full stop, Hugging his own pretty Body with his hands under his arms, Stood staring rown'd him, like a Catt let out of a Baskett. At last, like the creature Balaam Rode on, he opened his mouth and said: have You any Ribinen for Hatbands to sell I pray? The Questions and Answers about the pay being past, the Ribin is bro't and opened. Bumpkin Simpers, cryes its confounded Gay I vow; and beckning to the door, in comes Jone Tawdry, dropping about 50 curtsees, and stands by him: hee shows her the Ribin. *Law You*, sais shee, *its right Gent*, do You take it, *tis dreadfull pretty*. Then she enquires. *have You any hood silk I pray?* wch being brought and bought. Have You any *thred silk to sew it w^th* says shee, wch being accomodated wth they Departed. They Generaly stand after they come in a great while speachless, and sometimes dont say a word till they are askt what they want, which I Impute to the Awe they stand in of the merchants, who they are constantly almost Indebted too; and must take what they bring without Liberty to choose for themselves; but they serve them as well, making the merchants stay long enough for their pay.

We may Observe here the great necessity and bennifitt both of Education and Conversation: for these people have as Large a portion of mother witt, and sometimes a Larger, than those who have bin brought up in Cities; But for want of emprovements, Render themselves almost Ridiculos, as above. I should be glad if they would leave such follies, and am sure all that Love Clean Houses (at least) would be glad on't too.

They are generaly very plain in their dress, throuout all ye Colony, as I saw, and follow one another in their modes; that You may know where they belong, especially the women, meet them where you will.

Their Cheif Red Letter day is St. Election, wch is annualy Observed according to Charter, to choose their Goven^r: a blessing they can never be thankfull enough for, as they will find if ever it be their hard fortune to loose it.[5] The present Governor in Conecticott is the Honble John Winthrop, Esq. A Gentleman of an Ancient and Honourable Family, whose Father was Govenor here sometime before, and his Grand father had bin Govr of the Massachusetts. This gentleman is a very curteous and afable person, much Given to Hospitality, and has by his Good services Gain'd the affections of the people as much as any who had bin before him in that post.

Decr 6th. Being by this time well Recruited and rested after my

Journy, my business lying unfinished by some concerns at New York depending thereupon, my Kinsman, Mr. Thomas Trowbridge of New Haven, must needs take a Journy there before it could be accomplished, I resolved to go there in company wth him, and a man of the town wch I engaged to wait on me there. Accordingly, Dec. 6th we set out from New Haven, and about 11 same morning came to Stratford ferry; wch crossing, about two miles on the other side Baited our horses and would have eat a morsell ourselves. But the Pumpkin and Indian mixt Bred had such an Aspect, and the Bare-legg'd Punch so awkerd or rather Awfull a sound, that we left both, and proceeded forward, and about seven at night come to Fairfield, where we met with good entertainment and Lodg'd; and early next morning set forward to Norowalk from its halfe Indian name *North-walk*, when about 12 at noon we arrived, and Had a Dinner of Fryed Venison, very savoury. Landlady wanting some pepper in the seasoning, bid the Girl hand her the spice in the litte *Gay* cupp on ye shelfe. From hence we Hasted towards Rye, walking and Leading our Horses neer a mile together, up a prodigios high Hill; and so Riding till about nine at night. and there arrived and took up our Lodgings at an ordinary, wch a French family kept. Here being very hungry, I desired a fricasee wch the Frenchman undertakeing, managed so contrary to my notion of Cookery, that I hastned to Bed superless; And being shewd the way up a pair of stairs wch had such a narrow passage that I had almost stopt by the Bulk of my Body, But arriving at my apartment found it to be a little Lento Chamber furnisht amongst other Rubbish with a High Bedd and a Low one, a Long Table, a Bench and a Bottomless chair, – Little Miss went to scratch up my Kennell wch Russelled as if shee'd bin in the Barn amongst the Husks, and supose such was the contents of the tickin – nevertheless being exceeding weary, down I laid my poor Carkes (never more tired) and found my Covering as scanty as my Bed was hard. Annon I heard another Russelling noise in Y^e Room – called to know the matter – Little miss said shee was making a bed for the men; who, when they were in Bed, complained their leggs lay out of it by reason of its shortness – my poor bones complained bitterly not being used to such Lodgings, and so did the man who was with us; and poor I made but one Grone, which was from the time I went to bed to the time I Riss, which was about three in the morning, Setting up by the Fire till Light, and having discharged our ordinary wch was as dear as if we had had far Better fare – we took our leave of Monsier and about seven in the morn come to New Rochell a french town, where we had a good

Breakfast. And in the strength of that about an how'r before sunsett got to York.

. . .

The Cittie of New York is a pleasant well compacted place, situated on a Commodius River wch is a fine harbour for shipping. The Buildings Brick Generaly, very stately and high, though not altogether like ours in Boston. The Bricks in some of the Houses are of divers Coullers and laid in Checkers, being glazed look very agreeable. The inside of them are neat to admiration, the wooden work, for only the walls are plasterd, and the Sumers and Gist are plained and kept very white scowr'd as so is all the partitions if made of Bords. The fire places have no Jambs (as ours have) But the Backs run flush with the walls, and the Hearth is of Tyles and is as farr out into the Room at the Ends as before the fire, wch is Generally Five foot in the Low'r rooms, and the peice over where the mantle tree should be is made as ours with Joyners work, and as I supose is fasten'd to iron rodds inside. The House where the Vendue was, had Chimney Corners like ours, and they and the hearths were laid wth the finest tile that I ever see, and the stair cases laid all with white tile which is ever clean, and so are the walls of the Kitchen wch had a Brick floor. They were making Great preparations to Receive their Governor, Lord Cornbury from the Jerseys, and for that End raised the militia to Gard him on shore to the fort.

They are Generaly of the Church of England and have a New England Gentleman for their minister, and a very fine church set out with all Customary requsites. There are also a Dutch and Divers Conventicles as they call them, viz. Baptist, Quakers, &c. They are not strict in keeping the Sabbath as in Boston and other places where I had bin, But seem to deal with great exactness as farr as I see or Deall with. They are sociable to one another and Curteos and Civill to strangers and fare well in their houses. The English go very fasheonable in their dress. But the Dutch, especially the middling sort, differ from our women in their habitt go loose, were French muches^k wch are like a Capp and a head band in one, leaving their ears bare, which are sett out wth Jewells of a large size and many in number. And their fingers hoop't with Rings, some with large stones in them of many Coullers as were their pendants in their ears, which You should see very old women wear as well as Young.

They have Vendues very frequently, and make their Earnings very well by them, for they treat with good Liquor Liberally, and the Customers Drink as Liberally and Generally pay for't as well, by

k Kerchiefs (from the French her handkerchief (*mouchoir*).

paying for that which they Bidd up Briskly for, after the sack has gone plentifully about, tho' sometimes good penny worths are got there. Their Diversions in the Winter is Riding Sleys about three or four Miles out of Town, where they have Houses of entertainment at a place called the Bowery, and some go to friends Houses who handsomely treat them. Mr. Burroughs carry'd his spouse and Daughter and myself out to one Madame Dowes, a Gentlewoman that lived at a farm House, who gave us a handsome Entertainment of five or six Dishes and choice Beer and metheglin, Cyder, &c. all which she said was the produce of her farm. I believe we mett 50 or 60 slays that day – they fly with great swiftness and some are so furious that they'le turn out of the path for none except a Loaden Cart. Nor do they spare for any diversion the place affords, and sociable to a degree, they'r Tables being as free to their Naybours as to themselves.

Having here transacted the affair I went upon and some other that fell in the way, after about a fortnight's stay there I left New York with no Little regrett.

. . .

Descending the Mountainos passage that almost broke my heart in ascending before, we come to Stamford, a well compact Town, but miserable meeting house, wch we passed, and thro' many and great difficulties, as Bridges which were exceeding high and very tottering and of vast Length, steep and Rocky Hills and precipices, (Buggbears to a fearful female travailer.) About nine at night we come to Norrwalk, having crept over a timber of a Broken Bridge about thirty foot long, and perhaps fifty to ye water. I was exceeding tired and cold when we come to our Inn, and could get nothing there but poor entertainment, and the Impertinant Bable of one of the worst of men, among many others of which our Host made one, who, had he bin one degree Impudenter, would have outdone his Grandfather. And this I think is the most perplexed night I have yet had. From hence, Saturday, Dec. 23, a very cold and windy day, after an Intolerable night's Lodging, wee hasted forward only observing in our way the Town to be situated on a Navigable river wth indiferent Buildings and people more refind than in some of the Country towns wee had passed, tho' vicious enough, the Church and Tavern being next neighbours. Having Ridd thro a difficult River wee come to Fairfield where wee Baited and were much refreshed as well with the Good things wch gratified our appetites as the time took to rest our wearied Limbs, wch Latter I employed in enquiring concerning the Town and manners of the people, &c. This is a considerable town, and filld as they say with wealthy people – have a spacious meeting house and good Buildings. But the Inhabitants are Litigious, nor do they well agree with their minister, who (they say) is a very worthy Gentleman.

They have aboundance of sheep, whose very Dung brings them great gain, with part of which they pay their Parsons sallery, And they Grudg that, prefering their Dung before their minister. They Lett out their sheep at so much as they agree upon for a night: the highest Bidder always caries them, And they will sufficiently Dung a Large quantity of Land before morning. But were once Bitt by a sharper who had them a night and sheared them all before morning – from hence we went to Stratford, the next Town, in which I observed but few houses, and those not very good ones. But the people that I conversed with were civill and good natured. Here we staid till late at night, being to cross a Dangerous River ferry, the River at that time full of Ice; but after about four hours waiting with great difficulty wee got over. My fears and fatigues prevented my here taking any particular observation. Being got to Milford, it being late in the night, I could go no further; my fellow travailer going forward, I was invited to Lodg at Mrs. —, a very kind and civill Gentlewoman, by whom I was handsomely and kindly entertained till the next night. The people here go very plain in their apparel (more plain that I had observed in the towns I had passed) and seem to be very grave and serious. They told me there was a singing Quaker lived there, or at least had a strong inclination to be so. His spouse not at all affected that way. Some of the singing Crew come there one day to visit him, who being then abroad, they sat down (to the woman's no small vexation) Humming and singing and groneing after their conjuring way – Says the woman are you singing quakers? Yea says They – Then take my squalling Brat of a child here and sing to it says she for I have almost split my throat wth singing to him and cant get the Rogue to sleep. They took this as a great Indignity, and mediately departed. Shaking the dust from their Heels left the good woman and her Child among the number of the wicked.

This is a Seaport place and accomodated with a Good Harbour, But I had not opportunity to make particular observations because it was Sabbath day – This Evening.

December 24. I set out with the Gentlewomans son who she very civilly offered to go with me when she see no parswasions would cause me to stay which she pressingly desired, and crossing a ferry having but nine miles to New Haven, in a short time arrived there and was Kindly received and well accommodated amongst my Friends and Relations.

The Government of Connecticut Collony begins westward

towards York at Stanford (as I am told) and so runs Eastward towards Boston (I mean in my range, because I dont intend to extend my description beyond my own travails) and ends that way at Stonington – And has a great many Large towns lying more northerly. It is a plentiful Country for provisions of all sorts and its Generally Healthy. No one that can and will be dilligent in this place need fear poverty nor the want of food and Rayment.

January 6th Being now well Recruited and fitt for business I discoursed the persons I was concerned with, that we might finnish in order to my return to Boston. They delay^{d} as they had hitherto done hoping to tire my Patience. But I was resolute to stay and see an End of the matter let it be never so much to my disadvantage – So January 9th they come again and promise the Wednesday following to go through with the distribution of the Estate which they delayed till Thursday and then come with new amusements. But at length by the mediation of that holy good Gentleman, the Rev. Mr. James Pierpont, the minister of New Haven, and with the advice and assistance of other our Good friends we come to an accommodation and distribution, which having finished though not till February, the man that waited on me to York taking the charge of me I sit out for Boston.

. . .

March 3d wee got safe home to Boston, where I found my aged and tender mother and my Dear and only Child[1] in good health with open arms redy to receive me, and my Kind relations and friends flocking in to welcome mee and hear the story of my transactions and travails I having this day bin five months from home and now I cannot fully express my Joy and Satisfaction. But desire sincearly to adore my Great Benefactor for thus graciously carying forth and returning in safety his unworthy handmaid.

[1] Madam Knight's daughter Elizabeth, then about seventeen.

William Byrd II, 'History of the Dividing Line Betwixt Virginia and North Carolina Run in the Year of our Lord 1728'

William Byrd (1674–1744) was born on 28 March 1674 on that part of the family estate at the fall of the James River called Westover and now covered by the growth of the city he planted, Richmond. Unlike Cotton Mather or Sarah Kemble Knight, likewise native-born, he lived often and happily in England. He resided there on five occasions, the two longest for his education under the direction of an English grandfather between the ages of seven and twenty-two and for his appointment as colonial agent of Virginia between the ages of thirty-three and forty. He was already a member of the Royal Society when he returned to Virginia at twenty-two; he was the affectionate friend of English aristocrats and literati when he returned at forty, determined to make Westover yield the style and pleasures he enjoyed in London. At forty-seven he settled in Virginia for good with his second wife, always hoping for further time abroad which never came. When he died aged seventy, he had spent exactly half his life in England. Whatever disappointment Byrd felt, the elegance, gaiety and urbanity he enjoyed in London were not at all in conflict with the obligation which he recognized to develop his own country and set his own lands in order. His family called him 'The Black Swan' and indeed he swanned about as much as he might; but at the same time felt the patriotism of his class and colony. He opposed the authoritarianism of Governor Spotswood, took sides with the American planters in their struggle to determine their own local government and taxation, sought better and easier land grant arrangements for the western frontier, and answered to his own sense of occasion in all his public and private roles. His private diaries, decoded and published only since 1941, reveal a voracious reader, an authentic amateur of English, French, Latin and Greek literature, and a wise and decent human being. That he took his Americanized religion calmly does not mean that he took it lightly; free from the moral and ascetic constrictions of the chilly northern Calvinism, he was nonetheless constant to his faith. If he sometimes missed out his morning or evening prayers, he almost never neglected to read the allotted portion of scripture in Hebrew and Latin. One can detect, in those diaries, a foreshadowing of the liberal patrician stance of Washington or of Jefferson in the next generation. His relaxed, assured and Christian humanistic lively mindedness has nevertheless a quality all its own.

Byrd's style derives much of its tone and texture from his experience of the brilliant first quarter of the eighteenth century in England and from his sense of identity with Wycherley, Congreve, the Earl of Orrery and so forth. He cannot bring himself to be dull. What preoccupies him in the American Westover manuscripts, however, is incomparably more interesting than the dinners, theatre expeditions, incidental gambling, dalliance and the like recorded in his private diaries. His more recent American editors obviously enjoy him a good deal but tend to dismiss him as sub-Augustan, too modestly on his behalf suggesting that his importance to American letters is directly proportional to the paucity of competitors. An undefensive reading will, however, find in him not only amused social commentary but an imagination genuinely awakened by the natural possibilities of the land about him. The section excerpted below reads generally like a somewhat detached observation: Byrd often waits comfortably in the house of a gentleman and receives reports as the more professional part of his surveying party struggles in difficult professional work in the dismal swamp. From time to time, however, he writes with the warmth of adventurous discovery, naming the plants and trees not simply like a virtuoso but like a trained forester, describing the differences in the production of turpentine for Virginia and for Carolina evergreens, detailing the terrain of unexplored areas with the warmth of adventurous discovery. He is himself shrewd in distinguishing between 'communicating ... dear-bought Experience' and 'conversation ... like whip-sillabub ... very pretty, but nothing in it'. The elements of bought experience and an imagination for America make Byrd a considerable prose writer.

My text is taken from the edition of *The Writings of Colonel William Byrd of Westover in Virginia Esqr.* edited by John Spencer Bassett, New York, 1901, which reprinted the 1841 edition without corrections of orthography.

History of the Dividing Line:

Run in the Year 1728

Before I enter upon the Journal of the Line betwen Virginia and North Carolina, it will be necessary to clear the way to it, by shewing how the other British Colonies on the Main have, one after the other, been carved out of Virginia, by Grants from his Majesty's Royal Predecessors. All that part of the Northern American Continent now under the Dominion of the King of Great Britain, and Stretching quite as far as the Cape of Florida, went *at first under the General Name of Virginia*.

The only Distinction, in those early Days, was, that all the Coast to the Southward of Chesapeake Bay was called South Virginia, and all to the Northward of it, North Virginia.

The first Settlement of this fine Country was owing to that great Ornament of the British Nation, Sir Walter Raleigh, who obtained a Grant thereof from Queen Elizabeth of ever-glorious Memory, by Letters Patent, dated March the 25th, 1584.

But whether that Gentleman ever made a Voyage thither himself is uncertain; because those who have favour'd the Public with an Account of His Life mention nothing of it. However, thus much may be depended on, that Sir Walter invited sundry persons of Distinction to Share in his Charter, and join their Purses with his in the laudable project of fitting out a Colony to Virginia.

Accordingly, 2 Ships were Sent away that very Year, under the Command of his good Friends Amidas and Barlow, to take possession of the Country in the Name of his Roial Mistress, the Queen of England.

These worthy Commanders, for the advantage of the Trade Winds, shaped their Course first to the Charibbe Islands, thence stretching away by the Gulph of Florida, dropt Anchor not far from Roanoak Inlet. They ventured ashoar near that place upon an Island now called Colleton island, where they set up the Arms of England, and claimed the Adjacent Country in Right of their Sovereign Lady, the Queen; and this Ceremony being duly performed, they kindly invited the neighbouring Indians to traffick with them.

These poor people at first approacht the English with great Caution, having heard much of the Treachery of the Spaniards, and not knowing but these Strangers might be as treacherous as they. But, at length, discovering a kind of good nature in their looks, they ventured to draw near, and barter their Skins and Furs, for the Bawbles and Trinkets of the English.

These first Adventurers made a very profitable Voyage, raising at least a Thousand per cent. upon their Cargo. Amongst other Indian Commodities, they brought over Some of that bewitching Vegetable, Tobacco. And this being the first that ever came to England, Sir Walter thought he could do no less than make a present of Some of the brightest of it to His Roial Mistress, for her own Smoaking.

The Queen graciously accepted of it, but finding her Stomach sicken after two or three Whiffs, it was presently whispered by the earl of Leicester's faction, that Sir Walter had certainly Poison'd Her. But Her Majesty soon recovering her Disorder, obliged the Countess of Nottingham and all her Maids to Smoak a whole Pipe out amongst them.

As it happen'd some Ages before to be the fashion to Santer to the Holy Land, and go upon other Quixot Adventures, so it was now grown the Humour to take a Trip to America. The Spaniards had lately discovered Rich Mines in their Part of the West Indies, which made their Maritime Neighbours eager to do so too. This Modish Frenzy being still more Inflam'd by the Charming Account given of Virginia, by the first Adventurers, made many fond of removeing to such a Paradise.

Happy was he, and still happier She, that cou'd get themselves transported, fondly expecting their Coarsest Utensils, in that happy place, would be of Massy Silver.

This made it easy for the Company to procure as many Volunteers as they wanted for their new Colony; but like most other Undertakers who have no Assistance from the Public, they Starved the Design by too much Frugality; for, unwilling to Launch out at first into too much Expense, they Ship't off but few People at a Time, and Those but Scantily provided. The Adventurers were, besides, Idle and extravagant, and expected they might live without work in so plentiful a Country.

These Wretches were set Ashoar not far from Roanoak Inlet, but by some fatal disagreement, or Laziness, were either Starved or cut to Pieces by the Indians.

Several repeated Misadventures of this kind did, for some time, allay the Itch of Sailing to this New World; but the Distemper broke out again about the Year 1606. Then it happened that the Earl of Southampton and several other Persons, eminent for their Quality and Estates, were invited into the Company, who apply'd themselves once more to People the then almost abandon'd Colony. For this purpose they embarkt about an Hundred men, most of them Riprobates of good Familys, and related to some of the company, who were men of Quality and Fortune.

The Ships that carried them made a Shift to find a more direct way to Virginia, and ventured thro the Capes into the Bay of Chesapeak. The same Night they came to an Anchor at the Mouth of Powatan, the same as James River, where they built a Small Fort at a Place call'd Point Comfort.

This Settlement stood its ground from that time forward in spite of all the Blunders and Disagreement of the first Adventurers, and the many Calamitys that befel the Colony afterwards.

The six gentlemen who were first named of the company by the crown, and who were empowered to choose an annual President from among themselves, were always engaged in Factions and Quarrels, while the rest detested Work more than Famine. At this rate the Colony must have come to nothing, had it not been for the vigilance and Bravery of Capt. Smith, who struck a Terrour into all the Indians round about. This Gentleman took some pains to perswade the men to plant Indian corn, but they lookt upon all Labor as a Curse. They chose rather to depend upon the Musty Provisions that were sent from England: and when they fail'd they were forct to take more pains to Seek for Wild Fruits in the Woods, than they would have taken in tilling the Ground. Besides, this Exposd them to be knockt on the head by the Indians, and gave them Fluxes into the Bargain, which thind the Plantation very much. To Supply this mortality, they were reinforct the year following with a greater number of People, amongst which were fewer Gentlemen and more Labourers, who, however, took care not to kill themselves with Work.[1]

These found the First Adventurers in a very starving condition, but relievd their wants with the fresh Supply they brought with them. From Kiquotan they extended themselves as far as James-Town, where like true Englishmen, they built a Church that cost no more than Fifty Pounds, and a Tavern that cost Five hundred.[2]

They had now made peace with the Indians, but there was one thing wanting to make that peace lasting. The Natives coud, by no means, perswade themselves that the English were heartily their Friends, so long as they disdained to intermarry with them. And, in earnest, had the English consulted their own Security and the good of the Colony – Had they intended either to Civilize or Convert these Gentiles, they would have brought their Stomachs to embrace this prudent Alliance.

The Indians are generally tall and well-proportion'd, which may make full Amends for the Darkness of their Complexions. Add to this, that they are healthy & Strong, with Constitutions untainted by Lewdness, and not enfeebled by Luxury. Besides, Morals and all considered, I cant think the Indians were much greater Heathens than the first Adventurers, who, had they been good Christians, would have had the Charity to take this only method of converting the Natives to Christianity. For, after all that can be said, a sprightly Lover is the most prevailing Missionary that can be sent amongst these, or any other Infidels.

Besides, the poor Indians would have had less reason to Complain that the English took away their Land, if they had received it by way of Portion with their Daughters. Had such Affinities been contracted in the Beginning, how much Bloodshed had been prevented, and how populous would the Country have been, and, consequently, how considerable? Nor wou'd the Shade of the Skin have been any reproach at this day; for if a Moor may be washt white in 3 Generations, Surely an Indian might have been blancht in two.

. . .

About the same time New England was pared off from Virginia by Letters Patent, bearing date April the 10th, 1608.[3] Several Gentlemen of the Town and Neighbourhood of Plymouth obtain'd this Grant, with the Ld Chief Justice Popham at their Head.

Their Bounds were Specified to Extend from 38 to 45 Degrees of Northern Latitude, with a Breadth of one Hundred Miles from the Sea Shore. The first 14 Years, this Company encounter'd many Difficulties, and lost many men, tho' far from being discouraged, they sent over Numerous Recruits of Presbyterians, every year, who for all that, had much ado to stand their Ground, with all their Fighting and Praying.

But about the year 1620, a Large Swarm of Dissenters fled thither from the Severities of their Stepmother, the Church. These Saints conceiving the same Aversion to the Copper Complexion of the Natives, with that of the first Adventurers to Virginia, would, on no Terms, contract Alliances with them, afraid perhaps, like the Jews of Old, lest they might be drawn into Idolatry by those Strange Women.

Whatever disgusted them I cant say, but this false delicacy creating in the Indians a Jealousy that the English were ill affected towards them, was the Cause that many of them were cut off, and the rest Exposed to various Distresses.

This Reinforcement was landed not far from Cape Codd, where, for their greater Security they built a Fort, and near it a Small Town, which in Honour of the Proprietors, was call'd New Plymouth. But they Still had many discouragements to Struggle with, tho' by being well Supported from Home, they by Degrees Triumph't over them all.

Their Bretheren, after this, flockt over so fast, that in a few Years they extended the Settlement one hundred Miles along the Coast, including Rhode Island and Martha's Vineyard.

Thus the Colony throve apace, and was throng'd with large Detachments of Independents and Presbyterians, who thought themselves persecuted at home.

Tho' these People may be ridiculd for some Pharisaical Particularitys in their Worship and Behaviour, yet they were very useful Subjects, as being Frugal and Industrious, giving no Scandal or bad Example, at least by any Open and Public Vices. By which excellent Qualities they had much the Advantage of the Southern Colony, who thought their being Members of the Establish't Church sufficient to Sanctifie very loose and Profligate Morals. For this Reason New England improved much faster than Virginia, and in Seven or Eight Years New Plimouth, like Switzerland, seemed too Narrow a Territory for its Inhabitants.

For this Reason, several Gentlemen of Fortune purchas'd of the Company that Canton of New England now called Massachuset colony. And King James confirm'd the Purchase by his Royal Charter, dated March the 4th, 1628. In less than 2 years after, above 1000 of the Puritanical Sect removed thither with considerable Effects, and these were followed by such Crowds, that a Proclamation was issued in England, forbidding any more of his Majesty's Subjects to be Shipt off. But this had the usual Effect of things forbidden, and serv'd only to make the Wilful Independents flock over the faster...

In the Year 1630, the famous City of Boston was built, in a Commodious Situation for Trade and Navigation, the same being on a Peninsula at the Bottom of Massachuset Bay.

This Town is now the most considerable of any on the British Continent, containing at least 8,000 houses and 40,000 Inhabitants. The Trade it drives, is very great to Europe, and to every Part of the West Indies, having near 1,000 Ships and lesser Vessels belonging to it.

Altho the Extent of the Massachuset Colony reach't near one Hundred and Ten Miles in Length, and half as much in Breadth, yet many of its Inhabitants, thinking they wanted Elbow-room, quitted their Old Seats in the Year 1636, and formed 2 New Colonies: that of Connecticut and New Haven. These King Charles the 2d erected into one Government in 1664[4] and gave them many Valuable Priviledges, and among the rest, that of chusing their own Governors. The Extent of these united Colonies may be about Seventy Miles long and fifty broad.

Besides these Several Settlements, there Sprang up still another, a little more Northerly, called New Hampshire. But that consisting of no more than two Counties, and not being in condition to Support the Charge of a Distinct Government, was glad to be incorporated with that of Massachuset, but upon Condition, however, of being Named in all Public Acts, for fear of being quite lost and forgot in the Coalition.

In like manner New Plymouth joyn'd itself to Massachuset, except only Rhode Island, which, tho' of small Extent, got itself erected into a Separate government by a Charter from King Charles the 2d, soon after the Restoration, and continues so to this day.

These Governments all continued in Possession of their Respective Rights and Priviledges till the Year 1683[5] when that of Massachuset was made Void in England by a Quo Warranto.

In Consequence of which the King was pleased to name Sir Edmund Andros His first Governor of that Colony. This Gentleman, it seems, ruled them with a Rod of Iron till the Revolution, when they laid unhallowed Hands upon Him, and sent him Prisoner to England.

This undutiful proceeding met with an easy forgiveness at that happy Juncture. King William and his Royal Consort were not only pleasd to overlook this Indignity offered to their Governor, but being made sensible how unfairly their Charter had been taken away, most graciously granted them a new one.

By this some new Franchises were given them, as an Equivalent for those of Coining Money and Electing a governour, which were taken away. However, the other Colonies of Connecticut and

Rhode Island had the luck to remain in Possession of their Original Charters, which to this Day have never been calld in Question.

. . .

Another Limb lopt off from Virginia was New York, which the Dutch seized very unfairly, on pretence of having Purchasd if from Captain Hudson, the first Discoverer. Nor was their way of taking Possession of it a whit more justifiable than their pretended Title.

Their West India Company tamperd with some worthy English skippers (who had contracted with a Swarm of English Dissenters to transport them to Hudson river) by no means to land them there, but to carry 'em some leagues more northerly.

This Dutch Finesse took Exactly, and gave the Company time soon after to seize the Hudson River for themselves. But Sr Samuel Argall, then governor of Virginia, understanding how the King's Subjects had been abused by these Republicans, marcht thither with a good Force, and obligd them to renounce all pretensions to that Country. The worst of it was, the Knight depended on their Parole to Ship themselves to Brasile, but took no measures to make this Slippery Peope as good as their Word.

No sooner was the good Governor retired, but the honest Dutch began to build Forts and strengthen themselves in their ill-gotten Possessions; nor did any of the King's Liege People take the trouble to drive these Intruders thence. The Civil War in England, And the Confusions it brought forth, allowed no Leisure to such distant Considerations. Tho tis strange that the Protector, who neglected no Occasion to mortify the Dutch, did not afterwards call them to Account for this breach of Faith. However, after the Restoration, the King sent a Squadron of his Ships of War, under the Command of Sir Robert Carr, and reduced that Province to his Obedience.

Some time after, His Majesty was Pleasd to grant that Country to his Royal Highness, the Duke of York, by Letters Patent, dated March the 12th, 1664. But to shew the Modesty of the Dutch to the Life, tho they had no Shaddow of Right to New York, yet they demanded Surinam, a more valuable Country, as an Equivalent for it, and our able Ministers at that time had the Generosity to give it them.

But what wounded Virginia deepest was the cutting off MARY-LAND from it, by Charter from King Charles the 1st, to sir George Calvert, afterwards Ld Baltimore, bearing date the 20th of June, 1632. The Truth of it is, it begat much Speculation in those days, how it came about that a good Protestant King should bestow so bountiful a Grant upon a Zealous Roman catholic. But 'tis probable it was one fatal Instance amongst many other of his Majesty's complaisance to the Queen.

However that happened, 'tis certain this Province afterwards provd a Commodious Retreat for Persons of that Communion. The Memory of the Gun-Powder-Treason-Plot was Still fresh in every body's mind, and made England too hot for Papists to live in, without danger of being burnt with the Pope, every 5th of November; for which reason Legions of them transplanted themselves to Maryland in Order to be Safe, as well from the Insolence of the Populace as the Rigour of the Government.

Not only the Gun-Powder-Treason, but every other Plot, both pretended and real, that has been trump't up in England ever Since, has helpt to People his Lordship's Propriety.

But what has provd most Serviceable to it was the Grand Rebellion against King Charles the 1st, when every thing that bore the least tokens of Popery was sure to be demolisht, and every man that Profest it was in Jeopardy of Suffering the same kind of Martyrdom the Romish Priests do in Sweden.

Soon after the Reduction of New York, the Duke was pleasd to grant out of it all that Tract of Land included between Hudson and Delaware Rivers, to the Lord Berkley and Sir George Carteret, by deed dated June the 24th, 1664. And when these Grantees came to make Partition of this Territory, His Lordp's Moiety was calld West Jersey and that to Sir George, East Jersey.

But before the Date of this Grant, the Swedes began to gain Footing in part of that Country; tho, after they saw the Fate of New York, they were glad to Submit to the King of England, on the easy Terms of remaining in their Possessions, and rendering a Moderate Quit-rent. Their Posterity continue there to this Day, and think their Lot cast in a much fairer Land than Dalicarlia.[a]

The Proprietors of New Jersey, finding more Trouble than Profit in their new Dominions, made over their Right to several other Persons, who obtained a fresh Grant from his Royal Highness, dated March 14th, 1682.

Several of the Grantees, being Quakers and Anabaptists, faild not to encourage many of their own Perswasion to remove to this Peaceful Region. Amongst them were a Swarm of Scots Quakers, who were not tolerated to exercise the Gifts of the Spirit in their own Country.

Besides the hopes of being Safe from Persecution in this Retreat, the New Proprietors inveigled many over by this tempting Account

[a] The name of a Swedish province.

of the Country: that it was a Place free from those 3 great Scourges of Mankind, Priests, Lawyers, and Physicians. Nor did they tell a Word of Lye, for the People were yet too poor to maintain these Learned Gentlemen, who, every where, love to be paid well for what they do; and, like the Jews, cant breathe in a Climate where nothing is to be got.

The Jerseys continued under the Government of these Proprietors till the Year 1702, when they made a formal Surrender of the Dominion to the Queen, reserving however the Property of the Soil to themselves. So soon as the Bounds of New Jersey came to be distinctly laid off, it appeared that there was still a Narrow Slipe of Land, lying betwixt that Colony and Maryland. Of this, William Penn, a Man of much Worldly Wisdom, and some Eminence among the Quakers, got early Notice, and, by the Credit he had with the Duke of York, obtain a Patent for it, Dated March the 4th, 1680.

It was a little Surprising to some People how a Quaker should be so much in the good Graces of a Popish Prince; tho, after all, it may be pretty well Accounted for. This Ingenious Person had not been bred a Quaker; but, in his Earlier days, had been a Man of Pleasure about the Town. He had a beautiful form and very taking Address, which made him Successful with the Ladies, and Particularly with a Mistress of the Duke of Monmouth. By this Gentlewoman he had a Daughter, who had Beauty enough to raise her to be a Dutchess, and continued to be a Toast full 30 Years.

But this Amour had like to have brought our Fine Gentleman in Danger of a Duell, had he not discreetly shelterd himself under this peaceable Perswasion. Besides, his Father having been a Flag-Officer in the Navy, while the Duke of York was Lord High Admiral, might recommend the Son to his Favour. This piece of secret History I thought proper to mention, to wipe off the Suspicion of his having been Popishly inclind.[6]

This Gentleman's first Grant confind Him within pretty Narrow Bounds, giving him only that Portion of Land which contains Buckingham, Philadelphia and Chester Counties. But to get these Bounds a little extended, He pusht His Interest still further with His Royal Highness, and obtain a fresh Grant of the three Lower Counties, called New-Castle, Kent and Sussex, which still remain within the New York Patent, and had been luckily left out of the Grant of New Jersey.

The Six Counties being thus incorporated, the Proprietor dignifyd the whole with the Name of Pensilvania.

The Quakers flockt over to this Country in Shoals, being averse to go to Heaven the same way with the Bishops. Amongst them were not a few of good Substance, who went Vigorously upon every kind of Improvement; and thus much I may truly say in their Praise, that by Diligence and Frugality, For which this Harmless Sect is remarkable, and by haveing no Vices but such as are Private, they have in a few Years made Pensilvania a very fine Country.

The truth is, they have observed exact Justice with all the Natives that border upon them; they have purchasd all their Lands from the Indians; and tho they paid but a Trifle for them, it has procured them the Credit of being more righteous than their Neighbours. They have likewise had the Prudence to treat them kindly upon all Occasions, which has savd them from many Wars and Massacres wherein the other Colonies have been indiscreetly involved. The Truth of it is, a People whose Principles forbid them to draw the Carnal Sword, were in the Right to give no Provocation.

Both the French and the Spaniards had, in the Name of their Respective Monarchs, long ago taken Possession of that Part of the Northern Continent that now goes by the Name of Carolina; but finding it Produced neither Gold nor Silver, as they greedily expected, and meeting such returns from the Indians as their own Cruelty and Treachery deserved, they totally abandond it. In this deserted Condition that country lay for the Space of 90 Years, till King Charles the 2d, finding it a DERELICT, granted it away to the Earl of Clarendon and others, by His Royal Charter, dated March the 24th, 1663. The Boundary of that Grant towards Virginia was a due West Line from Luck-Island, (the same as Colleton Island), lying in 36 degrees N. Latitude, quite to the South Sea.

But afterwards Sir William Berkeley, who was one of the Grantees and at that time Governour of Virginia, finding a Territory of 31 Miles in Breadth between the Inhabited Part of Virginia and the above-mentioned Boundary of Carolina, advisd the Lord Clarendon of it. And His Lordp had Interest enough with the King to obtain a Second Patent to include it, dated June the 30th, 1665.

This last Grant describes the Bounds between Virginia and Carolina in these Words: 'To run from the North End of Corotuck-Inlet, due West to Weyanoke Creek, lying within or about the Degree of Thirty-Six and Thirty Minutes of Northern Latitude, and from thence West, in a direct Line, as far as the South-Sea.'[7] Without question, this Boundary was well known at the time the Charter was Granted, but in a long Course of years Weynoke Creek lost its name, so that it became a Controversy where it lay. Some Ancient Persons in Virginia affirmd it was the same with Wicocon, and others again in Carolina were as Positive it was Nottoway River.

In the mean time, the People on the Frontiers Enterd for Land, & took out Patents by Guess, either from the King or the Lords Proprietors. But the Crown was like to be the loser by this Incertainty, because the Terms both of taking up and seating Land were easier much in Carolina. The Yearly Taxes to the Public were likewise there less burdensome, which laid Virginia under a Plain disadvantage.

This Consideration put that Government upon entering into Measures with North Carolina, to terminate the Dispute, and settle a Certain Boundary between the two colonies. All the Difficulty was, to find out which was truly Weyanoke Creek. The Difference was too Considerable to be given up by either side, there being a Territory of 15 Miles betwixt the two Streams in controversy.

However, till that Matter could be adjusted, it was agreed on both sides, that no Lands at all Should be granted within the disputed Bounds. Virginia observed this Agreement punctually, but I am sorry I cant say the Same of North-Carolina. The great Officers of that Province were loath to lose the Fees accrueing from the Grants of Land, and so private Interest got the better of Public Spirit; and I wish that were the only Place in the World where such politicks are fashionable.

. . .

Accordingly an Order was sent by the late King to Mr. Gooch, afterwards Lievt Governor of Virginia, to pursue those Preliminaries exactly. In Obedience thereunto, he was pleased to appoint Three of the Council of that colony to be Commissioners on the Part of Virginia, who, in Conjunction with others to be named by the Governor of North Carolina, were to settle the Boundary between the 2 Governments, upon the Plan of the above-mentioned Articles.

Two Experienct Surveyors were at the same time directed to wait upon the Commissioners, Mr. Mayo, who made the Accurate Mapp of Barbadoes, and Mr. Irvin, the Mathematick Professor of William and Mary Colledge. And because a good Number of Men were to go upon this Expedition, a Chaplain was appointed to attend them, and the rather because the People on the Frontiers of North-Carolina, who have no Minister near them, might have an Opportunity to get themselves and their Children baptizd.

. . .

In the Mean time, the requisite Preparations were made for so long and tiresome a Journey: and because there was much work to be done and some Danger from the Indians, in the uninhabited Part of the Country, it was necessary to provide a Competent Number of Men.

Accordingly, seventeen able Hands were listed on the Part of Virginia, who were most of them Indian Traders and expert Woodsmen.

27. These good Men were ordered to come armed with a Musquet and a Tomahack, or large Hatchet, and provided with a Sufficient Quantity of Ammunition.

They likewise brought Provisions of their own for ten days, after which time they were to be furnisht by the Government. Their March was appointed to be on the 27th of February, on which day one of the Commissioners met them at their Rendezvous, and proceeded with them as far as Colo Allen's. This Gentleman is a great oeconomist, and Skilld in all the Arts of living well at an easy expense.

28. They proceeded in good Order through Surry County, as far as the Widdow Allen's who had copied Solomon's complete housewife exactly. At this Gentlewoman's House, the other two Commissioners had appointed to join them, but were detained by some Accident at Williamsburg, longer than their appointment.

29. They pursued their March thro the Isle of Wight and observd a most dreadful Havock made by a late Hurricane, which happend in August, 1726. The Violence of it had not reachd above a Quarter of a Mile in Breadth. But within that Compass had levelld all before it. Both Trees and Houses were laid flat on the Ground, and several things hurld to an incredible distance. Tis happy such violent Gusts are confined to so narrow a Channel because they carry desolation wherever they go.[8] In the Evening they reacht Mr. Godwin's, on the South Branch of Nansemond River, where they were treated with abundance of Primitive Hospitality.

March 1. This Gentleman was so kind as to shorten their Journey, by setting them over the river. They coasted the N E Side of the Dismal for several miles together, and found all the Grounds bordering upon it very full of Sloughs. The Trees that grew near it lookt very Reverend, with the long Moss that hung dangling from their Branches. Both cattle and Horses eat this Moss greedily in Winter when other Provender is Scarce, tho it is apt to scowr them at first. In that moist Soil too grew abundance of that kind of Myrtle which bears the Candle-Berries. There was likewise, here and there, a Gall-bush, which is a beautiful Evergreen, and may be cut into any Shape. It derives its Name from its Berries turning Water black, like the Galls of an oak.

When this Shrub is transplanted into Gardens, it will not thrive without frequent watering.

The two other commissioners came up with them just at their Journey's end, and that evening they arrivd all together at Mr.

Craford's, who lives on the South Branch of Elizabeth-River, over against Norfolk. Here the Commissioners left the Men with all the Horses and heavy Baggage, and crosst the River with their Servants only, for fear of making a Famine in the Town.

Norfolk has most the ayr of a Town of any in Virginia. There were then near 20 Brigantines and Sloops riding at the Wharves, and oftentimes they have more. It has all the advantages of Situation requisite for Trade and Navigation. There is a Secure Harbour for a good Number of Ships of any Burthen. Their River divides itself into 3 several Branches, which are all Navigable. The Town is so near the sea, that its Vessels may Sail in and out in a few Hours. Their Trade is Chiefly to the West-Indies, whither they export abundance of Beef, Pork, Flour and Lumber. The worst of it is, they contribute much towards debauching the Country by importing abundance of Rum, which, like Ginn in Great Britain, breaks the Constitution, Vitiates the Morals, and ruins the Industry of most of the Poor people of this Country.

This Place is the Mart for most of the Commodities produced in the Adjacent Parts of North Carolina. They have a pretty deal of Lumber from the Borderers on the Dismal, who make bold with the King's Land there abouts, without the least Ceremony. They not only maintain their Stocks upon it, but get Boards, Shingles and other Lumber out of it in great Abundance.

The Town is built on a level Spot of Ground upon Elizabeth River, the Banks whereof are neither so high as to make the landing of Goods troublesome, or so low as to be in Danger of over flowing. The Streets are Straight, and adorned with several Good Houses, which Encrease every Day. It is not a Town of Ordinarys and Publick Houses, like most others in this Country, but the Inhabitants consist of Merchants, Ship-Carpenters and other useful Artisans, with Sailors enough to manage their Navigation. With all these Conveniences, it lies under the two great disadvantages that most of the Towns in Holland do, by having neither good Air nor good Water. The two Cardinal Vertues that make a Place thrive, Industry and Frugality, are seen here in Perfection; and so long as they can banish Luxury and Idleness, the Town will remain in a happy and flourishing Condition.

The Method of building Wharffs here is after the following Manner. They lay down long Pine Logs, that reach from the Shore to the Edge of the Channel. These are bound fast together by Cross-Pieces notcht into them, according to the Architecture of the Log-Houses in North Carolina. A wharff built thus will stand several Years, in spight of the Worm, which bites here very much, but may be soon repaired in a Place where so many Pines grow in the Neighbourhood.

The Commissioners endeavourd, in this Town, to list Three more men to serve as Guides in that dirty Part of the Country, but found that these People knew just enough of that frightful Place to avoid it.

They had been told that those Netherlands were full of Bogs, of Marshes and Swamps, not fit for Human Creatures to engage in, and this was Reason enough for them not to hazard their Persons. So they told us, flat and plain, that we might een daggle thro the mire by Our-Selves for them.

The worst of it was, we coud not learn from any body in this Town, what Rout to take to Coratuck Inlet; till at last we had the fortune to meet with a Borderer upon North Carolina, who made a rought Sketch of that Part of the Country. Thus, upon seeing how the Land lay, we determind to march directly to Prescot Landing upon N W River, and proceed from thence by Water to the Place where our Line was to begin.

4. In Pursuance of this Resolution we crost the River this Morning to Powder-Point, where we all took Horse; and the Grandees of the Town, with geat Courtesy, conducted us Ten Miles on our way, as far as the long Bridge built over the S Branch of the River.

. . .

We rowd down N W River about 18 miles, as far as the Mouth of it, where it empties itself into Albemarle Sound. It was a really Delightful Sight, all the way, to see the Banks of the River adornd with Myrtle, Laurel and Bay-Trees, which preserve their Verdure the Year round, tho it must be ownd that these beautiful Plants, sacred to Venus and Appollo, grow commonly in very dirty Soil. The River is, in most Places, fifty or Sixty Yards wide, without spreading much wider at the Mouth. Tis remarkable it was never known to Ebb and flow till the year 1713, when a Violent Storm opend a new Inlet, about 5 Miles South of the old one; since which Convulsion, the Old Inlet is almost choakd up by the Shifting of the Sand, and grows both Narrower and and Shoaller every day.

It was dark before we could reach the Mouth of the River, where our wayward Stars directed us to a Miserable Cottage. The Landlord was lately removed, Bag and Baggage, from Maryland, thro a Strong Antipathy he had to work and paying his Debts. For want of our Tent, we were obligd to Shelter our Selves in this wretched Hovel, where we were almost devourd by Vermin of Various kinds. However, we were above complaining, being all Philosophers enough to improve such Slender Distresses into Mirth and good Humour.

5. The Day being now come, on which we had agreed to meet the Commissioners of North Carolina, we embarkd very early, which we coud the easier do, having no Temptation to stay where we were. We Shapt our Course along the South End of Knot's Island, there being no Passage open on the North.

Farther Still to the Southward of us, we discovered two Smaller Islands, that go by the names of Bell's and Churche's Isles. We also saw a small New England Sloop riding in the Sound, a little to the South of our Course. She had come in at the New-Inlet, as all other Vessels have done since the opening of it. This Navigation is a little difficult, and fit only for Vessels that draw no more than ten feet Water.

The Trade hither is engrosst by the Saints of New England, who carry off a great deal of Tobacco, without troubling themselves with paying that Impertinent Duty of a Penny a Pound.

It was just Noon before we arrivd at Coratuck Inlet, which is now so shallow that the Breakers fly over it with a horrible Sound, and at the same time afford a very wild Prospect. Or the North side of the Inlet, the High Land terminated in a Bluff Point, from which a Spit of Sand extended itself towards the South-East, full half a Mile. The Inlet lies between that Spit and another on the South of it, leaving an Opening of not quite a Mile, which at this day is not practicable for any Vessel whatsoever. And as shallow as it now is, it continues to fill up more and more, both the Wind and Waves rolling in the Sands from the Eastern Shoals.

About two a Clock in the Afternoon we were joind by two of the Carolina Commissioners, attended by Mr. S—n, their Surveyor. The other two were not quite so punctual, which was the more unlucky for us, because there could be no sport till they came. These Gentlemen, it seems, had the Carolina-Commission in their keeping, notwithstanding which they coud not forbear paying too much regard to a Proverb – fashionable in ther Country, – not to make more hast than good Speed.

However, that we who were punctual might not spend our precious time unprofitably, we took the Several bearings of the Coast. We also surveyd part of the Adjacent High Land, which had scarcely any Trees growing upon it, but Cedars. Among the Shrubs, we were shewed here and there a Bush of Carolina-Tea calld Japon, which is one Species of the Phylarrea. This is an Evergreen, the Leaves whereof have some resemblance to Tea, but differ very widely both in Tast and Flavour.

We also found some few Plants of the Spired Leaf Silk grass, which is likewise an Evergreen, bearing on a lofty Stemm a large Cluster of Flowers of a Pale Yellow. Of the Leaves of this Plant the People thereabouts twist very strong Cordage.

A vertuoso might divert himself here very well, in picking up Shells of various Hue and Figure, and amongst the rest, that Species of Conque Shell which the Indian Peak is made of.[b] The Extremities of these Shells are Blue and the rest white, so that Peak of both these Colours are drilld out of one and the same Shell, serving the Natives both for Ornament and Money, and are esteemd by them far beyond Gold and Silver.

The Cedars were of Singular use to us in the Absence of our Tent, which we had left with the rest of the Baggage for fear of overloading the Periaugas. We made a Circular Hedge of the Branches of this Tree, Wrought so close together as to fence us against the Cold Winds. We then kindled a rouseing fire in the Center of it, and lay round it, like so many Knights Templars. But, as comfortable as this Lodging was, the Surveyors turnd out about 2 in the Morning to try the Variation by a Meridian taken from the North Star, and found it to be somewhat less than three degrees West.

The Commissioners of the Neighbouring Colony came better provided for the Belly than the Business. They brought not above two men along with them that would put their Hands to any thing but the Kettle and the Frying-Pan. These spent so much of their Industry that way, that they had as little Spirit as Inclination for Work.

6. At Noon, having a Perfect Observation, we found the Latitude of Coratuck Inlet to be 36 Degrees and 31 Minutes.

Whilst we were busied about these Necessary Matters, our Skipper row'd to an Oyster Bank just by, and loaded his Periauga with Oysters as Savoury and well-tasted as those from Colchester or Walfleet, and had the advantage of them, too, by being much larger and fatter.

. . .

While we continued here, we were told that on the South Shore, not far from the Inlet, dwelt a Marooner, that Modestly call'd himself a Hermit, tho' he forfeited that Name by Suffering a wanton Female to cohabit with Him.

His Habitation was a Bower, cover'd with Bark after the Indian Fashion, which in that mild Situation protected him pretty well from the Weather. Like the Ravens, he neither plow'd nor sow'd, but Subsisted chiefly upon Oysters, which his Handmaid made a Shift to gather from the Adjacent Rocks. Sometimes, too, for Change of

[b] Wampum.

Dyet, he sent her to drive up the Neighbour's Cows, to moisten their Mouths with a little Milk. But as for raiment, he depended mostly upon his Length of Beard, and She upon her Length of Hair, part of which she brought decently forward, and the rest dangled behind quite down to her Rump, like one of Herodotus's East Indian Pigmies.

Thus did these Wretches live in a dirty State of Nature, and were mere Adamites, Innocence only excepted.

7. This Morning the Surveyors began to run the Dividing line from the Cedar-Post we had driven into the Sand, allowing near 3 Degrees for the Variation. Without making this Just allowance, we should not have obeyd his Majesty's order in running a Due West Line. It seems the former Commissioners had not been so exact, which gave our Friends of Carolina but too just an Exception to their Proceedings.

The Line cut Dosier's Island, consisting only of a Flat Sand, with here and there an humble Shrub growing upon it. From thence it crost over a narrow Arm of the Sound into Knot's Island, and there Split a Plantation belonging to William Harding.

The Day being far spent, we encampt in this Man's Pasture, tho' it lay very low, and the Season now inclin'd People to Aguish Distempers. He sufferd us to cut Cedar-Branches for our Enclosure, and other Wood for Firing, to correct the moist Air and drive away the Damps. Our Landlady, in the Days of her Youth, it seems, had been a Laundress in the Temple, and talkt over her Adventures in that Station, with as much pleasure as an Old Soldier talks over his Battles and Distempers, and I believe with as many Additions to the Truth.

The Soil is good in many Places of this Island, and the Extent of it pretty large. It lyes in the form of a Wedge: the South End of it is Several Miles over, but towards the North it Sharpens into a Point. It is a Plentiful Place for Stock, by reason of the wide Marshes adjacent to it, and because of its warm Situation. But the Inhabitants pay a little dear for this Convenience, by losing as much Blood in the Summer Season by the infinite Number of Mosquetas, as all their beef and Pork can recruit in the Winter.

. . .

8. By break of Day we sent away our Largest Periauga, with the Baggage, round the South end of Knot's Island, with Orders to the Men to wait for us in the Mouth of North River. Soon after, we embarkt ourselves on board the smaller Vessel, with Intent, if possible, to find a Passage round the North End of the Island.

We found this Navigation very difficult, by reason of the Continued Shoals, and often stuck fast aground; for tho' the Sound spreads many miles, yet it is in most places extremely Shallow, and requires a Skilful Pilot to Steer even a Canoe safe over it. It was almost as hard to keep our Temper as to keep the Channel, in this provoking Situation. But the most impatient amongst us strokt down their Choler and swallow'd their curses, lest, if they suffer'd them to break out, they might sound like Complaining, which was expressly forbid, as the first Step to Sedition.

At a distance we descry'd Several Islands to the Northward of us, the largest of which goes by the Name of Cedar Island. Our periauga stuck so often that we had a fair chance to be benighted in this wide Water, which must certainly have been our Fate, had we not luckily spied a Canoe that was giving a Fortune-teller a cast from Princess Anne County over to North Carolina. But, as conjurers are Sometimes mistaken, the Man mistrusted we were Officers of Justice in pursuit of a Young Wench he had carry'd off along with him. We gave the Canoe Chase for more than an Hour and when we came up with her, threatend to make them all prisoners unless they would direct us into the right Channel.

By the Pilotage of these People we row'd up an Arm of the Sound, call'd the Back-Bay, till we came to the Head of it. There we were stoppt by a miry Pocoson full half a Mile in Breadth, thro' which we were oblig'd to daggle on foot, plungeing now and then, tho' we pickt our Way, up to the Knees in Mud. At the End of this Charming walk we gain'd the Terra Firma of Princess Anne County. In that Dirty Condition we were afterwards oblig'd to foot it two Miles, as far as John Heath's Plantation, where we expected to meet the Surveyors & the men who waited upon them.

. . .

All the People in the Neighbourhood flockt to John Heath's, to behold such Rarities as they fancied us to be. The Men left their belov'd Chimney Corners, the good women their Spinning Wheels, and some, of more Curiosity than Ordinary, rose out of their sick Beds, to come and stare at us. They lookt upon us as a Troop of Knight Errants, who were running this great Risque of our Lives, as they imagin'd, for the Public Weal; and some of the gravest of them question'd much whether we were not all Criminals, condemned to this dirty work for Offences against the State.

What puzzled them most was, what cou'd make our men so very Light-hearted under such intolerable Drudgery. 'Ye have little reason to be merry, My Masters', said one of them, with a very solemn Face, 'I fancy the Pocoson you must Struggle with to-morrow will make you change your Note, and try what Metal you are made of. Ye are, to be sure, the first of Human Race that ever had the Boldness to attempt it, and I dare say will be the last. If, therefore, you have any Worldly Goods to dispose of, My Advice is that you make your Wills this very Night, for fear you die Intestate to-Morrow.' But, alas! these fright-full Tales were so far from disheartening the men, that they serv'd only to whet their Resolution.

9. The Surveyors enter'd Early upon their Business this Morning, and ran the Line thro' Mr. Eyland's Plantation, as far as the Banks of North River. They passt over it in the Periauga, and landed in Gibbs' Marsh, which was a mile in Breadth, and tolerably firm. They trudg'd thro' this Marsh without much difficulty as far as the High Land, which promis'd more Fertility than any they had seen in these lower Parts. But this firm Land lasted not long before they came upon the dreadful Pocoson they had been threaten'd with. Nor did they find it one Jot better than it had been painted to them. The Beavers and Otters had render'd it quite impassable for any Creature but themselves.

Our poor Fellows had much ado to drag their Legs after them in this Quagmire, but disdaining to be baulkt, they cou'd hardly be persuaded from pressing forward by the Surveyors, who found it absolutely Necessary to make a Traverse in the Deepest Place, to prevent their Sticking fast in the Mire, and becoming a Certain Prey to the Turkey-Buzzards.

This Horrible Day's Work Ended two Miles to the Northward of Mr. Merchant's Plantation, divided from N W River by a Narrow Swamp, which is causeway'd over. We took up our Quarters in the open Field, not far from the House, correcting, by a Fire as large as a Roman-Funeral-Pile, the Aguish Exhalations arising from the Sunken Grounds that Surrounded us...

10. The Sabbath happen'd very opportunely to give some ease to our jaded People, who rested religiously from every work, but that of cooking the Kettle. We observed very few corn-fields in our Walks, and those very small, which seem'd the Stranger to us, because we could see no other Tokens of Husbandry or Improvement. But, upon further Inquiry, we were given to understand People only made Corn for themselves and not for their Stocks, which know very well how to get their own Living.

Both Cattle and Hogs ramble in the Neighbouring Marshes and Swamps, where they maintain themselves the whole Winter long, and are not fetch'd home till the Spring. Thus these Indolent Wretches, during one half of the Year, lose the Advantage of the Milk of their cattle, as well as their Dung, and many of the poor

Creatures perish in the Mire, into the bargain, by this ill Management.

Some, who pique themselves more upon Industry than their Neighbours, will, now and then, in complement to their Cattle, cut down a Tree whose Limbs are loaden with the Moss aforemention'd. The trouble wou'd be too great to Climb the Tree in order to gather this Provender, but the Shortest way (which in this Country is always counted the best) is to fell it, just like the Lazy Indians, who do the same by such Trees as bear fruit, and so make one Harvest for all. By this bad Husbandry Milk is so Scarce, in the Winter Season, that were a Big-belly'd Woman to long for it, She would lose her Longing. And, in truth, I believe this is often the Case, and at the same time a very good reason why so many People in this Province are markt with a Custard Complexion.

The only Business here is raising of Hogs, which is manag'd with the least Trouble, and affords the Diet they are most fond of. The Truth of it is, the Inhabitants of N Carolina devour so much Swine's flesh, that it fills them full of gross Humours. For want too of a constant Supply of Salt, they are commonly obliged to eat it Fresh, and that begets the highest taint of Scurvy. Thus, whenever a Severe Cold happens to Constitutions thus Vitiated, tis apt to improve into the Yaws, called there very justly the country-Distemper. This has all the Symptoms of the Pox, with this Aggravation, that no Preparation of Mercury will touch it. First it seizes the Throat, next the Palate, and lastly shews its spite to the poor Nose, of which tis apt in a small time treacherously to undermine the Foundation.

This Calamity is so common and familiar here, that it ceases to be a Scandal, and in the disputes that happen about Beauty, the Noses have in some Companies much ado to carry it. Nay, tis said that once, after three good Pork years, a Motion had like to have been made in the House of Burgesses, that a Man with a Nose shou'd be incapable of holding any Place of Profit in the Province; which Extraordinary Motion could never have been intended without Some Hopes of a Majority.

Thus, considering the foul and pernicious Effects of Eating Swine's Flesh in a hot Country, it was wisely forbidden and made an Abomination to the Jews, who liv'd much in the same Latitude with Carolina.

11. We ordered the Surveyors early to their Business, who were blesst with pretty dry Grounds for three Miles together.

. . .

We had encampt so early, that we found time in the Evening to walk near half a Mile into the Woods. There we came upon a Family of Mulattoes, that call'd themselvs free, tho' by the Shyness of the Master of the House, who took care to keep least in Sight, their Freedom seem'd a little Doubtful. It is certain many Slaves Shelter themselves in this Obscure Part of the World, nor will any of their righteous Neighbours discover them. On the Contrary, they find their Account in Settling such Fugitives on some out-of-the-way-corner of their Land, to raise Stocks for a mean and inconsiderable Share, well knowing their Condition makes it necessary for them to Submit to any Terms.

Nor were these worthy Borderers content to Shelter Runaway Slaves, but Debtors and Criminals have often met with the like Indulgence. But if the Government of North Carolina has encourag'd this unneighbourly Policy in order to increase their People, it is no more than what Ancient Rome did before them, which was made a City of Refuge for all Debtors and Fugitives, and from that wretched Beginning grew up in time to be Mistress of a great Part of the World. And, considering how Fortune delights in bringing great things out of Small, who knows but Carolina may, one time or other, come to be the Seat of some other great Empire?

12. Every thing had been so soakt with the Rain, that we were oblig'd to lie by a good Part of the Morning and dry them. However, that time was not lost, because it gave the Surveyors an Opportunity of Platting off their Work, and taking the Course of the River. It likewise helpt to recruit the Spirits of the Men, who had been a little harass'd with Yesterday's March. Notwithstanding all this, we crosst the River before Noon, and advanc'd our Line 3 Miles. It was not possible to make more of it, by reason good Part of the way was either Marsh or Pocoson...

In the Evening we took up our Quarters in Mr. Ballance's Pasture, a little above the Bridge built over N W River. There we discharg'd the two Periaugas, which in truth had been very Servicable in transporting us over the Many Waters in that Dirty and Difficult Part of our Business.

Our Landlord had a tolerable good House and Clean Furniture, and yet we cou'd not be tempted to lodge in it. We chose rather to lye in the open Field, for fear of growing too tender. A clear Sky, spangled with Stars, was our Canopy, which being the last thing we saw before we fell asleep, gave us Magnificent Dreams. The Truth of it is, we took so much pleasure in that natural kind of Lodging, that I think at the foot of the Account Mankind are great Losers by the Luxury of Feather-Beds and warm apartments...

13. Early this Morning our Chaplain repair'd to us with the Men

we had left at Mr. Wilson's. We had sent for them the Evening before to relieve those who had the Labour-Oar from Corotuck-Inlet. But to our great surprise, they petition'd not to be reliev'd, hoping to gain immortal Reputation by being the first of Mankind that Ventur'd thro' the great Dismal. But the rest being equally Ambitious of the same Honour, it was but fair to decide their Pretensions by Lot. After Fortune had declar'd herself, those which she had excluded offer'd Money to the Happy Persons to go in their Stead. But Hercules would have as soon sold the Glory of cleansing the Augean Stables, which was pretty near the same Sort of Work.

. . .

Tis hardly credible how little the Bordering inhabitants were acquainted with this mighty Swamp, notwithstanding they had liv'd their whole lives within Smell of it. Yet, as great Strangers as they were to it, they pretended to be very exact in their Account of its Dimensions, and were positive it could not be above 7 or 8 Miles wide, but knew no more of the Matter than Star-gazers know of the Distance of the Fixt Stars. At the Same time, they were Simple enough to amuse our Men with Idle Stories of the Lyons, Panthers and Alligators, they were like to encounter in that dreadful Place.

In short, we saw plainly there was no Intelligence of this Terra Incognita to be got, but from our own Experience. For that Reason it was resolv'd to make the requisite Dispositions to enter it next Morning. We allotted every one of the Surveyors for this painful Enterprise, with 12 Men to attend them. Fewer than that cou'd not be employ'd in clearing the way, carrying the Chain, marking the Trees, and bearing the necessary Bedding and Provisions.

. . .

14. Before nine of the Clock this Morning, the Provisions, Bedding and other Necessaries, were made up into Packs for the Men to carry on their Shoulders into the Dismal. They were victuall'd for 8 days at full Allowance, Nobody doubting but that wou'd be abundantly Sufficient to carry them thro' that Inhospitable Place; nor Indeed was it possible for the Poor Fellows to Stagger under more. As it was, their Loads weigh'd from 60 to 70 Pounds, in just Proportion to the Strength of those who were to bear them.

Twou'd have been unconscionable to have Saddled them with Burthens heavier than that, when they were to lugg them thro' a filthy Bogg, which was hardly practicable with no Burthen at all.

Besides this Luggage at their Backs, they were oblig'd to measure the distance, mark the Trees, and clear the way for the Surveyors every Step they went. It was really a Pleasure to see with how much

Cheerfulness they undertook, and with how much Spirit they went thro' all this Drudgery. For their Greater Safety, the Commissioners took care to furnish them with Peruvian-Bark, Rhubarb and Hipocoacanah, in case they might happen, in that wet Journey, to be taken with fevers or Fluxes.

Altho' there was no need of Example to inflame Persons already so cheerful, yet to enter the People with better grace, the Author and two more of the Commissioners accompanied them half a Mile into the Dismal. The Skirts of it were thinly Planted with Dwarf Reeds and Gall-Bushes, but when we got into the Dismal itself, we found the Reeds grew there much taller and closer, and, to mend the matter was so interlac'd with bamboe-briars, that there was no scuffling thro' them without the help of Pioneers. At the same time, we found the Ground moist and trembling under our feet like a Quagmire, insomuch that it was an easy Matter to run a Ten-Foot-Pole up to the Head in it, without exerting any uncommon Strength to do it.

Two of the Men, whose Burthens were the least cumbersome, had orders to march before, with their Tomahawks, and clear the way, in order to make an Opening for the Surveyors. By their Assistance we made a Shift to push the Line half a Mile in 3 Hours, and then reacht a small piece of firm Land, about 100 Yards wide, Standing up above the rest like an Island. Here the people were glad to lay down their Loads and take a little refreshment, while the happy man, whose lot it was to carry the Jugg of Rum, began already, like Aesop's Bread-Carriers, to find it grow a good deal lighter.

After reposing about an Hour, the Commissioners recommended Vigour and Constancy to their Fellow-Travellers, by whom they were answer'd with 3 Cheerful Huzzas, in Token of Obedience. This Ceremony was no sooner over but they took up their Burthens and attended the Motion of the Surveyors, who, tho' they workt with all their might, could reach but one Mile farther, the same obstacles still attending them which they had met with in the Morning.

However small this distance may seem to such as are us'd to travel at their Ease, yet our Poor Men, who were oblig'd to work with an unwieldy Load at their Backs, had reason to think it a long way; Especially in a Bogg where they had no firm Footing, but every Step made a deep Impression, which was instantly fill'd with Water. At the same time they were labouring with their Hands to cut down the Reeds, which were Ten-feet high, their Legs were hampered with the Bryars. Besides, the Weather happen'd to be very warm, and the tallness of the Reeds kept off every Friendly Breeze from coming to refresh them. And, indeed, it was a little provoking to hear the Wind whistling among the branches of the White Cedars, which grew here and there amongst the Reeds, and at the same time not have the Comfort to feel the least Breath of it.

. . .

15. The Surveyors pursued their work with all Diligence, but Still found the Soil of the Dismal so Spongy that the Water ouzed up into every footstep they took. To their Sorrow, too, they found the Reeds and Bryars more firmly interwoven than they did the day before. But the greatest Grievance was from large Cypresses, which the Wind had blown down and heap'd upon one another. On the Limbs of most of them grew Sharp Snags, Pointing every way like so many Pikes, that requir'd much Pains and Caution to avoid.

These Trees being Evergreens, and Shooting their Large Tops Very high, are easily overset by every Gust of Wind, because there is no firm Earth to Steddy their roots. Thus many of them were laid prostrate to the great Encumbrance of the way. Such Variety of Difficulties made the Business go on heavily, insomuch that, from Morning till Night, the Line could advance no further than 1 Mile and 31 Poles. Never was Rum, that cordial of Life, found more necessary than it was in this Dirty Place. It did not only recruit the People's Spirits, now almost Jaded with Fatigue, but serv'd to correct the Badness of the Water, and at the same time to resist the Malignity of the Air. Whenever the Men wanted to drink, which was very often, they had nothing more to do but to make a Hole, and the Water bubbled up in a Moment. But it was far from being either clear or well tasted, and had besides a Physical Effect, from the tincture it receiv'd from the Roots of the Shrubbs and Trees that grew in the Neighbourhood.

. . .

There is but little Wool in that Province, tho' Cotton grows very kindly, and, so far South, is Seldom nippt by the Frost. The Good Women mix this with their Wool for their outer Garments; tho', for want of Fulling, that kind of Manufacture is Open and Sleazy. Flax likewise thrives there extreamly, being perhaps as fine as any in the World, and I question not might, with a little care, and pains, be brought to rival that of Egypt; and yet the Men are here so intolerable Lazy, they seldom take the trouble to propagate it.

16. The Line was this day carry'd one Mile and half and 16 Poles. The Soil continued soft and Miry, but fuller Trees, especially White cedars. Many of these too were thrown down and piled in Heaps, high enough for a good Muscovite Fortification. The worst of it was, the Poor Fellows began now to be troubled with Fluxes, occasion'd

by bad Water and moist Lodgings: but chewing of Rhubarb kept that Malady within Bounds.

. . .

There fell a great deal of Rain in the Night, accompany'd with a Strong Wind. The fellow-feeling we had for the poor Dismalites, on Account of this unkind Weather, render'd the Down we laid upon uneasy. We fancy'd them half-drown'd in their Wet Lodging, with the Trees blowing down about their Ears. These Were the Gloomy Images our Fears Suggested; tho' twas so much uneasiness clear gain. They happen'd to come of much better, by being luckily encampt on the dry piece of Ground afore-mention'd.

17. They were, however, forct to keep the Sabbath in Spite of their teeth, contrary to the Dispensation our Good Chaplain had given them. Indeed, their Short allowance of Provision would have justify'd their making the best of their way, without distinction of days. Twas certainly a Work both of Necessity and Self-preservation, to save themselves from Starving. Nevertheless, the hard Rain had made every thing so thoroughly wet, that it was quite impossible to do any Business. They therefore made a vertue of what they could not help, and contentedly rested in their dry Situation.

Since the Surveyors had enter'd the Dismal, they had laid Eyes on no living Creature: neither Bird nor Beast, Insect nor Reptile came in View. Doubtless, the Eternal Shade that broods over this mighty Bog, and hinders the sun-beams from blessing the Ground, makes it an uncomfortable Habitation for any thing that has life. Not so much as a Zealand Frog cou'd endure so Aguish a Situation.

It had one Beauty, however, that delighted the Eye, tho' at the Expense of all the other Senses: the Moisture of the Soil preserves a continual Verdure, and makes every Plant an Evergreen, but at the same time the foul Damps ascend without ceasing, corrupt the Air, and render it unfit for Respiration. Not even a Turkey-Buzzard will venture to fly over it, no more than the Italian Vultures will over the filthy Lake Avernus, or the Birds in the Holy-Land over the Salt Sea, where Sodom and Gomorrah formerly stood.

In these sad Circumstances, the kindest thing we cou'd do for our Suffering Friends was to give them a place in the Litany. Our Chaplain, for his Part, did his Office, and rubb'd us up with a Seasonable Sermon. This was quite a new thing to our Brethren of North Carolina, who live in a climate where no clergyman can Breathe, any more than Spiders in Ireland.

For want of men in Holy Orders, both the Members of the Council and Jutices of the Peace are empower'd by the Laws of that Country to marry all those who will not take One another's Word; but for the ceremony of Christening their children, they trust that to chance. If a Parson come in their way, they will crave a Cast of his office, as they call it, else they are content their Offspring should remain as Arrant Pagans as themselves. They account it among their greatest advantages that they are not Priest-ridden, not remembering that the Clergy is rarely guilty of Bestriding such as have the misfortune to be poor.

One thing may be said for the Inhabitants of that Province, that they are not troubled with any Religious Fumes, and have the least Superstition of any People living. They do not know Sunday from any other day, any more than Robinson Crusoe did, which would give them a great Advantage were they given to be industrious. But they keep so many Sabbaths ever week, that their disregard of the Seventh Day has no manner of cruelty in it, either to Servants or Cattle.

It was with some difficulty we cou'd make our People quit the good chear they met with at this House, so it was late before we took our Departure; but to make us amends, our Landlord was so good as to conduct us Ten Miles on our Way, as far as the Cypress Swamp, which drains itself into the Dismal... Here we flatter'd ourselves we should by this time meet with good Tydings of the Surveyors, but had reckon'd, alas! without our Host: on the Contrary, we were told the Dismal was at least Thirty Miles wide at that Place. However, as nobody could say this on his own Knowledge, we Order'd Guns to be fired and a Drum to be beaten, but receiv'd no Answer, unless it was from that prating Nymph Echo, who, like a loquacious Wife, will always have the last Word, and Sometimes return three for one.

18. It was indeed no Wonder our Signal was not heard at that time, by the People in the Dismal, because, in Truth, they had not then penetrated one Third of their way. They had that Morning fallen to work with great Vigour; and, finding the Ground better than Ordinary, drove on the Line 2 Miles and 38 poles. This was reckon'd an Herculean day's Work, and yet they would not have Stopp'd there, had not an impenetrable cedar Thicket chekt their Industry.

. . .

19. We Ordered Several Men to Patrole on the Edge of the Dismal, both towards the North and towards the South, and to fire Guns at proper Distances. This they perform'd very punctually, but cou'd hear nothing in return, nor gain any Sort of Intelligence. In the mean time whole Flocks of Women and Children flew hither to Stare at us, with as much curiosity as if we had lately Landed from Bantam or Morocco.

The Dividing Line

Some Borderers, too, had a great Mind to know where the Line wou'd come out, being for the most part Apprehensive lest their Lands Should be taken into Virginia. In that case they must have submitted to some Sort of Order and Government; whereas, in N Carolina, every One does what seems best in his own Eyes. There were some good Women that brought their children to be Baptiz'd, but brought no Capons along with them to make the solemnity cheerful. In the mean time it was Strange that none came to be marry'd in such a Multitude, if it had only been for the Novelty of having their Hands Joyn'd by one in Holy Orders. Yet so it was, that tho' our chaplain Christen'd above an Hundred, he did not marry so much as one Couple dureing the whole Expedition. But marriage is reckon'd a Lay contract in Carolina, as I said before, and a Country Justice can tie the fatal Knot there, as fast as an Archbishop.[9]

None of our Visiters could, however, tell us any News of the Surveyors, nor Indeed was it possible any of them shou'd at that time, They being still laboring in the Midst of the Dismal.

It seems they were able to carry the Line this Day no further than one mile and 61 Poles, and that whole distance was thro' a Miry cedar Bogg, where the ground trembled under their Feet most frightfully. In many places too their Passage was retarded by a great number of fallen Trees, that lay Horsing upon one Another.

Tho' many circumstances concurr'd to make this an unwholesome Situation, yet the Poor men had no time to be sick, nor can one conceive a more Calamitous Case than it would have been to be laid up in that uncomfortable Quagmire. Never were Patients more tractable, or willing to take Physick, than these honest Fellows; but it was from a Dread of laying their Bones in a Bogg that wou'd soon spew them up again. That Consideration also put them upon more caution about their Lodging.

They first cover'd the Ground with Square Pieces of Cypress bark, which now, in the Spring, they cou'd easily Slip off the Tree for that purpose. On this they Spread their Bedding; but unhappily the Weight and Warmth of their Bodies made the Water rise up betwixt the Joints of the Bark, to their great Inconvenience. Thus they lay not only moist, but also exceedingly cold, because their Fires were continually going out. For no sooner was the Trash upon the Surface burnt away, but immediately the Fire was extinguisht by the Moisture of the Soil, Insomuch that it was great part of the Centinel's Business to rekindle it again in a Fresh Place, every Quarter of an Hour. Nor cou'd they indeed do their duty better, because Cold was the only Enemy they had to Guard against in a miserable Morass, where nothing can inhabit.

21. The Surveyors and their Attendants began now in good Earnest to be alarm'd with Apprehensions of Famine, nor could they forbear looking with Some Sort of Appetite upon a dog that had been the faithful Companion of their Travels.

Their Provisions were now near exhausted. They had this Morning made the last Distribution, that so each might Husband his small Pittance as he pleas'd. Now it was that the fresh Colour'd Young Man began to tremble every Joint of Him, having dreamed, the Night before, that the Indians were about to Barbacue him over live coals.

The Prospect of Famine determin'd the People, at last, with one consent, to abandon the Line for the Present, which advanced but slowly, and make the best of their way to firm Land. Accordingly they sat off very early, and, by the help of the Compass which they carried along with them, Steer'd a direct Westwardly Course. They marcht from Morning till Night, and Computed their Journey to amount to about 4 Miles, which was a great way, considering the difficulties of the Ground. It was all along a Cedar-Swamp, so dirty and perplext, that if they had not travell'd for their Lives, they cou'd not have reacht so far.

On their way they espied a Turkey-Buzzard, that flew prodigiously high to get above the Noisome Exhalations that ascend from that filthy place. This they were willing to understand as a good Omen, according to the Superstitions of the Ancients, who had great Faith in the Flight of Vultures. However, after all this tedious Journey, they could yet discover no End of their toil, which made them very pensive, especially after they had eat the last Morsel of their Provisions. But to their unspeakable comfort, when all was husht in the Evening, they heard the Cattle low, and the Dogs bark, very distinctly, which, to Men in that distress, was more delightful Music than Faustina or Farinelli cou'd have made.

. . .

22. Our Patrole happen'd not to go far enough to the Northward this Morning, if they had, the People in the Dismal might have heard the Report of their Guns. For this Reason they return'd without any Tydings, which threw us into a great tho' unnecessary Perplexity. This was now the Ninth day since they enter'd into that inhospitable Swamp, and consequently we had reason to believe their Provisions were quite Spent.

We knew they workt hard, and therefore would eat heartily, so long as they had wherewithal to recruit their Spirits, not imagining the

Swamp so wide as they found it. Had we been able to guess where the Line wou'd come out, we wou'd have sent men to meet them with a fresh Supply; but as we cou'd know nothing of that, and as we had neither Compass nor Surveyor to guide a Messenger on such an Errand, we were unwilling to expose him to no Purpose; Therefore, all we were able to do for them, in so great an Extremity, was to recommend them to a Merciful Providence.

However long we might think the time, yet we were cautious of Shewing our uneasiness, for fear of Mortifying our Landlord. He had Done his best for us, and therefore we were unwilling he should think us dissatisfy'd with our Entertainment. In the midst of our concern, we were most agreeably surpriz'd, just after Dinner, with the News that the Dismalites were all Safe. These blessed Tidings were brought to us by Mr. Swan, the Carolina-Surveyor, who came to us in a very tatter'd condition.

After very Short Salutations, we got about Him as if He had been a Hottentot, and began to Inquire into his Adventures. He gave us a Detail of their uncomfortable Voyage thro' the Dismal, and told us, particularly, they had pursued their Journey early that Morning, encouraged by the good Omen of seeing the Crows fly over their Heads; that, after an Hour's march over very Rotten Ground, they, on a Sudden, began to find themselves among tall Pines, that grew in the Water, which in Many Places was Knee-deep. This Pine Swamp, into which that of Coropeak drain'd itself, extended near a Mile in Breadth; and tho' it was exceedingly wet, yet it was much harder at Bottom than the rest of the Swamp; that about ten in the Morning, they recovered firm Land, which they embraced with as much Pleasure as Shipwreckt Wretches do the shoar... They all lookt very thin, and as ragged as the Gibeonite Ambassadors did in the days of Yore. Our Surveyors told us they had measur'd Ten Miles in the Dismal, and Computed the Distance they had Marcht since to amount to about five more, So they made the whole Breadth to be 15 Miles in all.

. . .

In the mean time, we who stay'd behind had nothing to do, but to make the best observations we cou'd upon that Part of the Country. The Soil of our Landlord's Plantation, tho' none of the best, seem'd more fertile than any thereabouts, where the Ground is near as Sandy as the Desarts of Affrica, and consequently barren. The Road leading from thence to Edenton, being in distance about 27 Miles, lies upon a Ridge call'd Sandy-Ridge, which is so wretchedly Poor that it will not bring Potatoes.

The Pines in this Part of the country are of a different Species from those that grow in Virginia: their bearded Leaves are much longer and their Cones much larger. Each Cell contains a Seed of the Size and Figure of a black-ey'd Pea, which, Shedding in November, is very good Mast for Hogs, and fattens them in a Short time... The Trees also abound more with Turpentine, and consequently yield more Tarr, than either the Yellow or the White Pine; And for the same reason make more durable Timber for building. The Inhabitants hereabouts pick up Knots of Lightwood in Abundance, which they burn into tar, and then carry it to Norfolk or Nansimond for a Market. The Tar made in this method is the less Valuable, because it is said to burn the Cordage, tho' it is full as good for all other uses, as that made in Sweden and Muscovy.

Surely there is no place in the World where the Inhabitants live with less Labour than in N Carolina. It approaches nearer to the Description of Lubberland than any other, by the great felicity of the Climate, the easiness of raising Provisions, and the Slothfulness of the People.

Indian Corn is of so great increase, that a little Pains will Subsist a very large Family with Bread, and then they may have meat without any pains at all, by the Help of the Low Grounds, and the great Variety of Mast that grows on the High-land. The Men, for their Parts, just like the Indians, impose all the Work upon the poor Women. They make their Wives rise out of their Beds early in the Morning, at the same time that they lye and Snore, till the Sun has run one third of his course, and disperst all the unwholesome Damps. Then, after Stretching and Yawning for half an Hour, they light their Pipes, and, under the Protection of a cloud of Smoak, venture out into the open Air; tho', if it happens to be never so little cold, they quickly return Shivering into the Chimney corner. When the weather is mild, they stand leaning with both their arms upon the corn-field fence, and gravely consider whether they had best go and take a Small Heat at the Hough: but generally find reasons to put it off till another time.

Thus they loiter away their Lives, like Solomon's Sluggard, with their Arms across, and at the Winding up of the Year Scarcely have Bread to Eat.

To speak the Truth, tis a thorough Aversion to Labor that makes People file off to N Carolina, where Plenty and a Warm Sun confirm them in their Disposition to Laziness for their whole Lives.

. . .

The Method of burning Tar in Sweden and Muscovy Succeeds not well in this Warmer Part of the World. It seems they kill the

Pine-Trees, by barking them quite round at a certain Height, which in those cold countreys brings down the Turpentine into the Stump in a Year's time. But experience has taught us that in warm Climates the Turpentine will not so easily descend, but is either fixt in the upper parts of the Tree, or fryed out by the intense Heat of the Sun...

Because the Spring was now pretty forward, and the Rattle-Snakes began to crawl out of their Winter-Quarters, and might grow dangerous, both to the Men and their Horses, it was determin'd to proceed no farther with the Line till the Fall. Besides, the Uncommon Fatigue the People had undergone for near 6 Weeks together, and the Inclination they all had to visit their Respective Familys, made a Recess highly reasonable.

. . .

6. Thus we finish'd our Spring Campaign, and having taken leave of our Carolina-Friends, and agreed to meet them again the Tenth of September following, at the same Mr. Kinchin's, in order to continue the Line, we crosst Meherin River near a Quarter of a Mile from the House. About ten Miles from that we halted at Mr. Kindred's Plantation, where we Christen'd two Children.

. . .

7. In the Morning we despacht a runner to the Nottoway Town, to let the Indians know we intended them a Visit that Evening, and our honest Landlord was so kind as to be our Pilot thither, being about 4 Miles from his House.

Accordingly in the Afternoon we marcht in good Order to the Town, where the Female Scouts, station'd on an Eminence for that purpose, had no sooner spy'd us, but they gave Notice of our Approach to their Fellow-Citizens by continual Whoops and Cries, which cou'd not possibly have been more dismal at the Sight of their most implacable Enemys.

This Signal Assembled all their Great Men, who receiv'd us in a Body, and conducted us into the Fort. This Fort was a Square Piece of Ground, inclos'd with Substantial Puncheons, or Strong Palisades, about ten feet high, and leaning a little outwards, to make a Scalade more difficult.

Each side of the Square might be about 100 Yards long, with Loop-holes at proper Distances, through which they may fire upon the Enemy.

Within this Inclosure we found Bark Cabanes Sufficient to lodge all their people, in Case they should be obliged to retire thither. These Cabanes are no other but Close Arbours made of Saplings, arched at the top, and cover'd so well with Bark as to be proof against all

Weather. The fire is made in the Middle, according to the Hibernian Fashion, the Smoak whereof finds no other Vent but at the Door, and so keeps the whole family Warm, at the Expense both of their Eyes and Complexion.

The Indians have no standing Furniture in their Cabanes but Hurdles to repose their Persons upon, which they cover with Mats or Deer-skins. We were conducted to the best Appartments in the Fort, which just before had been made ready for our Reception, and adorn'd with new Mats, that were sweet and clean.

The Young Men had Painted themselves in a Hideous Manner, not so much for Ornament as Terror. In that frightful Equipage they entertain'd us with Sundry War-Dances, wherein they endeavour'd to look as formidable as possible. The Intrument they danct to was an Indian-drum, that is, a large Gourd with a Skin bract tort over the Mouth of it. The Dancers all Sang to this Musick, keeping exact Time with their feet, while their Heads and Arms were screw'd into a thousand Menacing Postures.

Upon this occasion the Ladies had array'd themselves in all their finery. They were Wrapt in their Red and Blue Match-Coats, thrown so Negligently about them, that their Mehogony Skins appear'd in Several Parts, like the Lacedaemonian Damsels of Old. Their Hair was breeded with white and Blue Peak, and hung gracefully in a large Roll upon their Shoulders.

This peak Consists of Small Cylinders cut out of a Conque-Shell, drill'd through and Strung like Beads. It serves them both for Money and Jewels, the Blue being of much greater Value than the White, for the same reason that Ethiopian Mistresses in France are dearer than French, because they are more Scarce. The Women wear Necklaces and Bracelets of these precious Materials, when they have a mind to appear lovely. Tho' their compexions be a little Sad-Colour'd, yet their Shapes are very Strait and well proportion'd. Their Faces are Seldom handsome, yet they have an Air of Innocence and Bashfulness, that with a little less dirt wou'd not fail to make them desirable. Such Charms might have had their full Effect upon Men who had been so long deprived of female conversation, but that the whole Winter's Soil was so crusted on the Skins of those dark Angels, that it requir'd a very strong Appetite to approach them. The Bear's oyl, with which they anoint their Persons all over, makes their Skins Soft, and at the Same time protects them from every Species of Vermin that use to be troublesome to other uncleanly People.

We were unluckily so many, that they cou'd not well make us the Complement of Bed-fellows, according to the Indian Rules of Hospitality, tho' a grave Matron whisper'd one of the Commissioners very civily in the Ear, that if her Daughter had been but one year Older, she should have been at his Devotion.

It is by no means a loss of Reputation among the Indians, for Damsels that are Single to have Intrigues with the Men; on the contrary, they count it an Argument of Superior Merit to be liked by a great Number of Gallants. However, like the Ladys that Game they are a little Mercenary in their Amours, and seldom bestow their Favours out of Stark Love and Kindness. But after these Women have once appropriated their Charms by Marriage, they are from thenceforth faithful to their Vows, and will hardly ever be tempted by an Agreeable Gallant, or be provokt by a Brutal or even by a fumbling Husband to go astray.

The little Work that is done among the Indians is done by the poor Women, while the men are quite idle, or at most employ'd only in the Gentlemanly Diversions of Hunting and Fishing.

In this, as well as in their Wars, they now use nothing but Fire-Arms, which they purchase of the English for Skins. Bows and Arrows are grown into disuse, except only amongst their Boys. Nor is it ill Policy, but on the contrary very prudent, thus to furnish the Indians with Fire-Arms, because it makes them depend entirely upon the English, not only for their Trade, but even for their subsistence. Besides, they were really able to do more mischief, while they made use of Arrows, of which they wou'd let Silently fly Several in a Minute with Wonderful Dexterity, whereas now they hardly ever discharge their Fire-locks more than once, which they insidiously do from behind a Tree, and then retire as nimbly as the Dutch Horse us'd to do now and then formerly in Flanders.

We put the Indians to no expense, but only of a little Corn for our Horses, for which in Gratitude we cheer'd their hearts with what Rum we had left, which they love better than they do their Wives and Children.

Tho' these Indians dwell among the English, and see in what Plenty a little Industry enables them to live, yet they chuse to continue in their Stupid Idleness, and to Suffer all the Inconveniences of Dirt, Cold, and Want, rather than to disturb their heads With care, or defile their Hands with labour.

I am sorry I can't give a Better Account of the State of the Poor Indians with respect to Christianity, altho' a great deal of Pains has been and still continues to be taken with them. For my Part, I must be of Opinion, as I hinted before, that there is but one way of Converting these poor Infidels, and reclaiming them from Barbarity, and that is,

Charitably to intermarry with them, according to the Modern Policy of the most Christian King in Canada and Louisiana.

Had the English done this at the first Settlement of the Colony, the Infidelity of the Indians had been worn out at this Day, with their Dark Complexions, and the Country had swarm'd with People more than it does with Insects.

It was certainly an unreasonable Nicety, that prevented their entering into so good-Natur'd an Alliance. All Nations of men have the same Natural Dignity, and we all know that very bright Talents may be lodg'd under a very dark Skin. The principal Difference between one People and another proceeds only from the Different Opportunities of Improvement.

The Indians by no means want understanding, and are in their Figure tall and well-proportion'd. Even their Copper-colour'd Complexion wou'd admit of Blanching, if not in the first, at the farthest in the Second Generation.

I may safely venture to say, the Indian Women would have made altogether as Honest Wives for the first Planters, as the Damsels they us'd to purchase from aboard the Ships. It is Strange, therefore, that any good Christian Shou'd have refused a wholesome, Straight Bed-fellow, when he might have had so fair a Portion with her, as the Merit of saving her Soul...

About 10 a Clock we marched out of Town in good order, & the War Captains saluted us with a Volley of Small-Arms. From thence we proceeded over Black-water Bridge to colo' Henry Harrisons, where we congratulated each other upon our Return into Christendom.

Thus ended our Progress for this Season, which we may justly say was attended with all the Success that could be expected. Besides the Punctual Performance of what was Committed to us, we had the Pleasure to bring back every one of our Company in perfect Health. And this we must acknowledge to be a Singular Blessing, considering the Difficulties and Dangers to which they had been expos'd.

Jonathan Edwards, 'Personal Narrative'

Jonathan Edwards (1703–58) was born at East Windsor, Connecticut in 1703, the grandson of Solomon Stoddard. His grandfather was called 'Pope' Stoddard not to comment on his liturgy but to suggest his authority and that authority not only over the parish in Northampton, Massachusetts, but over the whole coastal plain from Rhode Island to New York. There is in the relationship of Edwards to his impressive religious forebear a reminder of Mather's to his, as there is a reminder of Mather's precociousness in Edwards's. As a young man Edwards interested himself in the natural sciences, natural philosophy and natural religion. He entered Yale College at thirteen, read Newton and Locke 'with more pleasure than the most greedy miser finds when gathering up handfuls of silver and gold' and filled his notebooks with studies in natural history, psychology, and metaphysics. He graduated at seventeen and, after two years' study of theology and a brief pastorate in New York City, returned to Yale as senior tutor. In 1727 he was made his grandfather's associate minister at Northampton (recognizing unusual promise and an impressive beginning with speedy family preferment). Edwards succeeded his grandfather on Stoddard's death in 1729. With his wife Sarah Pierpont whom he loved early and long, he remained at Northampton for twenty-four years. At Northampton commenced Edwards's fame as an evangelical minister, a fame which reached international proportions, in the Great Awakening of religious enthusiasm from 1735 to 1750. In that period Edwards developed his stunning philosophical and emotional insights into religious experience, applying Lockean sensationalism to Calvinist theology so as to give warmth to a faith he considered had been over-intellectualized and schematized into aridity. In 1751 after a dispute with his congregation he was forced to resign his pastorate. He transferred to the western frontier parish of Stockbridge, Massachusetts, where for the next seven years he served as a missionary to the Indians. During those years, well outside the centres of power in the church, he wrote his most searching philosophical defences of Calvinist theology in full-scale reconsideration of free will and determinism, good and evil. Taken together the books of those years of virtual exile constitute a large and profound, although unfinished, protestant *summa theologica*. In 1758 he very reluctantly accepted the presidency of the College of New Jersey, later to be called Princeton University, writing to the trustees to explain his reluctance, 'I have a constitution, in many respects peculiarly unhappy, attended with ... a low tide of spirits ... a disagreeable darkness and stiffness, most unfitting me for conversation, but more especially for the government of a college.' The justice of this self-analysis was not to be tried, however. He died of smallpox in Princeton a few months after his arrival.

The *Personal Narrative* was found in Edwards's papers and printed fifty years after his death. The original manuscript has not survived so his readers are obliged to rely upon transcribers who from the middle of the nineteenth century regularized the text in various ways. The least defective because the least corrected was included in a pious life written by the congregational minister Samuel Hopkins.

The heterogeneity of American prose which we have been describing makes it unusually susceptible to arrangement into dualities. Scholars and critics all too often fall into the declaration of antitheses – Smith versus Bradford, Mather versus Byrd, even

Jonathan Edwards (1703–58)

Rowlandson versus Knight. This not entirely absurd habit has led to a frequent contrasting of Edwards's autobiography with that of his contemporary Benjamin Franklin. The comparison of the two texts almost makes itself: Franklin's startling rise from provincial poverty to wealth, fame and general admiration in contrast to Edwards's clerically protected entry into the company of spiritual teachers and his subsequent downfall and isolation among the Indians; Franklin's worldly and sophisticated progressivism in contrast to Edwards's despairing certainty of human depravity; Franklin's rigorous demands upon his own energies to improve his world in contrast to Edwards's equally rigorous use of his powers to reformulate the dependent relationship of man to God; Franklin's attractive and cheerful annexation of the title *philosophe* in contrast to Edwards's self-demanding subordination of himself to his God. So long as the comparison suggests the intractibility of American prose to analysis in terms of single causes or single theses, it is perhaps innocent. If offered, however, to urge upon readers a simple choice of lowbrow or highbrow, paleface or redskin, progressive or conservative, it is worse than defective. No modern reader will understand the direction of American prose down to the modern day by offering the victory to one or another of these strains; the dynamism of American writing derives from the tension between the energies of each.

My text is that included in *Memoirs of the Rev. Jonathan Edwards compiled by Samuel Hopkins D.D.*, edited by John Hawksley, London, James Black, 1815.

I

I had a variety of concerns and exercises about my soul from my childhood; but had two more remarkable seasons of awakening, before I met with that change by which I was brought to those new dispositions, and that new sense of things, that I have since had. The first time was when I was a boy, some years before I went to college, at a time of remarkable awakening in my father's congregation. I was then very much affected for many months, and concerned about the things of religion, and my soul's salvation; and was abundant in duties. I used to pray five times a day in secret, and to spend much time in religious talk with other boys; and used to meet with them to pray together. I experienced I know not what kind of delight in religion. My mind was much engaged in it, and had much self-righteous pleasure; and it was my delight to abound in religious duties. I with some of my school-mates joined together, and built a booth in a swamp, in a very retired spot, for a place of prayer. – And besides, I had particular secret places of my own in the woods, where I used to retire by myself; and was from time to time much affected. My affections seemed to be lively and easily moved, and I seemed to be in my element when engaged in religious duties. And I am ready to think, many are deceived with such affections, and such a kind of delight as I then had in religion, and mistake it for grace.

But in process of time, my convictions and affections wore off; and

178

I entirely lost all those affections and delights, and left off secret prayer, at least as to any constant performance of it; and returned like a dog to his vomit, and went on in the ways of sin. Indeed I was at times very uneasy, especially towards the latter part of my time at college; when it pleased God to seize me with a pleurisy; in which he brought me nigh to the grave, and shook me over the pit of hell. And yet, it was not long after my recovery, before I fell again into my old ways of sin. But God would not suffer me to go on with any quietness; I had great and violent inward struggles, till, after many conflicts with wicked inclinations, repeated resolutions, and bonds that I laid myself under by a kind of vows to God, I was brought wholly to break off all former wicked ways, and all ways of known outward sin; and to apply myself to seek salvation, and practise many religious duties; but without that kind of affection and delight which I had formerly experienced. My concern now wrought more by inward struggles and conflicts, and self-reflections. I made seeking my salvation the main business of my life. But yet, it seems to me, I sought after a miserable manner; which has made me sometimes since to question, whether ever it issued in that which was saving; being ready to doubt, whether such miserable seeking ever succeeded. I was indeed brought to seek salvation in a manner that I never was before; I felt a spirit to part with all things in the world, for an interest in Christ. My concern continued and prevailed, with many exercising thoughts and inward struggles; but yet it never seemed to be proper to express that concern by the name of terror.

From my childhood up, my mind had been full of objections against the doctrine of God's sovereignty, in choosing whom he would to eternal life, and rejecting whom he pleased; leaving them eternally to perish, and be everlastingly tormented in hell. It used to appear like a horrible doctrine to me. But I remember the time very well, when I seemed to be convinced, and fully satisfied, as to this sovereignty of God, and his justice in thus eternally disposing of men, according to his sovereign pleasure. But I never could give an account how, or by what means, I was thus convinced, not in the least imagining at the time, nor a long time after, that there was any extraordinary influence of God's Spirit in it; but only that now I saw further, and my reason apprehended the justice and reasonableness of it. However, my mind rested in it; and it put an end to all those cavils and objections. And there has been a wonderful alteration in my mind, with respect to the doctrine of God's sovereignty, from that day to this; so that I scarce ever have found so much as the rising of an objection against it, in the most absolute sense, in God shewing mercy to whom he will shew mercy, and hardening whom he will. God's absolute sovereignty and justice, with respect to salvation and damnation, is what my mind seems to rest assured of, as much as of any thing that I see with my eyes; at least it is so at times. But I have often, since that first conviction, had quite another kind of sense of God's sovereignty than I had then.[1] I have often since had not only a conviction, but a *delightful* conviction. The doctrine has very often appeared exceedingly pleasant, bright, and sweet. Absolute sovereignty is what I love to ascribe to God. But my first conviction was not so.

The first instance that I remember of that sort of inward, sweet delight in God and divine things that I have lived much in since, was on reading those words, 1 Tim. i. 17. *Now unto the King eternal, immortal, invisible, the only wise God, be honour and glory for ever and ever, Amen.* As I read the words, there came into my soul, and was as it were diffused through it, a sense of the glory of the Divine Being; a new sense, quite different from any thing I ever experienced before. Never any words of scripture seemed to me as these words did. I thought with myself, how excellent a Being that was, and how happy I should be, if I might enjoy that God, and be wrapt up to him in heaven, and be as it were swallowed up in him for ever! I kept saying, and, as it were, singing over these words of scripture to myself; and went to pray to God that I might enjoy him, and prayed in a manner quite different from what I used to do; with a new sort of affection. But it never came into my thought, that there was any thing spiritual, or of a saving nature in this.

From about that time I began to have a new kind of apprehensions and ideas of Christ, and the work of redemption, and the glorious way of salvation by him. An inward sweet sense of these things, at times, came into my heart; and my soul was led away in pleasant views and contemplations of them. And my mind was greatly engaged to spend my time in reading and meditating on Christ, on the beauty and excellency of his person, and the lovely way of salvation by free grace in him. I found no books so delightful to me as those that treated of these subjects...

Not long after I first began to experience these things, I gave an account to my father of some things that had passed in my mind. I was pretty much affected by the discourse we had together; and when the discourse was ended, I walked abroad alone, in a solitary place in my father's pasture, for contemplation. And as I was walking there, and looking up on the sky and clouds, there came into my mind so sweet a sense of the glorious *majesty* and *grace* of God, that I know not how to express. – I seemed to see them both in a sweet conjunction; majesty and meekness joined together: it was a sweet, and gentle, and holy majesty; and also a majestic meekness; an awful sweetness; a high, and great, and holy gentleness.

After this my sense of divine things gradually increased, and became more and more lively, and had more of that inward sweetness. The apearance of every thing was altered; there seemed to be, as it were, a calm, sweet cast, or appearance of divine glory, in almost every thing. God's excellency, his wisdom, his purity, and love, seemed to appear in every thing; in the sun, moon, and stars; in the clouds, and blue sky; in the grass, flowers, trees; in the water, and all nature; which used greatly to fix my mind. I often used to sit and view the moon for continuance; and in the day, spent much time in viewing the clouds and sky, to behold the sweet glory of God in these things: in the mean time, singing forth, with a low voice, my contemplations of the Creator and Redeemer. And scarce any thing among all the works of nature, was so sweet to me as thunder and lightning; formerly, nothing had been so terrible to me. Before, I used to be uncommonly terrified with thunder, and to be struck with terror when I saw a thunder-storm rising; but now, on the contrary, it rejoiced me. I felt God, so to speak, at the first appearance of a thunder-storm; and used to take the opportunity, at such times, to fix myself in order to view the clouds, and see the lightnings play, and hear the majestic and awful voice of God's thunder, which oftentimes was exceedingly entertaining, leading me to sweet contemplations of my great and glorious God. While thus engaged, it always seemed natural to me to sing, or chaunt forth my meditations; or, to speak my thoughts in soliloquies with a singing voice.[2]

I felt then great satisfaction, as to my good state; but that did not content me. I had vehement longings of soul after God and Christ, and after more holiness, where-with my heart seemed to be full and ready to break; which often brought to my mind the words of the Psalmist, Psal. cxix. 28. *My soul breaketh for the longing it hath*. I often felt a mourning and lamenting in my heart, that I had not turned to God sooner, that I might have had more time to grow in grace. My mind was greatly fixed on divine things; almost perpetually in the contemplation of them. I spent most of my time in thinking of divine things, year after year; often walking alone in the woods, and solitary places, for meditation, soliloquy, and prayer, and converse with God; and it was always my manner, at such times, to sing forth my contemplations, I was almost constantly in ejaculatory prayer, wherever I was. Prayer seemed to be natural to me, as the breath by which the inward burnings of my heart had vent. The delights which I now felt in the things of religion, were of an exceedingly different kind from those before-mentioned, that I had when a boy; and what I then had no more notion of, than one born blind has of pleasant and beautiful colours. They were of a more inward, pure, soul-animating, and refreshing nature. Those former delights never reached the heart; and did not arise from any sight of the divine excellency of the things of God; or any taste of the soul-satisfying and life-giving good there is in them.

My sense of divine things seemed gradually to increase, till I went to preach at New York,[3] which was about a year and a half after they began; and while I was there, I felt them, very sensibly, in a much higher degree than I had done before. My longings after God and holiness were much increased. Pure and humble, holy and heavenly christianity, appeared exceedingly amiable to me. I felt a burning desire to be in every thing a complete christian, and conformed to the blessed image of Christ; and that I might live, in all things, according to the pure, sweet, and blessed rules of the gospel. I had an eager thirsting after progress in these things; which put me upon pursuing and pressing after them... I now sought an increase of grace and holiness, and a holy life, with much more earnestness than ever I sought grace before I had it. I used to be continually examining myself, and studying and contriving for likely ways and means how I should live holily, with far greater diligence and earnestness than ever I pursued any thing in my life; but yet with too great a dependence on my own strength, which afterwards proved a great damage to me. My experience had not then taught me, as it has done since, my extreme feebleness and impotence, every manner of way; and the bottomless depths of secret corruption and deceit there were in my heart. However, I went on with my eager pursuit after more holiness and conformity to Christ.

The heaven I desired was a heaven of holiness; to be with God, and to spend my eternity in divine love, and holy communion with Christ. My mind was very much taken up with contemplations on heaven, and the enjoyments there; and living there in perfect holiness, humility, and love; and it used at that time to appear a great part of the happiness of heaven, that there the saints could express their love to Christ. It appeared to me a great clog and burden, that what I felt within, I could not express as I desired. The inward ardour of my soul seemed to be hindered and pent up, and could not freely flame out as it would. I used often to think, how in heaven this principle should freely and fully vent and express itself. Heaven appeared exceedingly delightful, as a world of love; and that all happiness consisted in living in pure, humble, heavenly, divine love.

I remember the thoughts I used then to have of holiness; and said sometimes to myself, 'I do certainly know that I love holiness, such as the gospel prescribes.' It appeared to me, that there was nothing in it but what was ravishingly lovely; the highest beauty and amiableness – a *divine* beauty; far purer than any thing here upon earth; and that every thing else was like mire and defilement in comparison of it.

Holiness, as I then wrote down some of my contemplations on it, appeared to me to be of a sweet, pleasant, charming, serene, calm nature; which brought an inexpressible purity, brightness, peacefulness and ravishment to the soul. In other words, that it made the soul like a field or garden of God, with all manner of pleasant flowers: all pleasant, delightful, and undisturbed; enjoying a sweet calm, and the gently vivifying beams of the sun. The soul of a true christian, as I then wrote my meditations, appeared like such a little white flower as we see in the spring of the year; low and humble on the ground, opening its bosom, to receive the pleasant beams of the sun's glory; rejoicing, as it were, in a calm rapture; diffusing around a sweet fragrancy: standing peacefully and lovingly, in the midst of other flowers round about; all in like manner opening their bosoms, to drink in the light of the sun. There was no part of creature-holiness, that I had so great a sense of its loveliness, as humility, brokenness of heart, and poverty of spirit; and there was nothing that I so earnestly longed for. My heart panted after this, – to lie low before God, as in the dust; that I might be nothing, and that God might be ALL, that I might become as a little child.

While at New York, I sometimes was much affected with reflections on my past life, considering how late it was before I began to be truly religious; and how wickedly I had lived till then: and once so as to weep abundantly, and for a considerable time together.

On January 12, 1723, I made a solemn dedication of myself to God, and wrote it down; giving up myself, and all that I had, to God; to be for the future in no respect my own; to act as one that had no right to himself, in any respect. And I solemnly vowed to take God for my whole portion and felicity; looking on nothing else as any part of my happiness, nor acting as if it were; and his law for the constant rule of my obedience: engaging to fight with all my might, against the world, the flesh, and the devil, to the end of my life. But I have reason to be infinitely humbled, when I consider, how much I have failed of answering my obligation.

. . .

Jonathan Edwards (1703–58)

I very frequently used to retire into a solitary place, on the banks of Hudson's River, at some distance from the city, for contemplation on divine things, and secret converse with God; and had many sweet hours there. Sometimes Mr. Smith and I walked there together, to converse on the things of God; and our conversation used to turn much on the advancement of Christ's kingdom in the world, and the glorious things that God would accomplish for his church in the latter days. I had then, and at other times, the greatest delight in the holy scriptures, of any book whatsoever. Oftentimes in reading it, every word seemed to touch my heart. I felt a harmony between something in my heart, and those sweet and powerful words. I seemed often to see so much light exhibited by every sentence, and such a refreshing food communicated, that I could not get along in reading; often dwelling long on one sentence, to see the wonders contained in it; and yet almost every sentence seemed to be full of wonders.

I came away from New York in the month of April, 1723, and had a most bitter parting with Madam Smith and her son. My heart seemed to sink within me at leaving the family and city, where I had enjoyed so many sweet and pleasant days. I went from New York to Weathersfield, by water; and as I sailed away, I kept sight of the city as long as I could. However, that night after this sorrowful parting, I was greatly comforted in God at Westchester, where we went ashore to lodge; and had a pleasant time of it all the voyage to Saybrook. It was sweet to me to think of meeting dear christians in heaven, where we should never part more. At Saybrook we went ashore to lodge on Saturday, and there kept the Sabbath; where I had a sweet and refreshing season, walking alone in the fields.

After I came home to Windsor, I remained much in a like frame of mind, as when at New York; only sometimes I felt my heart ready to sink with the thoughts of my friends at New York. My support was in contemplations on the heavenly state; as I find in my Diary of May 1, 1723.[4] It was a comfort to think of that state, where there is fulness of joy; where reigns heavenly, calm, and delightful love, without alloy; where there are continually the dearest expressions of this love; where is the enjoyment of the persons loved, without ever parting; where those persons who appear so lovely in this world, will really be inexpressibly more lovely, and full of love to us. And how sweetly will the mutual lovers join together to sing the praises of God and the Lamb! How will it fill us with joy to think, that this enjoyment, these sweet exercises, will never cease, but will last to all eternity! – I continued much in the same frame, in the general, as when at New York, till I went to Newhaven as tutor of the college;[5] particularly once at Bolton, on a journey from Boston, while walking out alone in the fields. After I went to Newhaven I sunk in religion; my mind being diverted from my eager pursuits after holiness, by some affairs that greatly perplexed and distracted my thoughts.

In September, 1725, I was taken ill at Newhaven, and while endeavouring to go home to Windsor, was so ill at the North Village, that I could go no further; where I lay sick for about a quarter of a year. In this sickness God was pleased to visit me again with the sweet influences of his Spirit. My mind was greatly engaged there on divine, pleasant contemplations, and longings of soul. I observed that those who watched with me,[a] would often be looking out wishfully for the morning; which brought to my mind those words of the Psalmist, and which my soul with delight made its own language, *My soul waiteth for the Lord, more than they that watch for the morning, I say, more than they that watch for the morning;* and when the light of day came in at the windows it refreshed my soul from one morning to another. It seemed to be some image of the light of God's glory.

. . .

Since I came to this town,[b] I have often had sweet complacency in God, in views of his glorious perfections, and the excellency of Jesus Christ. God has appeared to me a glorious and lovely being, chiefly on the account of his holiness. The holiness of God has always appeared to me the most lovely of all his attributes. The doctrines of God's absolute sovereignty, and free grace, in shewing mercy to whom he would shew mercy; and man's absolute dependence on the operations of God's Holy Spirit, have very often appeared to me as sweet and glorious doctrines. These doctrines have been much my delight. God's sovereignty has ever appeared to me great part of his glory. It has often been my delight to approach God, and adore him as a sovereign God, and ask sovereign mercy of him.

I have loved the doctrines of the gospel; they have been to my soul like green pastures. The gospel has seemed to me the richest treasure; the treasure that I have most desired, and longed that it might dwell richly in me. The way of salvation by Christ has appeared, in a general way, glorious and excellent, most pleasant and most beautiful. It has often seemed to me, that it would, in a great measure, spoil heaven, to receive it in any other way. That text has often been affecting and delightful to me, Isa. xxxii. 2. *A man shall be as an hiding place from the wind, and a covert from the tempest; as rivers of water in a dry place; as the shadow of a great rock in a weary land.*

---

[a] His mother came to New Haven to nurse him through the dangerous illness.
[b] Northampton, Massachusetts.

It has often appeared to me delightful, to be united to Christ; to have him for my head, and to be a member of his body; also to have Christ for my teacher and prophet. I very often think with sweetness, and longings, and pantings of soul, of being a little child, taking hold of Christ, to be led by him through the wilderness of this world. That text, Matt. xviii. 3. had often been sweet to me, *Except ye be converted, and become as little children, ye shall not enter into the kingdom of heaven.* I love to think of coming to Christ, to receive salvation of him, poor in spirit, and quite empty of self, humbly exalting him alone; cut off entirely from my own root, in order to grow into, and out of Christ: to have God in Christ to be all in all; and to live by faith on the Son of God, a life of humble, unfeigned confidence in him. That scripture has often been sweet to me, Psal. cxv. 1. *Not unto us, O Lord, not unto us, but unto thy name give glory, for thy mercy, and for thy truth's sake.* And those words of Christ, Luke, x. 21. *In that hour Jesus rejoiced in spirit, and said, I thank thee, O Father, Lord of heaven and earth, that thou has hid these things from the wise and prudent, and hast revealed them unto babes: even so, Father, for so it seemed good in thy sight.* That sovereignty of God which Christ rejoiced in, seemed to me worthy of such joy; and that rejoicing seemed to shew the excellency of Christ, and of what spirit he was.

. . .

The sweetest joys and delights I have experienced, have not been those that have arisen from a hope of my own good estate, but in a direct view of the glorious things of the gospel. When I enjoy this sweetness, it seems to carry me above the thoughts of my own estate; it seems at such times a loss that I cannot bear, to take off my eye from the glorious, pleasant object I behold without me, to turn my eye in upon myself, and my own good estate.

. . .

Once, as I rode out into the woods for my health, in 1737, having alighted from my horse in a retired place, as my manner commonly has been, to walk for divine contemplation and prayer, I had a view, that for me was extraordinary, of the glory of the Son of God, as Mediator between God and man, and his wonderful, great, full, pure and sweet grace and love, and meek and gentle condescension. This grace that appeared so calm and sweet, appeared also great above the heavens. The person of Christ appeared ineffably excellent, with an excellency great enough to swallow up all thought and conception – which continued, as near as I can judge, about an hour; which kept me, the greater part of the time, in a flood of tears, and weeping aloud. I felt an ardency of soul to be, what I know not otherwise how to express, emptied and annihilated; to lie in the dust, and to be full of Christ alone; to love him with a holy and pure love; to trust in him; to live upon him; to serve and follow him; and to be perfectly sanctified and made pure, with a divine and heavenly purity. I have, several other times, had views very much of the same nature, and which have had the same effects.

I have, many times, had a sense of the glory of the third person in the Trinity, in his office of Sanctifier; in his holy operations, communicating divine light and life to the soul. God, in the communications of his Holy Spirit, has appeared as an infinite fountain of divine glory and sweetness; being full, and sufficient to fill and satisfy the soul; pouring forth itself in sweet communications; like the sun in its glory, sweetly and pleasantly diffusing light and life. And I have sometimes had an affecting sense of the excellency of the word of God, as a word of life; as the light of life; a sweet, excellent, life-giving word; accompanied with a thirsting after that word, that it might dwell richly in my heart.

Often, since I lived in this town, I have had very affecting views of my own sinfulness and vileness; very frequently to such a degree as to hold me in a kind of loud weeping, sometimes for a considerable time together; so that I have often been forced to shut myself up. I have had a vastly greater sense of my own wickedness, and the badness of my heart, than ever I had before my conversion.[6] It has often appeared to me, that if God should mark iniquity against me, I should appear the very worst of all mankind; of all that have been, since the beginning of the world to this time: and that I should have by far the lowest place in hell. When others, that have come to talk with me about their soul-concerns, have expressed the sense they have had of their own wickedness, by saying that it seemed to them, that they were as bad as the devil himself, I thought their expressions seemed exceedingly faint and feeble, to represent my wickedness.

My wickedness, as I am in myself, has long appeared to me perfectly ineffable, and swallowing up all thought and imagination; like an infinite deluge, or mountains over my head. I know not how to express better what my sins appear to me to be, than by heaping infinite upon infinite, and multiplying infinite by infinite. Very often, for these many years, these expressions are in my mind, and in my mouth, 'Infinite upon infinite – Infinite upon infinite!' – When I look into my heart, and take a view of my wickedness, it looks like an abyss infinitely deeper than hell. And it appears to me, that were it not for free grace, exalted and raised up to the infinite height of all the fulness and glory of the great Jehovah, and the arm of his power and grace stretched forth in all the majesty of his power, and in all the glory of his sovereignty, I should appear sunk down in my sins below hell itself; far beyond the sight of every thing, but the eye of sovereign grace, that can pierce even down to such a depth. And yet it seems to me, that my conviction of sin is exceedingly small, and faint; it is enough to amaze me, that I have no more sense of my sin. I know certainly, that I have very little sense of my sinfulness. When I have had turns of weeping and crying for my sins, I thought I knew at the time, that my repentence was nothing to my sin.

I have greatly longed of late for a broken heart,[7] and to lie low before God; and, when I ask for humility, I cannot bear the thoughts of being no more humble than other christians. It seems to me, that though their degrees of humility may be suitable for them, yet it would be a vile self-exaltation in me, not to be the lowest in humility of all mankind. Others speak of their longing to be 'humbled to the dust'; that may be a proper expression for them, but I always think of myself, that I ought (and it is an expression that has long been natural for me to use in prayer) 'to lie infinitely low before God'. And it is affecting to think, how ignorant I was, when a young christian, of the bottomless, infinite depths of wickedness, pride, hypocrisy, and deceit, left in my heart.

I have a much greater sense of my universal, exceeding dependence on God's grace and strength, and mere good pleasure, of late, than I used formerly to have; and have experienced more of an abhorrence of my own righteousness. The very thought of any joy arising in me, on any consideration of my own amiableness, performances, or experiences, or any goodness of heart or life, is nauseous and detestable to me. And yet I am greatly afflicted with a proud and self-righteous spirit, much more sensibly than I used to be formerly. I see that serpent rising and putting forth its head continually, every where, all around me.

Though it seems to me, that, in some respects, I was a far better christian, for two or three years after my first conversion, than I am now; and lived in a more constant delight and pleasure; yet, of late years, I have had a more full and constant sense of the absolute sovereignty of God, and a delight in that sovereignty; and have had more of a sense of the glory of Christ, as a mediator revealed in the gospel. On one Saturday night, in particular, I had such a discovery of the excellency of the gospel above all other doctrines, that I could not but say to myself, 'This is my chosen light, my chosen doctrine': and of Christ, 'This is my chosen Prophet.' It appeared sweet, beyond all expression, to follow Christ, and to be taught, and enlightened, and instructed by him; to learn of him, and live to him. Another Saturday night, (Jan. 1739)[8] I had such a sense, how sweet and blessed a thing it was to walk in the way of duty; to do that which was right and meet to be done, and agreeable to the holy mind of God; that it caused me to break forth into a kind of loud weeping, which held me some time, so that I was forced to shut myself up, and fasten the doors. I could not but, as it were, cry out 'How happy are they which do that which is right in the sight of God! They are blessed indeed, they are the happy ones!' I had, at the same time, a very affecting sense, how meet and suitable it was that God should govern the world, and order all things according to his own pleasure; and I rejoiced in it, that God reigned, and that his will was done.

Benjamin Franklin, 'The Autobiography of Benjamin Franklin'

Benjamin Franklin (1706–90) was born in Boston. Whether or not he attended Madam Knight's school, he got little of the formal education in the English model on which the city and its neighbouring Cambridge prided itself. By his own account, he was sent to grammar school at eight, was removed to 'a school for writing and arithmetic' at nine, and was withdrawn from school altogether at ten and 'taken home to assist [his] father in his business, which was that of a tallow-chandler' (p. 196). At twelve he was apprenticed as printer to his older brother James, whose newspaper the *New England Courant* was the fourth newspaper established in the colonies. His indentures would have required him to work for James until aged twenty-one but, as Franklin's notes to the *Autobiography* (notes constituting a working outline for that book) put it: 'Differences arise between my Brother and me'; there ensued 'The final Breach... My leaving him and going to New York (return to eating flesh); thence to Pennsylvania.' Franklin arrived in Philadelphia in October 1723, sought and got employment as a printer and after various activities, including a two-year stay in London, became the owner of a printing firm. He made a common-law marriage with Deborah Reed in 1730, his only marriage, which lasted forty-four years. The success of his printing firm enabled him to retire in 1748, when he was forty-two. Characteristically Franklin acknowledged to the end of his life the publishing basis on which his autodidactic understanding of the world and his economic security in it rested; he drafted his will to begin, 'I, Benjamin Franklin, of Philadelphia, printer...' Franklin's state of mind on the point of retiring from business he set forth in a letter to Cadwallader Colden:

> I am in a fair way of having no other tasks than such as I shall like to give myself, and of enjoying what I look upon as a great happiness, leisure to read, study, make experiments, and converse at large with such ingenious and worthy men as are pleased to honor me with their friendship or acquaintance, on such points as may produce something for the common benefit of mankind, uninterrupted by the little cares and fatigues of business.

From 1748 to his death in 1790, Franklin grasped every possible opportunity to adorn his polis and his nation with common benefits. He was postmaster, city commissioner, clerk of the Pennsylvania Assembly, agent of the province of Pennsylvania in England, delegate to the Second Continental Congress, diplomat and finally United States Minister Plenipotentiary in Paris; he invented bifocal spectacles, the lightning rod, the Franklin open stove; he established the first colonial circulating library, helped devise the local fire company and police force, founded the first colonial fire insurance company, the first colonial hospital, the American Philosophical Society, 'The Pennsylvania Society for Promoting the Abolition of Slavery, for the Relief of Free Negroes Unlawfully Held in Bondage, and for Improving the Condition of the African Race', and the first thoroughly secular university, the University of Pennsylvania; with John Jay and John Adams he arranged the terms and signed the Treaty of Paris that ended the Revolution. Back in Philadelphia in 1785 he became president of her executive council for three years, ending his public career as a member of the Constitutional Convention. The last act of his life was to write a satirical defence of slavery, disguising himself in the persona of an Algerian pirate, in response to a racist speech by a convention delegate from Georgia. At his death, the largest company of Americans ever to assemble, it was said, came together to pay tribute to him.

Those Americans who dislike Benjamin Franklin and his *Autobiography* – and they are not few – dislike the absence of mystery, of tragedy, of anxiety and of imaginative awe in his life and works. It is possible to find offensive, for example, in the second part of that work Franklin's succinct and ironic summary of his religious beliefs:

> I had been religiously educated as a Presbyterian; and 'tho some of the dogmas of that persuasion, such as the eternal decrees of God, election, reprobation, etc., appeared to me unintelligible, others doubtful, and I early absented myself from the public assemblies of the sect, Sunday being my studying day, I was never without some religious principles. I never doubted, for example, the existence of the Deity, that he made the world and governed it by his providence, that the most acceptable service of God was the doing of good to man, that our souls are immortal, and that all crimes will be punished and virtues rewarded either here or hereafter.

The rejection of theological doctrines as they appear 'unintelligible', the comic composure of 'Sunday being my studying day', the secure aplomb of enunciating the doctrine of good works as 'the most acceptable service', the crucial reserve in the phrase 'here or hereafter' implying an ultimate form of humanism at the very heart of a declaration of faith – all these have seemed deeply disagreeable to those who especially respond to Jonathan Edwards. Others have disliked the *Autobiography* not only for its over-secure rationalism but for its decisive grip on the concept of personal identity as an aggregation of consciously adopted representative roles, its parading the various Franklins from penniless youth to entrepreneurial maturity before the reader (and before William, the son assumed to be the immediate reader to whom the memoir is addressed), from the likewise adopted posture of the cultivated elderly gentleman 'expecting a week's uninterrupted leisure in my present country retirement'. Franklin's cool certainty that a life consists of a series of consciously assumed and manipulated roles, for example, inevitably attracted the hostility of Herman Melville, who portrayed him in *Israel Potter*:

> Having carefully weighed the world, Franklin could act any part in it. By nature turned to knowledge, his mind was often grave, but never serious....This philosophical levity of tranquillity, so to speak, is shown in his easy variety of pursuits. Printer, postmaster, almanac maker, essayist, chemist, orator, tinker, statesman, humorist, philosopher, parlor man, political economist, professor of housewifery, ambassador, projector, maxim-monger, herb-doctor, wit: – Jack of all trades, master of each and mastered by none – the type and genius of his land, Franklin was everything but a poet.

Melville's catalogue of poses, consistently depressing Franklin's value by an epithetic thumb on the scales, may nonetheless serve to make again the point that American colonial prose is anything but unitary in nature. Were it to tend to produce nothing but cascading Franklins, we might shiver; since it lies in our power to read Edwards as well as Franklin, there is no need to fear that the forces of tragic understanding and poetic irrationality will not be heard in America.

My text is the first printed text edited by John Bigelow from the manuscript in 1868.

Part One

Twyford, at the Bishop of St. Asaph's 1771

Dear Son,

    I have ever had a Pleasure in obtaining any little Anecdotes of my

Ancestors. You may remember the Enquiries I made among the Remains of my Relations when you were with me in England; and the Journey I took for that purpose. Now imagining it may be equally agreeable to you to know the Circumstances of *my* Life, many of which you are yet unacquainted with; and expecting a Weeks uninterrupted Leisure in my present Country Retirement, I sit down to write them for you. To which I have besides some other Inducements. Having emerg'd from the Poverty and Obscurity in which I was born and bred, to a State of Affluence and some Degree of Reputation in the World, and having gone so far thro' Life with a considerable Share of Felicity, the conducing Means I made use of, which, with the Blessing of God, so well succeeded, my Posterity may like to know, as they may find some of them suitable to their own Situations, and therefore fit to be imitated. That Felicity, when I reflected on it, has induc'd me sometimes to say, that were it offer'd to my Choice, I should have no Objection to a Repetition of the same Life from its Beginning, only asking the Advantage Authors have in a second Edition to correct some Faults of the first.[1] So would I if I might, besides corr[ectin]g the Faults, change some sinister Accidents and Events of it for others more favourable, but tho' this were deny'd, I should still accept the Offer. However, since such a Repetition is not to be expected, the next Thing most like living one's Life over again, seems to be a *Recollection* of that Life; and to make that Recollection as durable as possible, the putting it down in Writing. Hereby, too, I shall indulge the Inclination so natural in old Men, to be talking of themselves and their own past Actions, and I shall indulge it, without being troublesome to others who thro' respect to Age might think themselves oblig'd to give me a Hearing, since this may be read or not as any one pleases. And lastly, (I may as well confess it, since my Denial of it will be believ'd by no body) perhaps I shall a good deal gratify my own *Vanity*. Indeed I scarce ever heard or saw the introductory Words, *Without Vanity I may say*, &c. but some vain thing immediately follow'd. Most People dislike Vanity in others whatever Share they have of it themselves, but I give it fair Quarter wherever I meet with it, being persuaded that it is often productive of Good to the Possessor and to others that are within his Sphere of Action: And therefore in many Cases it would not be quite absurd if a Man were to thank God for his Vanity among the other Comforts of Life.

And now I speak of thanking God, I desire with all Humility to acknowledge, that I owe the mention'd Happiness of my past Life to his kind Providence, which led me to the Means I us'd and gave them

Success. My Belief of this, induces me to *hope*, tho' I must not *presume*, that the same Goodness will still be exercis'd towards me in continuing that Happiness, or in enabling me to bear a fatal Reverse, which I may experience as others have done, the Complexion of my future Fortune being known to him only: and in whose Power it is to bless to us even our Afflictions.

The Notes one of my Uncles (who had the same kind of Curiosity in collecting Family Anecdotes) once put into my Hands, funish'd me with several Particulars relating to our Ancestors. From these Notes I learnt that the Family had liv'd in the same Village, Ecton in Northamptonshire, for 300 Years, and how much longer he knew not (perhaps from the Time when the Name *Franklin* that before was the Name of an Order of People, was assum'd by them for a Surname when others took Surnames all over the Kingdom) on a Freehold of about 30 Acres, aided by the Smith's Business which had continued in the Family till his Time, the eldest Son being always bred to that Business. A Custom which he and my Father both followed as to their eldest Sons. When I search'd the Register at Ecton, I found an Account of their Births, Marriages and Burials, from the Year 1555 only, there being no Register kept in that Parish at any time preceding. By that Register I perceiv'd that I was the youngest Son of the youngest Son for 5 Generations back.

My Grandfather Thomas, who was born in 1598, lived at Ecton till he grew too old to follow Business longer, when he went to live with his Son John, a Dyer at Banbury in Oxfordshire, with whom my Father serv'd an Apprenticeship. There my Grandfather died and lies buried. We saw his Gravestone in 1758. His eldest Son Thomas liv'd in the House at Ecton, and left it with the Land to his only Child, a Daughter, who with her Husband, one Fisher of Wellingborough sold it to Mr. Isted, now Lord of the Manor there. My Grandfather had 4 Sons that grew up, viz. Thomas, John, Benjamin and Josiah. I will give you what Account I can of them at this distance from my Papers, and if they are not lost in my Absence, you will among them find many more Particulars. Thomas was bred a Smith under his Father, but being ingenious, and encourag'd in Learning (as all his Brothers like wise were) by an Esquire Palmer then the principal Gentleman in that Parish, he qualify'd for the Business of Scrivener, became a considerable Man in the County Affairs, was a chief Mover of all publick Spirited Undertakings, for the County, or Town of Northampton and his own Village, of which many Instances were told us at Ecton and he was much taken Notice of and patroniz'd by the then Lord Halifax. He died in 1702, Jan. 6, old Stile, just 4 Years to a Day before I was born.[2] The Account we receiv'd of his Life and Character from some old People at Ecton, I remember struck you, as something extraordinary from its Similarity to what you knew of mine. Had he died on the same Day, you said one might have suppos'd a Transmigration.

John was bred a Dyer, I believe of Woollens. Benjamin, was bred a Silk Dyer, serving an Apprenticeship at London. He was an ingenious Man, I remember him well, for when I was a Boy he came over to my Father in Boston, and lived in the House with us some Years. He lived to a great Age. His Grandson Samuel Franklin now lives in Boston. He left behind him two Quarto Volumes, M.S. of his own Poetry, consisting of little occasional Pieces address'd to his Friends and Relations... I was nam'd after this Uncle, there being a particular Affection between him and my Father...

This obscure Family of ours was early in the Reformation, and continu'd Protestants thro' the Reign of Queen Mary, when they were sometimes in Danger of Trouble on Account of their Zeal against Popery. They had got an English Bible, and to conceal and secure it, it was fastned open with Tapes under and within the Frame of a Joint Stool. When my Great Great Grandfather read in it to his Family, he turn'd up the Joint Stool upon his Knees, turning over the Leaves then under the Tapes. One of the Children stood at the Door to give Notice if he saw the Apparitor coming, who was an Officer of the Spiritual Court. In that Case the Stool was turn'd down again upon its feet, when the Bible remain'd conceal'd under it as before. This Anecdote I had from my Uncle Benjamin. The Family continu'd all of the Church of England till about the End of Charles the 2ds Reign, when some of the Miniters that had been outed for Noncon-formity, holding Conventicles in Northamptonshire, Benjamin and Josiah adher'd to them, and so continu'd all their Lives. The rest of the Family remain'd with the Episcopal Church.

Josiah, my Father, married young, and carried his Wife with three Children unto New England, about 1682. The Conventicles having been forbidden by Law, and frequently disturbed, induced some considerable Men of his Acquaintance to remove to that Country, and he was prevail'd with to accompany them thither, where they expected to enjoy their Mode of Religion with Freedom. By the same Wife he had 4 Children more born there, and by a second Wife ten more, in all 17, of which I remember 13 sitting at one time at his Table, who all grew up to be Men and Women, and married. I was the youngest Son and the youngest Child but two, and was born in Boston, N. England.

Autobiography

My Mother the 2d Wife was Abiah Folger, a Daughter of Peter Folger, one of the first Settlers of New England, of whom honourable mention is made by Cotton Mather, in his Church History of that Country, (entitled Magnalia Christi Americana) as a *godly learned Englishman*, if I remember the words rightly. I have heard that he wrote sundry small occasional Pieces, but only one of them was printed which I saw now many Years since. It was written in 1675, in the homespun Verse of that Time and People, and address'd to those then concern'd in the Government there. It was in favour of Liberty of Conscience, and in behalf of the Baptists, Quakers, and other Sectaries, that had been under Persecution; ascribing the Indian Wars and other Distresses, that had befallen the Country to that Persecution, as so many Judgments of God, to punish so heinous an Offence; and exhorting a Repeal of those uncharitable Laws. The whole appear'd to me as written with a good deal of Decent Plainness and manly Freedom. The six last concluding Lines I remember, tho' I have forgotten the two first of the Stanza, but the Purport of them was that his Censures proceeded from *Goodwill*, and therefore he would be known as the Author,

> because to be a Libeller, (says he)
>   I hate it with my Heart.
> From Sherburne Town where now I dwell,
>   My Name I do put here,
> Without Offence, your real Friend,
>   It is Peter Folgier.

My elder Brothers were all put Apprentices to different Trades. I was put to the Grammar School at Eight Years of Age, my Father intending to devote me as the Tithe of his Sons to the Service of the Church. My early Readiness in learning to read (which must have been very early, as I do not remember when I could not read) and the Opinion of all his Friends that I should certainly make a good Scholar, encourag'd him in this Purpose of his. My Uncle Benjamin too approv'd of it, and propos'd to give me all his Shorthand Volumes of Sermons I suppose as a Stock to set up with, if I would learn his Character. I continu'd however at the Grammar School not quite one Year, tho' in that time I had risen gradually from the Middle of the Class of that Year to be the Head of it, and farther was remov'd into the next Class above it, in order to go with that into the third at the End of the Year. But my Father in the mean time, from a View of the Expence of a College Education which, having so large a Family, he could not well afford, and the mean Living many so educated were afterwards able to obtain, Reasons that he gave to his Friends in my

Hearing, altered his first Intention, took me from the Grammar School, and sent me to a School for Writing and Arithmetic kept by a then famous Man, Mr. Geo. Brownell, very successful in his Profession generally, and that by mild encouraging Methods. Under him I acquired fair Writing pretty soon, but I fail'd in the Arithmetic, and made no Progress in it.

At Ten Years old, I was taken home to assist my Father in his Business, which was that of a Tallow Chandler and Sope-Boiler. A Business he was not bred to, but had assumed on his Arrival in New England and on finding his Dying Trade would not maintain his Family, being in little Request. Accordingly I was employed in cutting Wick for the Candles, filling the Dipping Mold, and the Molds for cast Candles, attending the Shop, going of Errands, &c. I dislik'd the Trade and had a strong Inclination for the Sea; but my Father declar'd against it; however, living near the Water, I was much in and about it, learnt early to swim well, and to manage Boats, and when in a Boat or Canoe with other Boys I was commonly allow'd to govern, especially in any case of Difficulty; and upon other Occasions I was generally a Leader among the Boys, and sometimes led them into Scrapes, of which I will mention one Instance, as it shows an early projecting public Spirit, tho' not then justly conducted. There was a Salt Marsh that bounded part of the Mill Pond, on the Edge of which at Highwater, we us'd to stand to fish for Minews. By much Trampling, we had made it a mere Quagmire. My Proposal was to build a Wharf there fit for us to stand upon, and I show'd my Comrades a large Heap of Stones which were intended for a new House near the Marsh, and which would very well suit our Purpose. Accordingly in the Evening when the Workmen were gone, I assembled a Number of my Playfellows, and working with them diligently like so many Emmets, sometimes two or three to a Stone, we brought them all away and built our little Wharff. The next moring the Workmen were surpiz'd at Missing the Stones; which were found in our Wharff; Enquiry was made after the Removers; we were discovered and complain'd of; several of us were corrected by our Fathers; and tho' I pleaded the Usefulness of the Work, mine convinc'd me that nothing was useful which was not honest.

I think you may like to know Something of his Person and Character. He had an excellent Constitution of Body, was of middle Stature, but well set and very strong. He was ingenious, could draw prettily, was skill'd a little in Music and had a clear pleasing Voice, so that when he play'd Psalm Tunes on his Violin and sung withal as he sometimes did in an Evening after the Business of the Day was over, it was extreamly agreable to hear. He had a mechanical Genius too, and on occasion was very handy in the Use of other Tradesmen's Tools. But his great Excellence lay in a sound Understanding, and solid judgment in prudential Matters, both in private and publick Affairs. In the latter indeed he was never employed, the numerous Family he had to educate and the straitness of his Circumstances, keeping him close to his Trade, but I remember well his being frequently visisted by leading People, who consulted him for his Opinion in affairs of the Town or of the Church he belong'd to and show'd a good deal of Respect for his Judgment and Advice. He was also much consulted by private Persons about their Affairs when any Difficulty occur'd, and frequently chosen an Arbitrator between contending Parties. At his Table he lik'd to have as often as he could, some sensible Friend or Neighbour, to converse with, and always took care to start some ingenious or useful Topic for Discourse, which might tend to improve the Minds of his Children. By this means he turn'd our Attention to what was good, just, and prudent in the Conduct of Life; and little or no Notice was ever taken of what related to the Victuals on the Table, whether it was well or ill drest, in or out of season, of good or bad flavour, preferable or inferior to this or that other thing of the kind; so that I was bro't up in such a perfect Inattention to those Matters as to be quite Indifferent what kind of Food was set before me; and so unobservant of it, that to this Day, if I am ask'd I can scarce tell, a few Hours after Dinner, what I din'd upon. This has been a Convenience to me in travelling, where my Companions have been sometimes very unhappy for want of a suitable Gratification of their more delicate because better instructed Tastes and Appetites.

My Mother had likewise an excellent Constitution. She suckled all her 10 Children. I never knew either my Father or Mother to have any Sickness but that of which they dy'd, he at 89 and she at 85 Years of age. They lie buried together at Boston, where I some Years since plac'd a Marble stone over their Grave...

By my rambling Digressions I perceive my self to be grown old. I us'd to write more methodically. But one does not dress for private Company as for a publick Ball. 'Tis perhaps only Negligence.

To return. I continu'd thus employ'd in my Father's Business for two Years, that is till I was 12 Years old; and my Brother John, who was bred to that Business having left my Father, married and set up for himself at Rhodeisland, there was all Appearance that I was destin'd to supply his Place and be a Tallow Chandler. But my Dislike to the Trade continuing, my Father was under Apprehensions that if he did not find one for me more agreably, I should break away and get to Sea, as his Son Josiah had done to his great Vexation. He therefore sometimes took me to walk with him, and see Joiners, Bricklayers, Turners, Braziers, &c. at their Work, that he might observe my Inclination, and endeavour to fix it on some Trade or other on Land. It has ever since been a Pleasure to me to see good Workmen handle their Tools; and it has been useful to me, having learnt so much by it, as to be able to do little Jobs my self in my House, when a Workman could not readily be got; and to construct little Machines for my Experiments while the Intention of making the Experiment was fresh and warm in my Mind. My Father at last fix'd upon the Cutlers Trade, and my Uncle Benjamin's Son Samuel who was bred to that Business in London being about that time establish'd in Boston, I was sent to be with him some time on liking. But his Expectations of a Fee with me displeasing my Father, I was taken home again.

From a Child I was fond of Reading, and all the little Money that came into my Hands was ever laid out in Books. Pleas'd with the Pilgrim's Progress, my first Collection was of John Bunyan's Works, in separate little Volumes. I afterwards sold them to enable me to buy R. Burton's Historical Collections; they were small Chapmen's Books and cheap, 40 or 50 in all. My Father's little Library consisted chiefly of Books in polemic Divinity, most of which I read, and have since often regretted, that at a time when I had such a Thirst for Knowledge, more proper Books had not fallen in my Way, since it was now resolv'd I should not be a Clergyman. Plutarch's Lives there was, in which I read abundantly, and I still think that time spent to great Advantage. There was also a Book of Defoe's, called an Essay on Projects, and another of Dr. Mather's, call'd Essays to do Good which perhaps gave me a Turn of Thinking that had an Influence on some of the principal future Events of my Life.[3]

This Bookish Inclination at length determin'd my Father to make me a Printer, tho' he had already one Son, (James) of that Profession. In 1717 my Brother James return'd from England with a Press and Letters to set up his Business in Boston. I lik'd it much better than that of my Father, but still had a Hankering for the Sea. To prevent the apprehended Effect of such an Inclination, my Father was impatient to have me bound to my Brother. I stood out some time, but at last was persuaded and signed the Indentures, when I was yet but 12 Years old. I was to serve as an Apprentice till I was 21 Years of Age, only I was to be allow'd Journeyman's Wages during the last Year. In a little time I made great Proficiency in the Business, and became a useful Hand to my Brother. I now had Access to better Books. An Acquaintance with the Apprentices of Booksellers, enabled me sometimes to borrow a small one, which I was careful to return soon and clean. Often I sat up in my Room reading the greatest Part of the Night, when the Book was borrow'd in the Evening and to be return'd early in the Morning lest it should be miss'd or wanted. And after some time an ingenious Tradesman Mr. Matthew Adams who had a pretty Collection of Books, and who frequented our Printing House, took Notice of me, invited me to his Library, and very kindly lent me such Books as I chose to read. I now took a Fancy to Poetry, and made some little Pieces. My Brother, thinking it might turn to account encourag'd me, and put me on composing two occasional Ballads. One was called the *Light House Tragedy*, and contain'd an Account of the drowning of Capt. Worthilake with his Two Daughters; the other was a Sailor Song on the Taking of *Teach* or Blackbeard the Pirate. They were wretched Stuff, in the Grubstreet Ballad Stile, and when they were printed he sent me about the Town to sell them. The first sold wonderfully, the Event being recent, having made a great Noise. This flatter'd my Vanity. But my Father discourag'd me, by ridiculing my Performances, and telling me Verse-makers were generally Beggars; so I escap'd being a Poet, most probably a very bad one...

There was another Bookish Lad in the Town, John Collins by Name, with whom I was intimately acquainted. We sometimes disputed, and very fond we were of Argument, and very desirous of confuting one another. Which disputacious Turn, by the way, is apt to become a very bad Habit, making People often extreamly disagreable in Company, by the Contradiction that is necessary to bring it into Practice, and thence, besides souring and spoiling the Conversation, is productive of Disgusts and perhaps Enmities where you may have occasion for Friendship. I had caught it by reading my Father's Books of Dispute about Religion. Persons of good Sense, I have since observ'd, seldom fall into it, except Lawyers, University Men, and Men of all Sorts that have been bred at Edinborough. A Question was once some how or other started between Collins and me, of the Propriety of educating the Female Sex in Learning, and their Abilities for Study. He was of Opinion that it was improper; and that they were naturally unequal to it. I took the contrary Side, perhaps a little for Dispute sake.[4] He was naturally more eloquent, had a ready Plenty of Words, and sometimes as I thought bore me down more by his Fluency than by the Strength of his Reasons. As we parted without settling the Point, and were not to see one another again for sometime, I sat down to put my Arguments in Writing, which I copied fair and sent to him. He answer'd and I reply'd. Three or four Letters of a Side had pass'd, when my Father happen'd to find my Papers, and read them. Without entring into the Discussion, he took occasion to talk to me about the Manner of my Writing, observ'd that tho' I had the Advantage of my Antagonist in correct Spelling and pointing (which I ow'd to the Printing House) I fell far short in elegance of Expression, in Method and in Perspicuity, of which he convinc'd me by several Instances. I saw the Justice of his Remarks, and thence grew more attentive to the *Manner* in Writing, and determin'd to endeavour at Improvement.

About this time I met with an odd Volume of the Spectator. It was the third. I had never before seen any of them. I bought it, read it over and over, and was much delighted with it. I thought the Writing excellent, and wish'd if possible to imitate it. With that View, I took some of the Papers, and making short Hints of the Sentiment in each Sentence, laid them by a few Days, and then without looking at the Book, try'd to compleat the Papers again, by expressing each hinted Sentiment at length and as fully as it had been express'd before, in any suitable Words, that should come to hand.

Then I compar'd my Spectator with the Original, discover'd some of my Faults and corrected them. But I found I wanted a Stock of Words or a Readiness in recollecting and using them, which I thought I should have acquir'd before that time, if I had gone on making Verses, since the continual Occasion for Words of the same Import but of different Length, to suit the Measure, or of different Sound for the Rhyme, would have laid me under a constant Necessity of searching for Variety, and also have tended to fix that Variety in my Mind, and make me Master of it. Therefore I took some of the Tales and turn'd them into Verse: And after a time, when I had pretty well forgotten the Prose, turn'd them back again. I also sometimes jumbled my Collections of Hints into Confusion, and after some Weeks, endeavour'd to reduce them into the best Order, before I began to form the full Sentences, and compleat the Paper. This was to teach me Method in the Arrangement of Thoughts. By comparing my work afterwards with the original, I discover'd many faults and amended them; but I sometimes had the Pleasure of Fancying that in certain Particulars of small Import, I had been lucky enough to improve the Method or the Language and this encourag'd me to think I might possibly in time come to be a tolerable English Writer, of which I was extreamly ambitious.

My Time for these Exercises and for Reading, was at Night, after Work or before Work began in the Morning; or on Sundays, when I contrived to be in the Printing House alone, evading as much as I could the common Attendance on publick Worship, which my Father used to exact of me when I was under his Care: And which indeed I still thought a Duty; tho' I could not, as it seemed to me, afford the Time to practise it.

When about 16 Years of Age, I happen'd to meet with a Book, written by one Tryon, recommending a Vegetable Diet. I determined to go into it. My Brother being yet unmarried, did not keep House, but boarded himself and his Apprentices in another Family. My refusing to eat Flesh occasioned an Inconveniency, and I was frequently chid for my singularity. I made my self acquainted with Tryon's Manner of preparing some of his Dishes, such as Boiling Potatoes or Rice, making Hasty Pudding, and a few others, and then propos'd to my Brother, that if he would give me Weekly half the Money he paid for my Board I would board my self. He instantly agreed to it, and I presently found that I could save half what he paid me. This was an additional Fund for buying Books: But I had another Advantage in it. My Brother and the rest going from the Printing House to their Meals, I remain'd there alone, and dispatching presently my light Repast, (which often was no more than a Bisket or a Slice of Bread, a Handful of Raisins or a Tart from the Pastry Cook's, and a Glass of Water) had the rest of the Time till their Return, for Study, in which I made the greater Progress from that greater Clearness of Head and quicker Apprehension which usually attend Temperance in Eating and Drinking. And now it was that being on some Occasion made asham'd of my Ignorance in Figures, which I had twice failed in learning when at School, I took Cocker's Book of Arithmetick, and went thro' the whole by my self with great Ease. I also read Seller's and Sturmy's Books of Navigation, and became acquainted with the little Geometry they contain, but never proceeded far in that Science. And I read about this Time Locke on Human Understanding, and the Art of Thinking by Messrs. du Port Royal.

While I was intent on improving my Language, I met with an English Grammar (I think it was Greenwood's) at the End of which there were two little Sketches of the Arts of Rhetoric and Logic, the latter finishing with a Specimen of a Dispute in the Socratic Method. And soon after I procur'd Xenophon's Memorable Things of Socrates, wherein there are many Instances of the same Method. I was charm'd with it, adopted it, dropt my abrupt Contradiction, and positive Argumentation, and put on the humble Enquirer and Doubter. And being then, from reading Shaftsbury and Collins, become a real Doubter in many Points of our Religious Doctrine, I found this Method safest for my self and very embarassing to those against whom I used it, therefore I took a Delight in it, practis'd it continually and grew very artful and expert in drawing People even of superior Knowledge into Concessions the Consequences of which they did not foresee, entangling them in Difficulties out of which they could not extricate themselves, and so obtaining Victories that neither my self nor my Cause always deserved.

I continu'd this Method some few Years, but gradually left it, retaining only the Habit of expressing my self in Terms of modest Diffidence, never using when I advance any thing that may possibly be disputed, the Words, *Certainly, undoubtedly*, or any others that give the Air of Positiveness to an Opinion; but rather say, I conceive, or I apprehend a Thing to be so or so, It appears to me, or I should think it so or so for such and such Reasons, or I imagine it to be so, or it is so if I am not mistaken. This Habit I believe has been of great Advantage to me, when I have had occasion to inculcate my Opinions and persuade Men into Measures that I have been from time to time engag'd in promoting. And as the chief Ends of Conversation are to *inform*, or to be *informed*, to *please* or to *persuade*, I wish wellmeaning sensible Men would not lessen their Power of doing Good by a Positive assuming Manner that seldom fails to disgust, tends to create Opposition, and to defeat every one of those Purposes for which Speech was given us, to wit, giving or receiving Information, or Pleasure: For if you would *inform*, a positive dogmatical Manner in advancing your Sentiments, may provoke Contradiction and prevent a candid Attention. If you wish Information and Improvement from the Knowledge of others and yet at the same time express your self as firmly fix'd in your present Opinions, modest sensible Men, who do not love Disputation, will probably leave you undisturb'd in the Possession of your Error; and by such a Manner you can seldom hope to recommend your self in *pleasing* your Hearers, or to persuade those whose Concurrence you desire. Pope says, judiciously,

> Men should be taught as if you taught them not,
> And things unknown propos'd as things forgot,

farther recommending it to us,

> To speak tho' sure, with seeming Diffidence.

And he might have coupled with this Line that which he has coupled with another, I think less properly,

> For Want of Modesty is Want of Sense.

If you ask why, *less properly*, I must repeat the Lines;

> Immodest Words admit of *no* Defence;
> *For* Want of Modesty is Want of Sense.

Now is not *Want of Sense* (where a Man is so unfortunate as to want it) some Apology for his *Want of Modesty*? and would not the Lines stand more justly thus?

> Immodest Words admit *but this* Defence.
> That Want of Modesty is Want of Sense.

This however I should submit to better Judgments.

My Brother had in 1720 or 21, begun to print a Newspaper. It was the second that appear'd in America, and was called *The New England Courant*.[5] The only one before it, was *the Boston News Letter*. I remember his being dissuaded by some of his Friends from the Undertaking, as not likely to succeed, one Newspaper being in their Judgment enough for America. At this time 1771 there are not less than five and twenty. He went on however with the Undertaking, and after having work'd in composing the Types and printing of the Sheets I was employ'd to carry the Papers thro' the Streets to the Customers. He had some ingenious Men among his Friends who amus'd themselves by writing little Pieces for this Paper, which gain'd it Credit, and made it more in Demand; and these Gentlemen often visited us. Hearing their Conversations, and their Accounts of the Approbation their Papers were receiv'd with, I was excited to try my Hand among them. But being still a Boy, and suspecting that my Brother would object to printing any Thing of mine in his Paper if he knew it to be mine, I contriv'd to disguise my Hand, and writing an anonymous Paper I put it in at Night under the Door of the Printing House. It was found in the Morning and communicated to his Writing Friends when they call'd in as usual. They read it, commented on it in my Hearing, and I had the exquisite Pleasure, of finding it met with their Approbation, and that in their different Guesses at the Author none were named but Men of some Character among us for Learning and Ingenuity.

I suppose now that I was rather lucky in my Judges: And that perhaps they were not really so very good ones as I then esteem'd them. Encourag'd however by this, I wrote and convey'd in the same Way to the Press several more Papers, which were equally approv'd, and I kept my Secret till my small Fund of Sense for such Performances was pretty well exhausted, and then I discovered it; when I began to be considered a little more by my Brother's Acquaintance, and in a manner that did not quite please him, as he thought, probably with reason, that it tended to make me too vain.[6] And perhaps this might be one Occasion of the Differences that we frequently had about this Time. Tho' a Brother, he considered himself as my Master, and me as his Apprentice; and accordingly expected the same Services from me as he would from another; while I thought he demean'd me too much in some he requir'd of me, who from a Brother expected more Indulgence. Our Disputes were often brought before our Father, and I fancy I was either generally in the right, or else a better Pleader, because the Judgment was generally in my favour: But my Brother was passionate and had often beaten me, which I took extreamly amiss; and thinking my Apprenticeship very tedious, I was continually wishing for some Opportunity of shortening it, which at length offered in a manner unexpected.[7]

One of the Pieces in our News-Paper, on some political Point which I have now forgotten, gave Offence to the Assembly. He was taken up, censur'd and imprison'd for a Month by the Speaker's Warrant, I suppose because he would not discover his Author. I too was taken up and examin'd before the Council; but tho' I did not give them any Satisfaction, they contented themselves with admonishing me, and dismiss'd me; considering me perhaps as an Apprentice who was bound to keep his Master's Secrets. During my Brother's Confinement, which I resented a good deal, notwithstanding our private Differences, I had the Management of the Paper, and I made bold to give our Rulers some Rubs in it, which my Brother took very kindly, while others began to consider me in an unfavourable Light, as a young Genius that had a Turn for Libelling and Satyr. My Brother's Discharge was accompany'd with an Order of the House, (a very odd one) *that James Franklin should no longer print the Paper called the New England Courant*. There was a Consultation held in our Printing House among his Friends what he should do in this Case. Some propos'd to evade the Order by changing the Name of the Paper; but my Brother seeing Inconveniences in that, it was finally concluded on as a better Way, to let it be printed for the future under the Name of *Benjamin Franklin*. And to avoid the Censure of the Assembly that might fall on him, as still printing it by his Apprentice, the Contrivance was, that my old Indenture shoud be return'd to me with a full Discharge on the Back of it, to be shown on Occasion; but to secure to him the Benefit of my Service I was to sign new Indentures for the Remainder of the Term, which were to be kept private. A very flimsy Scheme it was, but however it was immediately executed, and the Paper went on accordingly under my Name for several Months. At length a fresh Difference arising between my Brother and me, I took upon me to assert my Freedom, presuming that he would not venture to produce the new Indentures. It was not fair in me to take this Advantage, and this I therefore reckon one of the first Errata of my Life: But the Unfairness of it weigh'd little with me, when under the Impressions of Resentment, for the Blows his Passion too often urg'd him to bestow upon me. Tho' he was otherwise not an ill-natur'd Man: Perhaps I was too saucy and provoking.

When he found I would leave him, he took care to prevent my getting Employment in any other Printing-House of the Town, by going round and speaking to every Master, who accordingly refus'd to give me Work. I then thought of going to New York as the nearest Place where there was a Printer... My Friend Collins therefore undertook to manage a little for me. He agreed with the Captain of a New York Sloop for my Passage, under the Notion of my being a young Acquaintance of his that had got a naughty Girl with Child, whose Friends would compel me to marry her, and therefore I could not appear or come away publickly. So I sold some of my Books to raise a little Money, Was taken on board privately, and as we had a fair Wind in three Days I found my self in New York near 300 Miles from home, a Boy of but 17, without the least Recommendation to or Knowledge of any Person in the Place, and with very little Money in my Pocket.

My Inclinations for the Sea, were by this time worne out, or I might now have gratify'd them. But having a Trade, and supposing my self a pretty good Workman, I offer'd my Service to the Printer of the Place, old Mr. Wm. Bradford, (who had been the first Printer in Pensilvania, but remov'd from thence upon the Quarrel of Geo. Keith). He could give me no Employment, having little to do, and Help enough already: But, says he, my Son at Philadelphia has lately lost his principal Hand, Aquila Rose, by Death. If you go thither I believe he may employ you. Philadelphia was 100 Miles farther. I set out, however, in a Boat for Amboy, leaving my Chest and Things to follow me round by Sea. In crossing the Bay we met with a Squall that tore our rotten Sails to pieces, prevented our getting into the Kill, and drove us upon Long Island. In our Way a drunken Dutchman, who was a Passenger too, fell over board; when he was sinking I reach'd thro' the Water to his shock Pate and drew him up so that we got him in again. His Ducking sober'd him a little, and he went to sleep, taking first out of his Pocket a Book which he desir'd I would dry for him. It prov'd to be my old favourite Author Bunyan's Pilgrim's Progress in Dutch, finely printed on good Paper with copper Cuts, a Dress better than I had ever seen it wear in its own Language. I have since found that it has been translated into most of the Languages of Europe, and suppose it has been more generally read than any other Book except perhaps the Bible. Honest John was the first that I know of who mix'd

Narration and Dialogue, a Method of Writing very engaging to the Reader, who in the most interesting Parts finds himself as it were brought into the Company, and present at the Discourse. Defoe in his Cruso, his Moll Flanders, Religious Courtship, Family Instructor, and other Pieces, has imitated it with Success. And Richardson has done the same in his Pamela, &c.

...

In the Evening I found my self very feverish, and went in to Bed. But having read somewhere that cold Water drank plentifully was good for a Fever, I follow'd the Prescription, sweat plentifully most of the Night, my Fever left me, and in the Morning crossing the Ferry, I proceeded on my Journey, on foot, having 50 Miles to Burlington, where I was told I should find Boats that would carry me the rest of the Way to Philadelphia.

It rain'd very hard all the Day, I was thoroughly soak'd and by Noon a good deal tir'd, so I stopt at a poor Inn, where I staid all Night, beginning now to wish I had never left home. I cut so miserable a Figure too, that I found by the Questions ask'd me I was suspected to be some runaway Servant, and in danger of being taken up on that Suspicion. However I proceeded the next Day, and got in the Evening to an Inn within 8 or 10 Miles of Burlington, kept by one Dr. Brown.

He entred into Conversation with me while I took some Refreshment, and finding I had read a little, became very sociable and friendly. Our Acquaintance continu'd as long as he liv'd. He had been, I imagine, an itinerant Doctor, for there was not Town in England, or Country in Europe, of which he could not give a very particular Account. He had some Letters, and was ingenious, but much of an Unbeliever, and wickedly undertook some Years after to travesty the Bible in doggrel Verse as Cotton had done Virgil. By this means he set many of the Facts in a very ridiculous Light, and might have hurt weak minds if his Work had been publish'd: but it never was. At his House I lay that Night, and the next Morning reach'd Burlington. But had the Mortification to find that the regular Boats were gone, a little before my coming, and no other expected to go till Tuesday, this being Saturday. Wherefore I return'd to an old Woman in the Town of whom I had bought Gingerbread to eat on the Water, and ask'd her Advice; she invited me to lodge at her House till a Passage by Water should offer: and being tired with my foot Travelling, I accepted the Invitation. She understanding I was a Printer, would have had me stay at that Town and follow my Business, being ignorant of the Stock necessary to begin with. She was very hospitable, gave me a Dinner of

Ox Cheek with great Goodwill, accepting only of a Pot of Ale in return. And I tho't my self fix'd till Tuesday should come. However walking in the Evening by the Side of the River a Boat came by, which I found was going towards Philadelphia, with several People in her. They took me in, and as there was no Wind, we row'd all the Way; and about Midnight not having yet seen the City, some of the Company were confident we must have pass'd it, and would row no farther, the others knew not where we were, so we put towards the Shore, got into a Creek, landed near an old Fence with the Rails of which we made a Fire, the Night being cold, in October, and there we remain'd till Daylight. Then one of the Company knew the Place to be Cooper's Creek a little above Philadelphia, which we saw as soon as we got out of the Creek, and arriv'd there about 8 or 9 a Clock, on the Sunday morning, and landed at the Market street Wharff.

I have been the more particular in this Description of my Journey, and shall be so of my first Entry into that City, that you may in your Mind compare such unlikely Beginnings with the Figure I have since made there. I was in my Working Dress, my best Cloaths being to come round by Sea. I was dirty from my Journey; my Pockets were stuff'd out with Shirts and Stockings; I knew no Soul, nor where to look for Lodging. I was fatigu'd with Travelling, Rowing and Want of Rest. I was very hungry, and my whole Stock of Cash consisted of a Dutch Dollar and about a Shilling in Copper. The latter I gave the People of the Boat for my Passage, who at first refus'd it on Account of my Rowing; but I insisted on their taking it, a Man being sometimes more generous when he has but a little Money than when he has plenty, perhaps thro' Fear of being thought to have but little.

Then I walk'd up the Street, gazing about, till near the Market House I met a Boy with Bread. I had made many a Meal on Bread, and inquiring where he got it, I went immediately to the Baker's he directed me to in second Street; and ask'd for Bisket, intending such as we had in Boston, but they it seems were not made in Philadelphia, then I ask'd for a threepenny Loaf, and was told they had none such: so not considering or knowing the Difference of Money and the greater Cheapness nor the Names of his Bread, I bad him give me three penny worth of any sort. He gave me accordingly three great Puffy Rolls. I was surpriz'd at the Quantity, but took it, and having no room in my Pockets, walk'd off, with a Roll under each Arm, and eating the other. Thus I went up Market Street as far as fourth Street, passing by the Door of Mr. Read, my future Wife's Father, when she standing at the Door saw me, and thought I made as I certainly did a most awkward ridiculous Appearance. Then I turn'd and went down

Chestnut Street and part of Walnut Street, eating my Roll all the Way, and coming round found my self again at Market Street Wharff, near the Boat I came in, to which I went for a Draught of the River Water, and being fill'd with one of my Rolls, gave the other two to a Woman and her Child that came down the River in the Boat with us and were waiting to go farther. Thus refresh'd I walk'd again up the Street, which by this time had many clean dress'd People in it who were all walking the same Way; I join'd them, and thereby was led into the great Meeting House of the Quakers near the Market. I sat down among them, and after looking round a while and hearing nothing said, being very drowzy thro' Labour and want of Rest the preceding Night, I fell fast asleep, and continu'd so till the Meeting broke up, when one was kind enough to rouse me. This was therefore the first House I was in or slept in, in Philadelphia.

Walking again down towards the River, and looking in the Faces of People, I met a young Quaker Man whose Countenance I lik'd, and accosting him requested he would tell me where a Stranger could get Lodging. We were then near the Sign of the Three Mariners. Here, says he, is one Place that entertains Strangers, but it is not a reputable House; if thee wilt walk with me, I'll show thee a better. He brought me to the Crooked Billet in Water-Street. Here I got a Dinner. And while I was eating it, several sly Questions were ask'd me, as it seem'd to be suspected from my youth and Appearance, that I might be some Runaway. After Dinner my Sleepiness return'd: and being shown to a Bed, I lay down without undressing, and slept till Six in the Evening; was call'd to Supper; went to Bed again very early and slept soundly till the next Morning. Then I made my self as tidy as I could, and went to Andrew Bradford the Printer's. I found in the Shop the old Man his Father, whom I had seen at New York, and who travelling on horse back had got to Philadelphia before me. He introduc'd me to his Son, who receiv'd me civilly, gave me a Breakfast, but told me he did not at present want a Hand, being lately supply'd with one. But there was another Printer in town lately set up, one Keimer, who perhaps might employ me; if not, I should be welcome to lodge at his House, and he would give me a little Work to do now and then till fuller Business should offer.

The old Gentleman said, he would go with me to the new Printer: And when we found him, Neighbour, says Bradford, I have brought to see you a young Man of your Business, perhaps you may want such a One. He ask'd me a few Questions, put a Composing Stick in my Hand to see how I work'd, and then said he would employ me soon, tho' he had just then nothing for me to do. And taking old Bradford whom he had never seen before, to be one of the Towns People that had a Good Will for him, enter'd into a Conversation on his present Undertaking and Prospects; while Bradford not discovering that he was the other Printer's Father, on Keimer's saying he expected soon to get the greatest Part of the Business into his own Hands, drew him on by artful Questions and starting little Doubts, to explain all his Views, what Interest he rely'd on, and in what manner he intended to proceed. I who stood by and heard all, saw immediately that one of them was a crafty old Sophister, and the other a mere Novice. Bradford left me with Keimer, who was greatly surpriz'd when I told him who the old Man was.

. . .

These two Printers I found poorly qualified for their Business. Bradford had not been bred to it, and was very illiterate; and Keimer tho' something of a Scholar, was a mere Compositor, knowing nothing of Presswork. He had been one of the French Prophets[a] and could act their enthusiastic Agitations. At this time he did not profess any particular Religion, but something of all on occasion; was very ignorant of the World, and had, as I afterwards found, a good deal of the Knave in his Composition. He did not like my Lodging at Bradford's while I work'd with him. He had a House indeed, but without Furniture, so he could not lodge me: But he got me a Lodging at Mr. Read's before-mentioned, who was the Owner of his House. And my Chest and Clothes being come by this time, I made rather a more respectable Appearance in the Eyes of Miss Read, than I had done when she first happen'd to see me eating my Roll in the Street.

I began now to have some Acquaintance among the young People of the Town, that were Lovers of Reading with whom I spent my Evenings very pleasantly and gaining Money by my Industry and Frugality, I lived very agreably, forgetting Boston as much as I could, and not desiring that any there should know where I resided, except my Friend Collins who was in my Secret, and kept it when I wrote to him. At length an Incident happened that sent me back again much sooner than I had intended.

I had a Brother-in-law, Robert Holmes, Master of a Sloop, that traded between Boston and Delaware. He being at New Castle 40 Miles below Philadelphia, heard there of me, and wrote me a Letter, mentioning the Concern of my Friends in Boston at my abrupt Departure, assuring me of their Goodwill to me, and that every thing

---

[a] A group of French Protestant refugees in England in 1706, prone to trances and revelations, who proclaimed a messianic kingdom soon to come.

would be accommodated to my Mind if I would return, to which he exhorted me very earnestly. I wrote an Answer to his Letter, thank'd him for his Advice, but stated my Reasons for quitting Boston fully, and in such a Light as to convince him I was not so wrong as he had apprehended.

Sir William Keith Governor of the Province, was then at New Castle, and Capt. Holmes happening to be in Company with him when my Letter came to hand, spoke to him of me, and show'd him the Letter. The Governor read it, and seem'd surpriz'd when he was told my Age. He said I appear'd a young Man of promising Parts, and therefore should be encouraged: The Printers at Philadelphia were wretched ones, and if I would set up there, he made no doubt I should succeed; for his Part, he would procure me the publick Business, and do me every other Service in his Power. This my Brother-in-Law afterwards told me in Boston. But I knew as yet nothing of it; when one Day Keimer and I being at Work together near the Window, we saw the Governor and another Gentleman (which prov'd to be Col. French, of New Castle) finely dress'd, come directly across the Street to our House, and heard them at the Door. Keimer ran down immediately, thinking it a Visit to him. But the Governor enquir'd for me, came up, and with a Condescension and Politeness I had been quite unus'd to, made me many Compliments, desired to be acquainted with me, blam'd me kindly for not having made my self known to him when I first came to the Place, and would have me away with him to the Tavern where he was going with Col. French to taste as he said some excellent Madeira. I was not a little surpriz'd, and Keimer star'd like a Pig poison'd. I went however with the Governor and Col. French, to a Tavern the Corner of Third Street, and over the Madeira he propos'd my Setting up my Business, laid before me the Probabilities of Success, and both he and Col. French assur'd me I should have their Interest and Influence in procuring the Publick Business of both Governments. On my doubting whether my Father would assist me in it, Sir William said he would give me a Letter to him, in which he would state the Advantages, and he did not doubt of prevailing with him. So it was concluded I should return to Boston in the first Vessel with the Governor's Letter recommending me to my Father. In the mean time the Intention was to be kept secret, and I went on working with Keimer as usual, the Governor sending for me now and then to dine with him, a very great Honour I thought it, and conversing with me in the most affable, familiar, and friendly manner imaginable.

About the End of April 1724. a little Vessel offer'd for Boston. I took Leave of Keimer as going to see my Friends. The Governor gave me an ample Letter, saying many flattering things of me to my Father[8] and strongly recommending the Project of my setting up at Philadelphia, as a Thing that must make my Fortune. We struck on a Shoal in going down the Bay and sprung a Leak, we had a blustring time at Sea, and were oblig'd to pump almost continually, at which I took my Turn. We arriv'd safe however at Boston in about a Fortnight. I had been absent Seven Months and my Friends had heard nothing of me; for my Br. Holmes was not yet return'd; and had not written about me. My unexpected Appearance surpriz'd the Family; all were however very glad to see me and made me Welcome, except my Brother. I went to see him at his Printing House: I was better dress'd than ever while in his Service, having a genteel new Suit from Head to foot, a Watch, and my Pockets lin'd with near Five Pounds Sterling in Silver. He receiv'd me not very frankly, look'd me all over, and turn'd to his Work again. The Journey-Men were inquisitive where I had been, what sort of a Country it was, and how I lik'd it? I prais'd it much, and the happy Life I led in it; expressing strongly my Intention of returning to it; and one of them asking what kind of Money we had there, I produc'd a handful of Silver and spread it before them, which was a kind of Raree-Show they had not been us'd to, Paper being the Money of Boston. Then I took an Opportunity of letting them see my Watch: and lastly, (my Brother still grum and sullen) I gave them a Piece of Eight to drink and took my Leave. This Visit of mine offended him extreamly. For when my Mother some time after spoke to him of a Reconciliation, and of her Wishes to see us on good Terms together, and that we might live for the future as Brothers, he said, I had insulted him in such a Manner before his People that he could never forget or forgive it. In this however he was mistaken.

My Father receiv'd the Governor's Letter with some apparent Surprize; but said little of it to me for some Days; when Capt. Homes returning, he show'd it to him, ask'd if he knew Keith, and what kind of a Man he was: Adding his Opinion that he must be of small Discretion, to think of setting a Boy up in Business who wanted yet 3 Years of being at Man's Estate. Homes said what he could in favour of the Project; but my Father was clear in the Impropriety of it; and at last gave a flat Denial to it. Then he wrote a civil Letter to Sir William thanking him for the Patronage he had so kindly offered me, but declining to assist me as yet in Setting up, I being in his Opinion too young to be trusted with the Management of a Business so important, and for which the Preparation must be so expensive.

My Friend and Companion Collins, who was a Clerk at the

Post-Office, pleas'd with the Account I gave him of my new Country, determin'd to go thither also: And while I waited for my Fathers Determination, he set out before me by Land to Rhode-island, leaving his Books which were a pretty Collection of Mathematicks and Natural Philosophy, to come with mine and me to New York where he propos'd to wait for me. My Father, tho' he did not approve Sir William's Proposition was yet pleas'd that I had been able to obtain so advantageous a Character from a Person of such Note where I had resided, and that I had been so industrious and careful as to equip my self so handsomely in so short a time; therefore seeing no Prospect of an Accommodation between my Brother and me, he gave his Consent to my Returning again to Philadelphia, advis'd me to behave respectfully to the People there, endeavour to obtain the general Esteem, and avoid lampooning and libelling to which he thought I had too much Inclination; telling me, that by steady Industry and a prudent Parsimony, I might save enough by the time I was One and Twenty to set me up, and that if I came near the Matter he would help me out with the rest. This was all I could obtain, except some small Gifts as Tokens of his and my Mother's Love, when I embark'd again for New-York, now with their Approbation and their Blessing.

The Sloop putting in at Newport, Rhodeisland, I visited my Brother John, who had been married and settled there some Years. He received me very affectionately, for he always lov'd me. A Friend of his, one Vernon, having some Money due to him in Pensilvania, about 35 Pounds Currency, desired I would receive it for him, and keep it till I had his Directions what to remit it in. Accordingly he gave me an Order. This afterwards occasion'd me a good deal of Uneasiness. At Newport we took in a Number of Passengers for New York: Among which were two young Women, Companions, and a grave, sensible Matron-like Quaker-Woman with her Attendants. I had shown an obliging readiness to do her some little Services which impress'd her I suppose with a degree of Good-will towards me. Therefore when she saw a daily growing Familiarity between me and the two Young Women, which they appear'd to encourage, she took me aside and said, Young Man, I am concern'd for thee, as thou has no Friend with thee, and seems not to know much of the World, or of the Snares Youth is expos'd to; depend upon it those are very bad Women, I can see it in all their Actions, and if thee art not upon they Guard, they will draw thee into some Danger: they are Strangers to thee, and I advise thee in a friendly Concern for thy Welfare, to have no Acquaintance with them. As I seem'd at first not to think so ill of them as she did, she mention'd some Things she had observ'd and heard that had escap'd my Notice; but now convinc'd me she was right. I thank'd her for her kind Advice, and promis'd to follow it. When we arriv'd at New York, they told me where they liv'd, and invited me to come and see them: but I avoided it. And it was well I did: For the next Day, the Captain miss'd a Silver Spoon and some other Things that had been taken out of his Cabbin, and knowing that these were a Couple of Strumpets, he got a Warrant to search their Lodgings, found the stolen Goods, and had the Thieves punish'd. So tho' we had escap'd a sunken Rock which we scrap'd upon in the Passage, I thought this Escape of rather more Importance to me.

At New York I found my Friend Collins, who had arriv'd there some Time before me. We had been intimate from Children, and had read the same Books together. But he had the Advantage of more time for reading, and Studying and a wonderful Genius for Mathematical Learning in which he far outstript me. While I liv'd in Boston most of my Hours of Leisure for Conversation were spent with him, and he continu'd a sober as well as an industrious Lad; was much respected for his Learning by several of the Clergy and other Gentlemen, and seem'd to promise making a good Figure in Life: but during my Absence he had acquire'd a Habit of Sotting with Brandy; and I found by his own Account and what I heard from others, that he had been drunk every day since his Arrival at New York, and behav'd very oddly. He had gam'd too and lost his Money, so that I was oblig'd to discharge his Lodgings, and defray his Expences to and at Philadelphia; Which prov'd extreamly inconvenient to me. The then Governor of N York, Burnet, Son of Bishop Burnet hearing from the Captain that a young Man, one of his Passengers, had a great many Books, desired he would bring me to see him. I waited upon him accordingly, and should have taken Collins with me but that he was not sober. The Governor treated me with great Civility, show'd me his Library, which was a very large one, and we had a good deal of Conversation about Books and Authors. This was the second Governor who had done me the Honour to take Notice of me, which to a poor Boy like me was very pleasing.

We proceeded to Philadelphia. I received on the Way Vernon's Money, without which we could hardly have finish'd our Journey. Collins wish'd to be employ'd in some Counting House; but whether they discover'd his Dramming by his Breath, or by his Behaviour, tho' he had some Recommendations, he met with no Success in any Application, and continu'd Lodging and Boarding at the same House with me and at my Expence. Knowing I had that Money of Vernon's he was continually borrowing of me, still promising Repayment as soon as he sould be in Business. At length he had got so much of it, that I was distress'd to think what I should do, in case of being call'd on to remit it. His Drinking continu'd about which we sometimes quarrel'd, for when a little intoxicated he was very fractious. Once in a Boat on the Delaware with some other young Men, he refused to row in his Turn: I will be row'd home, says he. We will not row you, says I. You must or stay all Night on the Water, says he, just as you please. The others said, Let us row; what signifies it? But my Mind being soured with his other Conduct, I continu'd to refuse. So he swore he would make me row, or throw me overboard; and coming along stepping on the Thwarts towards me, when he came up and struck at me I clapt my Hand under his Crutch, and rising pitch'd him head-foremost into the River. I knew he was a good Swimmer, and so was under little Concern about him; but before he could get round to lay hold of the Boat, we had with a few Strokes pull'd her out of his Reach. And ever when he drew near the Boat, we ask'd if he would row, striking a few Strokes to slide her away from him. He was ready to die with Vexation, and obstinately would not promise to row; however seeing him at last beginning to tire, we lifted him in; and brought him home dripping wet in the Evening. We hardly exchang'd a civil Word afterwards; and a West India Captain who had a Commission to procure a Tutor for the Sons of a Gentleman at Barbadoes, happening to meet with him, agreed to carry him thither. He left me then, promising to remit me the first Money he should receive in order to discharge the Debt. But I never heard of him after.

The Breaking into this Money of Vernon's was one of the first great Errata of my Life. And this Affair show'd that my Father was not much out in his Judgment when he suppos'd me too young to manage Business of Importance. But Sir William, on reading his Letter, said he was too prudent. There was great Difference in Persons, and Discretion did not always accompany Years, nor was Youth always without it. And since he will not set you up, says he, I will do it my self. Give me an Inventory of the Things necessary to be had from England, and I will send for them. You shall repay me when you are able; I am resolv'd to have a good Printer here, and I am sure you must succeed. This was spoken with such an Appearance of Cordiality, that I had not the least doubt of his meaning what he said. I had hitherto kept the Proposition of my Setting up a Secret in Philadelphia, and I still kept it. Had it been known that I depended on the Governor, probably some Friend that knew him better would have advis'd me not to rely on him, as I afterwards heard it as his known Character to be liberal of Promises which he never meant to keep. Yet unsolicited as he was by me, how could I think his generous Offers insincere? I believ'd him one of the best Men in the World.

I presented him an Inventory of a little Printing House, amounting by my Computation to about £100 Sterling. He lik'd it, but ask'd me if my being on the Spot in England to chuse the Types and see that every thing was good of the kind, might not be of some Advantage. Then, says he, when there, you may make Acquaintances and establish Correspondencies in the Bookselling and Stationary Way. I agreed that this might be advantageous. Then says he, get yourself ready to go with Annis; which was the annual Ship, and the only one at that Time usually passing between London and Philadelphia. But it would be some Months before Annis sail'd, so I continu'd working with Keimer, fretting about the Money Collins had got from me, and in daily Apprehensions of being call'd upon by Vernon, which however did not happen for some Years after.

I believe I have omitted mentioning that in my first Voyage from Boston, being becalm'd off Block Island, our People set about catching Cod and hawl'd up a great many. Hitherto I had stuck to my Resolution of not eating animal Food; and on this Occasion, I consider'd with my Master Tryon, the taking every Fish as a kind of unprovok'd Murder, since none of them had or ever could do us any Injury that might justify the Slaughter. All this seem'd very reasonable. But I had formerly been a great Lover of Fish, and when this came hot out of the Frying Pan, it smelt admirably well. I balanc'd some time between Principle and Inclination: till I recollected, that when the Fish were opened, I saw smaller Fish taken out of their Stomachs: Then thought I, if you eat one another, I don't see why we mayn't eat you. So I din'd upon Cod very heartily and continu'd to eat with other People, returning only now and than occasionally to a vegetable Dict. So convenient a thing it is to be a *reasonable Creature*, since it enables one to find or make a Reason for every thing one has a mind to do.

Keimer and I liv'd on a pretty good familiar Footing and agreed tolerably well: for he suspected nothing of my Setting up. He retain'd a great deal of his old Enthusiasms, and lov'd Argumentation. We therefore had many Disputations. I us'd to work him so with my Socratic Method, and had trapann'd him so often by Questions apparently so distant from any Point we had in hand, and yet by degrees led to the Point, and brought him into Difficulties and Contradictions that at last he grew ridiculously cautious, and would hardly answer me the most common Question, without asking first,

What do you intend to infer from that? However it gave him so high an Opinion of my Abilities in the Confuting Way, that he seriously propos'd my being his Colleague in a Project he had of setting up a new Sect. He was to preach the Doctrines, and I was to confound all Opponents. When he came to explain with me upon the Doctrines, I found several Conundrums which I objected to unless I might have my Way a little too, and introduce some of mine. Keimer wore his Beard at full Length, because somewhere in the Mosaic Law it is said, *thou shalt not mar the Corners of thy Beard.* He likewise kept the seventh day Sabbath; and these two Points were Essentials with him. I dislik'd both, but agreed to admit them upon Condition of his adopting the Doctrine of using no animal Food. I doubt, says he, my Constitution will not bear that. I assur'd him it would, and that he would be the better for it. He was usually a great Glutton, and I promis'd my self some Diversion in half-starving him. He agreed to try the Practice if I would keep him Company. I did so and we held it for three Months. We had our Victuals dress'd and brought to us regularly by a Woman in the Neighbourhood, who had from me a List of 40 Dishes to be prepar'd for us at different times, in all which there was neither Fish Flesh nor Fowl, and the whim suited me the better at this time from the Cheapness of it, not costing us above 18*d*. Sterling each, per Week. I have since kept several Lents most strictly, Leaving the common Diet for that, and that for the common, abruptly, without the least Inconvenience: So that I think there is little in the Advice of making those Changes by easy Gradations. I went on pleasantly, but poor Keimer suffer'd grievously, tir'd of the Project, long'd for the Flesh Pots of Egypt, and order'd a roast Pig. He invited me and two Women Friends to dine with him, but it being brought too soon upon table, he could not resist the Temptation, and ate it all up before we came.

I had made some Courtship during this time to Miss Read. I had a great Respect and Affection for her, and had some Reason to believe she had the same for me: but as I was about to take a long Voyage, and we were both very young, only a little above 18. it was thought most prudent by her Mother to prevent our going too far at present, as a Marriage if it was to take place would be more convenient after my Return, when I should be as I expected set up in my Business. Perhaps too she thought my Expectations not so wellfounded as I imagined them to be.

My chief Acquaintances at this time were, Charles Osborne, Joseph Watson, and James Ralph; All Lovers of Reading. The two first were Clerks to an eminent Scrivener or Conveyancer in the Town, Charles

Brogden; the other was Clerk to a Merchant. Watson was a pious sensible young Man, of great Integrity. The others rather more lax in their Principles of Religion, particularly Ralph, who as well as Collins had been unsettled by me, for which they both made me suffer. Osborne was sensible, candid, frank, sincere, and affectionate to his Friends; but in litterary Matters too fond of Criticising. Ralph, was ingenious, genteel in his Manners, and extreamly eloquent; I think I never knew a prettier Talker. Both of them great Admirers of Poetry, and began to try their Hands in little Pieces. Many pleasant Walks we four had together on Sundays into the Woods near Skuylkill, where we read to one another and conferr'd on what we read.

Ralph was inclin'd to pursue the Study of Poetry, not doubting but he might become eminent in it and make his Fortune by it, alledging that the best Poets must when they first began to write, make as many Faults as he did. Osborne dissuaded him, assur'd him he had no Genius for Poetry, and advis'd him to think of nothing beyond the Business he was bred to; that in the mercantile way tho' he had no Stock, he might by his Diligence and Punctuality recommend himself to Employment as a Factor, and in time acquire wherewith to trade on his own Account. I approv'd the amusing one's self with Poetry now and then, so far as to improve one's Language, but no farther. On this it was propos'd that we should each of us at our next Meeting produce a Piece of our own Composing, in order to improve by our mutual Observations, Criticisms and Corrections. As Language and Expression was what we had in View, we excluded all Considerations of Invention, by agreeing that the Task should be a Version of the 18th Psalm, which describes the Descent of a Deity. When the Time of our Meeting drew nigh, Ralph call'd on me first, and let me know his Piece was ready. I told him I had been busy, and having little Inclination had done nothing. He then show'd me his Piece for my Opinion; and I much approv'd it, as it appear'd to me to have great Merit. Now, says he, Osborne never will allow the least Merit in any thing of mine, but makes 1000 Criticisms out of mere Envy. He is not so jealous of you. I wish therefore you would take this Piece, and produce it as yours. I will pretend not to have had time, and so produce nothing: We shall then see what he will say to it. It was agreed, and I immediately transcrib'd it that it might appear in my own hand. We met. Watson's Performance was read: there were some Beauties in it: but many Defects. Osborne's was read: It was much better. Ralph did it Justice, remark'd some Faults, but applauded the Beauties. He himself had nothing to produce. I was backward, seem'd desirous of being excus'd, had not had sufficient Time to correct; &c.

but no Excuse could be admitted, produce I must. It was read and repeated; Watson and Osborne gave up the Contest; and join'd in applauding it immoderately. Ralph only made some Criticisms and propos'd some Amendments, but I defended my Text. Osborne was against Ralph, and told him he was no better a Critic than Poet; so he dropt the Argument. As they two went home together, Osborne express'd himself still more strongly in favour of what he thought my Production, having restrain'd himself before as he said, lest I should think it Flattery. But who would have imagin'd, says he, that Franklin had been capable of such a Performance; such Painting, such Force! such Fire! he has even improv'd the Original! In his common Conversation, he seems to have no Choice of Words; he hesitates and blunders; and yet, good God, how he writes! When we next met, Ralph discover'd the Trick, we had plaid him, and Osborne was a little laught at. This Transaction fix'd Ralph in his Resolution of becoming a Poet. I did all I could to dissuade him from it, but He continued scribbling Verses, till Pope cur'd him. He became however a pretty good Prose Writer. More of him hereafter.

. . .

The Governor, seeming to like my Company, had me frequently to his House; and his Setting me up was always mention'd as a fix'd thing. I was to take with me Letters recommendatory to a Number of his Friends, besides the Letter of Credit to furnish me with the necessary Money for purchasing the Press and Types, Paper, &c. For these Letters I was appointed to call at different times,when they were to be ready, but a future time was still named. Thus we went on till the Ship whose Departure too had been several times postponed was on the Point of sailing. Then when I call'd to take my Leave and Receive the Letters, his Secretary, Dr. Bard, came out to me and said the Governor was extreamly busy, in writing, but would be down at Newcastle before the Ship, and there the Letters would be delivered to me.

Ralph, tho' married and having one Child, had determined to accompany me in this Voyage. It was thought he intended to establish a Correspondence, and obtain Goods to sell on Commission. But I found afterwards, that thro' some Discontent with his Wifes Relations, he purposed to leave her on their Hands, and never return again. Having taken leave of my Friends, and interchang'd some Promises with Miss Read, I left Philadelphia in the Ship, which anchor'd at Newcastle. The Governor was there. But when I went to his Lodging, the Secretary came to me from him with the civillest Message in the World, that he could not then see me being engag'd in

Business of the utmost Importance; but should send the Letters to me on board, wish'd me heartily a good Voyage and a speedy Return, &c. I return'd on board, a little puzzled, but still not doubting.

Mr. Andrew Hamilton, a famous Lawyer of Philadelphia, had taken Passage in the same Ship for himself and Son; and with Mr. Denham a Quaker Merchant, and Messrs. Onion and Russel Masters of an Iron Work in Maryland, had engag'd the Great Cabin; so that Ralph and I were forc'd to take up with a Birth in the Steerage: And none on board knowing us, were considered as ordinary Persons. But Mr. Hamilton and his Son (it was James, since Governor) return'd from New Castle to Philadelphia, the Father being recall'd by a great Fee to plead for a seized Ship. And just before we sail'd Col. French coming on board, and showing me great Respect, I was more taken Notice of, and with my Friend Ralph invited by the other Gentlemen to come into the Cabin, there being now Room. Accordingly we remov'd thither.

Understanding that Col. French had brought on board the Governor's Dispatches, I ask'd the Captain for those Letters that were to be under my Care. He said all were put into the Bag together; and he could not then come at them; but before we landed in England, I should have an Opportunity of picking them out...

When we came into the Channel, the Captain kept his Word with me, and gave me an Opportunity of examining the Bag for the Governor's Letters. I found none upon which my Name was put, as under my Care; I pick'd out 6 or 7 that by the Hand writing I thought might be the promis'd Letters, especially as one of them was directed to Basket the King's Printer, and another to some Stationer. We arriv'd in London the 24th of December, 1724. I waited upon the Stationer who came first in my Way, delivering the Letter as from Gov. Keith. I don't know such a Person, says he: but opening the Letter, O, this is from Riddlesden; I have lately found him to be a compleat Rascal, and I will have nothing to do with him, nor receive any Letters from him. So putting the Letter into my Hand, he turn'd on his Heel and left me to serve some Customer. I was surprized to find these were not the Governor's Letters. And after recollecting and comparing Circumstances, I began to doubt his Sincerity. I found my Friend Denham, and opened the whole Affair to him. He let me into Keith's Character, told me there was not the least Probability that he had written any Letters for me, that no one who knew him had the smallest Dependance on him, and he laught at the Notion of the Governor's giving me a Letter of Credit, having as he said no Credit to give. On my expressing some Concern about what I should do: He advis'd me to endeavour getting some Employment in the Way of my Business. Among the Printers here, says he, you will improve yourself; and when you return to America, you will set up to greater Advantage.

We both of us happen'd to know, as well as the Stationer, that Riddlesden the Attorney, was a very Knave. He had half ruin'd Miss Read's Father by drawing him in to be bound for him. By his Letter it appear'd, there was a secret Scheme on foot to the Prejudice of Hamilton, (Suppos'd to be then coming over with us,) and that Keith was concern'd in it with Riddlesden. Denham, who was a Friend of Hamilton's, thought he ought to be acquainted with it. So when he arriv'd in England, which was soon after, partly from Resentment and Ill-Will to Keith and Riddlesden, and partly from Good Will to him: I waited on him, and gave him the Letter. He thank'd me cordially, the Information being of Importance to him. And from that time he became my Friend, greatly to my Advantage afterwards on many Occasions.

. . .

Ralph and I were inseparable Companions. We took Lodgings together in Little Britain at 3s. 6d. per Week, as much as we could then afford. . .

I immediately got into Work at Palmer's then a famous Printing House in Bartholomew Close; and here I continu'd near a Year. I was pretty diligent; but spent with Ralph a good deal of my Earnings in going to Plays and other Places of Amusement. We had together consum'd all my Pistoles, and now just rubb'd on from hand to mouth. He seem'd quite to forget his Wife and Child, and I by degrees my Engagements with Miss Read, to whom I never wrote more than one Letter, and that was to let her know I was not likely soon to return. This was another of the great Errata of my Life, which I should wish to correct if I were to live it over again. In fact, by our Expences, I was constantly kept unable to pay my Passage.

At Palmer's I was employ'd in composing for the second Edition of Woollaston's Religion of Nature. Some of his Reasonings not appearing to me well-founded, I wrote a little metaphysical Piece, in which I made Remarks on them. It was entitled, *A Dissertation on Liberty and Necessity, Pleasure and pain.* I inscrib'd it to my Friend Ralph. I printed a small Number. It occasion'd my being more consider'd by Mr. Palmer, as a young Man of some Ingenuity, tho' he seriously expostulated with me upon the Principles of my Pamphlet which to him appear'd abominable. My printing this Pamphlet was another Erratum.[9]

While I lodg'd in Little Britain I made an Acquaintance with one Wilcox a Bookseller, whose Shop was at the next Door. He had an immense Collection of second-hand Books. Circulating Libraries were not then in Use; but we agreed that on certain reasonable Terms which I have now forgotten, I might take, read and return any of his Books. This I esteem'd a great Advantage, and I made as much use of it as I could.

My Pamphlet by some means falling into the Hands of one Lyons, a Surgeon, Author of a Book intituled *The Infallibility of Human Judgment*, it occasioned an Acquaintance between us; he took great Notice of me, call'd on me often, to converse on those Subjects, carried me to the Horns a pale Ale-House in [blank] Lane, Cheapside, and introduc'd me to Dr. Mandevile, Author of the Fable of the Bees who had a Club there, of which he was the Soul, being a most facetious entertaining Companion. Lyons too introduc'd me, to Dr. Pemberton, at Batson's Coffee House, who promis'd to give me an Opportunity some time or other of seeing Sir Isaac Newton, of which I was extreamly desirous; but this never happened.

I had brought over a few Curiosities among which the principal was a Purse made of the Asbestos, which purifies by Fire. Sir Hans Sloane heard of it, came to see me, and invited me to his House in Bloomsbury Square, where he show'd me all his Curiosities, and persuaded me to let him add that to the Number, for which he paid me handsomely.

In our House there lodg'd a young Woman; a Millener, who I think had a Shop in the Cloisters. She had been genteelly bred, was sensible and lively, and of most pleasing Conversation. Ralph read Plays to her in the Evenings, they grew intimate, she took another Lodging, and he follow'd her. They liv'd together some time, but he being still out of Business, and her Income not sufficient to maintain them with her Child, he took a Resolution of going from London, to try for a Country School, which he thought himself well qualify'd to undertake, as he wrote an excellent Hand, and was a Master of Arithmetic and Accounts. This however he deem'd a Business below him, and confident of future better Fortune when he should be unwilling to have it known that he once was so meanly employ'd he chang'd his Name, and did me the Honour to assume mine. For I soon after had a Letter from him, acquainting me, that he was settled in a small Village in Berkshire, I think it was, where he taught reading and writing to 10 or a dozen Boys at 6 pence each per Week, recommending Mrs. T. to my Care, and desiring me to write to him directing for Mr. Franklin Schoolmaster at such a Place. He continu'd to write frequently, sending me large Specimens of an Epic Poem, which he was then composing, and desiring my Remarks and Corrections. These I gave him from time to time, but endeavour'd rather to discourage his Proceeding. One of Young's Satires was then just publish'd. I copy'd and sent him a great Part of it, which set in a strong Light the Folly of pursuing the Muses with any Hope of Advancement by them. All was in vain. Sheets of the Poem continu'd to come by every Post. In the mean time Mrs. T. having on his Account lost her Friends and Business, was often in Distresses, and us'd to send for me, and borrow what I could spare to help her out of them. I grew fond of her Company, and being at this time under no Religious Restraints, and presuming on my Importance to her, I attempted Familiarities, (another Erratum) which she repuls'd with a proper Resentment, and acquainted him with my Behaviour. This made a Breach between us, and when he return'd again to London, he let me know he thought I had cancel'd all the Obligations he had been under to me. So I found I was never to expect his Repaying me what I lent to him or advanc'd for him. This was however not then of much Consequence, as he was totally unable. And in the Loss of his Friendship I found my self reliev'd from a Burthen. I now began to think of getting a little Money beforehand; and expecting better Work, I left Palmer's to work at Watts's near Lincoln's Inn Fields, a still greater Printing House. Here I continu'd all the rest of my Stay in London.

At my first Admission into this Printing House, I took to working at Press, imagining I felt a Want of the Bodily Exercise I had been us'd to in America, where Presswork is mix'd with Composing. I drank only Water; the other Workmen, near 50 in Number, were great Guzzlers of Beer. On occasion I carried up and down Stairs a large Form of Types in each hand, when others carried but one in both Hands. They wonder'd to see from this and several Instances that the Water-American as they call'd me was *stronger* than themselves who drank *strong* Beer. We had an Alehouse Boy who attended always in the House to supply the Workmen. My Companion at the Press, drank every day a Pint before Breakfast, a Pint at Breakfast with his Bread and Cheese; a Pint between Breakfast and Dinner; a Pint at Dinner; a Pint in the Afternoon about Six o'Clock, and another when he had done his Day's-Work. I thought it a detestable Custom. But it was necessary, he suppos'd, to drink *strong* Beer that he might be *strong* to labour. I endeavour'd to convince him that the Bodily Strength afforded by Beer could only be in proportion to the Grain or Flour of the Barley dissolved in the Water of which it was made; that there was more Flour in a Penny-worth of Bread, and therefore if he would eat that with a Pint of Water, it would give him more Strength than a Quart of Beer. He drank on however, and had 4 or 5 Shillings to pay out of his Wages every Saturday Night for that muddling Liquor; an Expence I was free from. And thus these poor Devils keep themselves always under.

Watts after some Weeks desiring to have me in the Composing Room, I left the Pressmen. A new *Bienvenu* or Sum for Drink, being 5s., was demanded of me by the Compositors. I thought it an Imposition, as I had paid below. The Master thought so too, and forbad my Paying it. I stood out two or three Weeks, was accordingly considered as an Excommunicate, and had so many little Pieces of private Mischief done me, by mixing my Sorts, transposing my Pages, breaking my Matter, &c. &c. if I were ever so little out of the Room, and all ascrib'd to the Chapel Ghost, which they said ever haunted those not regularly admitted, that notwithstanding the Master's Protection, I found myself oblig'd to comply and pay the Money; convinc'd of the Folly of being on ill Terms with those one is to live with continually. I was now on a fair Footing with them, and soon acquir'd considerable Influence. I propos'd some reasonable Alterations in their Chapel[b] Laws, and carried them against all Opposition. From my Example a great Part of them, left their muddling Breakfast of Beer and Bread and Cheese, finding they could with me be supply'd from a neighbouring House with a large Porringer of hot Water-gruel, sprinkled with Pepper, crumb'd with Bread, and a Bit of Butter in it, for the Price of a Pint of Beer, viz, three halfpence. This was a more comfortable as well as cheaper Breakfast, and kept their Heads clearer. Those who continu'd sotting with Beer all day, were often, by not paying, out of Credit at the Alehouse, and us'd to make Interest with me to get Beer, *their Light*, as they phras'd it, *being out*. I watch'd the Pay table on Saturday Night, and collected what I stood engag'd for them, having to pay some times near Thirty Shillings a Week on their Accounts. This, and my being esteem'd a pretty good Riggite, that is a jocular verbal Satyrist, supported my Consequence in the Society. My constant Attendance, (I never making a St. Monday), recommended me to the Master; and my uncommon Quickness at Composing, occasion'd my being put upon all work of Dispatch which was generally better paid. So I went on now very agreably.

. . .

At Watts's Printinghouse I contracted an Acquaintance with an ingenious young Man, one Wygate, who having wealthy Relations,

[b] Franklin's note: 'A Printing House is always called a Chappel by the Workmen.'

had been better educated than most Printers, was a tolerable Latinist, spoke French, and lov'd Reading. I taught him, and a Friend of his, to swim, at twice going into the River, and they soon became good Swimmers. They introduc'd me to some Gentlemen from the Country who went to Chelsea by Water to see the College and Don Saltero's Curiosities. In our Return, at the Request of the Company, whose Curiosity Wygate had excited, I stript and leapt into the River, and swam from near Chelsea to Blackfryars, performing on the Way many Feats of Activity both upon and under Water, that surpriz'd and pleas'd those to whom they were Novelties. I had from a Child been ever delighted with this Exercise, had studied and practis'd all Thevenot's Motions and Positions, added some of my own, aiming at the graceful and easy, as well as the Useful. All these I took this Occasion of exhibiting to the Company, and was much flatter'd by their Admiration. And Wygate, who was desirious of becoming a Master, grew more and more attach'd to me, on that account, as well as from the Similarity of our Studies. He at length propos'd to me travelling all over Europe together, supporting ourselves everywhere by working at our Business. I was once inclin'd to it. But mentioning it to my good Friend Mr. Denham, with whom I often spent an Hour, when I had Leisure. He dissuaded me from it, advising me to think only of returning to Pensilvania, which he was now about to do.

. . .

He now told me he was about to return to Philadelphia, and should carry over a great Quantity of Goods in order to open a Store there: He propos'd to take me over as his Clerk, to keep his Books (in which he would instruct me) copy his Letters, and attend the Store. He added, that as soon as I should be acquainted with mercantile Business he would promote me by sending me with a Cargo of Flour and Bread &c. to the West Indies, and procure me Commissions from others; which would be profitable, and if I manag'd well, would establish me handsomely. The Thing pleas'd me, for I was grown tired of London, remember'd with Pleasure the happy Months I had spent in Pennsylvania, and wish'd again to see it. Therefore I immediately agreed, on the Terms of Fifty Pounds a Year, Pensilvania Money; less indeed than my present Gettings as a Compostor, but affording a better Prospect.

I now took Leave of Printing, as I thought for ever, and was daily employ'd in my new Business; going about with Mr. Denham among the Tradesmen, to purchase various Articles, and seeing them pack'd up, doing Errands, calling upon Workmen to dispatch, &c. and when all was on board, I had a few Days Leisure. On one of these Days I was to my Surprize sent for by a great Man I knew only by Name, a Sir William Wyndham and I waited upon him. He had heard by some means or other of my Swimming from Chelsey to Blackfryars, and of my teaching Wygate and another young Man to swim in a few Hours. He had two Sons about to set out on their Travels; he wish'd to have them first taught Swimming; and propos'd to gratify me handsomely if I would teach them. They were not yet come to Town and my Stay was uncertain, so I could not undertake it. But from this Incident I thought it likely, that if I were to remain in England and open a Swimming School, I might get a good deal of Money. And it struck me so strongly, that had the Overture been sooner made me, probably I should not so soon have returned to America. After many Years, you and I had something of more Importance to do with one of these Sons of Sir William Wyndham, become Earl of Egremont, which I shall mention in its Place.

Thus I spent about 18 Months in London. Most Part of the Time, I work'd hard at my Business, and spent but little upon my self except in seeing Plays and in Books. My Friend Ralph had kept me poor. He owed me about 27 Pounds; which I was now never likely to receive; a great Sum out of my small Earnings. I lov'd him notwithstanding, for he had many amiable Qualities. Tho' I had by no means improv'd my Fortune. But I had pick'd up some very ingenious Acquaintance whose Conversation was of great Advantage to me, and I had read considerably.

We sail'd from Gravesend on the 23rd of July 1726. For the Incidents of the Voyage, I refer you to my Journal, where you will find them all minutely related. Perhaps the most important Part of that Journal is the *Plan* to be found in it which I formed at Sea, for regulating my future Conduct in Life. It is the more remarkable, as being form'd when I was so young, and yet being pretty faithfully adhered to quite thro' to old Age. We landed in Philadelphia the 11th of October, where I found sundry Alterations. Keith was no longer Governor, being superceded by Major Gordon: I met him walking the Streets as a common Citizen. He seem'd a little asham'd at seeing me, but pass'd without saying any thing. I should have been as much asham'd at seeing Miss Read, had not her Friends, despairing with Reason of my Return, after the Receipt of my Letter, persuaded her to marry another, one Rogers, a Potter, which was done in my Absence. With him however she was never happy, and soon parted from him, refusing to cohabit with him, or bear his Name It being now said that he had another Wife. He was a worthless Fellow tho' an excellent Workman which was the Temptation to her Friends. He got into Debt, and ran away in 1727 or 28. Went to the West Indies, and died there. Keimer had got a better House, a Shop well supply'd with Stationary, plenty of new Types, a number of Hands tho' none good, and seem'd to have a great deal of Business.

Mr. Denham took a Store in Water Street, where we open'd our Goods. I attended the Business diligently, studied Accounts, and grew in a little Time expert at selling. We lodg'd and boarded together, he counsell'd me as a Father, having a sincere Regard for me: I respected and lov'd him: and we might have gone on together very happily: But in the Beginning of Feby. 1726/7 when I had just pass'd my 21st Year, we both were taken ill. My Distemper was a Pleurisy, which very nearly carried me off: I suffered a good deal, gave up the Point in my own mind, and was rather disappointed when I found my Self recovering: regretting in some degree that I must now some time or other have all that disagreable Work to do over again. I forget what his Distemper was. It held him a long time, and at length carried him off. He left me a small Legacy in a nuncupative Will, as a Token of his Kindness for me, and he left me once more to the wide World. For the Store was taken into the Care of his Executors, and my Employment under him ended: My Brother-in-law Holmes, being now at Philadelphia, advis'd my Return to my Business. And Keimer tempted me with an Offer of large Wages by the Year to come and take the Management of his Printing-House, that he might better attend his Stationer's Shop. I had heard a bad Character of him in London, from his Wife and her Friends, and was not fond of having any more to do with him. I try'd for farther Employment as a Merchant's Clerk; but not readily meeting with any, I clos'd again with Keimer.

I found in *his* House these Hands; Hugh Meredith a Welsh-Pensilvanian, 30 Years of Age, bred to Country Work: honest, sensible, had a great deal of solid Observation, was something of a Reader, but given to drink: Stephen Potts, a young Country Man of full Age, bred to the Same: of uncommon natural Parts, and great Wit and Humour, but a little idle. These he had agreed with at extream low Wages, per Week, to be rais'd a Shilling every 3 Months, as they would deserve by improving in their Business, and the Expectation of these high Wages to come on hereafter was what he had drawn them in with. Meredith was to work at Press, Potts at Bookbinding, which he by Agreement, was to teach them, tho' he knew neither one nor t'other. John—a wild Irishman brought up to no Business, whose Service for 4 Years Keimer had purchas'd from the Captain of a Ship. He too was to be made a Pressman. George Webb, an Oxford

Scholar, whose Time for 4 Years he had likewise bought, intending him for a Compositor: of whom more presently. And David Harry, a Country Boy, whom he had taken Apprentice. I soon perceiv'd that the Intention of engaging me at Wages so much higher than he had been us'd to give, was to have these raw cheap Hands form'd thro' me, and as soon as I had instructed them, then, they being all articled to him, he should be able to do without me. I went on however, very chearfully; put his Printing House in Order, which had been in great Confusion, and brought his Hands by degrees to mind their Business and to do it better.

It was an odd Thing to find an Oxford Scholar in the Situation of a bought Servant. He was not more than 18 Years of Age, and gave me this Account of himself; that he was born in Gloucester, educated at a Grammar School there, had been distinguish'd among the Scholars for some apparent Superiority in performing his Part when they exhibited Plays; belong'd to the Witty Club there, and had written some Pieces in Prose and Verse which were printed in the Gloucester Newspapers. Thence he was sent to Oxford; there he continu'd about a Year, but not well-satisfy'd, wishing of all things to see London and become a Player. At length receiving his Quarterly Allowance of 15 Guineas, instead of discharging his Debts, he walk'd out of Town, hid his Gown in a Furz Bush, and footed it to London, where having no Friend to advise him, he fell into bad Company, soon spent his Guineas, found no means of being introduc'd among the Players, grew necessitous, pawn'd his Cloaths and wanted Bread. Walking the Street very hungry, and not knowing what to do with himself, a Crimp's Bill[c] was put into his Hand, offering immediate Entertainment and Encouragement to such as would bind themselves to serve in America. He went directly, sign'd the Indentures, was put into the Ship and came over; never writing a Line to acquaint his Friends what was become of him. He was lively, witty, good-natur'd, and a pleasant Companion, but idle, thoughtless and imprudent to the last Degree.

. . .

Our Printing-House often wanted Sorts, and there was no Letter Founder in America. I had seen Types cast at James's in London, but without much Attention to the Manner: However I now contriv'd a Mould, made use of the Letters we had, as Puncheons, struck the matrices in Lead, and thus supply'd in a pretty tolerable way all Deficiencies. I also engrav'd several Things on occasion. I made the

---

[c] A crimp was one whose business was to secure men for military or naval service, or to persuade them to become indentured servants in exchange for transport to the colonies.

Ink, I was Warehouse-man and every thing, in short quite a Factotum.

But however serviceable I might be, I found that my Services became every Day of less Importance, as the other Hands improv'd in the Business. And when Keimer paid my second Quarter's Wages, he let me know that he felt them too heavy, and thought I should make an Abatement. He grew by degrees less civil, put on more of the Master, frequently found Fault, was captious and seem'd ready for an Out-breaking. I went on nevertheless with a good deal of Patience, thinking that his incumber'd Circumstances were partly the Cause. At length a Trifle snapt our Connexion. For a great Noise happening near the Courthouse, I put my Head out of the Window to see what was the Matter. Keimer being in the Street look'd up and saw me, call'd out to me in a loud Voice and angry Tone to mind my Business, adding some reproachful Words. that nettled me the more for their Publicity, all the Neighbours who were looking out on the same Occasion being Witnesses how I was treated. He came up immediately into the Printing-House, continu'd the Quarrel, high Words pass'd on both Sides, he gave me the Quarter's Warning we had stipulated, expressing a Wish that he had not been oblig'd to so long a Warning: I told him his Wish was unnecessary for I would leave him that Instant; and so taking my Hat walk'd out of Doors; desiring Meredith whom I saw below to take care of some Things I left, and bring them to my Lodging.

Meredith came accordingly in the Evening, when we talk'd my Affair over. He had conceiv'd a great Regard for me, and was very unwilling that I should leave the House while he remain'd in it. He dissuaded me from returning to my native Country which I began to think of. He reminded me that Keimer was in debt for all he possess'd, that his Creditors began to be uneasy, that he kept his Shop miserably, sold often without Profit for ready Money, and often trusted without keeping Accounts. That he must therefore fail; which would make a Vacancy I might profit of. I objected my Want of Money. He then let me know, that his Father had a high Opinion of me, and from some Discourse that had pass'd between them, he was sure would advance Money to set us up, if I would enter into Partnership with him. My Time, says he, will be out with Keimer in the Spring. By that time we may have our Press and Types in from London: I am sensible I am no Workman. If you like it, Your Skill in the Business shall be set against the Stock I furnish; and we will share the Profits equally. The Proposal was agreable, and I consented. His Father was in Town, and approv'd of it, the more as he saw I had great Influence with his Son, had prevail'd on him to abstain long from Dramdrinking, and he hop'd might break him of that wretched Habit entirely, when we came to be so closely connected. I gave an Inventory to the Father, who carry'd it to a Merchant; the Things were sent for; the Secret was to be kept till they should arrive, and in the mean time I was to get work if I could at the other Printing House. But I found no Vacancy there, and so remain'd idle a few Days, when Keimer, on a Prospect of being employ'd to print some Paper-money, in New Jersey, which would require Cuts and various Types that I only could supply, and apprehending Bradford might engage me and get the Jobb from him, sent me a very civil Message, that old Friends should not part for a few Words, the Effect of sudden Passion, and wishing me to return. Meredith persuaded me to comply, as it would give more Opportunity for his Improvement under my daily Instructions. So I return'd, and we went on more smoothly than for some time before. The New Jersey Jobb was obtain'd. I contriv'd a Copper-Plate Press for it, the first that had been seen in the Country. I cut several Ornaments and Checks for the Bills. We went together to Burlington, where I executed the Whole to Satisfaction, and he received so large a Sum for the Work, as to be enabled thereby to keep his Head much longer above Water.

. . .

Before I enter upon my public Appearance in Business it may be well to let you know the then State of my Mind, with regard to my Principles and Morals, that you may see how far those influenc'd the future Events of my Life. My Parents had early given me religious Impressions, and brought me through my Childhood piously in the Dissenting Way. But I was scarce 15 when, after doubting by turns of several Points as I found them disputed in the different Books I read, I began to doubt of Revelation it self. Some Books against Deism fell into my Hands; they were said to be the Substance of Sermons preached at Boyle's Lectures. It happened that they wrought an Effect on me quite contrary to what was intended by them: For the Arguments of the Deists which were quoted to be refuted, appeared to me much stronger than the Refutations. In short I soon became a thorough Deist. My Arguments perverted some others, particularly Collins and Ralph: but each of them having afterwards wrong'd me greatly without the least Compunction and recollecting Keith's Conduct towards me, (who was another Freethinker) and my own towards Vernon and Miss Read which at Times gave me great Trouble, I began to suspect that this Doctrine tho' it might be true, was not very useful.

My London Pamphlet, which had for its Motto those Lines of
Dryden

> —Whatever is, is right.—
> Tho' purblind Man
> Sees but a Part of the Chain, the nearest Link,
> His Eyes not carrying to the equal Beam,
> That poizes all, above.[10]

And from the Attributes of God, his infinite Wisdom, Goodness
and Power concluded that nothing could possibly be wrong in the
World, and that Vice and Virtue were empty Distinctions, no such
Things existing: appear'd now not so clever a Performance as I once
thought it; and I doubted whether some Error had not insinuated
itself unperceiv'd into my Argument, so as to infect all that follow'd,
as is common in metaphysical Reasonings. I grew convinc'd that
Truth, Sincerity and Integrity in Dealings between Man and Man,
were of the utmost Importance to the Felicity of Life, and I form'd
written Resolutions, (which still remain in my Journal Book) to
practice them ever while I lived. Revelation had indeed no weight
with me as such; but I entertain'd an Opinion, that tho' certain
Actions might not be bad *because* they were forbidden by it, or good
because it commanded them; yet probably those Actions might be
forbidden *because* they were bad for us, or commanded *because* they
were beneficial to us, in their own Natures, all the Circumstances of
things considered. And this Persuasion, with the kind hand of
Providence, or some guardian Angel, or accidental favourable Circumstances and Situations, or all together, preserved me (thro' this
dangerous Time of Youth and the hazardous Situations I was sometimes in among Strangers, remote from the Eye and Advice of my
Father) without any *wilful* gross Immorality or Injustice that might
have been expected from my Want of Religion. I say *wilful*, because
the Instances I have mentioned, had something of *Necessity* in them,
from my Youth, Inexperience, and the Knavery of others. I had
therefore a tolerable Character to begin the World with, I valued it
properly, and determin'd to preserve it.

We had not been long return'd to Philadelphia, before the New
Types arriv'd from London. We settled with Keimer, and left him by
his Consent before he heard of it. We found a House to hire near the
Market, and took it. To lessen the Rent, (which was then but £24 a
Year tho' I have since known it let for 70) We took in Tho' Godfrey a
Glazier and his Family, who were to pay a considerable Part of it to us,
and we to board with them. We had scarce opened our Letters and put
our Press in Order, before George House, an Acquaintance of Mine,

brought a Country-man to us; whom he had met in the Street enquiring for a Printer. All our Cash was now expended in the Variety of Particulars we had been obliged to procure and this Countryman's Five Shillings being our first Fruits, and coming so seasonably, gave me more Pleasure than any Crown I have since earn'd; and from the Gratitude I felt towards House, has made me often more ready than perhaps I should otherwise have been to assist young Beginners.

There are Croakers in every Country always boding its Ruin. Such a one then lived in Philadelphia, a Person of Note, an elderly Man, with a wise Look, and very grave Manner of speaking. His Name was Samuel Mickle. This Gentleman, a Stranger to me, stopt one Day at my Door, and asked me if I was the young Man who had lately opened a new Printing House: Being answer'd in the Affirmative; he said he was sorry for me, because it was an expensive Undertaking and the Expence would be lost; for Philadelphia was a sinking Place, the People already half Bankrupts or near being so; all Appearances of the contrary, such as new Buildings and the Rise of Rents being to his certain Knowledge fallacious, for they were in fact among the Things that would soon ruin us. And he gave me such a Detail of Misfortunes, now existing or that were soon to exist, that he left me half-melancholy. Had I known him before I engag'd in this Business, probably I never should have done it. This Man continu'd to live in this decaying Place; and to declaim in the same Strain, refusing for many Years to buy a House there, because all was going to Destruction, and at last I had the Pleasure of seeing him give five times as much for one as he might have bought it for when he first began his Croaking.

I should have mention'd before, that in the Autumn of the preceding Year I had form'd most of my ingenious Acquaintance into a Club for mutual Improvement, which we call'd the Junto. We met on Friday Evenings. The Rules I drew up requir'd that every Member in his Turn should produce one or more Queries on any Point of Morals, Politics or Natural Philosophy, to be discuss'd by the Company, and once in three Months produce and read an Essay of his own Writing on any Subject he pleased. Our Debates were to be under the Direction of a President, and to be conducted in the sincere Spirit of Enquiry after Truth, without Fondness for Dispute, or Desire of Victory; and to prevent Warmth all Expressions of Positiveness in Opinion, or of direct Contradiction, were after some time made contraband and prohibited under small pecuniary Penalties....

And the club continu'd almost as long and was the best School of Philosophy, Morals and Politics that then existed in the Province; for our Queries which were read the Week preceding their Discussion, put us on Reading with Attention upon the several Subjects, that we might speak more to the purpose: and here too we acquired better Habits of Conversation, every thing being studied in our Rules which might prevent our disgusting each other. From hence the long Continuance of the Club, which I shall have frequent Occasion to speak farther of hereafter; But my giving this Account of it here, is to show something of the Interest I had, every one of these exerting themselves in recommending Business to us... And this Industry visible to our Neighbours began to give us Character and Credit; particularly I was told, that mention being made of the new Printing Office at the Merchants every-night-Club, the general Opinion was that it must fail, there being already two Printers in the Place, Keimer and Bradford; but Doctor Baird (whom you and I saw many Years after at his native Place, St. Andrews in Scotland) gave a contrary Opinion; for the Industry of that Franklin, says he, is superior to any thing I ever saw of the kind: I see him still at work when I go home from Club; and he is at Work again before his Neighbours are out of bed. This struck the rest, and we soon after had Offers from one of them to Supply us with Stationary. But as yet we did not chuse to engage in Shop Business.

I mention this Industry the more particularly and the more freely, tho' it seems to be talking in my own Praise, that those of my Posterity who shall read it, may know the Use of that Virtue, when they see its Effects in my Favour throughout this Relation.

George Webb, who had found a Female Friend that lent him wherewith to purchase his Time of Keimer, now came to offer himself as a Journeyman to us. We could not then imploy him, but I foolishly let him know, as a Secret, that I soon intended to begin a Newspaper, and might then have Work for him. My Hopes of Success as I told him were founded on this, that the then only Newspaper, printed by Bradford was a paltry thing, wretchedly manag'd, and no way entertaining; and yet was profitable to him. I therefore thought a good Paper could scarcely fail of good Encouragement.

. . .

Our first Papers made a quite different Appearance from any before in the Province, a better Type and better printed: but some spirited Remarks of my Writing on the Dispute then going on between Govr. Burnet and the Massachusetts Assembly, struck the principal People, ocasion'd the Paper and the Manager of it to be much talk'd of, and in a few Weeks brought them all to be our Subscribers. Their Example was follow'd by many, and our Number went on growing continually. This was one of the first good Effects of my having learnt a little to scribble. Another was, that the leading Men, seeing a News Paper now in the hands of one who could also handle a Pen, thought it convenient to oblige and encourage me. Bradford still printed the Votes and Laws and other Publick Business. He had printed an Address of the House to the Governor in a coarse blundering manner; We reprinted it elegantly and correctly, and sent one to every Member. They were sensible of the Difference, it strengthen'd the Hands of our Friends in the House, and they voted us their Printers for the Year ensuing.

Among my Friends in the House I must not forget Mr. Hamilton before mentioned, who was now returned from England and had a Seat in it. He interested himself[11] for me strongly in that Instance, as he did in many others afterwards, continuing his Patronage till his Death. Mr. Vernon about this time put me in mind of the Debt I ow'd him: but did not press me. I wrote him an ingenuous Letter of Acknowledgments, crav'd his Forbearance a little longer which he allow'd me, and as soon as I was able I paid the Principal with Interest and many Thanks. So that *Erratum* was in some degree corrected.

But now another Difficulty came upon me, which I had never the least Reason to expect. Mr. Meredith's Father, who was to have paid for our Printing House according to the Expectations given me, was able to advance only one Hundred Pounds, Currency, which had been paid, and a Hundred more was due to the Merchant; who grew impatient and su'd us all. We gave Bail, but saw that if the Money could not be rais'd in time, the Suit must come to a Judgment and Execution, and our hopeful Prospects must with us be ruined, as the Press and Letters must be sold for Payment, perhaps at half Price. In this distress two true Friends whose Kindness I have never forgotten nor ever shall forget while I can remember any thing, came to me separately unknown to each other, and without any Application from me, offering each of them to advance me all the Money that should be necessary to enable me to take the whole Business upon my self if that should be practicable, but they did not like my continuing the Partnership with Meredith, who as they said was often seen drunk in the Streets, and playing at low Games in Alehouses, much to our Discredit. These two Friends were William Coleman and Robert Grace. I told them I could not propose a Separation while any Prospect remain'd of the Merediths fulfilling their Part of our Agreement. Because I thought myself under great Obligations to them for what they had done and would do if they could. But if they finally fail'd in their Performance, and our Partnership must be dissolv'd, I should then think myself at Liberty to accept the Assistance of my Friends.

Thus the matter rested for some time. When I said to my Partner, perhaps your Father is dissatisfied at the part you have undertaken in this Affair of ours, and is unwilling to advance for you and me what he would for you alone: If that is the Case, tell me, and I will resign the whole to you and go about my Business. No says he, my Father has really been disappointed and is really unable; and I am unwilling to distress him farther. I see this is a Business I am not fit for. I was bred a Farmer, and it was a Folly in me to come to Town and put my Self at 30 Years of Age an Apprentice to learn a new Trade. Many of our Welsh People are going to settle in North Carolina where Land is cheap: I am inclin'd to go with them, and follow my old Employment. You may find Friends to assist you. If you will take the Debts of the Company upon you, return to my Father the Hundred Pound he has advanc'd, pay my little personal Debts, and give me Thirty Pounds and a new Saddle, I will relinquish the Partnership and leave the whole in your Hands. I agreed to this Proposal. It was drawn up in Writing, sign'd and seal'd immediately. I gave him what he demanded and he went soon after to Carolina; from whence he sent me next Year two long Letters, containing the best Account that had been given of that Country, the Climate, Soil, Husbandry, &c. for in those Matters he was very judicious. I printed them in the papers, and they gave grate Satisfaction to the Publick.

As soon as he was gone, I recurr'd to my two Friends; and because I would not give an unkind Preference to either, I took half what each had offered and I wanted, of one, and half of the other; paid off the Company Debts, and went on with the Business in my own Name, advertising that the Partnership was dissolved. I think this was in or about the Year 1729.

. . .

I now open'd a little Stationer's Shop. I had in it Blanks of all Sorts the correctest that ever appear'd among us, being assisted in that by my Friend Brientnal; I had also Paper, Parchment, Chapmen's Books, &c. One Whitemash a Compositor I had known in London, an excellent Workman now came to me and work'd with me constantly and diligently, and I took an Apprentice the Son of Aquila Rose. I began now gradually to pay off the Debt I was under for the Printing-House. In order to secure my Credit and Character as a Tradesman, I took care not only to be in *Reality* Industrious and frugal, but to avoid all *Appearances* of the Contrary. I drest plainly; I was seen at no Places of idle Diversion; I never went out a-fishing or shooting; a Book, indeed, sometimes debauch'd me from my Work; but that was seldom, snug, and gave no Scandal: and to show that I was not above my Business, I sometimes brought home the Paper I purchas'd at the Stores, thro' the Streets on a Wheelbarrow. Thus being esteem'd an industrious thriving young Man, and paying duly for what I bought, the Merchants who imported Stationary solicited my Custom, others propos'd supplying me with Books, and I went on swimmingly.

. . .

I had hitherto continu'd to board with Godfrey who lived in Part of my House with his Wife and Children, and had one Side of the Shop for his Glazier's Business, tho' he work'd little, being always absorb'd in his Mathematics. Mrs. Godfrey projected a Match for me with a Relation's Daughter, took Opportunities of bringing us often together, till a serious Courtship on my Part ensu'd, the Girl being in herself very deserving. The old Folks encourag'd me by continual Invitations to Supper, and by leaving us together, till at length it was time to explain. Mrs. Godfrey manag'd our little Treaty. I let her know that I expected as much Money with their Daughter as would pay off my Remaining Debt for the Printinghouse, which I believe was not then above a Hundred Pounds. She brought me Word they had no such Sum to spare. I said they might mortgage their House in the Loan office. The Answer to this after some Days was, that they did not approve the Match; that on Enquiry of Bradford they had been inform'd the Printing Business was not a profitable one, the Types would soon be worn out and more wanted, that S. Keimer and D. Harry had fail'd one after the other, and I should probably soon follow them; and therefore I was forbidden the House, and the Daughter shut up. Whether this was a real Change of Sentiment, or only Artifice, on a Supposition of our being too far engag'd in Affection to retract, and therefore that we should steal a Marriage, which would leave them at Liberty to give or withold what they pleas'd, I know not: But I suspected the latter, resented it, and went no more. Mrs. Godfrey brought me afterwards some more favourable Accounts of their Disposition, and would have drawn me on again: but I declared absolutely my Resolution to have nothing more to do with that Family. This was resented by the Godfreys, we differ'd, and they removed, leaving me the whole House, and I resolved to take no more Inmates.

But this Affair having turn'd my Thoughts to Marriage, I look'd round me, and made Overtures of Acquaintance in other Places; but soon found that the Business of a Printer being generally thought a poor one, I was not to expect Money with a Wife unless with such a one, as I should not otherwise think agreable. In the mean time, that hard-to-be-govern'd Passion of Youth, had hurried me frequently into Intrigues with low Women that fell in my Way, which were attended with some Expence and great Inconvenience, besides a continual Risque to my Health by a Distemper which of all Things I dreaded, tho' by great good Luck I escaped it.

A friendly Correspondence as Neighbours and old Acquaintances, had continued between me and Mrs. Read's Family, who all had a regard for me from the time of my first Lodging in their House. I was often invited there and consulted in their Affairs, wherein I sometimes was of service. I pity'd poor Miss Read's unfortunate Situation, who was generally dejected, seldom chearful, and avoided Company. I consider'd my Giddiness and Inconstancy when in London as in a great degree the Cause of her Unhappiness; tho' the Mother was good enough to think the Fault more her own than mine, as she had prevented our Marrying before I went thither, and persuaded the other Match in my Absence. Our mutual Affection was revived, but there were now great Objections to our Union. That Match was indeed look'd upon as invalid, a preceding Wife being said to be living in England; but this could not easily be prov'd, because of the Distance. And tho' there was a Report of his Death, it was not certain. Then tho' it should be true, he had left many Debts which his Successor might be call'd on to pay. We ventured however, over all these Difficulties, and I [took] her to Wife Sept. 1. 1730. None of the Inconveniences happened that we had apprehended, she prov'd a good and faithful Helpmate, assisted me much by attending the Shop, we throve together, and have ever mutually endeavour'd to make each other happy. Thus I corrected that great *Erratum* as well as I could.[12]

About this Time our Club meeting, not at a Tavern, but in a little Room of Mr. Grace's set apart for that Purpose; a Proposition was made by me that since our Books were often referr'd to in our Disquisitions upon the Queries, it might be convenient to us to have them all together where we met, that upon Occasion they might be consulted; and by thus clubbing our Books to a common Library, we should, while we lik'd to keep them together, have each of us the Advantage of using the Books of all the other Members, which would be nearly as beneficial as if each owned the whole. It was lik'd and agreed to, and we fill'd one End of the Room with such Books as we could best spare. The Number was not so great as we expected; and tho' they had been of great Use, yet some Inconveniencies occurring for want of due Care of them, the Collection after about a Year was separated, and each took his Books home again.

And now I set on foot my first Project of a public Nature, that for a Subscription Library. I drew up the Proposals, got them put into Form by our great Scrivener Brockden, and by the help of my Friends in the Junto, procur'd Fifty Subscribers of 40*s*. each to begin with and 10*s*. a Year for 50 Years. the Term our Company was to continue. We afterwards obtain'd a Charter, the Company being increas'd to 100. This was the Mother of all the N American Subscription Libraries now so numerous. It is become a great thing itself, and continually increasing. These Libraries have improv'd the general Conversation of the Americans, made the common Tradesmen and Farmers as intelligent as most Gentlemen from other Countries, and perhaps have contributed in some degree to the Stand so generally made throughout the Colonies in Defence of their Privileges.[13]

Patrick Tailfer, Hugh Anderson and David Douglas, 'A True and Historical Narrative of the Colony of Georgia in America'

Dr Patrick Tailfer (*fl*. eighteenth century) was born and educated in Scotland. He arrived in Georgia in August 1734, with a group of well-off intending settlers who financed their own transportation costs and those of their servants. He had received a land grant of five hundred acres in October the previous year, the maximum grant allowed by the Trustees of the colony. When he arrived in Georgia he found his land to be seventy miles from Savannah in a region thought unlikely to lead to success in agriculture. He himself never cultivated those holdings, although some members of his group did build a fort in the area and plant unsuccessful settlements around it. Instead Dr Tailfer rented a house in Savannah and began to practise medicine. For a time he was the only physician in the city and soon became a prosperous one, although he also hired out his indentured servants to supplement his income. He married the sister of Robert Williams, a merchant of means and reputation. He himself soon was the acknowledged leader of the critics of the Trustees, the so-called 'malcontents'. His very prosperity strongly suggests that he was less 'malcontent' than politically ambitious, especially since he had good hopes of gaining for the Georgia settlers a greater degree of self-government than they enjoyed under the Royal Charter. During the year 1740 Tailfer let it be known that he intended to leave Georgia with some of his followers and move to Charlestown, South Carolina, which he called 'a Land of Liberty'. By January 1741, he was practising medicine in that city and preparing the publication of the *Narrative*.

Hugh Anderson was a well-educated man of station and wealth when he applied to the Trustees for permission to migrate to Georgia with his wife, five children and five servants. He was given a land grant as well as a town lot in Savannah, having especially requested the town lot because, he said, his wife was the granddaughter of an Earl 'tenderly brought up, and would require some society'. Prior to his departure, he was appointed 'Inspector of the Public Garden and Mulberry plantation', a position which may have been unsalaried. He arrived in Georgia in June 1737, three years after Tailfer and Douglas. He at once applied himself with energy to creating a profitable plantation but was soon convinced that although the colony could in the long run prosper, its immediate difficulties could be overcome only by greatly increased public support from England. Within two years, Anderson left Savannah for Charlestown, having been invited to give weekly subscription lectures on natural philosophy, natural history, agriculture and gardening. By 1741 he was the head of a school in Charlestown.

Of David Douglas less is known. He very likely came over to Georgia with the group that included Patrick Tailfer, but it is not clear whether he had a land grant. In 1736 he was granted a town lot in Savannah. In 1740 he petitioned for a land grant on Wilmington Island. His request was at first denied but that decision was later apparently rescinded. Nevertheless in 1741 he too was living in Charlestown, South Carolina.

It is difficult to judge what part each author finally played in the writing of the

Narrative. The principal role is usually assigned to Tailfer who had a known capacity for irony. His irony did not extend, of course, to noticing anything remarkable in urging the recognition of the natural political rights of land-holding colonists so that they might enslave blacks. A less major but substantial role is usually also urged for Anderson. The first edition appeared early in 1741 in Charlestown, South Carolina, published by private subscription. A second London edition appeared in December 1741.

My text is taken from the London edition, reprinted from a collection of Colonial tracts made by Peter Chance and published in Washington, 1834.

To His Excellency
James Oglethorpe, Esq;

General and Commander in Chief of His Majesty's Forces in South Carolina and Georgia; and one of the Honourable Trustees for Establishing the Colony of GEORGIA in AMERICA, &c.

May it please Your Excellency,

As the few surviving Remains of the Colony of *Georgia* find it necessary to present the World (and in particular *Great-Britain*) with a true State of that Province, from its first Rise, to its present Period; Your Excellency (of all Mankind) is best entitled to the Dedication, as the principal Author of its present Strength and Affluence, Freedom and Prosperity: And tho' incontestable Truths will recommend the following *NARRATIVE* to the patient and attentive Reader; yet your Name, *SIR*, will be no little Ornament to the Frontispiece, and may possibly engage some courteous Perusers a little beyond it.

THAT Dedication and Flattery are synonimous, is the Complaint of every Dedicator, who concludes himself ingenuous and fortunate, if he can discover a less trite and direct Method of flattering than is usually practised; but we are happily prevented from the least Intention of this kind, by the repeated Offerings of the *Muses* and *News-Writers* to Your Excellency, in the publick Papers: 'Twere presumptuous even to dream of equalling or encreasing them: We therefore flatter ourselves, that Nothing we can advance will in the least shock Your Excellency's Modesty; not doubting but your Goodness will pardon any Deficiency of Elegance and Politeness, on account of our Sincerity, and the serious Truths we have the Honour to approach you with.

WE have seen the ancient Custom of sending forth Colonies, for the Improvement of any distant Territory, or new Acquisition, continued down to ourselves: but to Your Excellency alone it is owing, that the World is made acquainted with a Plan, highly refined from those of all former Projectors. They fondly imagin'd it necessary to communicate to such young Settlements the fullest Rights and Properties, all the Immunities of their Mother Countries, and Privileges rather more extensive: By such Means, in deed, these Colonies flourish'd with early Trade and Affluence; but Your Excellency's Concern for our perpetual Welfare could never permit you to propose such transitory Advantages for us: You considered Riches like a Divine and Philosopher, as the *Irritamenta Malorum*, and knew that they were disposed to inflate weak Minds with Pride; to pamper the Body with Luxury, and introduce a long Variety of Evils. Thus have you *Protected us from ourselves*, as Mr. *Waller* says, by keeping all Earthly Comforts from us: You have afforded us the Opportunity of arriving at the Integrity of the *Primitive Times*, by intailing a more than *Primitive Poverty* on us: The Toil, that is necessary to our bare Subsistence, must effectually defend us from the Anxieties of any further Ambition: As we have no Properties, to feed Vain-Glory and beget Contention; so we are not puzzled with any System of Laws, to ascertain and establish them: The valuable Virtue of Humility is secured to us, by your Care to prevent our procuring, or so much as seeing any *Negroes* (the only human Creatures proper to improve our Soil) lest our Simplicity might mistake the poor *Africans* for greater Slaves than ourselves: And that we might fully receive the Spiritual Benefit of those wholesome Austerities; you have wisely denied us the Use of such Spiritous Liquors, as might in the least divert our Minds from the Contemplation of our Happy Circumstances.

OUR Subjects swells upon us; and did we allow ourselves to indulge our Inclination, without considering our weak Abilities, we should be tempted to launch out into many of Your Excellency's extraordinary Endowments, which do not so much regard the Affair in Hand: But as this would lead us beyond the Bounds of a Dedication; so would it engross a Subject too extensive for us, to the Prejudice of other Authors and Panegyrists; We shall therefore confine ourselves to that remarkable Scene of Your Conduct, whereby *Great-Britain* in general, and the Settlers of *Georgia*, in particular, are laid under such inexpressible Obligations.

BE pleased then, *Great SIR*, to accompany our heated Imaginations, in taking a View of this Colony of *Georgia*! this Child of your auspicious Politicks! arrived at the utmost Vigor of its Constitution, at a Term when most former States have been struggling through the Convulsions of their Infancy. This early Maturity, however, lessens our Admiration, that Your Excellency lives to see (what few Founders ever aspired after) the great Decline and almost final Termination of it. So many have finish'd their Course during the Progress of the Experiment, and such Numbers have retreated from the Fantoms of Poverty and Slavery which their cowardly Imaginations pictur'd to them; that you may justly vaunt with the boldest Hero of them all,

—Like Death you reign
O'er silent Subjects and a desart Plain.
Busiris.

YET must your Enemies (if you have any) be reduced to confess, that no ordinary Statesman could have digested, in the like Manner, so capacious a Scheme, such a copious Jumble of Power and Politicks. We shall content ourselves with observing, that all those beauteous Models of Government which the little States of *Germany* exercise, and those extensive Liberties which the Boors of *Poland* enjoy, were design'd to concenter in your System; and were we to regard the Modes of Government, we must have been strangely unlucky to have miss'd of the best, where there was an Appearance of so great a Variety; for under the Influence of our *Perpetual Dictator*, we have seen something like *Aristocracy, Oligarchy,* as well as the *Triumvirate, Decemvirate,* and *Consular Authority* of famous Republicks, which have expired many Ages before us: What Wonder then we share the same Fate? Do their Towns and Villages exist but in Story and Rubbish? We are all over Ruins; our Publick-Works, Forts, Wells, High-Ways, Light-House, Store and Water-Mills, &c. are dignified like theirs, with the same venerable Desolation. The Logg-House, indeed, is like to be the last forsaken Spot of Your Empire; yet even this, through the Death, or Desertion of those who should continue to inhabit it, must suddenly decay; the Bankrupt Jailor himself shall be soon denied the Privilege of human Conversation; and when this last Moment of the Spell expires, the whole shall vanish like the Illusion of some *Eastern Magician.*

BUT let not this solitary Prospect impress Your Excellency with any Fears of having your Services to Mankind, and to the Settlers of *Georgia* in particular, buried in Oblivion; for it we diminutive Authors are allow'd to prophesy (as you know Poets in those Cases formerly did) we may confidently presage, That while the Memoirs of *America* continue to be read in *English, Spanish,* or the Language of the *Scots* High-Landers, Your Excellency's Exploits and Epocha will be transmitted to Posterity.

SHOULD Your Excellency apprehend the least Tincture of Flattery in any Thing already hinted, we may sincerely assure you, we intended nothing that our Sentiments did not very strictly attribute to your Merit; and, in such Sentiments, we have the Satisfaction of being fortified by all Persons of Impartiality and Discernment.

BUT to trespass no longer on those Minutes, which Your Excellency may suppose more significantly employ'd on the Sequel; let it suffice at present, to assure you, that we are deeply affected with your Favours; and tho' unable of ourselves properly to acknowledge them, we shall embrace every Opportunity of Recommending you to higher Powers, who (we are hopeful) will reward Your Excellency according to your MERIT.

May it please Your Excellency,
 Your Excellency's
  Most devoted Servants,
  The Land-Holders of GEORGIA,
  Authors of the following *Narrative*

Preface

The colony of Georgia has afforded so much subject of conversation to the world, that it is not to be questioned, but a true and impartial account of it, from its first settlement, to its present period, will be generally agreeable; and the more so, that the subject has hitherto been so much disguised and misrepresented in pamphlets, poems, gazettes, and journals.

If it is asked, Why this NARRATIVE has not been published to the world sooner? we assign two reasons, which (we doubt not) will be satisfactory.

First, a number of honourable gentlemen accepted the charge of Trustees for executing the purposes in His Majesty's most gracious Charter; gentlemen, whose honour and integrity we never did, or yet do, call in question: But, to our great misfortune, none of that honourable body (excepting Mr. Oglethorpe) ever had opportunity of viewing the situation and circumstances of the colony, and judging for themselves as to the necessities thereof. How far Mr. Oglethorpe's schemes were consistent with the welfare or prosperity of it, will best appear from the following NARRATIVE.

When experience gradually unfolded to us the alterations we found absolutely requisite to our subsisting, we made all dutiful and submissive applications to these our patrons, in whom we placed so much confidence: This course we judged the most proper and direct, and therefore repeated these our dutiful applications, both to the body of the Trustees and to Mr. Oglethorpe; but alas! our miseries could not alter his views of things, and therefore we could obtain no redress from him; and the honourable board we found were prejudiced against our petitions (no doubt) through misinformations and mis-representations; and this (we are confident) a further enquiry and time will convince them of.

The inviolable regard we paid to the honourable board, kept us from applying to any other power for redress, whilst the least hopes could be entertained of any from them: And we make no doubt, but that our moderation, in this respect, will recommend us to all persons of humanity.

A *second* reason is, that as we had daily occasion of seeing our supreme magistrates, who ruled over us with unlimited power, exer-cising illegal acts of authority, by threatenings, imprisonments, and other oppressions; therefore we had just reason to apprehend, that any further steps, to obtain relief, might subject us to the like effects of arbitrary power; so, until now, that a handful of us have made our escape to a LAND OF LIBERTY[a] (after having made shipwreck of our time and substance in that unhappy colony) we had it not in our power to represent the state of that settlement to the world, or to make our application to higher powers for redress.

We are hopeful, that the perusal of the following sheets will rectify two sorts of readers in their surprize in relation to the colony of Georgia, viz. those of Great Britain, who have never known this part of the world but by description; and those of America: The first are no doubt surprized, to think it possible, that so pleasant and temperate a clime; so fruitful a soil; such extensive privileges; all which were publickly given out; and such considerable sums of publick and private benefactions, have not satisfied and enriched us: Them we refer to the following Narrative for satisfaction. The American reader, on the other hand, must be equally surprized to find that such numbers should have been so fooled and blindfolded, as to expect to live in this part of America by cultivation of lands without Negroes, and much more without titles to their lands, and laid under a load of grievances and restrictions: And though these were redressed, how could persons in their senses ever imagine, that fifty acres of pine-barren, not value fifty six pences in property (and whereof many thousands may be purchased at half that rate in the neighbouring province) could maintain a family of white people, and pay such duties and quit-rents in a few years, as the richest grounds in Carolina,

[a] South Carolina.

or other provinces in America will never bear? To these last we shall only beg leave to observe, that such fatal artifice was used (we shall not say by whom) such specious pretences were made use of, and such real falsities advanced, and the smallest foundations of truth magnified to hyperbole; that we, who had no opportunity of knowing other ways, or means of learning the real truth, and being void of all suspicion of artifice or design, easily believed all these, and fell into the decoy.

The mind of man is naturally curious and enterprizing; we easily feed our wishes into realities, and affect and look upon every novelty in the most favourable light; how easy then is it, for cunning and artifice to lay hold on the weak sides of our fellow-creatures, as we catch fish with a hook baited to their particular gout?

To prove this charge, we shall only transcribe some passages from a piece of prose, and some from a piece of poesy; by which specimens, the reader may judge of some considerable number which were dispersed and vended of the same stamp.

The first are from a pamphlet printed at London, 1733, entitled *A New and Accurate Account of the Provinces of South Carolina and Georgia*. The author has not thought fit to favour us with his name; but it is easy to conceive, that we, who suspected no artifice or design, must conclude, that it came from the best authority, from the circumstances of its being dispersed publickly, and not being contradicted, and from the author's intimate acquaintance (at least so pretended) with all the Trustees' measures and designs. After a high encomium upon the Trustees, page 7, he says, 'The air of Georgia is healthy, being always serene and pleasant, never subject to excessive heat or cold, or sudden changes of weather; the winter is regular and short, and the summer cooled with refreshing breezes; it neither feels the cutting north-west wind that the Virginians complain of, nor the intense heats of Spain, Barbary, Italy, and Egypt. The soil will produce anything with very little culture.' Page 19, 'All sorts of corn yield an amazing increase; one hundred fold is the common estimate; though their husbandry is so slight that they can only be said to scratch the earth, and meerely to cover the seed: ALL the best sort of cattle and fowls are multiplied without number, and therefore without a price: Vines are natives here.' Page 21, 'The woods near Savannah are not hard to be cleared; many of them have no underwood, and the trees do not stand generally thick on the ground, but at considerable distances asunder; when you fall the timber for the use, or to make tar, the root will rot in four or five years; and in the mean time you may pasture the ground; but, if you would only destroy the timber, it is done by half a dozen strokes of an ax surrounding each tree a little above the root; in a year or two the water getting into the wound rots in the timber, and a brisk gust of wind fells many acres for you in an hour, of which you may make one bright bonfire. Such will be frequently here the fate of the pine, the wallnut, the cypress, the oak, and the cedar. Such an air and soil can only be described by a poetical pen, because there is no danger of exceeding the truth; therefore take Waller's description of an island in the neighbourhood of Carolina, to give you an idea of this happy climate:

'The Spring, which but salutes us here,
Inhabits there, and courts them all the Year;
Ripe Fruits and Blossoms on the same Tree live;
At once they promise what at once they give.
So sweet the Air, so moderate the Clime,
None sickly lives, or dies before his Time.
Heav'n sure has kept this Spot of Earth uncurst,
To shew how all Things were created first.'

Page 27, 'The Indians bring many a mile the whole deer's flesh, which they sell to the peope who live in the country, for the value of sixpence sterling; and a wild turkey of forty pounds weight, for the value of two pence.' In page 32, the author when recommending the Georgia adventure to gentlemen of decayed circumstances, who must labour at home or do worse, states the following objection, viz. 'If such people can't get bread here for their labour, how will their condition be mended in Georgia?' Which he solves in the following manner, 'The answer is easy; part of it is well attested, and part self-evident; they have land there for nothing, and that land so fertile, that, as is said before, they receive a hundredfold increase, for taking a very little pains: Give here in England ten acres of good land to one of those helpless persons, and I doubt not his ability to make it sustain him, and by his own culture, without letting it to another; but the difference between no rent, and rack'd rent, is the difference between eating and starving.' Page 32, 'These Trustees not only give land to the unhappy who go thither, but are also impowered to receive the voluntary contributions of charitable persons, to enable to furnish the poor adventurers with all necessaries for the expense of their voyage, occupying the land, and supporting them, till they find themselves comfortably settled; so that now the unfortunate will not be obliged to bind themselves to a long servitude to pay for their passage; for they may be carried *gratis* into a land of liberty and plenty, where they immediately find themselves in the possession of a competent estate, in an happier climate than they knew before, and they are unfortunate indeed, if here they cannot forget their sorrows.' Nay, as if such assertions as these were not powerful enough to influence poor people, calculations are subjoined, to demonstrate, that a family consisting of one poor man, his wife, and child of seven years old, may in Georgia earn sixty pounds sterling per annum, and this abstracted from silk, wine, &c. Page 41, 'Now this very family in Georgia, by raising rice and corn sufficient for its occasions, and by attending the care of their cattle and land (which almost every one is able to do in some tolerable degree for himself) will easily produce in gross value the sum of sixty pounds sterling per annum, nor is this to be wondered at, because of the valuable assistance it has from a fertile soil and a stock given gratis; which must always be remembered in this calculation.'

'The calculation of one hundred such families when formally extended, stands thus', – Page 43,

	l.	*s.*	*d.*
'In London one hundred poor men earn,	500	00	0
One hundred women, and one hundred children,	500	00	0
	1000	00	0
In Georgia an hundred families earn, One hundred men for labour,	1200	00	0
Ditto for care of their stock at leisure hours,	1200	00	0
One hundred women and one hundred children.	2400	00	0
Land and stock in themselves,	1200	00	0
Total,	6000	00	0

Q. E. D.'

But we must conclude this head, lest we tire the reader. We shall now beg leave to quote a few poetical accounts of this paradise of the world, and of the fatherly care and protection we might depend on from Mr. Oglethorpe. An hundred hackney Muses might be instanced; but we shall confine ourselves to the celebrated performance of the Rev. Mr. Samuel Wesly,[b] where we might well expect a sufficient stock of truth and religion, to counter-balance a poetical licence. *Vide* a poem entitled *Georgia, and Verses upon Mr. Oglethorpe's Second Voyage to Georgia.* Printed London, 1736.

[b] Wesley.

'See where beyond the spacious Ocean lies
A wide waste Land beneath the Southern Skies;
Where kindly Suns for Ages roll'd in vain,
Nor e'er the Vintage saw, or rip'ning Grain,
Where all Things into wild Luxuriance ran,
And burthen'd Nature ask'd the Aid of Man.
In this sweet Climate and prolifick Soil,
He bids the eager Swain indulge his Toil;
In free Possession to the Planter's Hand,
Consigns the rich uncultivated Land.
Go you, the Monarch cries, go settle there,
Whom *Britain* from her Plenitude can spare:
Go, your old wonted Industry pursue;
Nor envy *Spain* the Treasures of *Peru.*'

'But not content in Council here to join,
A further Labour, OGLETHORPE, is thine:
In each great Deed thou claim'st the foremost Part,
And Toil and Danger charm thy gen'rous Heart:
But chief for this thy warm Affections rise;
For oh! thou view'st it with a Parent's Eyes:
For this thou tempt'st the vast tremendous Main,
And Floods and Storms oppose their Threats in vain.'

'He comes, whose Life, while absent from your View,
Was one continued Ministry for you;
For you were laid out all his Pains and Art,
Won ev'ry Will and soften'd ev'ry Heart.
With what paternal Joy shall he relate,
How views its Mother Isle your little State:
Think while he strove your distant Coast to gain,
How oft he sigh'd and chid the tedious Main,
Impatient to survey, by Culture grac'd,
Your dreary Wood-Land and your rugged Waste.
Fair were the Scenes he feign'd, the Prospects fair;
and sure, ye *Georgians*, all he feign'd was there,
A Thousand Pleasures crowd into his Breast;
But one, one mighty Thought absorbs the rest,
And gives me Heav'n to see, the Patriot cries,
Another BRITAIN in the Desert rise.'

Again,
'With nobler Products see they GEORGIA teems,
Chear'd with the genial Sun's director Beams;
There the wild Vine to Culture learns to yield,
And purple Clusters ripen through the Field.
Now bid thy Merchants bring thy Wine no more
Or from the *Iberian* or the *Tuscan* Shore;
No more they need th' *Hungarian* Vineyards drain,
And *France* herself may drink her best *Champain*.

Behold! at last, and in a subject Land,
Nectar sufficient for thy large Demand:
Delicious Nectar, powerful to improve
Our hospitable Mirth and social Love:
This for thy jovial Sons. – Nor less the Care
Of thy young Province, to oblige the FAIR;
Here tend the Silk Worm in the verdant Shade,
The frugal Matron and the blooming Maid.'

From the whole, we doubt not, the reader will look upon us as sufficiently punished for our credulity: And indeed, who would not have been catched with such promises, such prospects? What might not the poor man flatter himself with, from such an alteration in his situation? And how much more might a gentleman expect from a plentiful stock of his own, and numbers of servants to set up with? Could a person, with the least faith, have questioned the committing his interests to such guardians, and such a tender father as Mr. Oglethorpe was believed to be? Whether he has acted that generous, that human[e], that fatherly part, the following NARRATIVE must determine.

As for those poetical licences touching the wine and silk; we do not transcribe them as a reflection upon the author; but as a satyr upon the mismanagement of those manufactures; since no measures were taken that seemed really intended for their advancement.

We no wise question the possibility of advancing such improvements in Georgia, with far less sums of money, properly applied, than the publick has bestowed. But not even the flourishing of wine and silk can make a colony of British subjects happy, if they are deprived of the liberties and properties of their birthright.

We have endeavoured to the utmost to be tender of characters; but as we undertake to write an account of facts and truths; there is no help for it, when those facts and truths press home.

It is a common satisfaction to sufferers, to expose to the publick the rocks upon which they split, and the misfortunes by which they suffered; and it may well be allowed us, to publish the causes to which we attribute the ruin of that settlement and ourselves; and more especially as we are prosecutors for justice from higher powers; which we doubt not receiving as the case deserves.

We hope the truth of the following NARRATIVE will recommend itself to the perusal of the candid reader. The fatal truth of this tragedy hath already been sealed with the death of multitudes of our fellow-creatures; but still (thanks to the providence of the Almighty) some survive to attest and confirm the truth of what is herein contained, against any persons or names, however great, however powerful. Our circumstances and sincerity will excuse our want of that politeness and accuracy of stile, which might have represented our case to greater advantage, to the courteous reader, whom we shall no longer detain from the subject in hand.

A True and Historical Narrative, &c.

Nothing is more difficult for authors, than to divest themselves of byass and partiality, especially when they themselves are parties or sufferers in the affair treated of.

It is possible, this may be supposed the case with us the publishers of this *Narrative*; it may be imagined, that the hardships, losses, and disappointments we have met with in the colony of Georgia, will naturally sour our humours, and engage us to represent everything in the worst light.

As the probability of those surmises is very obvious to us, we have, to the utmost of our power, guarded against the weak side of ourselves; and, to convince the world of our sincerity, shall no further descend into the grievances of particular persons, than is absolutely requisite for making our *General Narrative* intelligible; and to a faithful detail of publick vouchers, records, extracts, missives, memorials and representations, shall only adjoin so much of history, as may be necessary to recount the most material events, and complete the connexion.

We are hopeful, that an information, founded upon the strictest truth, will effectually introduce any further steps that Providence shall enable us to take towards procuring the redress of our grievances. While we had the least hopes of redress from our immediate superiors and patrons, we would not; and when we began to despair of relief by that channel, we durst not, make application to any other tribunal, unless we would expose ourselves to the dreadful effects of the resentment of those who had before reduced us to poverty by oppression: And indeed, in all the applications we made for redress, we were brow-beat, obstructed, threatened, and branded with opprobrious names, such as proud, idle, lazy, discontented and mutinous people, and several other appellations of that kind; and were always afterwards harrassed by all means whatsoever; several instances of which will appear to the reader in the sequel.

Our late retreat from that confinement, to a *Land of Liberty*, puts it in our power to speak the truth; and though our endeavours are too late to relieve the dead, the dying, and those many now dispersed in all the corners of His Majesty's dominions; yet they may be the means of ushering in sympathy and assistance to the survivors, and to multitudes of widows and orphans of the deceased, from the human[e] and generous.

As our sole design is to give a *plain narrative of the establishment and progress of the colony of Georgia, from its rise to its present period*; we shall court no other ornaments than those of truth and perspicuity; and shall endeavour to carry the reader's attention regularly, from the first to the last motions we make mention of.

. . .

GEORGIA lies in the 30 and 31 degrees of north latitude: The air generally clear, the rains being much shorter as well as heavier than in England; the dews are very great; thunder and lightning are expected almost every day in May, June, July, and August; they are very terrible, especially to a stranger: During those months, from ten in the morning to four in the afternoon, the sun is extremely scorching; but the sea-breeze sometimes blows from ten till three or four: The winter is nearly the same length as in England; but the mid-day sun is always warm, even when the mornings and evenings are very sharp, and the nights piercing cold.

The land is of four sorts; pine barren, oak land, swamp, and marsh. The pine land is of far the greatest extent, especially near the seacoasts: The soil of this is a dry whitish sand, producing shrubs of several sorts, and between them a harsh coarse kind of grass, which cattle do not love to feed upon; but here and there is a little of a better kind, especially in the Savannahs, (so they call the low watery meadows which are usually intermixed with pine lands:) It bears naturally two sorts of fruit; hurtle-berries much like those in England, and chinquopin nuts, a dry nut about the size of a small acorn: A laborious man may in one year clear and plant four or five acres of this land; it will produce, the first year, from two to four bushels of Indian corn, and from four to eight of Indian pease, per acre; the second year it usually bears much about the same; the third, less; the fourth, little or nothing: Peaches it bears well; likewise the white mulberry, which serves to feed the silk worms; the black is about the size of a black cherry, and has much the same flavour.

The oak land commonly lies in narrow streaks between pine land and swamps, creeks or rivers: The soil is a blackish sand, producing several kinds of oak, bay, laurel, ash, wallnut, sumach and gum trees, a sort of sycamore, dog trees and hickory: In the choicest part of this land grow parsimon trees, and a few black mulberry and American cherry trees: The common wild grapes are of two sorts, both red; the fox grape grows two or three only on a stalk, is thick-skinned, large stoned, of a harsh taste, and of the size of a small cherry; the cluster grape is of a harsh taste too, and about the size of a white currant. This land requires much labour to clear; but, when it is cleared, it will bear any grain, for three, four, or five years sometimes without laying any manure upon it: An acre of it generally produces ten bushels of Indian corn, besides five of pease, in a year; so that this is justly esteemed the most valuable land in the province, white people being incapable to clear and cultivate the swamps.

A swamp is any low watery place, which is covered with trees or canes: They are here of three sorts, cypress, river, and cane swamps. Cypress swamps are mostly large ponds, in and round which cypresses grow: Most river swamps are overflown on every side by the river which runs through or near them; if they were drained, they would produce good rice; as would the cane swamps also, which in the meantime are the best feeding for all sorts of cattle.

The marshes are of two sorts; soft wet marsh, which is all a quagmire, and absolutely good for nothing, and hard marsh, which is a firm sand; but however at some seasons is good for feeding cattle: Marshes of both sorts abound on the sea islands, which are very numerous, and contain all sorts of land; and upon these chiefly, near creeks and runs of watar, cedar trees grow.

. . .

We must likewise observe, that the proportion of pine barren to either good swamp or oak and hickory land, is at least six to one; that the far greater number of the small lots have none or very little oak land; and if they had swamp that would bear rice, white people are unable to clear them if they are covered with trees, and though only with canes, which is the easiest to cultivate; it were simply impossible to manufacture the rice by white men; the exercise being so severe, that no Negro can be employed in any other work or labour comparable to it, and many hundreds of them (notwithstanding all the care of their masters) yearly lose their lives by that necessary work.

Savannah stands on a flat bluff (so they term a high land hanging over a creek or river) which rises about forty feet perpendicular from the river, and commands it several miles both upwards and downwards, and if it was not for a point of woods which, for about four miles down the river, stretches itself out towards the south-east, one might have a view of the sea, and the island of Tybee: The soil is a white sand for above a mile in breadth south-east and north-west; beyond this, eastward, is a river swamp; westward, a small body of wood-land (in which was the old Indian town) separated by a creek from a large tract of land, which runs upwards along the side of the river, for the space of about five miles; and being, by far, the best near the town, is reserved for the Indians, as General Oglethorpe declares, as are also some of the islands in the river Savannah, and the three most valuable islands upon all the coast of that province, viz. Ossiba, St. Katherine, and Sapula. South-west of the town is a pine barren, that extends about fourteen miles to Vernon river.

On the east side of the own is situated the publick garden, (being ten acres inclosed) on a barren piece of land, where it is hardly possible for what is planted to live, but impossible to thrive; and from this garden were all the planters to have been furnished with mulberry trees. &c.

The plan of the town was beautifully laid out in wards, tythings, and publick squares left at proper distances for markets and publick buildings; the whole making an agreeable uniformity.

The publick works in this town are, 1st, a court house, being one handsome room, with a piache on three sides: This likewise serves for a church for divine service, none having been ever built, notwithstanding the Trustees, in their publick acts, acknowledge the receipt of about seven hundred pounds sterling, from charitable persons for that express purpose.[1]

2dly, Oppposite to the *court house* stands the *log house* or prison (which is the only one remaining of five or six that have been successively built in Savannah) that place of terror, and support of *absolute* power in Georgia.

3dly, Nigh thereto is a house built of logs, at a very great charge, as was said, for the Trustees' Steward; the foundation below ground is already rotten [In August, 1740, a new foundation was begun], as the whole fabrick must be in a short time; for, the roof being flat, the rain comes in at all parts of it.

4thly, The *store-house*, which has been many times altered and amended at a very great charge; and it now serves as a store for the private benefit of one or two, as before mentioned.

5thly, The *guard-house*, which was first built on the bluff, soon decayed; as did a second through improper management; this, now standing, being the third. Several flagg-staffs were likewise erected, the last of which, according to common report, cost 50*l*. sterling.

6thly, A *publick mill* for grinding corn, was first erected at a considerable expence, in one square of the own; but in about three years time (without doing the least service) it fell to the ground: In another square of the town, a second was set up, at a far greater expence, but never finished; and is now erased, and converted into a house for entertaining the Indians, and other such like uses.

7thly, Wells and pumps were made at a great charge; but they were immediately choaked up, and never rendered useful, though this grievance was frequently represented both to the General and magistrates; the want of wells obliging the inhabitants to use the river water, which all the summer over is polluted with putrid marshes, and the numberless insects that deposit their ova there, together with putrefied carcasses of animals and corrupted vegetables; and this, no doubt, occasioned much of the sickness that swept off many.

Several of the houses which were built by freeholders, for want of heirs male, are fallen to the Trustees (even to the prejudice of the lawful creditors of the deceased) and are disposed of as the General thinks proper.

At least two hundred lots were taken up in Savannah, about one hundred and seventy of which were built upon [Several of these had more than one house upon them]; a great many of these are now ruinous, and many more shut up and abandoned; so that the town appears very desolate, scarce one quarter part of its inhabitants being left, and most of those in a miserable condition, for want of the proper necessaries of life.

Having thus brought this Historical NARRATIVE within the compass proposed, and endeavoured to dispose the materials in as distinct a method and series as the necessary conciseness would allow: We readily admit that the design is far from being complete. To have acquainted the world with all the hardships and oppressions which have been exercised in the colony of Georgia must have required both a larger volume than we were capable of publishing, and more time than we could bestow: We therefore satisfy ourselves, that we have, with care and sincerity, executed so much of the design, as may pave the way to any others who can descend more minutely to particulars; and those, who are best acquainted with the affairs of that colony, will be most capable of judging how tenderly we have touched both persons and things.

It only remains, that we in a few paragraphs endeavour to exhibit to the view of the reader, the REAL causes of the ruin and desolation of the colony; and those briefly are the following.

1. The representing the climate, soil, &c. of Georgia in false and too flattering colours; at least, the not contradicting those accounts when publickly printed and dispersed, and satisfying the world in a true and genuine discription thereof.

2. The restricting the tenure of lands, from a fee simple to tail-male, cutting off daughters and all other relations.

3. The restraining the proprietor from selling, disposing of, or leasing any possesion.

4. The restricting too much the extent of possessions; it being impossible that fifty acres of good land, much less pine barren, could maintain a white family.

5. The laying the planter under a variety of restraints in clearing, fencing, planting, &c. which was impossible to be complied with.

6. The exacting a much higher quit-rent than the richest grounds in North America can bear.

7. But chiefly the denying the use of Negroes, and persisting in such denial after, by repeated applications, we had humbly remonstrated the impossibility of making improvements to any advantage with white servants.

8. The denying us the privilege of being judged by the laws of our mother country; and subjecting the lives and fortunes of all people in the colony, to one person or set of men, who assumed the privilege, under the name of a Court of Chancery, of acting according to their own will and fancy.

9. General Oglethorpe's taking upon him to nominate magistrates, appoint justices of the peace, and to do many other such things, without ever exhibiting to the people any legal commission or authority for so doing.

10. The neglecting the proper means for encouraging the silk and wine manufactures, and disposing of the liberal sums contributed by the publick, and by private persons, in such ways and channels as have been of little or no service to the colony.

11. The misapplying or keeping up sums of money which have been appointed for particular uses, such as building a church, &c. several hundreds of pounds sterling (as we are informed) having been lodged in Mr. Oglethorpe's hands for some years by past, for that purpose, and not one stone of it yet laid.

12. The assigning certain fixed tracts of land to those who came to settle in the colony, without any regard to the quality of the ground, occupation, judgment, ability, or inclination of the settler, &c. &c., &c.

By these and many other such hardships, the poor inhabitants of Georgia are scattered over the face of the earth; her plantations a wild; her towns a desart; her villages in rubbish; her improvements a by-word; and her liberties a jest: An object of pity to friends, and of insult, contempt and ridicule to enemies.

Thomas Jefferson, 'Autobiography. The Declaration of Independence'

Thomas Jefferson (1743–1826) was born on 13 April 1743 in Shadwell, Albemarle County, Virginia; he died at Montecello on 4 July 1826, on the fiftieth anniversary of the signing of the Declaration of Independence. At one time or another in his public life, he held every high office that his state and country could afford: member of the Virginia Legislature, Governor of Virginia, delegate to the Continental Congress, first American Secretary of State, second Minister Plenipotentiary to France, second Vice President, third President. His epitaph, of his own drafting, registers a personal sense of the value of his numerous achievements rather different from that list of signal honours, however. It reads: 'Here was buried / Thomas Jefferson / Author of the Declaration of Independence / Of the Statute of Virginia for religious freedom / And Father of the University of Virginia.' Jefferson was not in any usual sense an 'author' of colonial prose, although the modern edition of his prose writings will run to more than fifty volumes when it is finished. He published only eight titles in his lifetime and of those only the *Notes on the State of Virginia* is a book. Nonetheless Jefferson spoke so well for the emergent national culture in the Declaration of Independence that the imprint of that political document can be read in the consciousness of the writers who succeeded him. The phrasing of Jefferson's Declaration represents the end of one heterogeneous colonial culture and the commencement of a long effort to achieve a more homogenous national one. If the psychic, spiritual, ethical and aesthetic values of the New England historians left ineradicable marks upon the American character, no less profound marks were left by Jefferson's republicanism, his progress beyond religious toleration to a concept of religious freedom and his unfailing confidence in general and humane education. His epitaph truly registers his continuous most characteristic concerns and the first achievement for which he wished to be remembered is rightly his most enduring monument.

The very process of the harmonizing of regional and national interests in stepping away altogether from the mother country by asserting that the new country contained the best of England's achievements and hopes (indeed, the 'last, best hope of *man*') can be taken as a thread to follow through Jefferson's own life. After some years of private study and the sociable cheerful life of a Virginia patrician, Jefferson attended William and Mary College for two years and then commenced to study law. He continued to exemplify the sociable and carelessly intellectual life of his state; he was fond of riding, of observing wild life, playing the violin, reading the novels of Fielding, Smollett, and Sterne and the poems of Ossian, of learning foreign languages – in the end, he knew six – of reading mathematical, surveying and mechanics books, of studying political philosophy, law and government. He was elected to the Virginia House of Burgesses in 1769, where his first proposal was a bill allowing owners to free their slaves; in the spring of the year in which he died he was of the same libertarian mind, writing 'the mass of mankind has not been born with saddles on their backs, nor a favored few booted and spurred, ready to ride them'. That in his life Jefferson did not free his own few slaves is not the sign of hypocrisy some have automatically taken it to be; those whom he manumitted in his will he cared for in his estate management. When he was out of office, as he was during 1781–3, not having been a notably successful governor of his state, and after 1809 when he laid down the presidency he held for two terms, he indulged the intellectual tastes established earlier; he eagerly collected and read (often for fifteen hours a day) a large library, the sale of which helped stem bankruptcy in his last years, for he was an inefficient and too hospitable planter; he wrote about plants and animals; he designed his famous house at Montecello and the beautiful halls of the University; and he wrote the 25,000 letters that permit us to know him so thoroughly. In them, he expressed his hatred of Bonaparte; he applauded the South Americans who sought their liberty and Cortes's attempt to establish a liberal regime in Spain; he advised the Greek Coray, the Portuguese Correa, the Pole Kosciusko, the Spaniard De Onis, his French friends Lafayette, Du Pont de Nemours and Destutt de Tracy; he corresponded with Major Cartwright, Dugald Steward, and Alexander and Wilhelm von Humboldt.

Throughout his life Jefferson made the pursuit of happiness central to his political and social philosophy. If he began as a Virginian in his notion of felicity and never ceased to be one, he was able to imagine a nation of free men as well. That more comprehensive vision rested upon Jefferson's concepts of man as preeminently moral, rational and equal and of the state as designed to create the conditions for the fulfilment of man's nature or 'the pursuit of happiness'. Jefferson's first draft attempt at framing the central proposition in his concept of man for the Declaration of Independence read, 'We hold these truths to be sacred and undeniable; that all men are created equal and independent, that from that equal creation they derive rights inherent and inalienable, among which are the preservation of life, liberty and the pursuit of happiness' (p. 270). The words 'sacred and undeniable' better imply the truths about the nature of man held by Jefferson than his second version in the words 'self evident': Jefferson thought man by his very created nature 'endowed with a sense of right and wrong...as much a part of man as his leg or arm'. No man lacks that moral sense and upon every man's possession of it and strengthening of it by exercise and reason rests both his equality and his inalienable rights. There is a human nature; it is the same in all men; it is moral and improvable; a political policy is therefore valuable only as it allows men to realize and fulfil their nature. Jefferson's view of human nature is optimistic, to be sure, but it is also coherent; what is good for man can be determined from his nature. We have seen, however, what man's nature looked like to New England Puritans.

Jefferson's Massachusetts counterpart, John Adams, may serve as one final contrast to suggest how a republican nationalism expressed by Jefferson carries a new sense of American possibility forward to the next stage of American prose. Like Jefferson, John Adams, the second President of the United States, was assigned to the committee to draw up the Declaration of Independence; like Jefferson, he too died on the fiftieth anniversary of its signing. Had John Adams been the principal draughtsman of the Declaration, it would no doubt have contained its libertarian note; it would no doubt have incorporated the kind of political expertise he embodied in the preamble of the constitution he devised for his new Commonwealth of Massachusetts: 'The body politic is...a social compact, by which the whole people covenants with each citizen, and each citizen with the whole people, that all shall be governed by certain laws for the common good.' No concept of human innocence or human equality would have found expression in it, however, for Adams, although agnostic beyond expectation considering his heritage, believed neither in human innocence nor equality; nor would the third of that Lockean triad of inalienable rights, 'life, liberty and property', have been recast as 'the pursuit of happiness'. The renewed friendship between Adams and Jefferson after both had retired from public office led to one of the most interesting correspondences in the history of American letter writing, but that story of personal and intellectual rapprochement lies beyond the limits of this collection. As Adams is remembered for inscribing in the American political system the elaborate system of checks and balances he thought necessary to control greed and protect stability from man's depraved desires for power, Jefferson is remembered for inscribing there the cheerful national doctrines of free growth. Having done that, Jefferson could enter or leave public life with as little trouble of spirit as any natural leader ever exhibited.

My text is taken from *The Writings of Thomas Jefferson*, published by the order of the Joint Committee of Congress on the Library, ed. Henry A. Washington, Philadelphia, J. B. Lippincott and Co., 1869.

Autobiography

JANUARY 6, 1821. At the age of 77, I begin to make some memoranda, and state some recollections of dates and facts concerning myself, for my own more ready reference, and for the information of my family.[1]

The tradition in my father's family was, that their ancestor came to this country from Wales, and from near the mountain of Snowden, the highest in Great Britain. I noted once a case from Wales, in the law reports, where a person of our name was either plaintiff or defendant; and one of the same name was secretary to the Virginia Company. These are the only instances in which I have met with the name in that country. I have found it in our early records; but the first particular information I have of any ancestor was of my grandfather, who lived at the place in Chesterfield called Ozborne's and owned the lands afterwards the glebe of the parish. He had three sons; Thomas who died young, Field who settled on the waters of Roanoke and left numerous descendants, and Peter, my father, who settled on the lands I still own, called Shadwell, adjoining my present residence. He was born February 29, 1707–8, and intermarried 1739, with Jane Randolph, of the age of 19, daughter of Isham Randolph, one of the seven sons of that name and family, settled at Dungeoness in Goochland. They trace their pedigree far back in England and Scotland, to which let every one ascribe the faith and merit he chooses.[2]

My father's education had been quite neglected; but being of a strong mind, sound judgment, and eager after information, he read much and improved himself, insomuch that he was chosen, with Joshua Fry, Professor of Mathematics in William and Mary college, to continue the boundary line between Virginia and North Carolina, which had been begun by Colonel Byrd; and was afterwards employed with the same Mr. Fry, to make the first map of Virginia which had ever been made, that of Captain Smith being merely a conjectural sketch[3]... He died, August 17th, 1757, leaving my mother a widow, who lived till 1776, with six daughters and two sons, myself the elder. To my younger brother he left his estate on James River, called Snowden, after the supposed birth-place of the family: to myself, the lands on which I was born and live.

Thomas Jefferson (1743–1826)

He placed me at the English school at five years of age; and at the Latin at nine, where I continued until his death. My teacher, Mr. Douglas, a clergyman from Scotland, with the rudiments of the Latin and Greek languages, taught me the French; and on the death of my father, I went to the Reverend Mr. Maury, a correct classical scholar, with whom I continued two years; and then, to wit, in the spring of 1760, went to William and Mary college, where I continued two years. It was my great good fortune, and what probably fixed the destinies of my life, that Dr. William Small of Scotland, was then professor of Mathematics, a man profound in most of the useful branches of science, with a happy talent of communication, correct and gentlemanly manners, and an enlarged and liberal mind. He, most happily for me, became soon attached to me, and made me his daily companion when not engaged in the school; and from his conversation I got my first views of the expansion of science, and of the system of things in which we are placed. Fortunately, the philosophical chair became vacant soon after my arrival at college, and he was appointed to fill it *per interim*: and he was the first who ever gave, in that college, regular lectures in Ethics, Rhetoric and Belles lettres. He returned to Europe in 1762, having previously filled up the measure of his goodness to me, by procuring for me, from his most intimate friend, George Wythe, a reception as a student of law, under his direction, and introduced me to the acquaintance and familiar table of Governor Fauquier, the ablest man who had ever filled that office. With him, and at his table, Dr. Small and Mr. Wythe, his *amici omnium horarum*,[a] and myself, formed a *partie quarree*,[b] and to the habitual conversations on these occasions I owed much instruction. Mr. Wythe continued to be my faithful and beloved mentor in youth, and my most affectionate friend through life. In 1767, he led me into the practice of the law at the bar of the General court, at which I continued until the Revolution shut up the courts of justice.[4]

In 1769, I became a member of the legislature by choice of the county in which I live, and so continued until it was closed by the Revolution. I made one effort in that body for the permission of the emancipation of slaves, which was rejected: and indeed, during the regal government, nothing liberal could expect success. Our minds were circumscribed within narrow limits, by an habitual belief that it was our duty to be subordinate to the mother country in all matters of government, to direct all our labors in subservience to her interests, and even to observe a bigoted intolerance for all religions but hers.

[a] Constant friends.
[b] A foursome.

The difficulties with our representatives were of habit and despair, not of reflection and conviction. Experience soon proved that they could bring their minds to rights on the first summons of their attention. But the King's Council, which acted as another house of legislature, held their places at will, and were in most humble obedience to that will: the Governor too, who had a negative on our laws, held by the same tenure, and with still greater devotedness to it: and, last of all, the Royal negative closed the last door to every hope of amelioration.

On the 1st January, 1772, I was married to Martha Skelton widow of Bathurst Skelton, and daughter of John Wayles, then twenty-three years old.[5] Mr. Wayles was a lawyer of much practice, to which he was introduced more by his great industry, punctuality, and practical readiness, than by eminence in the science of his profession. He was a most agreeable companion, full of pleasantry and good humor, and welcomed in every society. He acquired a handsome fortune, and died in May, 1773, leaving three daughters: the portion which came on that event to Mrs. Jefferson, after the debts should be paid, which were very considerable, was about equal to my own patrimony, and consequently doubled the ease of our circumstances.

When the famous Resolutions of 1765, against the Stamp-act, were proposed, I was yet a student of law in Williamsburgh. I attended the debate, however, at the door of the lobby of the House of Burgesses, and heard the splendid display of Mr. Henry's talents as a popular orator. They were great indeed; such as I have never heard from any other man. He appeared to me to speak as Homer wrote...

In May, 1769, a meeting of the General Assembly was called by the Governor, Lord Botetourt. I had then become a member; and to that meeting became known the joint resolutons and address of the Lords and Commons, of 1768–9, on the proceedings in Massachusetts. Counter-resolutions, and an address to the King by the House of Burgesses, were agreed to with little opposition, and a spirit manifestly displayed itself of considering the cause of Massachusetts as a common one. The Governor dissolved us: but we met the next day in the Apollo[c] of the Raleigh tavern, formed ourselves into a voluntary convention, drew up articles of association against the use of any merchandise imported from Great Britain, signed and recommended them to the people, repaired to our several counties, and were re-elected without any other exception than of the very few who had declined assent to our proceedings.

Nothing of particular excitement occurring for a considerable time, our countrymen seemed to fall into a state of insensibility to our

[c] A public room in the Raleigh Tavern.

situation; the duty on tea, not yet repealed, and the declaratory act of a right in the British Parliament to bind us by their laws in all cases whatsoever, still suspended over us. But a court of inquiry held in Rhode Island in 1762, with a power to send persons to England to be tried for offences committed here, was considered, at our session of the spring of 1773, as demanding attention...We were all sensible that the most urgent of all measures was that of coming to an understanding with all the other colonies, to consider the British claims as a common cause to all, and to produce a unity of action: and, for this purpose, that a committee of correspondence in each colony would be the best instrument for intercommunication: and that their first measure would probably be, to propose a meeting of deputies from every colony, at some central place, who should be charged with the direction of the measures which should be taken by all. We, therefore, drew up the resolutions... [and] prepared a circular letter to the speakers of the other colonies, inclosing to each a copy of the resolutions, and left it in charge with their chairman to forward them by expresses...

The next event which excited our sympathies for Massachusetts, was the Boston port bill, by which that port was to be shut up on the 1st of June, 1774. This arrived while we were in session in the spring of that year. The lead in the House, on these subjects, being no longer left to the old members, Mr. Henry, R. H. Lee, Fr. L. Lee, three or four other members, whom I do not recollect, and myself, agreeing that we must boldly take an unequivocal stand in the line with Massachusetts, determined to meet and consult on the proper measures, in the council-chamber, for the benefit of the library in that room. We were under conviction of the necessity of arousing our people from the lethargy into which they had fallen, as to passing events; and thought that the appointment of a day of general fasting and prayer would be most likely to call up and alarm their attention. No example of such a solemnity had existed since the days of our distresses in the war of '55, since which a new generation had grown up. With the help, therefore, of Rushworth, whom we rummaged over for the revolutionary precedents and forms of the Puritans of that day, preserved by him, we cooked up a resolution, somewhat modernizing their phrases, for appointing the 1st day of June, on which the port-bill was to commence, for a day of fasting, humiliation, and prayer, to implore Heaven to avert from us the evils of civil war, to inspire us with firmness in support of our rights, and to turn the hearts of the King and Parliament to moderation and justice. To give greater emphasis to our proposition, we agreed to wait the next morning on

Mr. Nicholas, whose grave and religious character was more in unison with the tone of our resolution, and to solicit him to move it. We accordingly went to him in the morning. He moved it the same day; the 1st of June was proposed; and it passed without opposition. The Governor dissolved us, as usual. We retired to the Apollo, as before, agreed to an association, and instructed the committee of correspondence to propose to the corresponding committees of the other colonies, to appoint deputies to meet in Congress at such place, *annually*, as should be convenient, to direct, from time to time, the measures required by the general interest: and we declared that an attack on any one colony, should be considered as an attack on the whole. This was in May. We further recommended to the several counties to elect deputies to meet at Williamsburgh, the 1st of August ensuing, to consider the state of the colony, and particularly to appoint delegates to a general Congress, should that measure be acceded to by the committees of correspondence generally. It was acceded to; Philadelphia was appointed for the place, and the 5th of September for the time of meeting. We returned home, and in our several counties invited the clergy to meet assemblies of the people on the 1st of June, to perform the ceremonies of the day, and to address to them discourses suited to the occasion. The people met generally, with anxiety and alarm in their countenances, and the effect of the day, through the whole colony, was like a shock of electricity, arousing every man, and placing him erect and solidly on his centre. They chose, universally, delegates for the convention. Being elected one for my own county, I prepared a draught of instructions to be given to the delegates whom we should send to the Congress... In this I took the ground that, from the beginning, I had thought the only one orthodox or tenable, which was, that the relation between Great Britain and these colonies was exactly the same as that of England and Scotland, after the accession of James, and until the union, and the same as her present relations with Hanover, having the same executive chief, but no other necessary political connection; and that our emigration from England to this country gave her no more rights over us, than the emigrations of the Danes and Saxons gave to the present authorities of the mother country, over England. In this doctrine, however, I had never been able to get any one to agree with me but Mr. Wythe... Our other patriots, Randolph, the Lees, Nicholas, Pendleton, stopped at the half-way house of John Dickinson, who admitted that England had a right to regulate our commerce, and to lay duties on it for the purposes of regulation, but not of raising revenue. But for this ground there was no foundation in compact, in any acknowledged principles of colonization, nor in reason: expatriation being a natural right, and acted on as such, by all nations, in all ages. I set out for Williamsburg some days before that appointed for our meeting, but was taken ill of a dysentery on the road, and was unable to proceed. I sent on, therefore, to Williamsburgh, two copies of my draught, the one under cover to Peyton Randolph, who I knew would be in the chair of the convention, the other to Patrick Henry. Whether Mr. Henry disapproved the ground taken, or was too lazy to read it (for he was the laziest man in reading I ever knew) I never learned; but he communicated it to nobody. Peyton Randolph informed the convention he had received such a paper from a member, prevented by sickness from offering it in his place, and he laid it on the table for perusal. It was read generally by the members, approved by many, though thought too bold for the present state of things; but they printed it in pamphlet form, under the title of 'A Summary View of the Rights of British America'. It found its way to England, was taken up by the opposition, interpolated a little by Mr. Burke so as to make it answer opposition purposes, and in that form ran rapidly through several editions...The convention met on the 1st of August, renewed their association, appointed delegates to the Congress, gave them instructions very temperately and properly expressed, both as to style and matter, and they repaired to Philadelphia at the time appointed. The splendid proceedings of that Congress, at their first session, belong to general history, are known to every one, and need not therefore be noted here. They terminated their session on the 26th of October, to meet again on the 10th of May ensuing. The convention, at their ensuing session of March, '75, approved of the proceedings of Congress, thanked their delegates, and reappointed the same persons to represent the colony at the meeting to be held in May: and foreseeing the probability that Peyton Randolph, their president, and speaker also of the House of Burgesses, might be called off, they added me, in that event, to the delegation.

Mr. Randolph was, according to expectation, obliged to leave the chair of Congress, to attend the General Assembly summoned by Lord Dunmore, to meet on the 1st day of June, 1775. Lord North's conciliatory propositions, as they were called, had been received by the Governor, and furnished the subject for which this assembly was convened. Mr. Randolph accordingly attended, and the tenor of these propositions being generally known, as having been addressed to all the governors, he was anxious that the answer of our Assembly, likely to be the first, should harmonize with what he knew to be the sentiments and wishes of the body he had recently left. He feared that Mr. Nicholas, whose mind was not yet up to the mark of the times, would undertake the answer, and therefore pressed me to prepare it. I did so, and, with his aid, carried it through the House, with long and doubtful scruples from Mr. Nicholas and James Mercer, and a dash of cold water on it here and there, enfeebling it somewhat, but finally with unanimity, or a vote approaching it. This being passed, I repaired imediately to Philadelphia, and conveyed to Congress the first notice they had of it. It was entirely approved there. I took my seat with them on the 21st of June. On the 24th, a committee which had been appointed to prepare a declaration of the causes of taking up arms, brought in their report (drawn I believe by J. Rutledge) which, not being liked, the House recommitted it, on the 26th, and added Mr. Dickinson and myself to the committee.

. . .

I prepared a draught of the declaration committed to us. It was too strong for Mr. Dickinson. He still retained the hope of reconciliation with the mother country, and was unwilling it should be lessened by offensive statements. He was so honest a man, and so able a one, that he was greatly indulged even by those who could not feel his scruples. We therefore requested him to take the paper, and put it into a form he could approve. He did so, preparing an entire new statement, and preserving of the former only the last four paragraphs and half of the preceding one. We approved and reported it to Congress, who accepted it. Congress gave a signal proof of their indulgence to Mr. Dickinson, and of their great desire not to go too fast for any respectable part of our body, in permitting him to draw their second petition to the King according to his own ideas, and passing it with scarcely any amendment. The disgust against this humility was general; and Mr. Dickinson's delight at its passage was the only circumstance which reconciled them to it. The vote being passed, although further observation on it was out of order, he could not refrain from rising and expressing his satisfaction, and concluded by saying, 'there is but one word, Mr. President, in the paper which I disapprove, and that is the word *Congress*'; on which Ben Harrison rose and said, 'There is but one word in the paper, Mr. President, of which I approve, and that is the word *Congress*.'

On the 22d of July, Dr. Franklin, Mr. Adams, R. H. Lee, and myself, were appointed a committee to consider and report on Lord North's conciliatory resolution. The answer of the Virginia Assembly on that subject having been approved, I was requested by the committee to prepare this report, which will account for the similarity of feature in the two instruments.[6]

On the 15th of May, 1776, the convention of Virginia instructed their delegates in Congress, to propose to that body to declare the colonies independent of Great Britain, and appointed a committee to prepare a declaration of rights and plan of government.

In Congress, Friday, June 7, 1776.[d] The delegates from Virginia moved, in obedience to instructions from their constituents, that the Congress should declare that these United colonies are, and of right ought to be, free and independent states, that they are absolved from all allegiance to the British crown, and that all political connection between them and the state of Great Britain is, and ought to be, totally dissolved; that measures should be immediately taken for procuring the assistance of foreign powers, and a Confederation be formed to bind the colonies more closely together.

The House being obliged to attend at that time to some other business, the proposition was referred to the next day, when the members were ordered to attend punctually at ten o'clock.

Saturday, June 8. They proceeded to take it into consideration, and referred it to a committee of the whole, into which they immediately resolved themselves, and passed that day and Monday, the 10th, in debating on the subject.

It was argued by Wilson, Robert R. Livingston, E. Rutledge, Dickinson, and others –

That, though they were friends to the measures themselves, and saw the impossibility that we should ever again be united with Great Britain, yet they were against adopting them at this time:

That the conduct we had formerly observed was wise and proper now, of deferring to take any capital step till the voice of the people drove us into it:

That they were our power, and without them our declarations could not be carried into effect:

That the people of the middle colonies (Maryland, Delaware, Pennsylvania, the Jerseys and New York) were not yet ripe for bidding adieu to British connection, but that they were fast ripening, and, in a short time, would join in the general voice of America:

That the resolution, entered into by this House on the 15th of May, for suppressing the exercise of all powers derived from the crown,

---

[d] On this day, Richard Henry Lee of Virginia proposed the resolution that 'these united colonies are, and of right ought to be, free and independent states'. It was this proposal which was then debated.

had shown, by the ferment into which it had thrown these middle colonies, that they had not yet accommodated their minds to a separation from the mother country:

That some of them had expressly forbidden their delegates to consent to such a declaration, and others had given no instructions, and consequently no powers to give such consent:

That if the delegates of any particular colony had no power to declare such colony independent, certain they were, the others could not declare it for them; the colonies being as yet perfectly independent of each other:

That the assembly of Pennsylvania was now sitting above stairs, their convention would sit within a few days, the convention of New York was now sitting, and those of the Jerseys and Delaware counties would meet on the Monday following, and it was probable these bodies would take up the question of Independence, and would declare to their delegates the voice of their state:

That if such a declaration should now be agreed to, these delegates must retire, and possibly their colonies might secede from the Union:

That such a secession would weaken us more than could be compensated by any foreign alliance:

That in the event of such a division, foreign powers would either refuse to join themselves to our fortunes, or, having us so much in their power as that desperate declaration would place us, they would insist on terms proportionably more hard and prejudicial:

That we had little reason to expect an alliance with those to whom alone, as yet, we had cast our eyes:

That France and Spain had reason to be jealous of that rising power, which would one day certainly strip them of all their American possessions:

That it was more likely they should form a connection with the British court, who, if they should find themselves unable otherwise to extricate themselves from their difficulties, would agree to a partition of our teritories, restoring Canada to France, and the Floridas to Spain, to accomplish for themselves a recovery of these colonies:

That it would be not be long before we should receive certain information of the disposition of the French court, from the agent whom we had sent to Paris for that purpose:

That if this disposition should be favorable, by waiting the event of the present campaign, which we all hoped would be successful, we should have reason to expect an alliance on better terms:

That this would in fact work no delay of any effectual aid from such ally, as, from the advance of the season and distance of our situation, it was impossible we could receive any assistance during this campaign:

That it was prudent to fix among ourselves the terms on which we should form alliance, before we declared we would form one at all events:

And that if these were agreed on, and our Declaration of Independence ready by the time our Ambassador should be prepared to sail, it would be as well as to go into that Declaration at this day.

On the other side, it was urged by J. Adams, Lee, Wythe, and others, that no gentleman had argued against the policy or the right of separation from Britain, nor had supposed it possible we should ever renew our connection; that they had only opposed its being now declared:

That the question was not whether, by a Declaration of Independence, we should make ourselves what we are not; but whether we should declare a fact which already exists:

That, as to the people or parliament of England, we had always been independent of them, their restraints on our trade deriving efficacy from our acquiescence only, and not from any rights they possessed of imposing them, and that so far, our connection had been federal only, and was now dissolved by the commencement of hostilities:

That, as to the King, we had been bound to him by allegiance, but that this bond was now dissolved by his assent to the last act of Parliament, by which he declares us out of his protection, and by his levying war on us, a fact which had long ago proved us out of his protection; it being a certain position in law, that allegiance and protection are reciprocal, the one ceasing when the other is withdrawn:

That James the II. never declared the people of England out of his protection, yet his actions proved it, and the Parliament declared it:

No delegates then can be denied, or ever want, a power of declaring an existing truth:

That the delegates from the Delaware counties having declared their constituents ready to join, there are only two colonies, Pennsylvania and Maryland, whose delegates are absolutely tied up, and that these had, by their instructions, only reserved a right of confirming or rejecting the measure:

That the instructions from Pennsylvania might be accounted for from the times in which they were drawn, near a twelvemonth ago, since which the face of affairs has totally changed:

That within that time, it had become apparent that Britain was determined to accept nothing less than a *carte-blanche*, and that the King's answer to the Lord Mayor, Aldermen and Common Council of London, which had come to hand four days ago, must have satisfied every one of this point:

That the people wait for us to lead the way:

That *they* are in favour of the measure, though the instructions given by some of their *representatives* are not:

That the voice of the representatives is not always consonant with the voice of the people, and that this is remarkably the case in these middle colonies:

That the effect of the resolution of the 15th of May has proved this, which, raising the murmurs of some in the colonies of Pennsylvania and Maryland, called forth the opposing voice of the freer part of the people, and proved them to be the majority even in these colonies:

That the backwardness of these two colonies might be ascribed, partly to the influence of proprietary power and connections, and partly, to their having not yet been attacked by the enemy:

That these causes were not likely to be soon removed, as there seemed no probability that the enemy would make either of these the seat of this summer's war:

That it would be vain to wait either weeks or months for perfect unanimity, since it was impossible that all men should ever become of one sentiment on any question:

That the conduct of some colonies, from the beginning of this contest, had given reason to suspect it was their settled policy to keep in the rear of the confederacy, that their particular prospect might be better, even in the worst event:

That, therefore, it was necessary for those colonies who had thrown themselves forward and hazarded all from the beginning, to come forward now also, and put all again to their own hazard:

That the history of the Dutch Revolution, of whom three states only confederated at first, proved that a secession of some colonies would not be so dangerous as some apprehended:

That a declaration of Independence alone could render it consistent with European delicacy, for European powers to treat with us, or even to receive an Ambassador from us:

That till this, they would not receive our vessels into their ports, nor acknowledge the adjudications of our courts of admirality to be legitimate, in cases of capture of British vessels:

That though France and Spain may be jealous of our rising power, they must think it will be much more formidable with the addition of Great Britain; and will therefore see it their interest to prevent a coalition; but should they refuse, we shall be but where we are; whereas without trying, we shall never know whether they will aid us or not:

That the present campaign may be unsuccessful, and therefore we had better propose an alliance while our affairs wear a hopeful aspect:

That to wait the event of this campaign will certainly work delay, because, during the summer, France may assist us effectually, by cutting off those supplies of provisions from England and Ireland, on which the enemy's armies here are to depend; or by setting in motion the great power they have collected in the West Indies, and calling our enemy to the defence of the possessions they have there:

That it would be idle to lose time in settling the terms of alliance, till we had first determined we would enter into alliance:

That it is necessary to lose no time in opening a trade for our people, who will want clothes, and will want money too, for the payment of taxes:

And that the only misfortune is, that we did not enter into alliance with France six months sooner, as, besides opening her ports for the vent of our last year's produce, she might have marched an army into Germany, and prevented the petty princes there, from selling their unhappy subjects to subdue us.

It appearing in the course of these debates, that the colonies of New York, New Jersey, Pennsylvania, Delaware, Maryland, and South Carolina were not yet matured for falling from the parent stem, but that they were fast advancing to that state, it was thought most prudent to wait a while for them, and to postpone the final decision to July 1st; but, that this might occasion as little delay as possible, a committee was appointed to prepare a Declaration of Independence. The committee were John Adams, Dr. Franklin, Roger Sherman, Robert R. Livingston, and myself. Committees were also appointed, at the same time, to prepare a plan of confederation for the colonies, and to state the terms proper to be proposed for foreign alliance. The committee for drawing the Declaration of Independence, desired me to do it. It was accordingly done, and being approved by them, I reported it to the House on Friday, the 28th of June, when it was read, and ordered to lie on the table. On Monday, the 1st of July, the House resolved itself into a committee of the whole, and resumed the consideration of the original motion made by the delegates of Virginia, which, being again debated through the day, was carried in the affirmative by the votes of New Hampshire, Connecticut, Massachusetts, Rhode Island, New Jersey, Maryland, Virginia, North

Carolina and Georgia. South Carolina and Pennsylvania voted against it. Delaware had but two members present, and they were divided. The delegates from New York declared they were for it themselves, and were assured their constituents were for it; but that their instructions having been drawn near a twelvemonth before, when reconciliation was still the general object, they were enjoined by them to do nothing which should impede that object. They, therefore, thought themselves not justifiable in voting on either side, and asked leave to withdraw from the question; which was given them. The committee rose and reported their resolution to the House. Mr. Edward Rutledge, of South Carolina, then requested the determination might be put off to the next day, as he believed his colleagues, though they disapproved of the resolution, would then join in it for the sake of unanimity. The ultimate question, whether the House would agree to the resolution of the committee, was accordingly postponed to the next day, when it was again moved, and South Carolina concurred in voting for it.^c In the meantime, a third member had come post from the Delaware counties, and turned the vote of that colony in favor of the resolution. Members of a different sentiment attending that morning from Pennsylvania also, her vote was changed, so that the whole twelve colonies who were authorized to vote at all, gave their voices for it and within a few days^f the convention of New York approved of it, and thus supplied the void occasioned by the withdrawing of her delegates from the vote.

Congress proceeded the same day to consider the Declaration of Independence, which had been reported and lain on the table the Friday preceding, and on Monday referred to a committee of the whole. The pusillanimous idea that we had friends in England worth keeping terms with, still haunted the minds of many. For this reason, those passages which conveyed censures on the people of England were struck out, lest they should give them offence. The clause too, reprobating the enslaving the inhabitants of Africa, was struck out in complaisance to South Carolina and Georgia, who had never attempted to restrain the importation of slaves, and who, on the contrary, still wished to continue it. Our northern brethren also, I believe, felt a little tender under those censures; for though their people had very few slaves themselves, yet they had been pretty considerable carriers of them to others. The debates, having taken up the greater parts of the 2d, 3d, and 4th days of July, were, on the evening of the last, closed; the Declaration was reported by the

---

^c On 2 July 1776, Lee's original resolution was passed.
^f 9 July 1776.

committee, agreed to by the House and signed by every member present, except Mr. Dickinson.ᵍ As the sentiments of men are known not only by what they receive, but what they reject also, I will state the form of the Declaration as originally reported. The parts struck out by Congress shall be distinguished by a black line drawn under them;ʰ and those inserted by them shall be place in the margin, or in a concurrent column.

A Declaration by the Representatives of the United States of America, in *General* Congress assembled

When, in the course of human events, it becomes necessary for one people to dissolve the political bands which have connected them with another, and to assume among the powers of the earth the separate and equal station to which the laws of nature and of nature's God entitle them, a decent respect to the opinions of mankind requires that they should declare the causes which impel them to the separation.

We hold these truths to be self evident: that all men are created equal; that they are endowed by their creator with [*inherent and*] inalienable rights; that among these are life, liberty, and the pursuit of happiness; that to secure these rights, governments are instituted among men, deriving their just powers from the consent of the governed; that whenever any form of government becomes destructive of these ends, it is the right of the people to alter or to abolish it, and to institute new government, laying its foundation on such principles, and organizing its powers in such form, as to them shall seem most likely to effect their safety and happiness. Prudence, indeed, will dictate that governments long established should not be changed for light and transient causes; and accordingly all experience hath shown that mankind are more disposed to suffer while evils are sufferable, than to right themselves by abolishing the forms to which they are accustomed. But when a long train of abuses and usurpations, [*begun at a distinguished period and*] pursuing invariably the same object, evinces a design to reduce them under absolute despotism, it is their right, it is their duty to throw off such government, and to provide new guards for their future security. Such has been the patient sufferance of these colonies; and such is now the necessity which constrains them to [*expunge*] their former systems of government. The history of the present king of Great Britain is a history of [*unremitting*] injuries and usurpations, [*among which appears no solitary fact to contradict the uniform tenor of the rest, but all have*] in direct object the establishment of an absolute tyranny over these states. To prove this, let facts be submitted to a candid world [*for the truth of which we pledge a faith yet unsullied by falsehood*].

He has refused his assent to laws the most wholesome and necessary for the public good.

He has forbidden his governors to pass laws of immediate and pressing importance, unless suspended in their operation till his assent should be obtained; and, when so suspended, he has utterly neglected to attend to them.

He has refused to pass other laws for the accommodation of large districts of

alter

repeated

all having

ᵍ After the Declaration was passed, the Liberty Bell rang from the State House steeple in Philadelphia, and that night broadside copies were run off for public distribution.

ʰ In the text given, the parts struck out by Congress are printed in italics and enclosed in brackets.

people, unless those people would relinquish the right of representation in the legislature, a right inestimable to them and formidable to tyrants only.

He has called together legislative bodies at places unusual, uncomfortable, and distant from the depository of their public records, for the sole purpose of fatiguing them into compliance with his measures.

He has dissolved representative houses repeatedly [*and continually*] for opposing with manly firmness his invasions on the rights of the people.

He has refused for a long time after such dissolutions to cause others to be elected, whereby the legislative powers, incapable of annihilation, have returned to the people at large for their exercise, the state remaining, in the meantime, exposed to all the dangers of invasion from without and convulsions within.

He has endeavored to prevent the population of these states; for that purpose obstructing the laws for naturalization of foreigners, refusing to pass others to encourage their migrations hither, and raising the conditions of new appropriations of lands.

He has [*suffered*] the administration of justice [*totally to cease in some of these states*] refusing his assent to laws for establishing judiciary powers. *obstructed by*

He has made [*our*] judges dependent on his will alone for the tenure of their offices, and the amount and payment of their salaries.

He has erected a multitude of new offices [*by a self-assumed power*] and sent hither swarms of new officers to harass our people and eat out their substance.

He has kept among us in times of peace standing armies [*and ships of war*] without the consent of our legislatures.

He has affected to render the military independent of, and superior to, the civil power.

He has combined with others to subject us to a jurisdiction foreign to our constitutions and unacknowledged by our laws, giving his assent to their acts of pretended legislation for quartering large bodies of armed troops among us; for protecting them by a mock trial from punishment for any murders which they should commit on the inhabitants of these states; for cutting off our trade with all parts of the world; for imposing taxes on us without our consent; for depriving us [ ] of the benefits of trial by jury; for transporting us beyond seas to *in many cases* be tried for pretended offences; for abolishing the free system of English laws in a neighboring province, establishing therein an arbitrary government, and enlarging its boundaries, so as to render it at once an example and fit instrument for introducing the same absolute rule into these [*states*]; for taking away our *colonies* charters, abolishing our most valuable laws, and altering fundamentally the forms of our governments; for suspending our own legislatures, and declaring themselves invested with power to legislate for us in all cases whatsoever.

He has abdicated government here [*withdrawing his governors, and declaring us out of his allegiance and protection.*] *by declaring us out of his protection, and waging war against us.*

He has plundered our seas, ravaged our coasts, burnt our towns, and destroyed the lives of our people.

He is at this time transporting large armies of foreign mercenaries to complete the works of death, desolation and tyranny already begun with circumstances of cruelty and perfidy [ ] unworthy the head of a civilized nation. *scarcely paralleled in the most barbarous ages, and totally*

He has constrained our fellow citizens taken captive on the high seas, to bear arms against their country, to become the executioners of their friends and brethren, or to fall themselves by their hands.

He has [ ] endeavored to bring on the inhabitabnts of our frontiers, the merciless Indian savages, whose known rule of warfare is an undistinguished destruction of all ages, sexes and conditions [*of existence.*] *excited domestic insurrection among us. and has*

[*He has incited treasonable insurrections of our fellow citizens, with the allurements of forfeiture and confiscation of our property.*]

271

Thomas Jefferson (1743–1826)

He has waged cruel war against human nature itself, violating its most sacred rights of life and liberty in the persons of a distant people who never offended him, captivating and carrying them into slavery in another hemisphere, or to incur miserable death in their transportation thither. This piratical warfare, the opprobium of INFIDEL *powers, is the warfare of the* CHRISTIAN *king of Great Britain. Determined to keep open a market where* MEN *should be bought and sold, he has prostituted his negative for suppressing every legislative atempt to prohibit or to restrain this execrable commerce. And that this assemblage of horrors might want no fact of distinguished die, he is now exciting those very people to rise in arms among us, and to purchase that liberty of which he has deprived them, by murdering the people on whom he also obtruded them: thus paying off former crimes committed against the* LIBERTIES *of one people, with crimes which he urges them to commit against the* LIVES *of another.]*

In every stage of these oppressions we have petitioned for redress in the most humble terms: our repeated petitions have been answered only by repeated injuries.

A prince whose character is thus marked by every act which may define a tyrant is unfit to be ruler of a [ ] people [*who mean to be free. Future ages will scarcely believe that the hardiness of one man adventured, within the short compass of twelve years only, to lay a foundation so broad and so undisguised for tyranny over a people fostered and fixed in principles of freedom.*]

free

an unwarrant-able
us

Nor have we been wanting in attentions to our British brethren. We have warned them from time to time of attempts by their legislature to extend [*a*] jurisdiction over [*these our states*]. We have reminded them of the circumstances of our emigration and settlement here, [*no one of which could warrant so strange a pretension: that these were effected at the expense of our own blood and treasure, unassisted by the wealth or the strength of Great Britain: that in constituting indeed our several forms of government, we had adopted one common king, thereby laying a foundation for perpetual league and amity with them: but that submission to their parliament was no part of our constitution, nor ever in idea, if history may be credited: and,*]

have
and we have conjured them by
would inevit-ably

we [ ] appealed to their native justice and magnanimity [*as well as to*] the ties of our common kindred to disavow these usurpations which [*were likely to*] interrupt our connection and correspondence. They too have been deaf to the voices of justice and of consanguinity, [*and when occasions have been given them, by the regular course of their laws, of removing from their councils the disturbers of our harmony, they have, by their free election, re-established them in power. At this very time, too, they are permitting their chief magistrate to send over not only soldiers of our common blood, but Scotch and foreign mercenaries to invade and destroy us. These facts have given the last stab to agonizing affection, and manly spirit bids us to renounce forever these unfeeling brethren. We must endeavor to forget our former love for them,*]

We must therefore
and hold them as we hold the rest of man-kind, enemies in war, in peace friends.

and hold them as we hold the rest of mankind, enemies in war, in peace friends. We might have been a free and a great people together; but a communication of grandeur and of freedom, it seems, is below their dignity. Be it so, since they will have it. The road to happiness and to glory is open to us too. We will tread it apart from them, and] acquiesce in the necessity which denounces our [*eternal*] separation [ ]!

We therefore the representatives of the United States of America in General Congress assembled, do in the name, and by the authority of the good people of these [*states reject and renounce all allegiance and subjection to the kings of Great Britain and all others who may hereafter claim by, through or under them; we utterly dissolve all political connection which may heretofore*

We, therefore, the representatives of the United States of American in General Congress assembled, appealing to the supreme judge of the world for the rectitude of our intentions, do in the name, and by the authority of the good people of these colonies, solemnly publish and declare, that these united colonies are, and of right ought to be free and indepen-

have subsisted between us and the people or parliament of Great Britain: and finally we do assert and declare these colonies to be free and independent states,] and that as free and independent states, they have full power to levy war, conclude peace, contract alliances, establish commerce, and do all other acts and things which independent states may of right do.

And for the support of this declaration, we mutually pledge to each other our lives, our fortunes, and our sacred honour.

dent states; that they are absolved from all allegiance to the British crown, and that all political connection between them and the state of Great Britain is, and ought to be, totally dissolved and that as free and independent states, they have full power to levy war, conclude peace, contract alliances, establish commerce, and to do all other acts and things which independent states may of right do.

And for the support of this declaration, with a firm reliance on the protection of divine providence, we mutually pledge to each other our lives, our fortunes, and our sacred honor.

The Declaration thus signed on the 4th, on paper, was engrossed on parchment, and signed again on the 2d of August.

Notes

INTRODUCTION

1 Powhatan's Confederation. Powhatan was the Indian ruler of a tribal association centered in Virginia. John Smith heard of him soon after the English landing in 1607.

2 New Spain. In 1493 Alexander VI, a Spanish pope, divided the New World between Portugal and Spain so that all territory one hundred leagues west and south of the islands of Cape Verde fell to Spain and anything east of the line fell to Portugal. His division was unsatisfactory to both nations, who therefore redrew the line three hundred and seventy leagues west of the Cape Verde Islands, giving Portugal the hump of South America. New Spain was Central and South America, from Mexico to Patagonia, together with a scattering of Caribbean islands and as much of the southern fringe of North America as in contest with England could be held.

3 Roanoke Settlement. In the spring of 1585, Raleigh sent out a fleet of seven vessels under the command of his cousin, Sir Richard Grenville, to take possession of the territory Queen Elizabeth graciously allowed to be called Virginia, that is all the land from Florida to Newfoundland. One hundred men were designated as settlers. They selected Roanoke Island on the coast for their venture, but after one year returned home. A second group went out in 1587 and resettled Roanoke Island. It was not revisited for four years, by which time the colony had disappeared.

4 King Philip's War. In 1675 the Indians in Massachusetts united under a chief known as King Philip to attack outlying settlements in order to forestall colonial encroachment still further on their lands. Though many settlers were killed, the Indians were driven back along an expanded frontier.

5 Bacon's Rebellion. In 1676 Indians along the borders of Virginia and Maryland mounted attacks against the settlers, which the Virginia House of Burgesses under Governor Berkeley did little to prevent. Nathaniel Bacon defied the ruling clique to deal with the Indians in a popular movement which soon turned against the tyranny of the royal governor himself. After Bacon's death from exposure, the rebellion gradually collapsed. The English recalled Berkeley and appointed in succession to him Thomas, Lord Culpeper.

6 Culpeper's Rebellion. Thomas, Lord Culpeper did not prove more successful than Berkeley in satisfying both England and the Virginia colonists. His presenting to the Virginia Assembly at the instigation of the Board of Trade a new duty on tobacco led to the tobacco riots called Culpeper's Rebellion, in 1680.

7 Leisler's Rebellion. The people of New York staged a similar uprising against English governorship under the lead of Jacob Leisler in 1689.

8 John Robinson was pastor of the Scrooby congregation at its departure for Holland and the spiritual leader of the separatists in that country. He died before his intended departure for America. William Brewster, part of the withdrawal to

Holland, did accompany the pilgrims to America, where he became one of the principal spiritual and political leaders of the group.

9 Laudian persecution. Archbishop William Laud (1573–1645) was Charles I's chief minister in his attempt to strengthen the Church of England and bring the Puritan movement under the control of church and state. Laud's efforts included the dissolution of the preaching brotherhoods and other acts deemed intolerable persecution by the Puritans.

10 Antinomians. Those who held that by special grace direct contact with God could be obtained, removing from them obligation to the moral law taught by the church.

11 Typology. A variety of Scriptural hermeneutics in which Old Testament persons and events are held to prefigure New Testament persons and events, the Old Testament 'type' fulfilled in the New Testament 'anti-type'. The practice of detecting the patterns of God's behaviour towards man was extended to searching out similar prefigurations and fulfilments in later Christian experience.

12 Arminianism, named from James Arminius or Harmensen, a Dutch Protestant theologian who died in 1609, opposes Calvin's views, particularly on predestination, to argue the freedom of the will.

CAPTAIN JOHN SMITH

1 The motif of the good weak man on shipboard, whose spiritual strength prevails over others is a common motif in colonial histories, both New England and southern. The death at sea of an ungodly sailor and the rescue of one thought drowned who lives to become a useful member of the colony are equally common motifs. Sometimes the thematic point of the figure is to express God's providence. Here Smith creates for himself a godly supporter among human beings.

2 In both New England and southern chronicles the storm at sea is a conventional motif used to describe God's providence; it is sometimes linked to a leak in the vessel. Land phenomena equally prominent are the earthquake, the unanticipated quagmire and the like.

3 The theme of the discordant company of fortune seekers is particular to Smith; its mirror opposite, the company drawn together by adversity, is to be found in Bradford.

4 Both Smith and Bradford are careful to emphasize the patience, humanity and legality of the English dealings with Indians; both show some ready to pillage but restrained by other wiser settlers who arrange trade. Nonetheless, Smith's account involves unquestioning initial land-seizure; Bradford records initial land-purchase. Smith defends himself from many real and anticipated criticisms of his Indian dealings though he seems oblivious of other possible criticisms.

5 This scene is absent from the earlier account in *A True Relation* as is the scene describing Smith's teaching the Indians the use of the compass and thereby saving himself.

6 The casual exchange of an English boy for an Indian servant might seem one of the actions open to criticism but apparently regarded by Smith as unexceptional. The incorporation of Powhatan's speech, 'recalled' by Smith at a much later date, is not a fictitious addition to a literal text, meant to alter or corrupt historical truth, so much as it is an effort to draw a regal manner cloaking savage craftiness which Smith alone properly penetrates. Like all of Smith's embellishments of his first account, one of the points is his own superior acuity. Smith regularly invents dialogue to display his leadership. Bradford rarely invents dialogue; he writes one

imagined speech made in future time, however, on which comment will be made in place.

WILLIAM BRADFORD

1 Virtually identical instances of the godless sailor cast into the sea are recorded by Francis Higginson and John Winthrop.

2 The Biblical parallels to Jonah and to the prodigal son are clear. A similar event is recorded by Thomas Shepherd.

3 The structure of this brief artful chapter presents the arrival, a thanksgiving, a typologically significant summary of the environs and, to conclude, the imagined speech of future children of the pilgrims when they would come to reconsider the situation of their fathers, itself a renewed thanksgiving and prayer. The voyage contains the three episodes which reveal the 'spetiall worke of Gods providence' and occupies half the chapter. Bradford then intervenes in his own person to compress the account. His audience is those who desire strict and narrow truth. The thanksgiving, the kneeling in the new land, is the central focus of the chapter and prepares for Bradford's surveying them as from outside. When he then imagines the words that will be spoken in the future and by imputing speech expands a further thanksgiving, Bradford assumes an audience whose response he directs by vicariously making it up for them. At the end of this chapter Bradford drops the formal design of history in favour of the recording of annals.

4 Bradford accompanied the group. A fuller account of their exploration can be found in George Morton, *Mourt's Relation* (London, 1622).

5 Bradford's scrupulous fairness to the Indians is generally apparent in the history.

6 As Bradford knew, subsequent explorations and events would make many settlers doubt the wisdom of this choice of location. Once made it was not revoked, even after the settlement of Massachusetts Bay.

7 John Smith, as might be expected, attributed the suffering endured by the pilgrims to their refusal to use him as their guide: 'Nothing would be done for a Plantation till about some hundred of your Brownists of England Amsterdam and Leyden, went to New Plymouth: whose humorous ignorances caused them for more than a year, to endure a wonderful deal of misery with infinite patience; saying My Books and Maps were much better cheap to teach them than myself. Many others have used the like good husbandry; that have paid soundly in trying their self-willed conclusions.'

8 Samoset came from Morattiggon, or Monhegan Island, Maine, frequented by English fishing vessels. In 1622 the shallop sailed there in search of corn and came back with it.

9 The treaty was renewed in 1639 by Massasoit and his son Wamsutta, or Alexander. The peace lasted during their lives but ended in the life of Wamsutta's son, in the war known by the name of that son, King Philip. Bradford's attitude towards Indians reflects his hopes for their conversion, his own decency, and the period in which he writes; Mary Rowlandson's attitude, in contrast, reflects the doubtful benefits of Indian conversions and the time of King Philip's War.

10 Captain Hunt was master of one of the two ships in Captain John Smith's exploration of coastal New England in 1614. After Smith's departure, Hunt's ship 'staied to fit herselfe for Spaine with the dry fish'. It was then he kidnapped twenty-four Indians, took them to Malaga and sold 'the silly Saluages for Rials of

eight; but this vilde act kept him euer after from any more imploiment to those parts'.

11   Bradford's conception of marriage as a civil contract and not a religious sacrament is common in Puritanism.

MARY ROWLANDSON

1   The second remove was to Princeton, Massachusetts; the third to what is now New Braintree; the fourth, to modern Petersham; the fifth to Orange.

2   Mrs Rowlandson becomes the servant to Weetamoo, the widow of Massasoit's son Alexander. Weetamoo, known as the Queen of Pocasset, was one of the three squaws of Quinnapin; Mrs Rowlandson did not like her regal airs.

3   The rapidity of transitionless shifts from action to scriptural parallel and exposition in this remove is typical. Once Mrs Rowlandson's eyes are opened to the moral purpose of her sufferings in the third remove, her perception of her burden does not change.

4   The final remove, followed by an application of her experiences to the spiritual profit of her audience. During the last removes, while ransom is being arranged, the captors circle back towards Lancaster, Massachusetts.

COTTON MATHER

1   Mather's Diary for July 1693 records his decision to write the *Magnalia*: 'And because I foresaw an inexpressible deal of service like to be thereby done for the church of God, not only here but abroad in Europe, I formed a design to endeavour *The Church-History of this Country*. Laying my design before the neighboring ministers, they encouraged it; and accordingly I set myself to cry mightily unto the Lord that if my undertaking herein might be for His glory, He would grant me his assistance in it.' The task begun in that year was substantially finished in 1697.

2   Mather's sense of a double audience and double function for the *Magnalia* lies behind the tortuous mixture of praise and qualification, lament and thanksgiving in this paragraph. Both his English and American readers must be continually reminded of their natural depravity; his English readers must not lose sight of the efforts of the American church to recapture primitive purity under God's guidance.

3   Mather gives priority to church history over political history because he regards the establishment of churches as more heroic than the preservation of earthly empires, and also because his concept of heroism values exemplary martyrdom above victorious conquest.

4   If Mather apologizes for the *Magnalia* in contradictory terms – I was too busy as pastor to give this book my full attention and besides I was writing twenty other books now published and still others not yet published – he is no more than accurate here. His method of composition included the bringing together and expanding of earlier writings and the publication of numerous sermons; nonetheless he was virtually a private company for the manufacture of printed works. He self-consciously asked himself what to write, how to write; he asked other ministers whether to write on this subject or that; he only asked God Almighty whether to write at all.

5   Of the biographer, Mather wrote in *Parentator* (Boston, Mass., 1724): 'And if it has been determined that the name of historian shall be Virtues's secretary, I know not how the pen of an historian can be better employed than in reporting the virtuous tempers and actions of the men that have therein shown forth the virtues of

our blessed Redeemer, and been the epistles of Christ unto the rest of mankind. . .
The Best of Books does very much consist of such an history.'

6 These opening sentences already display Mather's fondness for the pun. The episode of the woman left behind at Grimsby is treated with more gallantry by Mather than by Bradford. The elaboration of the tempest to bring it nearer the storm on the Sea of Galilee which Jesus calmed is also a typical strategy.

7 Mather writes for Bradford a pious answer to unspecified protests, meant to do him credit. It reads more like Mather than Bradford. Nevertheless, Mather does distinguish between Bradford's own words when he gives them, his drift when he gives that, and quotations of his own invention.

8 Mather's uxoriousness is attributed to Bradford.

SARAH KEMBLE KNIGHT

1 She refers to Edward Ford, *Parismus, the renowned prince of Bohemia, his famous, delectable and pleasant history; containing his noble battails brought against the Persians, his love to Laurana, the King's daughter of Thessaly, and his stronge adventures in the desolate Island etc.* London, T. Creede, 1598, a popular romance which went through eighteen editions in its first hundred years.

2 The new secularism in Massachusetts endorsed by Madam Knight deplores the strictness praised only a few years earlier by Mather.

3 That Madam Knight records the episode with only a little surprise and almost complete approval suggests the totally different complexion of northern and southern slave holding.

4 The 'savagery' detailed is a matter of social mores. Madam Knight elsewhere notices that Indians live by their laws on their land unbothered by Englishmen living by their laws on their land. She writes less than three decades after Mrs Rowlandson but it would not occur to her to define savagery as diabolical wickedness.

5 Madam Knight so clearly assumes the capacity of the colonies to run themselves that she neither refers to nor challenges the right of England to make administrative law.

WILLIAM BYRD II

1 This very typical observation appears in the manuscript as a note and not in the text itself.

2 Smith describes the first church as a 'homely thing, like a barn, set upon crochets, covered with rafts, sedge and earth, so also was the walls'. Byrd anachronistically supplies the costly tavern. In 1623 Nathaniel Butler wrote a complaint against the Company that it had still failed to provide one.

3 Byrd strengthens his case inaccurately. The charters of both the London and Plymouth companies were dated 10 April 1606.

4 1622.

5 1684.

6 This unlikely story is recorded by no other contemporary.

7 Not the actual words, but Byrd is substantially correct.

8 Byrd notes ''tis happy', not that it is a special providence of God that the hurricane belt is so narrow, as Bradford or Mather would have noted.

9 Sarah Kemble Knight records the same secular attitude towards marriage in Connecticut.

JONATHAN EDWARDS

1 Edwards not only draws before and after portraits of himself understanding the doctrines of his faith and finding them reasonable, he also draws such portraits feeling the powerful attraction of those doctrines. His objections to double predestination vanished once and for all when his 'reason apprehended the justice and reasonableness of it'. His feelings that the doctrine is 'exceedingly pleasant, bright and sweet' are not continuous, however, though they occur 'very often'.

2 Edwards's chants of meditation choose natural images. His enthusiasm for lightning and thunderstorms is often contrasted with Franklin's utilitarian interest in them.

3 Edwards served as a minister in a Scotch Presbyterian church in New York City from August 1722 to May 1723. The record of his friendship with the Smith family indicates that he had not yet begun to suffer from the darkness of spirit he describes later.

4 Not the only indication that the older Edwards refers to a diary of the younger Edwards to retrieve his earlier religious experiences.

5 Edwards was senior tutor at Yale from 1724 to 6. Since the College was then between presidents, he had full charge of a student body of sixty.

6 Just as Edwards moves systematically through the contemplation of nature, the reading of Scripture and other useful books, and meditation on God, so he also describes the normal stages of true conversion; having recorded vocation, he here turns to conviction of sin. The organization of the *Personal Narrative*, that is, superimposes a thematic structure over the chronological structure.

7 Edwards is writing when the first revival at Northampton under his guidance is still prospering. His confessional tone plays into revival and draws on revival strategies; his prayer is to be put to the service of revival.

8 The inserted date marks the approach of the ebbing of Northampton's first revival, when Edwards is using all his energies to stem the lapse and refresh the movement. The visit of the English revivalist George Whitfield in 1740 succeeded in assisting the Great Awakening. Doubtless Edwards found no time then and little heart later to continue the *Personal Narrative*.

BENJAMIN FRANKLIN

1 Franklin composed an epitaph, not used on his gravestone, in similar terms about 1728: 'The Body of / B. Franklin, / Printer: / Like the Cover of an old Book, / Its contents torn out, / And stript of its Lettering and Gilding, / Lies here, Food for Worms. / But the Work shall not be wholly lost: / For it will, as he believ'd, appear once more, / In a new and more perfect Edition, / Corrected and amended / By the Author.'

2 The change from the Old Style or Julian calendar to the New Style or Gregorian calendar, adopted in many European countries in 1582, was made by England in 1752 by an act of Parliament dropping out eleven days so that Wednesday, September 2 was immediately followed by Thursday, September 14, and changing the beginning of the official year from March 25 to January 1. Colonial anniversaries and birthdays were correspondingly altered so that Franklin celebrated his birthday on January 17 instead of January 6, Washington his on February 22 not February 11.

3 Cotton Mather's *Bonifacius. An Essay upon the Good, that is to be Devised and Designed, by those Who Desire . . . to Do Good While they Live* (1710) not only strength-

ened Franklin's interest in moral self-improvement but supplied the name for his first satirical persona, Mrs Silence Do-good.

4 One of the Do-good letters quotes Defoe in favour of education for women. Franklin had his daughter Sally taught French and music as well as arithmetic and bookkeeping.

5 This is not quite correct. Save for a single issue of *Public Occurences* (25 Sept. 1690), *The Boston News-Letter* (24 April 1704) was the first colonial newspaper; *The Boston Gazette* (21 Dec. 1719) was the second; *The American Weekly* (Philadelphia, 22 Dec. 1719) was the third; and James's *New England Courant* (7 Aug. 1721) the fourth.

6 Fourteen Silence Do-good letters were printed between 12 April and 8 October 1722. In them, Franklin's earliest surviving publications, in the persona of a widow of a country minister writing to the publisher, he commented on manners and morals, satirized the students at Harvard College, scoffed at fashions and attacked hypocrisy in religion.

7 Franklin's note: 'I fancy his harsh and tyrannical Treatment of me, might be a means of impressing me with that Aversion to arbitrary Power that has stuck to me thro' my whole Life.'

8 Crossed out: 'and which I read before it was sealed'.

9 In 1779 Franklin recalled that after giving a few copies to friends he came to dislike the pamphlet and burned all the rest but one.

10 Franklin opens by quoting not Dryden but Pope's *Essay on Man*. He goes on to give the Dryden quotation from *Oedipus* which begins

    Whatever is, is in its Causes just
    Since all Things are by Fate, but purblind Man, etc.

11 Franklin's note: 'I got his Son once £500½.'

12 Lacking legal proof that John Rogers had a 'preceding wife' in England, Deborah was unable to have her marriage annulled; Pennsylvania had no law under which she could divorce him. Had she and Franklin married under Pennsylvania law and Rogers later reappeared, they could have been convicted of bigamy for which the punishment was the lash and imprisonment with hard labour for life. The common-law marriage they made was an adequate alternative and their two children were regarded as legitimate.

13 Franklin's note: 'My manner of acting to engage People in this and future Undertakings'. Apparently he intended to take up this topic next but in fact he ended the first book here.

PATRICK TAILFER, HUGH ANDERSON AND DAVID DOUGLAS

1 The authors clearly consider the failure to build a church with collected charitable monies a point telling shrewdly against the pious trustees and repeat it several times. It occurs again in the list of 'Real causes of the ruin and desolation of the colony'. Nonetheless the principal targets are land tenure, rum and slaves.

THOMAS JEFFERSON

1 The motive, 'the information of my family', is inoperative after the first few paragraphs. Jefferson's skill at political reportage is what justifies using the *Autobiography* as the source for the text of the Declaration and not any informal self-revelation.

2 Jefferson's scepticism concerning pedigree was life-long.

3 The persistent cross-referencing down the course of Virginia letters to Smith and Byrd resembles the persistent cross-referencing down Massachusetts letters to Bradford, Winthrop and the Mathers.

4 Jefferson enjoyed a long friendship with George Wythe and shared many views with him. He wrote to Wythe from Paris in 1786, for example, 'I think by far the most important bill in our whole code is that for the diffusion of knowledge among the people. No other sure foundation can be devised for the preservation of freedom and happiness. If anybody thinks that kings, nobles or priests are good conservators of public happiness, send him here. It is the best school in the universe to cure him of that folly.'

5 The marriage was a happy one, ended by the death of Martha in September 1781.

6 In the original manuscript these notes, written, Jefferson tells us later, 'whilst these things were going on', are on a paper different in size, quality and colour, from that of the rest.

A Select Booklist

The following is a guide to further reading in American colonial prose and not a comprehensive bibliography. The place of publication is London unless stated otherwise.

PRIMARY SOURCES

Bibliographical details of the texts in this collection can be found in the headnotes.

Captain John Smith

A True Relation. . .of Virginia (1608)
A Description of New England (1616)
Generale Historie of Virginia, New England, and The Summer Isles (1624)
Travels and Works, ed. Edward Arber, introduction A. G. Bradley (2 vols., Edinburgh, 1910)

William Bradford

Of Plymouth Plantation, annotated S. E. Morison (Boston, 1952)

Mary Rowlandson

Narratives of the Indian Wars, 1675–1699, ed. C. H. Lincoln (1913)

Cotton Mather

The Wonders of the Invisible World (1693)
Magnalia Christi Americana (1702)
Bonifacius (Boston, 1710)
The Christian Philosopher (1721)
Selections, ed. Kenneth B. Murdock (Boston, 1960)

Sarah Kemble Knight

Journal, ed. and published Theodore Dwight (Albany, 1825)

William Byrd II

The History of the Dividing Line (1728)
A Progress to the Mines in the Year 1732
A Journey to the Land of Eden (1733)
The Prose Works, ed. L. B. Wright (1966)
The Secret Diary (1709–12), ed. L. B. Wright and M. Tinling (1942)
The London Diary (1717–21), ed. L. B. Wright and M. Tinling (1958)

A select booklist

Jonathan Edwards

Sinners in the Hands of An Angry God (1741)
Freedom of the Will (1754)
The Great Christian Doctrine of Original Sin Defended (1753)
Concerning the End of which God Created the World (1765)
Representative Selections, ed. C. H. Faust and T. H. Johnson (New York, 1935)
The standard edition of *The Works* is in progress at Yale, general editor Perry Miller, now John E. Smith.

Benjamin Franklin

Do-good Papers (Boston, 1722)
Poor Richard's Almanack (1732–58)
Autobiography (1771)
Representative Selections, ed. C. E. Jorgensen and F. L. Mott (New York, 1962)
The standard edition of *The Papers*, ed., Leonard W. Labaree is now in progress at Yale.

Patrick Tailfer, Hugh Anderson and David Douglas

A True and Historical Narrative of the Colony of Georgia... (1741)
Clarence Ver Steeg has made a modern critical edition (Athens, Georgia, 1960)

Thomas Jefferson

The Basic Writings, ed. P. S. Foner (New York, 1944)
Life and Selected Writings, A. Koch and W. Peden (New York, 1944)
The standard edition of *The Papers* is that of Princeton, various editors.

MODERN ANTHOLOGIES

Among a growing number of useful collections, the following can be recommended as comprehensive and excellent: W. R. Benet and N. H. Pearson, *The Oxford Anthology of American Literature* (2 vols., Oxford, 1939);
Perry Miller and Thomas H. Johnson, *The Puritans* (New York, 2 vols., 1963);
Lazar Ziff, *The Literature of America: Colonial Period* (New York, 1970);
S. Bradley, R. C. Beatty, and E. H. Long, *The American Tradition in Literature* (4th edn, 2 vols., 1974); and H. T. Meserole, W. Sutton and B. Weber, *American Literature: Tradition and Innovation* (rev. edn, 4 vols., 1974)

SECONDARY MATERIAL
Biographical studies

The best modern collection of the lives of colonial writers is Everett Emerson, ed., *Major Writers of Early American Literature* (Madison, Wisc., 1972). Among the most reliable and interesting individual lives are the following: P. L. Barbour, *The Three Worlds of Captain John Smith* (Boston, 1964); S. E. Morison, *Builders of the Bay Colony* (Boston, 1964); Perry Miller, *Errand into the Wilderness* (Cambridge, Mass., 1957); Robert Middlekauf, *The Mathers: Three Generations of Puritan Intellectuals, 1597–1728* (New York, 1971); R. C. Beatty, *William Byrd* (1932) and Carl Dolmetsch, *William Byrd of Westover* (1974); Ola E. Winslow, *Jonathan Edwards* (1940) and A. O.

A select booklist

Aldridge, *Jonathan Edwards* (1964), both of which combine biography and criticism; Ronald W. Clark, *Benjamin Franklin* (New York, 1983); Dumas Malone, *Jefferson and His Times* (4 vols., 1982).

Critical studies, general

For the colonies in general, the first thorough studies by Moses Coit Tyler, *A History of American Literature, 1607–1765* (2 vols., New York, 1878) and *The Literary History of the American Revolution 1763–1783* (2 vols., New York, 1897) remain valuable. They are to be supplemented by the following studies: L. B. Wright, *The Elizabethan's America* (Cambridge, Mass., 1965), *The Atlantic Frontier* (New York, 1948) and *First Gentlemen of Virginia* (1940); Wallace Notestein, *The English People on the Eve of Colonialization, 1603–1670* (New York, 1962); W. F. Craven, *The Southern Colonies in the Seventeenth Century, 1607–1689* (New Orleans, 1970); Clarence Ver Steeg, *The Southern Colonies in the Eighteenth Century, 1689–1763* (New Orleans, 1970); John Richard Alden, *The South in the Revolution, 1763–1789* (New Orleans, 1970); J. S. Hubbell, *The South in American Literature, 1607–1900* (Durham, North Carolina, 1954); Perry Miller, *The New England Mind: the Seventeenth Century* (1939, reprinted 1961) and *The New England Mind: from Colony to Province* (1953, reprinted 1961); Adrienne Koch, *Power, Morals and the Founding Fathers, Essays in the Interpretation of the American Enlightenment* (Ithaca, New York, 1961); James Morton Smith ed., *Seventeenth-Century America: Essays in Colonial History* (Chapel Hill, 1959); Ray Billington, ed., *The Reinterpretation of Early American History* (San Merino, Calif., 1966); Sacvan Bercovitch ed., *Typology and Early American Literature* (Amherst, Mass., 1972) and *The American Puritan Imagination* (1974); Richard Bushman, *From Puritan to Yankee* (Cambridge, Mass., 1967); R. H. Niebuhr, *The Kingdom of God in America* (New York, 1957) and Peter Gay, *A Loss of Mastery* (Berkeley, Calif., 1966)

Critical studies, individual

In addition to the general studies the following studies of individual writers are helpful: (*for Smith*) Howard Mumford Jones, 'The literature of Virginia in the seventeenth century', *Memoirs of the American Academy of Arts and Sciences* XIX (1946); (*for Bradford*) R. S. Dunn, 'Seventeenth-century historians' in James Morton Smith ed., *Seventeenth-Century America*, Jasper Rosenmeier, '"With my owne eyes": William Bradford's of Plymouth Plantation' in Sacvan Berkovitch ed., *American Puritan Imagination*; David Levin, 'William Bradford: the value of Puritan historiography', in Everett Emerson, ed., *Major Writers*; and Ursula Brumm, 'Art and history in...Bradford's history of Plymouth Plantation', *Early American Literature* XX (1977); (*for Rowlandson*) P. D. Carleton, 'The Indian captivity', *American Literature* XV (1942); R. H. Pearce, 'The significance of captivity narrative', *American Literature* XIX (1947) and David Downing, 'Streams of Scripture comfort: Mary Rowlandson's typological use of the Bible', *Early American Literature* XV (1981); (*For Mather*) Sacvan Bercovitch, 'New England epic: Cotton Mather's *Magnalia Christi Americana*', *English Literary History* XXXIII (1966) and '*Cotton Mather*' in Everett Emerson, ed., *Major Writers*; Donald Shea, *Spiritual Autobiography in Early America* (Princeton, 1968); Austin Warren, *Connections* (Ann Arbor, 1970); (*for Knight*) Faye Vowell, 'A commentary on the Journal of Sarah Kemble Knight', *Emporia State Reseach Studies*, 1978; Alan Margolies, 'The editing and publication of the Journal of Madam Knight', *Biographical Society of America Papers* LVIII (1964); (*for Byrd*) Pierre Marambaud, *William Byrd of Westover* (1971) and M. Tinling, 'William Byrd of Westover, an American Pepys', *South Atlantic*

A select booklist

Quarterly LXXXIX (1940); (*for Edwards*) Alan Heimert, *Religion and the American Mind: from the Great Awakening to the Revolution* (Cambridge, Mass., 1966), David Minter, *The Interpreted Design as a Structural Principle in American Prose* (New Haven, Mass., 1969) and the studies of Roland Delattre, *Beauty and Sensibility in the Thought of Jonathan Edwards: An Essay in Aesthetics* (New Haven, Mass., 1968), William J. Schieck, *The Writings of Jonathan Edwards: Theory, Motif and Style* (Austin, Texas, 1975); (*for Franklin*) A. O. Aldridge, *Benjamin Franklin and Nature's God* (1967), J. A. Leo Lemay in Everett Emerson, ed., *Major Writers* and J. A. Sappenfield, *A Sweet Instruction* (1973); (*for Thomas Jefferson*) Edwin Gittleman, 'Jefferson's "Slave Narrative": the Declaration of Independence as a Literary Text', *Early American Literature* VIII (1974), Bernard Bailyn, *The Ideological Origins of the American Revolution* (Cambridge, Mass, 1967), Saul K. Padover, *A Jefferson Profile: As Revealed in his Letters* (New York, 1956); David Hawke, *A Transaction of Free Men* (New York, 1964); Julian Boyd, *The Declaration of Independence: The Evolution of the Text* (Princeton, 1945); Winthrop Jordan, *White Over Black* (Chapel Hill, 1969).